By The Grace of God

A True Story of Faith, Love, Prayers, and Miracles

PATRICIA LEE

ASPIRE
PUBLISHING HUB LLC.

Table of Contents

Dedication
2009

To you, Lord, I dedicate this book. Thank you for always being there, through it all. You stood by me when I had no one else, protected me, and loved us unconditionally. You made everything possible for me and your children. I give you all the praise; with you, Lord, nothing is impossible.

Mama, I dedicate this book to you with all my heart and soul. Thank you for your love, encouragement, and for being an exemplary mother. I love you deeply. Mama "I heard you."

To Poppi, the man who raised me, I dedicate this book. God bless you for your timeless, selfless love. Thank you for loving my mother, ensuring we had food to eat, keeping us warm, and being the father, I needed.

To my children, I dedicate this book to you with all my love. If given the chance to do it over, I would do it all for you.

To my brother, Rickey, I love you dearly. Thank you for protecting me and for your encouragement during tough times. Thank you for your unconditional love and for being the big brother everyone should have.

My main squeeze, Emory, my brother. Thank you for always keeping it real and honest.

Ozel, I love you for always being authentic and for being the big brother who never led me astray.

Evan, thank you for teaching me the coolest and latest dance steps from 1967.

Eddie Kelly, aka Fast Eddie, thank you for the memories and for being a man who steps up, even when it wasn't your responsibility. No one can match your James Brown splits. Thank you for loving my mother.

To my Ace Boon Coon, my dearest and closest friends, in both death and life, thank you for the memories and for always having my back. Sam, Michael, Ike, Jackie, Lawrence, Gramps,

J.D. Womack, Robert Howard, Spunky, and Melvin Causey, I dedicate this book to you with all my love. I know you're watching over me and would be proud. It's been real. I'm sending this to you. "Apples, Peaches, Pumpkin Pie" by Jay& the Techniques 1967 PEACE!

When I was a little girl, Mama told me that, though I may start life with many friends, if I ended up with one true friend, I'd be lucky. Mama was both right and wrong.

Matthew Sr., thank you for believing in me, for supporting my children when no one else would, and for buying us the house. "I love you just the way you are."

Ronnie, my love for you will always endure. Thank you for being so kind.

A special thanks to Father Marcan, a remarkable man who did amazing things for me. God bless you. Properly thanking you would require another book.

Thank you, Father Cunningham, for ensuring we had food to eat. Thank you, Westside Mothers, for being exactly what Detroit needed.

Tee Tee, I've never met a nicer guy. I'm heartbroken over what happened and wish I could change it. Thank you for the years you spent working on my cars in all weather, never charging a dime. I pray you find peace in heaven.

Mr. Berry Gordy, I dedicate this book to you. Through your divine vision, I found the will to live and overcome many obstacles to achieve great things. Thank you for Motown.

Marvin Gaye, the only man who has never disappointed me, says, "You're a Wonderful One."

Thank you, David Ruffin and Eddie Kendricks, for being lights in my life. "You're My Everything" from 1967.

Paul Williams, words cannot express my gratitude for the man who saved my life. May God's angels always protect you and your family, and may the light you left behind forever shine. "Don't Look Back," 1965.

A special acknowledgment to The Fabulous Funk Brothers: thank you for your unique funk that added life to Motown songs. Your groove and tempo taught me to dance and express myself through music, helping me navigate life and heartache. Your talent was instrumental in my journey.

It was a vibrant time to be alive in Detroit. PEACE.

I want to personally thank you for some of my favorite jams, like "Everybody Needs Love" by Gladys Knight and the Pips, 1967, and others by the Temptations and The Four Tops.

Smokey Robinson, your music and sweet lyrics are eternal. Thank you for "The Love I Saw in You Was Just a Mirage," 1967.

Thank you, Eddie Holland, for "Just Ain't Enough Love."

Laura Person, my dear friend, your loyalty and support have been my shelter through storms. Your care and understanding will never be forgotten.

To my sisters in the struggle, I dedicate this book to you. Eddie Mae, Marlene, and Pringle, your friendship and sisterhood have been my solace. Pamela, my love for you is unwavering.

Big Mama, thank you for your wisdom and support. May you rest in peace.

Pee Wee, you've always been there for me. Stay strong.

Mr. Coulter, thank you for your kindness in moving me and furnishing my home without expecting anything in return.

Erma, our friendship was love at first sight, characterized by a loyalty that's rare to find. Thank you for being my big sister and for all the nights you lent me your shoulder to cry on. I love you.

Bird, thank you for your encouragement, your love, and the personal care you've provided. RIP.

Margie and Little Dot, my love for you is deep and enduring. Your strength and beauty have always inspired me.

Elaine A., in my time of need, you provided a home. "Bless Your Heart."

Mother Waddles, a mother to us individually and collectively, thank you for the beds and your unwavering support.

I dedicate this book to all the old-school Detroiters for keeping it real. Your resilience kept me ahead of the game. Peace.

"Hey Love" by Stevie Wonder, summer 1967, encapsulates my feelings perfectly.

Mom and Dad, thank you for your love and support during the time when I needed guidance the most. Your encouragement and the safety net you provided have been invaluable.

Mrs. Wynn, your insight and wisdom have been a guiding light in my life. Thank you for always making me feel welcome.

Ma' Dear, your love and support during our times of need have left a lasting impact. I love you.

I dedicate this book to Robert Williams, Executive Director of the Repertory Theatre. Thank you for believing in me and for the countless hours spent on the phone encouraging me to finish my book. Even after more than twenty years of friendship, I suspect you might have borrowed some of my material.

Special thanks are extended to Detroit's own Sweet James and The Fantastic Four for helping me navigate the rough seas of life with their music. "Share Your Love with Me," 1967, and the DJs who played these life-affirming songs, you have my heartfelt gratitude.

A special acknowledgment goes to:

- Enchantment for "Thank You Girl," 1976,
- The Dramatics for "I'm Going by the Stars in Your Eyes," 1978, and "That's My Favorite Song," 1979,
- LJ Reynolds, "Key to the World," 1989,
- Detroit Emeralds for "Wear This Ring with Love," 1971,
- Just Brothers for "Things Will Be Better Tomorrow," 1965,
- Melvin Davis, whose "I Must Love You," 1966, holds a special place in my heart,
- Brothers of Soul for "I Guess That Don't Make Me a Loser," 1966,
- The Originals for "Baby, I'm For Real," 1969,
- Shades of Blue for "Oh How Happy," 1966,
- The Four Tops for "Baby, I Need Your Loving," 1965,
- The Holidays for "I'll Love You Forever," 1965,
- Little Daddy Walton and Sons for "Highway Blues" (year unknown),
- Pat Lewis for "Can't Shake It Loose," 1965, with a special thanks to Funk Brother James Jamison for his double bass play on this track,
- Kim Weston for "Take Me in Your Arms," 1965,
- The Dynamics for "Ice Cream Song," 1969,
- Little Junior Canaday for embodying the Blues,
- Little Sonny, for his harmonica skills,
- Jimmy McCloud, my personal friend, for singing the Blues,
- Johnnie Mae Matthews for "Ooh Wee," 1960s,
- The Contours for "Just a Little Misunderstanding," 1966,

- The Elgins for "Darlin' Baby," 1966,
- Jimmy Ruffin "As Long As There Is (LOVE) Love 1965,
- Jimmy Ruffin "What Become Of The Broken Hearted" 1966,
- Groovesville, Northern Sound, Golden World, United Soul, and Soulsville Recording Companies
- WJLB and CKLW radio stations,
- Jay Butler and Ernie Durham

The list of music, artists, and companies mentioned does not fully represent the rich musical heritage of Detroit. These are merely a few of my personal favorites.

Thank you, God, for without this music, I could not share my intimate story with you. For without this profound music, I would not have lived to tell it.

There is no infringement whatsoever. And I personally own all these records.

PART ONE

By The Grace of God A True Story of Faith, Love, Prayers, and Miracles

Chapter 1

"My life would not be in vain."

"Today is a day of gracious and glorious reflection, a day blessed by God. I counted my blessings, grateful to the Lord for waking me with a sound mind, watching over us through the night, and keeping us safe. I pray for His continued blessings on my children, for He is their Father.

Lying in bed, I rolled over and kneeled on the floor to pray the Lord's Prayer.

April 25, 1993, marks a significant milestone: my oldest son is scheduled to graduate from Eastern Michigan University at 9:00 a.m. He is the first among my mother's grandchildren to earn a college degree. Reflecting on my past and the time spent raising my children, I listened to the rain against my windows, deep in thought. Realizing how absorbed I had become, I startled myself. I began opening the blinds, moving through the house, and declaring, "It's time to get up." Peeking into the bedroom, I was greeted by my daughter Kyham, who, wiping sleep from her eyes, asked the time. "6:00," I replied. Her surprised response led to a playful exchange about staying up late watching videos. I urged her to focus on her studies with as much enthusiasm as she did her late-night habits.

I insisted we not be late, emphasizing the significance of the day and refusing to let anyone dampen my joy. I recounted the dreams I held for my children's success, now realized by my son's achievements. Overwhelmed with emotion, I spoke of the struggles I faced raising my children alone, starting as a teenager myself. My voice trembled, and tears streamed down my face as I expressed my pride in my son's hard work and dedication, leading to his receiving degrees in communications and real estate.

This day signifies more than his accomplishments; it represents the culmination of our collective struggles and triumphs. My son's graduation is a testament to his perseverance and our family's resilience against skepticism and adversity. It highlights the love and dedication I have for my children and the sacrifices I have made to ensure their success. My sister's envy cannot overshadow the pride and joy in my son's drug-free, accomplished path.

Beyond all else, they resented that I managed to raise you without their assistance. I recall the day my sister Geri warned my sons against turning to drug dealing and seeking her help thereafter. Mind you, they were mere boys at the time. She presumed to predict my children's future, unaware that God had a different plan in place. God, who answers all prayers, was with us. My prayers were answered, leading me to raise my hands in gratitude, exclaiming, "Thank you, Jesus! Thank you, Lord, for your unwavering support."

"Mama, don't cry," my daughter implored, misunderstanding my tears of joy for sorrow. I embraced her, whispering, "It's time to rise, my love." Her response, "I love you too, mama," warmed my heart.

The journey to my son's commencement was under a cloak of rain, darkening our path to Ypsilanti, Michigan. Parking atop the highest tower, we descended the steep hill, mindful not to ruin our carefully chosen attire. Despite the hurry, my umbrella was forgotten. Yet, locating Bowen Field House for the ceremony, scheduled for 8:45 AM with 2,500 students graduating, was effortless. My family's attendance was uncertain but irrelevant, as I had prepared a surprise for Edward—a reunion with our dear friend Laura Persons, who had traveled from Tuskegee, Alabama, after 17 years apart.

In 1977, Laura, who had been a motherly figure and sister to me, wished for us not to leave San Jose, California. However, circumstances dictate otherwise. Spotting Nina at the ceremony sparked a series of superficial exchanges with nothing of significance. Despite the familial tensions, Edward's graduation ceremony was a moment of pure joy, especially with Laura's unexpected presence. We captured this milestone with professional photography, a decision made to avoid relying on Nina and the potential for undue claims.

The celebration continued at Red Lobster, where family dynamics played out in subtle ways. Nina's attempt to assert dominance by arriving early and dining separately underscored her jealousy of Edward's achievement—a success she couldn't claim for her own child, despite her best efforts. This envy, exacerbated by alcohol, revealed the depth of her bitterness. Meanwhile, Geri, overcome by inebriation, momentarily shed her persona, offering Edward a generous yet prematurely dated gift.

Geri's indulgence in alcohol seemed to bolster her courage, leading her to an emotional display of boasting and bragging, as if trying to embody the role of the doting aunt for Edward's friends. Her actions, both transparent and overdone, failed to mask her true feelings. Nina, noticing the genuine joy at our table, decided to join, sitting beside Edward. She advised him to emulate others in the family, explicitly excluding me as a role model. I caught snippets of their conversation and was moved when Edward asserted his independence and gratitude towards me, the one who raised him. His public toast to me brought us all to tears, strengthening our family bond even amidst the tension.

Despite the dinner's earlier dramas, we enjoyed a heartfelt conclusion to the evening. My sons and I shared a tender goodbye, full of hugs and kisses, before they departed for the night's plans. The drive home was reflective and tearful, filled with gratitude for the journey and accomplishments we'd shared. I confided in Laura my deep thankfulness for the Lord's guidance through the trials of raising my children to this point, drug- and trouble-free, a testament to the values I instilled in them.

My thoughts then turned to my children's futures, notably free of the burden of early parenthood that I faced. With Andre and Terry in college and Kyham nearing high school graduation, our discussions on responsibility and choices seemed to have made a significant impact. As they slept, I found solace in Sam Cooke's "Bring it on Home to Me," a song that stirred memories of my mother and her influence on me. Reflecting on her life and wishing she could witness our triumphs brought a mix of sorrow and pride.

Recalling the summer of 1964, we settled into a green and white two-family flat around the bend facing Joy Road, at 8620 Joy Road to be exact. The neighborhood was well-maintained, with homeownership seemingly universal except for us. Despite financial constraints, Mama provided the best life she could. My older brother, having enlisted in the army in 1956, was a distant memory; often times I had to look in my mother's face to remember what he looked like. While Matthew sent letters, financial assistance was absent, despite knowing of our struggles—a fact that never seemed to fault him in our mother's eyes, though assistance would have eased her burdens.

In 1962, living on Mandalay Street brought hardships into sharp focus: empty cupboards, disconnected utilities, and a Mother's Day card from Matthew that, while visually appealing, underscored the absence of tangible support. Mama's quiet disappointment spoke volumes, yet she never solicited help from Matthew, perhaps out of pride or expectation that he should have offered without prompting.

Joyce, my oldest sister, succumbed to bone cancer at twelve before I was born. My mother's stories imbued me with a profound sense of loss and connection to Joyce, teaching me about pain from an early age.

Eileen, the third child, exemplified brilliance marred by poor judgment. Against Mama's advice, she married at sixteen to a twenty-five-year-old man, derailing her academic achievements for love—a decision that transformed her from an A student to mediocrity. Eileen's defiance was a testament to her stubbornness, a trait Mama often lamented.

My memories of Eileen are tender, filled with lessons in life's simple skills and moments of childhood wonder, like the awe of receiving my first two lady dimes—coins that held beauty in my young eyes.

Mama, despite reservations, consented to Eileen's marriage to Teddy on December 19, 1959, a union Eileen would come to lament. Despite her declarations of love for Teddy, Mama's pointed question lingered: "But does he love you?" This question underscored the complexity of love and the challenges of youthful decisions, themes that resonated through our family's narrative.

All my siblings shared the same father, except for me, and our ages spanned several years. Geri, the eldest of our four younger children, frequently exercised her authority. She was consistently hateful and bitter, seemingly resentful of her existence in the world, directing her animosity especially towards me. My childhood was shadowed by her daily reminders of disdain. Initially, a child might not recognize hatred in its entirety, but through experience, I learned quickly. Despite my mother's efforts to instill familial love and unity, Geri's capacity for love was hindered by her inability to love herself. Her actions and the memories of them linger vividly, as if they occurred just yesterday.

"Mama," struggling with chronic headaches that lasted from dawn till dusk, would often ask Geri to give me a glass of water, hearing my requests from my too-short stature to reach the faucet. However, Geri's indifference to Mama's suffering and her spiteful actions, like spitting in my water, were her form of rebellion. After drinking from those glasses for so long, I naively believed that was their natural state.

Nina, contrasting Geri, initially seemed kinder, not made of the same stern material. Our childhood involved simple pleasures like sliding down the basement stairs on a cardboard box and sharing the scarce toys we had, including a bicycle that we all took turns riding—except for Geri, who seemed preoccupied with her own bitterness.

Rickey, the youngest boy, holds a special place in my memories. Our closeness throughout life is filled with shared experiences and mutual respect. Despite being the oldest, I was taller, which bothered and amused us. Rickey, with his light, freckled complexion and sense of humor, was musically gifted. Our mother taught him to play guitar by ear, and I always encouraged him to play energetic tunes for me to dance to. Family gatherings often turned into impromptu dance and music sessions, with Mama leading in her traditional dance moves from her Georgia roots. While I lacked musical talent, I found my expression in dance, eager to compete with the best.

Eileen's talents were multifaceted, from her singing to her poetry and piano skills. Matthew and Nina also shared musical abilities, contributing to the choir under Mama's guidance, while the rest of me supported the pews. Mama's voice, a force of nature, could move any listener deeply, her songs flowing from her soul with an authenticity and warmth that could rival any professional singer.

Our family, each with unique talents and struggles, was bound by Mama's love and aspiration for us to achieve beyond her own accomplishments. Her voice, a symbol of strength and beauty, underscored our collective and individual journeys, encouraging us to find and nurture our own voices and talents.

Reflecting on Mama's once beautiful voice, it dawned on me that its melodic presence grew scarce after our move to Joy Road& Epworth. An undefined sorrow had enveloped her, as though life's essence was slipping through her grasp. Within our new home's walls, she seemed a shadow of her vibrant self, her zest for life dimmed into a mere whisper. Amidst the flux of good and bad days, the scale tipped unfavorably. In my prayers, I sought divine intervention to alleviate her burdens, yet the gradual fade of my closest ally unfolded before my young eyes. Mama gave all of herself to her children, knowing that I knew she did all she could to find us a decent place to live. And for that, I was grateful.

At eight and a half, with Rickey at eleven and Nina at fifteen, we witnessed this change. I had a wonderful stepfather; our household included Poppi, who had been a constant presence since our days on 15th Street. Standing tall at 6'1", he married Mama with seven kids when I was two years old. They loved each other very much, and it showed. Remembering the way he looked at Mama still makes my brown face blush today.

It was in his eyes that they shared mutual admiration for each other, and it was real. They had an undeniable soul connection and chemistry. My stepfather was born and raised in New Orleans, Louisiana. He was tall, light, handsome, and Creole. He was a very good-looking man and had served in the Navy. With predominantly Caucasian features, his distinguished appearance was marked by jet-black hair accented with a singular gray streak. His life, rich with experience, encompassed fluency in multiple languages, global travels, and accolades as a 1950s champion swimmer and war hero, honored with the Purple Heart.

Now, my mother was fine herself. She did not have to take a back seat to anyone. She didn't have any problems attracting friends; Mama was no slouch. But my mother was low-key, not a woman to run the streets. To look at her, you could not tell that she had seven children. Mama kept her waistline, had large hips, and sported a full bosom. Mama's skin was caramel in color, and she had beautiful brown moles on her face and shoulder-length hair. Mama told us that her friends asked how she was able to land a man like him, because men do not marry women with that many kids. Mama said that she put her hands on her hips, reared back on them, threw her head in the air, and said, "I asked God for him, and He answered my prayers." Not only did he love Mama, but he loved her children like his own, and we knew it.

Poppi was an only child, the son of a father who had once served in the United States Army and was now employed by the railroad company. His travels took him all across the country.

Poppi's mother was once a nun who left the convent to marry his father. Their marriage lasted only seven years. After their divorce, she returned to New Orleans, raising Poppi with a kindness that he mirrored in his interactions with us. Her visits were marked by generosity, bringing clothing and homemade pecan pralines, a testament to her large-heartedness despite her small stature.

Poppi was more than a stepfather; to me, he was the epitome of paternal love. His playful roughhousing with Rickey and the sweet homemade donuts he crafted brought joy into our lives. A cherished memory dates back to a winter in Elmhurst off Linwood, when I was five. Amid a harsh winter that saw our gas shut off and frost clinging to our windows, Poppi's nurturing spirit shone brightly. With Mama ill, he assumed the role of caregiver, preparing breakfast on a hot plate, warming water for my bath to stave off the cold, and ensuring my dress was heated before dressing me. Once outside, I looked back and could see the steam coming from my dress. His embrace offered additional warmth. His escort to school that day was a testament to the enduring bond he shared with Mama, a love that had blossomed since 1956.

Poppi's professional life as a chef at the Flaming Emerald downtown added another layer to his character. Positioned in the restaurant's front window, his culinary skills were a spectacle for passersby, embodying the passion and dedication he applied to all aspects of his life.

Mama owned an old mint green 1962 Chevrolet, a relic that struggled to run, while Poppi, my stepfather, relied on the Joy Road Bus for his commute. His arrivals home, sometimes after days or what seemed like weeks, were heralded by the sound of his whistling, a cheerful tune that could pierce any hour of the night or day. We would jump out of bed and run toward his sound. He often returned carrying gallons of milk, corn, beef, and sweet potatoes from the Eastern Market—a staple in our home—but never candy, citing its ill effects on health.

Despite Poppi's frequent absences and late-night arrivals while taking on a second job at the Eastern Market, Mama's demeanor suggested a deep-seated love and acceptance of his ways, markedly different from her own lifestyle. Mama abstained from drinking, smoking, and nightlife, opting instead for a home-centric life focused on her children. She embodied the teachings of Christianity, instilling in us the value of life, the importance of showing love and mercy, and the courage to face life's challenges—principles she preached but seemed to neglect in her struggle with declining health and relentless headaches.

With only Rickey and me at home, Nina, working at Gentleman Jim's downtown, became our unwitting provider. Her job there allowed us to dine well, introducing us to a world of culinary delights from shrimp and lobster to a variety of steaks and decadent desserts, all within the upscale ambiance of Gentleman Jim's. This restaurant, with its soft lighting, elegant flatware, and grand chandelier, offered more than just meals; it provided a glimpse into a life of refined tastes and manners, something Mama had always emphasized from an early age.

Nina, who had left school at fifteen to help support the family, worked tirelessly, her beauty and efficiency making her a favorite among patrons. Her sacrifices, pouring her earnings onto the kitchen table after long shifts, were a testament to her devotion to Mama and our family's well-being. Her contributions, though necessary, reversed the roles within our household, a shift that weighed heavily on Mama, who had always prided herself on providing for her children.

Nina's understanding of Mama's condition went beyond mere observation; she recognized the severity of Mama's health issues and urged her to seek medical attention, a conversation I accidentally overheard. This moment underscored Nina's deep concern and unwavering support for our mother, embodying the resilience and compassion that had been instilled in us. Her actions, born of love and responsibility, helped keep our family afloat during one of the most challenging periods of our lives.

The harsh reality of 1964 for a poor Black family in need of medical care was grim; options were limited and often inaccessible. Despite this, Mama agreed to seek help, her choices narrowed down to Receiving Hospital, known for its long waits and the paradox of harboring the best doctors that only money could attract. The hospital's reputation was such that, according to Mama, one had to be on death's doorstep to receive attention, and even then, it wasn't guaranteed.

Nina arranged to meet Mama downtown, promising a hospital visit followed by lunch as a treat, also seizing the opportunity to introduce Mama to George Beaver, a young man she had taken a liking to at Gentleman Jim's. Their budding relationship had reached a point where Nina wished for her mother's approval to invite George over, marking a significant step. Mama loved him right off, and she let him know.

Amid these plans, I faced my own challenges with yet another new school, Ruth Ruff Elementary on Livernois, feeling the familiar pangs of anxiety about making friends and the transient nature of our lives. However, a chance encounter with Pamela Elaine Gorman, a fellow student a year my senior, sparked an unexpected friendship. Pamela's family structure, with both parents in the home, was a novelty to me and contrasted starkly with my own experience. Despite my mother's strict rule about sleeping away from home, Pamela's offer of friendship and an invitation to stay over were welcome gestures of kindness.

Mama and Nina's journey to the hospital was a long ordeal, exacerbated by their wait to see a doctor, which was so prolonged that Eileen, who had joined them, had to leave early. The shadows of domestic strife loomed over Eileen's marriage to Teddy, with Mama suspecting abuse, though Eileen consistently denied it. Teddy's control extended to church attendance and a watchful presence over any family interactions, a tension palpable even to a child.

In Mama's absence, I found solace in Marvin Gaye's "Pretty Little Baby," playing it repeatedly on my portable record player. Music, a ubiquitous and joyous part of Detroit life, along with the simple pleasures of shopping downtown with Mama for records and treats, painted a vivid picture of our life amidst the city's vibrant Motown soundtrack.

As the day stretched on, I anxiously awaited Mama's return, hoping to learn about the doctor's findings and eager to share the news of my new friend. From my vantage point on the porch, I watched numerous buses pass without her alighting. The absence of Rickey, who was out shooting marbles, compounded my fear of being alone. To distract myself, I retrieved the mail, discovering a letter from Geri, my sister in the Air Force. Despite her two-year absence, I felt it hadn't been long enough since she left for service straight out of Northwestern High School, graduating with many Honors. While sifting through thoughts and the letter, our new downstairs neighbors were moving in when a white woman approached, introducing herself as Mama's social worker. Her inquiry about our family and living situation put me on guard, aware of Mama's strict rule against sharing personal details. As I attempted to retreat indoors, she followed, but Mama's timely arrival prevented any further intrusion.

Mama reluctantly allowed the social worker to inspect our home, a violation of privacy that clearly unsettled her. The worker's thorough search and subsequent questioning, while seated on our davenport—referred to as a "Dufole" back then—left a palpable tension. Eavesdropping, I learned of Mama's referral for further testing at Detroit Memorial Hospital. After the social worker's departure, I seized the moment to discuss my potential sleepover with my new friend, only to face the expected refusal, leaving me disheartened and resorting to my suitcase record player for solace.

In those moments of solitude, I found hope in the possibility of making new friends with the children of our new neighbors. Reflecting on simpler times, I cherished memories of going to the movies with Mama and Rickey, immersing ourselves in the vibrant world of cinema. Several times a day, we would watch multiple movies and the matinees. Our expeditions to the Riviera Theatre or to the Globe and Beverly Theatres were adventures, making every film a grand escape. Aunt Janie, Mama's sole surviving sibling, occasionally joined us, reinforcing the family bond amidst shared cinematic experiences.

The narrative of our family's history, marked by joy and tragedy alike, was a testament to resilience. Mama's recounting of her father and brothers' untimely deaths in 1950, her daughter's death in 1952, and her mother's death five months before I was born—a loss that deeply affected her—underscored the profound impact of familial bonds and the lingering grief of untimely separations. Through these stories, I gained insight into the complexities of life, love, and loss that shaped our family's journey.

In the days that followed, Mama's condition improved noticeably. Her sleep became more restful, and the headaches that had plagued her seemed to abate. On this particular day, she sent me across the street to Carpella's Market with a modest $5.00 to purchase a loaf of bread—Taystee's or Wonder Bread, both equally satisfying—and treated us to a foot-long chili dog with mustard and onions, plus a vanilla malt from the Dairy Queen on the corner of Epworth. As I waited in line, my attention was caught by a catchy tune blaring from a striking white convertible, the epitome of cool in my youthful eyes. The song, "Sally Go Round the Roses" by The Jaynettes, was new to me but an unmistakable jam, demanding a spot in my burgeoning music collection.

At home, music was a constant, a soulful companion that filled our space with everything from Jazz and Blues to the pulsating rhythms of Rock and Roll and the infectious beats of the British Invasion. My early introduction to music, facilitated by Mama's deep house cleaning rituals, allowed me to associate record labels with their unique sounds, fostering a lifelong passion.

One Saturday morning, the pungent smell of breakfast cooking was a gentle wake-up call. The aroma of sizzling bacon, scrambled eggs, hot buttery grits, and Mama's homemade Georgia biscuits, served with apple butter, filled the house. Adhering to Mama's strict morning routine, my siblings and I prepared for the day, knowing well the importance of gratitude before meals. Our family prayers were a testament to Mama's leadership and the values she instilled in us.

The music of Motown, Stax, local artists, and Chess Records filled the air. On any given day, you would hear music being played outside. Black people would put their speakers in the windows, facing outward toward the streets, and light it up. Detroit streets would be swaying and rocking to loud music with meaningful lyrics. Jams, jams, jams.

One behind the other, a steady stream of charcoal-smelling barbecue engulfed the air and filled your nostrils. Family men would be washing and waxing their cars, and children would be playing childish games. My favorite games were jump rope, jacks, bat and ball, and swinging on a swing.

It was a safe time… or so I thought…

Friday, August 16, 1964

That morning, Mama got me dressed for school as she always did. She dressed me in a ¾ sleeve, olive green, white cotton collar A-line dress with a slight bottom flare. Mama bought me a pair of white tights to match. I looked pretty because Mama said so. I wore my church shoes: black, patent leather with a cross strap at the ankle, and they had a small pump. Early morning, like every morning, Mama combed my hair. I had to hold my two fingers and both thumbs out so that she could loop and tie. Up, over, and around, she made green and white ribbons to bobby pin in my hair. Two ponytails and a bang. I was ready for school. "Don't splash in any water puddles like your brother," Mama said. "You are a young lady, and I want you to act accordingly." "Yes, ma'am," I answered.

Before leaving, Mama sat down in the living room on the edge of the blue tweed chair. I was busy looking for my loose-leaf notebook and waiting on Rickey. She called me over to her, fumbling through her change purse searching for money. Digging down to the very bottom, she searched for two pennies for me to buy Twin Pines milk in a bottle, and she gave me a nickel for penny candy. She knew how much I love banana splits. I noticed that every time she found a coin, she would take the coin in her hand and run her index finger around the rim of the coin to identify its marking. Mama did not really have to say anything because I could tell, as well as everyone else in the house, that something was wrong. We didn't know what. Mama laid her hand on my forehead and prayed for me that morning; it wasn't unusual. She hugged and kissed me goodbye. I left for school.

I walked up Whitfield to Northfield Street, where I waited a few minutes for Pam so that we could walk together. "3:00 pm school let out."

I had a good day at school. On the way home, Pam and I walked together, and she asked me if I could spend the night with her. Immediately, I told her no, I didn't think so because I knew that my mother wasn't going to let any of her kids stay away from home. She never did, and I knew better than to even ask. But I told her that I would anyway. Pam enticed me by saying what we were all going to do and how much fun we were going to have. One thing we planned to do was watch Dick Clark on American Bandstand, learn some new dances, and we were going to comb our baby dolls' hair. I was excited even though I knew that my chances were slim to none when it came to spending the night. Pam had four siblings under her, and they were her full responsibility. We talked about a lot of things on our walk home, and one thing we talked about and what we had in common was our mothers. Pam told me that her mother was in the hospital, maybe dying from breast cancer. I didn't know what that all meant, but I told her that I would pray for her mother anyway. We parted ways; Pam turned left, and I turned right. I was happy that entire day, so happy that I skipped all the way home without getting dirty.

Mama took the pep out of my skip…

I asked Mama, and she said no. I started to cry and tell Mama that she just didn't want me to have any friends. Pam was my only friend in the whole wide world. I promised her that I would be safe. I promised. Mama said no again. I continued to cry, holler, and stomp the floors like a damn fool. I guess any spoiled child would do that. I am surprised that I got away with clowning like that because my Mama would slap your ass into the middle of next week for showing out, but somehow that day I got away with it. Looking back now, Mama was tired and did not feel good, and I took advantage of the situation, not knowing then. She gave in and said I could go. "Oh lord, I was so happy!" I hugged and kissed Mama and told her thank you.

"It would be the worst mistake of my eight-and-a-half-year-old life." In passing, Mama had already met Pam's father at least three times before. One day, we were walking home from the Riviera Theater on Grand River after spending that Saturday afternoon at the movie theater watching "It Happened at the World's Fair," starring Elvis Presley. Mama thought she recognized him from her hometown of Macon, Georgia. She told him that she came to Detroit in 1926 when she was six years old. Another time, she stopped and talked to Mr. Gorman when he was outside watering his brown grass. We played outside his yard and couldn't help but listen to Mr. Gorman and Mama talk. For at least two hours, they went on and on, exchanging stories about the good old times back home. Mr. Gorman reminisced about how long his hair was, how slim he used to be, his love for pig feet, white women, and white lightning. Mama talked about her love for the blues. She compared the exceptional blues she heard coming from the juke joints to the Black Bottom blues she heard in Detroit. For a moment, there was silence between them; the conversation turned serious.

They confessed to each other how eternally grateful to God they were to be living in Detroit. He said that when the opportunity presented itself, he left, running from Georgia. Mama said that she loved Georgia. She also said that her father killed a white man with a headbutt; he didn't have any choice. They laughed when Mama mentioned the long train ride she had to endure. When the trip ended, she got off on Michigan Ave and walked along the red cobblestone street. It was a different time. Mama thought they were a nice family.

Normally, we took our clothes off when we came home from school, but Mama said I didn't have to that day. It was still light outside when Mama stood on the top of the crumbling porch, leaning over the edge. She made me cross the street in front of her, as she always did. She told me the dos and don'ts of life. I turned back and looked up at Mama, throwing my hand up. She waved her hand and leaned further, holding onto the green wooden banister. "Be careful," she said again as I walked down the block, checking every address in search of Pam's house. One and a half blocks down, on the right-hand side of the street, I found Pam's two-family flat that they owned. I arrived with my overnight bag, which held my baby doll, comb, brush, and barrettes. Pam lived upstairs too. The only difference between her house and mine was the color; hers was red brick. The address, 5111 Whitfield, would forever be engraved in my memory.

After being there for close to an hour, there was a knock at the door. Pam's younger brother, Vincent, who was six, ran and opened it. Two men were looking for Pam's older brother, Sam. I was combing my baby doll's hair in the dining room when the two men glanced over at me. That brief encounter scared me to death. Suddenly, I was overcome with fear. My mind and heart urged me to get up and leave right then. I can't explain the range of fear I felt. I became so afraid that my body started to tremble from the inside out. Never in my life had I experienced anything like that. Vincent slammed the door on them, saying that his brother was not home. The door shut, and I stood up to leave. I was so afraid that I told Pam I wanted to go out her back door. Pam asked why I wanted to leave; I couldn't explain what I felt. Pam begged me to stay. I tried not to show any emotion, but I just felt that I should leave right then. I sat back down, but the feelings did not waver.

All her brothers and sisters rallied around me and said, "Please don't go; stay with us." My eyes filled with water; I was so terrified of what was to come. I didn't know. I tried to feel at ease, but I couldn't. I stood up to leave again when I heard a knock on the door; it repeated itself. Something inside me screamed for me to leave and run. I heard my mother call me "Pat."

My hands were trembling; I didn't know what to expect next. I dropped my baby doll on the floor and started to run toward the back door, which had a set of stairs leading to the outside. But it was too late. I got up again, and as Vincent opened the door, the two men pushed past him and the other children. They ran toward me.

One man grabbed my arm near my elbow and yanked me upward toward him. I fought to get away, just like my dad had taught me. The kids tried to help me fight, but it was no use. He was bigger and stronger. The other man pushed and bullied the children away from me, herding them into the back bedroom. I was crying and fighting back with one arm. He shoved me into the bathroom. I heard two clicks; one of them locked the door, and with his other hand, he produced a steel gray pearl switchblade from behind his leg and snapped it open. He held it to my throat and told me to shut up, or he would kill me. I was sniffling and crying, terrified beyond words.

What does he want from me? I am a little girl. I am saying this in my mind.

He let go of my arm and opened the door to look out. I tried again to get away, but he pushed me so hard that I lost my balance. I stumbled and hit my back against the ledge of the bathroom window. There was a knock at the door. He extended; his left hand went out towards me with the knife. I was warned to stay back, or he would cut me to pieces. He opened the door and let the second man into the bathroom. They talked, and he let him out and locked the door again with me inside the small bathroom. I was shaking and crying for my mother. He held the knife to my throat and told me to lay down. I would not have felt bullied; I instantly got mad, and I hit him with my fist balled up. I missed it.

He stepped back, and then he lunged forward towards me. Grabbing me by both my shoulders and arms and crumbled my small body downward with his hands. He forced me down onto the cold, black, and white checkered marble floor. All his weight was on top of me. I struggled; I could not move. Panting like the dog that he was, I could smell his foul breath and heavy breathing. I had no win in this fight. He snatched my dress off me, he ripped the collar, and he was grabbing for my panties… I did not know why. No one ever checked my panties but my mother. I kept pushing his hands away from me. He was all over my small body. Fighting me like a boy, like I had seen my brother fight boys before. He covered my mouth with his smelly, sweaty hand. I struggled to stop him, but I couldn't stop him. I cried out from my soul, a cry that would resonate in the heavens. He tore my insides apart. I have never felt pain like that before!

He raped me for hours and hours. I cried helplessly. I prayed to God to help me, but he didn't, so I asked God to make him stop. He didn't.

This PATHETIC COWARD held my small hands together, above my head. I struggled to stop him; he grabbed my body with the other hand and forcibly turned me on my stomach.

This savage mother fucker brutally sodomized me. Over and over, and over again. I passed out from the pain. When I came, I was bloody from the waist down to the to the front and back.

When he finished, he got up off me and opened the door, and he let the second man in. I cried and begged for them to let me go; they passed me around in that bathroom back and forth between the two of them. Playing a game of whose turn was next. I heard one tell the other.

Man, she's a virgin. I didn't know what that meant. I never heard the word. One man sat on the edge of the tub; the other one sat on the toilet seat with the lid down. Their legs were stretched wide to control me in the middle. Their underwear was down and open, and I could smell the funk. I didn't want to look.

I kept my eyes turned away. I was shaking uncontrollably; it didn't matter to them. They destroyed my insides; together, they raped me; they took my virginity. I was brutally raped and sodomized and passed around in that bathroom like I was nothing. I could hear the kids beating on the door for them to let me out. I was crying out for someone to help me. No matter how hard I scratched, bit, clawed, cried, and prayed, my prayers went unanswered.

When they finished with me, they ran out of the house like the scum they were. The first man who raped me before he ran out of the house again threatened me with the knife. "If you tell anybody, I'll find you, and if I can't get to you, I know your brother."

I believe that I lost my mind… that night. I did not understand what happened to me, and I felt ashamed of what just happened to me. I tried with all my might to get up off the floor, but I was having trouble; my knees felt like they were busted open from a bad fall. Pam came in and tried to help me stand up. I was crying and laughing hysterically at the same time. I couldn't crawl. I was able to scoot my body over to the face bowl. I grabbed a hold of it, and I pulled myself up off the floor. Barely able to stand, I held on and faced the mirror that was steamed up. I wiped it with my bloody hand. My body was trembling, and I tried to pull myself together.

My face was swollen and cut above my lip. My white, bloody tights were pulled down around one ankle, and my shoes were sprawled underneath the four-leg bathtub. I could not assess all my injuries right then. I was hurting so bad on the inside of my body. The feeling was there.

It was real. I had to get away, run away, and hide. I held my dress together the best that I could. I tried hard to close my legs, but it hurt so bad. Eventually, after repeatedly trying to stand up, I did. The strength came from within. I did not know that I had it. Something arose on the inside of me and stayed there forever (determination). I made myself do it.

The bright red blood continued to trickle down the inside of my legs. I was dying. I was bleeding from my rectum and my vagina. But I was standing. Inside me, I wanted to die, and parts of me did that night. I couldn't understand what had happened to me. Mama never talked to me about anything like this. I did not pay any attention to what was down there. All I knew was to keep my body clean, and that is what I was taught, and that's what I did. I felt ashamed and embarrassed about what happened to me. I tried to find some self-dignity in the situation. I could not find my panties, so I pulled my tights up and put my arms in what was left of my dress.

I was looking for my ribbons to put back in my hair, and I found my blood-soaked ribbons lying next to the toilet. I fixed my hair the best I could, and I held my dress together. I knew that I had to walk past the same kids I came to play with to get out the front door. I was hoping that they had no knowledge of what happened to me. Cause I didn't.

Pam asked me not to tell her father or call the police because they would take them away from the house and put her father in jail. And her brother would be in trouble for not being home.

Right then and there, I knew that I was going to take it to my grave. No one will ever know what happened to me at Pam Gorman's house. Pam followed me out of the bathroom. She asked me not to leave her house and stay there until her big brother Sam got back. You will see that he won't let them hurt you anymore.

I asked Pam these questions: Do you know their names, who they are, and where they live? Without hesitation, the first boy was, and she called out their names, "Welton Smith and Donald Malone." "They're not boys," I said.

I walked past the kids; they were sprawled across the couch and sitting on the hardwood floor watching the small black-and-white TV. They didn't seem to notice me, and I was grateful. Once outside my head, space was in a fog. I could not get my sense of direction straight. I was in a state of confusion or shock. I looked up into the sky, and the same soft raindrops that fell from heaven earlier in the day washed away the blood stains on my dress and the smell of them left on my body. I wish the rain could have washed away my tears. I started to heave and vomit uncontrollably. It hurt so bad to keep my legs together; it felt as if they were disconnected from my body. I remember that I started laughing aloud and walking away, further and further away from Pam's house.

The streets were dark, quiet, and still. All I could hear was the sound of my small patent leather pumps clicking in the rain. My first thought was to kill myself. I couldn't stop crying. The tears blurred my vision, but I could still make out the lights ahead. Overwhelmed with sadness, I longed for my mama, yet I couldn't go home. Memories of the day flashed through my mind. The urge to end my life was overpowering; where I got the strength from, I don't know. But I forced one leg in front of the other and started running. I ran away from her house, headed towards Livernois Avenue, intending to throw myself into traffic to end the unbearable pain.

Behind me, Pam's entire family, including a stream of kids, was running, trying to catch me. I heard them calling my name through my tears. Just as I was about to step onto the busy highway of Livernois Avenue, someone grabbed me from behind and lifted me into their arms. They cradled and held me tight. I didn't know whose arms I was in, but my fear subsided. Ashamed, I buried my face and cried all the way back to Pam's house. It was then I realized it was her older brother, Sam, who had saved my life that night.

Sam was seventeen and had heard about what happened to me; someone was bragging in the streets. He blamed himself, as he had been instructed to stay home and babysit his younger siblings. I never blamed

Sam. The love, laughter, and friendship we shared over the years would last even beyond his death.

When we got back, I desperately wanted to bathe. I asked Pam to turn her back so she wouldn't see my body. She stayed in the bathroom with the door locked to give me privacy. I was in bad shape. The skin on my back was nearly gone, looking as though it had been scaled. My shoulders and arms were severely bruised and I could barely lift them. The skin on my tailbone and both heels, as well as the tops of my feet, was rubbed off. Both of my hands were cut and my legs felt lifeless and weak. The pain extended from my hips down. I lay on my side in the lower bunk bed in Pam's room, my back against the wall so I could see who came in and out. I was scared and had episodes of crying throughout the night; every time I dozed off, I would wake up shaking and crying. I was miserable and tired.

Sam reassured me that he was home and that he wouldn't let anyone hurt me again—and he kept his word. Sam was a compassionate young man who wore a suit of armor to shield himself from the true hurt, pain, and rejection he suffered from his stepfather. If Sam loved you, that was just how it was; he would do anything to make things right, anything to be accepted.

In the early morning, I was awakened by the sound of arguing outside, behind the house. Pam's bedroom window faced the backyard alley. Unable to get up to see, I was too frightened to move. Pam opened the dirty, dingy curtains and peered over the top of the tall garages.

Pam peeked out and beckoned me with her hand, urging, "Get up, get up! Sam and Welton are fighting outside. Sam has a knife!" Horrified, I prayed desperately for God to intervene, not against Sam but Welton. Pam helped me up, supporting me from behind as I struggled to see the fight with my swollen eyes. In the dim light of the alley, I could make out two figures struggling. Sam had forced Welton to his knees, gripping his head as if it were a football, and was repeatedly kneeing him under the chin. He dragged Welton through the alley, kicking and stomping on him, finally leaving him unconscious on the ground. I hoped he was dead, but he wasn't. While part of me was grateful for the punishment Welton received, it still wasn't enough for me… God, however, had a different plan.

That morning, my mother came to Pam's house to pick me up. Crawling out of bed, I couldn't sit or stand properly due to the pain. My body was sore, bruised, and I was still bleeding. Clutching a pillow in front of me, I made a quick stop at the bathroom to wash my face and hands, brush my teeth, and comb my hair—anything less would be unacceptable to Mama. From the top porch, I talked to Mama, who looked up at me under the bright sunlight, unable to see my injuries. When she asked if I was all right, I lied for the first time and said yes. Pam then asked if I could stay until Sunday to visit her mother in the hospital, and to my surprise, Mama agreed. I was relieved yet felt guilty for deceiving her.

Lying to my mother felt like lying to God. I was raised in Bible school to believe in miracles: that Jesus parted the Red Sea, John the Baptist baptized Jesus in the River Jordan, and that Jesus healed a crippled man by a pool. Mama had always taught me that nothing was impossible with God, and she had prayers stored up for me. I prayed for God's grace and mercy, to heal my body inside and out, to make me whole again. And He did.

I found a special healing in the water, using salt, water, and Vaseline. I took two or more baths a day, covering my bruises with long-sleeve blouses, long skirts, and knee-high socks. As time passed slowly, I moped around at home, feeling a change within me, parts of me shutting down. I was weighed down, still experiencing outbursts of quiet crying in my sleep and haunted by thoughts of that day. This continued into the next year and beyond.

Music was always a constant in our house. Mama had a beautiful singing voice—Billie Holiday had nothing on her. Whether she was making homemade biscuits or cleaning the house, there was always music playing. She would either sing herself or have the radio on, playing everything from blues, gospel, jazz, and more on our record player, which housed a collection of 78s to 45s.

In my room, I found solitude, playing my suitcase record player, searching for some understanding in the music. I had a nice collection of 45s myself. Mama noticed a change in me; she didn't know exactly what, but she sensed something was wrong. I stopped eating and talking. My posture changed; I walked with slumped shoulders and my head down. I became withdrawn, my voice dwindling to a whisper and then to complete silence. I couldn't tell anyone about my pain—I felt I had to protect everyone. The responsibility weighed heavily on me.

At night, I knelt as I was taught and said my prayers, and at the end of each one, I asked God to avenge the men who had wronged me. "And He did," I would say, reaffirming, "Vengeance is mine, saith the Lord. God really heard my prayers." The Almighty had a different plan for Welton Smith and Donald Malone.

On a crisp, cold morning in 1964, Mama announced that we didn't have to go to school and that she had a big surprise for me and Rickey. "So, take your bath and get dressed," she instructed. Rickey and I speculated excitedly about what it could be. Mama was always full of surprises. We walked up Joy Road to the Grand River bus stop, took the bus to Griswold and Grand River, and got off. Next, we visited Morrow's Nut House, where we got a quarter's worth of Spanish peanuts. Right next door was Awrey's Fresh Bakery, where Mama bought me a homemade cream puff sprinkled with powdered sugar, while Rickey enjoyed his favorite chocolate donut, licking off the icing as we walked up the slushy Woodward Avenue to catch another bus.

Our anticipation built as we arrived at the Fox Theater, where a long line had already formed. The bright marquee displayed the names of legends: Marvin Gaye, The Velvelettes, Willie Tyler and Lester, The Supremes, Martha Reeves and the Vandellas, The Miracles, The Four Tops, Little Stevie Wonder, The Contours, The Spinners, Shorty Long, and The Marvelettes. "Lord God, I thought I had gone to heaven!" I exclaimed. "Oh my God, Mama has taken us to the Motown Revue!" I was incredibly happy, overwhelmed by the prospect of seeing all my favorite singers live on stage.

When we reached the front, Mama paid for our tickets, and we walked in. I had never seen anything more beautiful in my life. Everything about the Motown Revue was massive and exquisite, a cultural phenomenon that I was now part of, uplifted by the vibrant performances of musical icons.

The stage was lit up with bright lights, the music was loud, and the crowd was thick. Everybody and their mama came out. People of all ages, young, old, and in-between. Our seats were two seats from the stage. Willie Tyler and his dummy, Lester, entertained until the real acts came out. Marvin Gaye, in his white three-piece suit, sang "Hitchhike." The Velvelettes were dressed in yellow sequence with matching shoes, and Mary Wells sang "Dear Lover." The Contours were dressed in a blue sequence with shiny patent leather shoes, and they sang my jam, "Just a Misunderstanding." Everyone connected to the Motown Review was there. One group behind the other. The Temptations in their red satin suits with matching shoes dancing to perfection sang "Your My Dream Come True," and Little Stevie Wonder had his harmonica, and he played Fingertips Parts 1 and 2. They dragged him off the stage. It was unbelievable. I ran to the stage like everyone else did. I hollered and lost my mind when Smokey Robinson touched my hand. "Oh my God!" I screamed. For the first time, I forgot it all and moved past what I was feeling. But the bus ride home would prove different. Mama took us to see the Motown Review at least twice a week on the weekends until they left.

1965

On this day, I had to find a way. I believe I have a way in mind. Pam's father kept a lot of medication in his bedroom; that's what I'll use to do it. "But damn, I hate swallowing pills." I hugged and kissed my mother, and I said goodbye to my brother. I walked out of the house like I was grown. I walked up Whitfield. I was spinning bullshit around in my head.

I took small steps towards my final destiny. With my shoulders slumped forward and my head hung down, I felt sad and heavy inside. Then I realized I was walking to the beat of the music being played outside. Speakers from the windows of heaven played a song—an unfamiliar tune—that set my soul on fire and saved my life. Prior to any of this happening to me, when I was seven, we belonged to the House of God Seventh-day Adventist Church on Canfield and Riopelle Street. I'd seen others terrain for the Holy Ghost, and I wanted to receive the Holy Ghost. "Oh boy, did I." One Saturday afternoon, I received the Holy Ghost when I was teaching myself how to play the tambourine. This beautiful, but very large, dome, which, when I looked up, led to the heavens, shining lights with lots of bright, magnificent colors, shined on me from above. I was encapsulated in God. Presents. I could move, but only through him. He was holding my hand. As I looked up, I could see the angels flying around, protecting me from what was to come.

Mama said that I was speaking in tongues and crying, out to God to help me. Then she said that I fell out by the altar. I soiled my panties. Mother Travis covered me with a white towel. It was talked about, and

Elder Travis declared that I did receive the Holy Ghost. I do believe that if I hadn't received it before, all of this would have happened to me.

I would have committed an unthinkable crime. And that was to harm myself. I took heed. How can I take something I cannot give? Right then God blocked out the noises of the world, and he propelled my ears upwards," and I heard Paul Williams from The Temptations sing "Don't Look Back, Keep on Walking." As the words magnified in my ears, I was listening, and I felt stronger and stronger. I threw my shoulders back, lifted my head, and felt determined to live.

The tears streamed down my face, and I felt released from something. Free from bondage. I was not going to let what happened to me destroy me. I was going to move forward with life and go on… I was going to have to live with what happened to me.

But at least I was going to live. I got my voice back, and sh*t changed. Whatever little girl I was before it all happened, I would never be again. I was like Eve when she bit into that apple, absorbing like a sponge. My mind, my eyes, and my thoughts changed. The world would never look the same. I stopped playing with baby dolls, I stopped wearing ponytails and ribbons, and I never wore green again. My territory was marked for the first time in my life.

I remember throwing up my guard. I built a brick wall as tall as it was deep; that part of me was locked away where no one would ever have access. I continued to suppress, and I joined a gang called The Whitfield Boys. Sam was the leader of the gang. We were harmless, a gang of broken-hearted misfits that hung together. We were tight; we did our dirt. Sam taught us how to watch our own backs by not taking silly risks and spinning idle time. "Don't get caught up," he would say. If only he had applied the same principle to his own life.

Although the kids in the gang knew what happened to me, they never broached the subject. Young and old, we kids had something in common. Some sort of pain was associated with us. Pam's mother died that year; she was thirty-two. It brought with it a sunny day when Mrs. Gorman was called home by God. The hospital informed us of Pam's mother's passing, a moment that filled me with sorrow for her children's uncertain future. After enduring over a year in the hospital and multiple surgeries, losing both breasts before the cancer spread to her brain, she left her children here. Pam and her siblings were enveloped in grief and desolation, while Mr. Gorman appeared unaffected, engaging in relationships freely. His behavior at the funeral, introducing his new girlfriend and her extensive family in the front row, displayed audacious disregard. Days later, he remarried, incorporating his new family into his home, drastically altering the dynamics and my visits there.

Michael Martin, aged twelve, and Ike, aged nine, were brothers. Together they witnessed their father kill their mother. Chalks, aged twelve, had a mother doing life in prison for a store robbery gone bad. Dickey Bird, aged seventeen, felt like his parents didn't understand him, so he became a car thief and spent time in jail. Diane, aged thirteen, was called the neighborhood hoe. She had her uncle first, her father, her cousins, and anyone else that wanted to. She was like a doorknob; everyone got a turn. Anntionette, aged sixteen, was hiding a secret in the closet. Corinthia, aged fifteen, was abandoned and abused by her mother. She beat and starved her, leaving Corinthia Jackson in the house without food and sometimes the water was cut off. She made her fend for her two younger brothers. She put her men before her children. Burnella London, aged ten, had a mother who had been institutionalized. My mother, aged forty, had been diagnosed with a brain tumor; she was going blind… "With a Child's Heart" by Little Stevie Wonder.

1965

There was love and loyalty between us. As time moved forward and I grew up, I would learn the difference. Mama used to say to me, "Pat, before you leave this world, you will do good to have one good friend left." And she was right.

In order for me to become a full Whitfield girl, certain protocol had to be met. The most important thing in the world was that you had to know how to skate. Thank God I already had a jump on that. You had to wear white pumpkin-seed tennis shoes and turn the tongue up. Whenever we got money, we all bought our shoes at Jupiter's for $1.79 and matched them with white cream bobby socks or windowpanes. Your hair had to be in a French roll, and you had to wear a sheer nylon scarf tied sideways around your neck. The Whitfield boys sported black leather jackets, brogan army boots, and a black greasy do-rag all year round.

I was hanging out, skipping school, sneaking out of the house, smoking cigarettes and weed, and drinking wine and beer. I was a delinquent. At night, we stood on the street corner underneath the streetlight, waiting for Sam and the others to get back from stealing Black Label Beer from the. store on Joy and Livernois. Then we harmonized to our favorite song by the Temptations, "Born to Love You." This was everybody's jam, period. It may not have been a hit worldwide like "My Girl," but it was a local hit in Detroit. Sam took the lead, I followed with bass, and everyone else blended in. We could not hold a real tune, but you couldn't tell us that we couldn't sing. Sam would pass the joint. It was like ten people to a hit. It scared me, but I hit it anyway.

1965

I spent my free time teaching myself how to skate better. These guys' reputations were notorious. They were legendary, and they knew it. I had to step my game up. Many nights I stayed out under the streetlights, listening to music coming from the neighbors' windows. Before long, I was skating my ass off, throwing hops, skating backward, and doing low downs. I took all my hurt and pain with me to the streets or to Orchard Gardens, the roller rink on Clarendon and Grand River. I was going to red light quarter parties, basement parties, and on occasion, I dropped a lot of aspirins and drank Thunderbird wine, Silver Satin with Kool-Aid, and King's Reward.

Skating in the streets and hanging out at Nardin Park taught me how to perfect new dance steps. I was bopping, doing the jerk, the pearl, the temptation walk, and the twine. I could dance, and so could my mama. On one occasion, I even hit a joint and passed it to Donald Goines. I didn't know who he was then. I was nine years old, hitting a joint. The age, I couldn't wait to get to. Secret Service came to Sam's house today and gave him his first warning to turn himself in after ignoring a written letter. Sam hid in the closet. He had been drafted by the United States Army, and after training, he might be sent to Vietnam. I could tell that he was scared; he was just a young man. My oldest brother, Matthew, was on his second tour in Vietnam.

They had a skating contest coming up at Orchard Garden, hosted by Disc Jockey Jay Butler from WJLB. The first prize was $100.00, and the second prize was a handful of the latest albums. The Whitfield Boys kicked ass and took names. They won hands down. Their outfits, along with black masks, stole the show. The routine was impeccable; they never missed a beat. I was proud of them. It helped with their ego, and they were the talk of the Westside. They skated to "Agent Double-O Soul," a 1965 jam by Edwin Starr.

Puberty set in, and it was a game-changer. I was developing at a rapid pace. Every day there was something new, a wonder! I didn't need Mama to tell me anything about what was going on with my body. I could have probably told her a thing or two. I blended in with everybody because I had a body like a full-grown woman, and I was big for my age. The more I ran the streets, the more I learned in the streets. And before long, I had a full understanding of what had happened to me.

Still, I couldn't shake the feelings that stayed with me: humiliation, anger, vengeance, degradation, disgust. All these negative things crept up inside of me and stayed. I was sad, but I knew how to mask my feelings. I suppressed them and kept on pushing. Trying hard to hide the pain, I realized all that street running wasn't for me. I got my act together.

Mama was glad about it. I went inside myself, and I stayed there. I shut down almost completely. Again. My voice was barely a whisper, my body demeanor was humbling. It was a dark period in my life. I was in a deep funk. I was going to end it all again. I couldn't take it anymore. I couldn't tell anyone what happened. Mama was in her own private hell. She would have blamed herself for the rest of her life. Or she would have gotten her Beretta out of her oatmeal box and blown their heads off, then called the police. They say that time heals all wounds.

"Time was standing still for me. I was still waiting on God's promise of vengeance."

February 25, 1965, four days after Malcolm X's assassination, marked one of the most severe snowstorms I'd ever witnessed, destined to make history. Rickey and I struggled to open the front door, only to be greeted by snow as high as the door itself, eleven inches of shimmering beauty, still descending rapidly. School was unmistakably canceled, but my thoughts were fixated on reaching Pam's house to watch Herman's Hermits perform "Mrs. Brown, You've Got a Lovely Daughter." The feat, however, was impossible. Thus, Mama, Rickey, and I spent the day indoors. I yearned for solitude to play my records and immerse myself in my emotions, seeking answers and understanding.

In the afternoons at Pam's house, we would gather to watch "Dark Shadows," "Shindig," "The Man from U.N.C.L.E.," "Swinging Time," and the "Robin Seymour Show," keeping abreast of emerging artists like Major Lance, The Mamas and the Papas, Sonny and Cher, and the legacy of Sam Cooke before his tragic murder three months before.

March 1965

Michael then shared a heartbreaking tale of his own loss; his mother had been tragically killed by his father in a senseless act of violence. This devastating event had left an indelible mark on him, shaping his worldview and his conversations around themes of grief and vengeance. Michael's strength and vulnerability in the face of such profound tragedy deeply moved me, intertwining our lives with threads of shared sorrow and unspoken understanding.

Despite these changes, our group continued to find solace in night skating at Orchard Gardens or singing on the porch until dawn. Our voices melding together, especially with Sam guiding mine to the bass notes, created a bond unbroken by adversity. We navigated our shared troubles, from basement parties to nights filled with dance, relying on each other for escape and camaraderie.

Home life took its own turns. The nights Mama was ill are vividly remembered, like the time we ventured downtown, seeking refuge in a hotel amidst the city's nightlife. Our innocence slightly breached, we absorbed the vibrant, albeit unsavory, language and laughter that night, a secret kept from Mama.

The return of Geri, however, brought an unwelcome tension. Her presence, now more imposing, disrupted the already fragile peace. My health deteriorated, with swollen, feverish lips confining me to sips through a straw, untreatable by hospital or home remedies. Geri's indifference to my condition and her confrontation over my academic performance escalated to a physical altercation, a vivid memory of struggle and defiance on our front porch, culminating in a fight that seemed to echo the tumult of our lives. When I stumbled and fell backward over the chair, she spat in my face and mouth. Eileen and my mother broke up the fight. I remember my mother telling her that she was wrong, that I was a child, and that she was a grown woman. She had no right to put her hands on me. She was hollering and screaming at my mother at the top of her lungs, like they had been sleeping together. My sister, Eileen, was very upset with Geri. They had some words. One thing about it, Geri knew she had been in a fight because I took all my frustrations out on her.

My brother Ricky was somewhere shooting marbles. Geri then stormed out of the house while cursing at my mother and slamming the door. My sister Eileen was pregnant and had been very sick with this baby. When her husband came to the house at the same time, he was rushing her to leave.

She was trying to comfort me and my mama. He then got angry because she wasn't moving fast enough for him, and on her way down the stairs, I went to the door to say goodbye, and I remember seeing him put his foot in her back and kick her down the stairs. When she hit the bottom of the stairs, there was blood everywhere. She had lost her baby.

My mother ran to get her gun, but I had moved it. I had moved the gun and hid it so I could kill the men who had raped me. I was just trying to figure out a way to do it. My sister was screaming and crying, and her children were screaming and crying. My mother was searching the house frantically, looking for the gun to kill him.

He grabbed my sister by the back of her head and threw her onto the porch. I told her to get in the car; she could hardly walk. She was crying and bleeding, and she didn't want to go. I was trying to fight him off with my sister. He then ran and snatched the kids from my arms and put them in the car. She said she didn't want to go, but she knew she had to go if she was ever to see her kids again.

1965

I could see a shadow walking towards us. I couldn't distinguish the figure; I felt instant fear. It looked like Welton Smith, and all of a sudden, I smelled his hands on my face. It was a creepy feeling, and I shook it off. Welton lived on Underwood, one block over. Dickie Bird said, "Yeah, that's him." Sam recognized the walk, and immediately, he broke into a run to kick his ass again. He caught up with Welton in the alley. I heard him say, " Where have you been hiding, motherfucker? I have been looking for you." All I could hear and see was Sam kicking Welton's ass. The streetlights provided enough light for me to see through the space between houses. Sam had Welton on his knees again, kneeing him in the face. He beat Welton's ass until it roped like okra. The Whitfield boys wanted to help, in fact, they said they wanted him dead. But Sam said, "No, this motherfucker is all mine." The Whitfield boys knew what happened to me, but Sam made them swear not to tell anyone. Donald Malone had once been a Whitfield boy, but not anymore. He lived across the street from Pam and stayed inside his aunt's house because he knew that the word on the street was that Sam was going to fuck him up on sight.

Sam couldn't go over there and get Donald Malone because, at that time, you didn't disrespect old people. Even though I was still afraid of them, there was something in me that wouldn't allow me to stay home. I had gone through a lot that night, and I asked Pat and Pam why they didn't help me. They said they did try to help, but Donald held a knife to their baby sister's throat, and they were afraid. We had a special bond that no one could shake, and we made a special pact that night. Sam was on a personal mission. I remember when I first met Michael Martin. He lived on Whitfield, sideways from Pam's house and down the street from mine. I lived on the corner facing Joy Road. He was thin and at least six feet tall. Michael had long, cold, black, beautiful curly hair that waved down his back. The only other person I'd seen with hair that long was Jackie Berry; she had hair down to the back of her knees. But when you spin her around, Jackie is a little hard on the eyes. She had a baby when she was 12 years old. Nevertheless, she was down, and she was also a Whitfield girl. They called him Bo-Rab, a nickname given to him by Sam because he could run so fast. But I called him Michael. It was love at first sight between the two of us. Yes, there is such a thing.

He had a younger brother named Ira, whom we affectionately called Ike because, despite his small stature, he possessed a formidable spirit. Together, they shared the duty of caring for their younger sister, Gloria. Michael, the eldest at twelve, bore the mantle of responsibility with maturity beyond his years. Ike, at nine, and Gloria, around five or six, completed their small, tightly-knit family. I spent countless hours with Michael and Ike, engaging in deep conversations that belied our young ages, forging a bond that felt more like family than friendship. Occasionally, they would visit my home, where my mother welcomed them with open arms and nourishing meals, earning her the affectionate title of 'mama' from them. Around them, my shyness was palpable; I found it difficult to meet Michael's gaze. However, Ike, sensing the mutual affection, teasingly dubbed me "sister-in-law."

Saturday Night– 1965

At Orchard Gardens, the excitement for the Roller-Skating Contest was palpable. The Whitfield girls and I dedicated our entire day to smoking cigarettes, styling our hair, selecting our outfits, and perfecting our routine. WJLB had significantly elevated the event's hype, making it the buzz of the town and fueling our motivation. The stakes were high, with the first prize at $200.00, the second at $100.00, and the third being a pair of tickets to the next roller rink party. We were impeccable, donning pleated skirts, pristine white blouses, and bobby socks. I, however, always sought to distinguish myself with a unique flair in both my attire and dance moves, a testament to my mother's teachings on leadership and individuality. Thus, I adorned myself with Nina's maroon mohair V-neck sweater over my blouse, often borrowing her fashionable clothes since she was frequently at work.

With our skates slung over our shoulders (mine carried by Michael, who held my hand with care and respect), we made our way to the Gardens. Inside, the atmosphere was electric, teeming with youth from every corner of the city. Disc Jockey Ernie Durham from WJLB called the first contestants, categorizing the competition into all-girl skaters, all-boys, and solo acts. The Whitfield girls skated to Pat Lewis's jam "I Can't Shake It Loose," facing off against the formidable Herman Garden Skaters. The competition was fierce, epitomized by our rivals' spirited performance to The Velvelettes' "Needle in a Haystack."

The boys' category was next, with the Whitfield boys skating to Eddie Holland's 1964 jam, "Just Ain't Enough Love," delivering an unforgettable performance filled with hops, splits, and spins. Their skill elicited screams of adoration from the crowd. Finally, in the solo category, Sam skated to Smokey Robinson's "Going to a Go-Go," securing our victory across all categories with his unmatched talent.

Victorious, we won first place in each category, collectively earning $300.00. Celebrations continued at Pam's house, where we deliberated on how to spend our winnings. As the night progressed, it transformed into an intimate gathering, underscored by shared drinks, smoking, and singing Temptations hits under the streetlight. That night also marked the beginning of something new for Michael and me, as we explored the nuances of French kissing—a revelation shared and explained by Pam.

As the evening waned, our connections deepened, not just among ourselves but with the whispers of love that floated amongst us, revealing the intertwined hearts within our group. This night, vibrant with the thrill of victory and the warmth of budding romances, encapsulated the essence of youth, friendship, and the unforgettable joy of shared experiences.

In 1966, the shadow of the Vietnam draft loomed large. Sam received his second draft notice from the Selective Service, leaving us all in disbelief. "Look," he exclaimed, pointing with his stubby fingernail at the document, "they didn't even spell my name right." Despite this, the message was unmistakable; the notice was indeed addressed to Chappelle Williams— Sam himself. Overwhelmed, he voiced his reluctance to participate in a war against those he had no quarrel with. His priority was to stay and look after his siblings to the best of his ability. However, he was acutely aware of the consequences of dodging the draft; in his own words, he knew they would not hesitate to "pick his black ass up."

Adding to the distress, Cindy, his girlfriend, was 17 and pregnant. On that same day, Tony Clark, a neighbor and peer from next door to Pam, also received his draft notice. On the cusp of turning eighteen, Tony was devastated, tearfully dreading the thought of leaving his mother and going to war. He shared that his principles did not align with taking lives. Having lost his father just a year before and with an older brother already serving, Tony's pain was profound.

Tony, an aspiring writer, would share his dreams and poetry with us, reading out loud from his kitchen window overlooking Pam's dingy yellow kitchen. Despite his mother's wishes for a better future for him, which precluded him from socializing with us as she desired, Tony found ways to stay connected. He would play music for us, placing his speakers facing outwards, making sure he remained part of our circle from a distance. Just one day after his eighteenth birthday, Tony had to report for duty, marking a significant and solemn milestone in our intertwined lives.

Fall was here, the leaves were changing fast, and all the beautiful colors enlightened my heart, soul, and spirit. It helped my frame of mind, and the bright colors made me feel better. We were spending most of our time skipping school, learning the latest dances, and hanging out.

Until the day the truant officer came to my house and presented my report card to my mother, I had managed to skip fifty-four days of school. My mother was surprised and shocked. The truant officer made an appointment for me to see a social worker, and from there, I was sent to counseling. They even had Mama take me to a psychologist. They all wanted to know what was wrong with me.

How do I tell someone what happened to me when I was eight and a half years old? The embarrassment and shame were overwhelming. I didn't have a voice to explain it to anyone. I knew the feelings of humiliation, guilt, and fear were something I had to bury deep down inside and learn to live with for the rest of my life. And I was trying to find out how to do that. I wanted to scream that to them. To the top of my lungs, I wanted to say that to them. I was trapped. I was suffering. And what made it so bad is that I felt like I set the trap for myself by going to Pam's when my mother didn't really want me to. Maybe she felt something was going to happen; maybe that's why God allowed what happened to me to happen. The burden of guilt was weighing heavily on my heart.

No one else could comprehend what transpired with me. My mother and brother remained oblivious, deliberately kept in the dark by my silence. They likely deemed me unhinged, a notion I largely disregarded. The sole concern that mattered to me was sparing my mother any additional anguish beyond what I had already inflicted. My heart was shattered and fragmented within me. Their inquiries about my reluctance to attend school met with my steadfast silence. Despite my mother's efforts, I engineered escapes from school, driven by the knowledge that some students recognized me as the girl who was rapped. How this information spread remains a mystery to me, but the palpable silence and piercing stares upon my entry into any classroom spoke volumes.

1966

A lot of time had gone by, and very little was being said in the house. Geri seemed to be running the whole show; she humiliated everyone around her and demeaned everyone in sight. She was never happy; she was a miserable human being, and she made everyone around her feel the same. Mama wasn't strong enough to fight back with words; the weaker Mama was, the stronger Geri got—the more Geri pushed.

One Saturday, there was a knock at the door, and Mama's friend came by to see her. They hugged each other like they hadn't seen each other in years. They sat at the kitchen table, talked, laughed, and reminisced about the good old days, only for me to find out they had been childhood friends.

Mama was cooking and making biscuits, and Isaac had gone across the street to Carpella's Market to get beer. Before he left, I asked him if he would let me cut his hair. He was a little short brown man that would put you in mind of Dracula; he had no front teeth and two long fangs. He talked really fast and seemed to be nervous all the time. I asked him again if I could cut his hair, and I kept saying, "Please, please, please let me cut your hair."

Finally, he agreed. Mama was making biscuits, and I was sitting in the living room watching Isaac drink his beer. The more he drank, the sleepier he got. He got so drunk that he finally fell asleep, and that was all I was waiting for. I then went to the bathroom, got Mama's big scissors, put soap on a washcloth, and put it all around the edges of his hairline. I had seen them cut hair like this on TV.

He immediately stood and screamed, indicating that I must have cut his skin as I continued to cut. "Mildred, look at what she's done to me." Mama came out of the kitchen and fell on her knees, laughing. "Look at what she's done to me, Mildred," he said.

All of Isaac's hair was on the floor. He started cussing and saying, "You should lock her up." He ran out of the house, and from that day to this, I haven't seen Isaac anymore. Mama, Ricky, and I laughed, ate Isaac's lunch, and went to the movies.

Right after this happened, Mama called her childhood friend Leonard Jones on the phone. She asked him to take her to the hospital and to keep an eye on me and Ricky while she was being seen. She didn't tell us why she had to go to the hospital on a Saturday. Leonard drove a little car, and he was always drinking Black Label Beer in the little bottle.

When we got to the receiving hospital, I watched Mama Walk into the emergency room entrance. Ricky and I stayed in the car with Leonard. Mama made us promise to be good. "That only goes so far."

Leonard had drunk so much beer and smoked so many Pall Mall cigarettes that he had dozed off into a drunken sleep. My brother Ricky, being as devilish as he was, whispered in my ear to reach up on the dashboard and get a cigarette. I got the cigarettes with no problem. We smoked and smoked until the car was hot-boxed, and the fire was long. My brother then told me to stick it in Leonard's ear, and I told him no. He said, "Do it, fool," so I did it.

Leonard's head was slouched on the headrest when he briefly rubbed his ear due to the heat. My brother advised me to elevate it above his nose. I said, "No," and he said, "Do it; I ain't going to tell anybody."

I took the cigarette and aimed for his nose. I was careful not to hit the sides. Leonard Jones had the biggest nostrils you have ever seen in your life. With perfect aim, I stuck the cigarette up his nose and left it. He jumped up and was brushing the fire out of his nose. He then started fussing at me, telling me that I was a bad girl and screaming to the top of his lungs. I jumped out of his car and started cursing at him.

My brother, Ricky, laughed so hard that he was on the floor in the back seat, crying. Just then, my mama walked across the street, and I didn't know whether to shit or go blind because I knew I was in trouble for talking back to a grown man. Mama chastised me for talking back to an adult and for burning him in the nose. She made me apologize. When Leonard told her all that I did to him, Mama couldn't keep a straight face; she had a good, hearty laugh. She laughed so hard that tears were rolling down her face. It was good to hear Mama laugh again, even if it was at his expense. When we got home that night, I watched Mama change the gauze stuffed inside her brassiere. Mama was bleeding from her breast nipples.

That Sunday, Mama's health took a worrying dip. She spent most of the day bedridden, battling severe headaches and bouts of vomiting. My attempts to comfort her felt inadequate against the backdrop of her suffering. Our night was disrupted by Mama's delusional insistence that an intruder was in our home, prompting a nocturnal odyssey on the Joy Road bus. This episode, a stark departure from her usual demeanor, revealed a dramatic shift in her condition. The noticeable change in her eye color and sensitivity to light were alarming signs we couldn't ignore.

Despite the turmoil, life's routines persisted. I longed to share my days with Mama, but her health remained a silent storm looming over our daily lives. A misunderstanding over a dime highlighted Mama's deteriorating eyesight, a revelation that filled me with dread.

As time progressed, specifically around November 1966, my life continued amidst these challenges. Sam, facing his imminent draft into the

Army, became my constant companion, cherishing each moment before his departure. Cindy hosted parties, her mother eyeing Sam as a potential son-in-law, hopeful for a union upon his return. Meanwhile, the local boys exploited their impending military service, promising fleeting romances. The aftermath saw many young women facing pregnancies alone, echoing the loneliness in Jimmy Hughes' 1964 hit "Steal Away."

Orchard Gardens announced another skating competition, fervently promoted across radio stations. This event marked our final gathering before Sam's departure. Once again, we entered the skating contest. The eve of the competition brought an unexpected encounter. In search of Ike, Pam and I stumbled upon Mike engaged in conversation with another girl. Our eyes met, igniting a flurry of emotions within me, leading to my abrupt departure. Despite my hurt feelings, the competition awaited. This year, it introduced new categories, prompting us to merge our groups for a collective effort. Despite Michael's attempt at reconciliation, I remained guarded, swayed only by Pam's assurances and Sam's heartfelt pleas, hinting at the transient nature of our time together.

The competition was fierce, especially against the renowned Petoskey skaters, whose performance fell short of expectations. Our selection of "She Blew a Good Thing" by The Poets underscored our synchronized prowess, earning us admiration. Similarly, Sam and his team, choosing "This Old Heart of Mine" by the Isley Brothers, captivated the audience with their spirited display.

The culmination of the evening was the couple skate, where Michael, seizing the spotlight, dedicated a song to me, a gesture that both embarrassed and touched me. The lyrics, he claimed, were a reflection of his heart, casting a spotlight on us both. Amidst the shared excitement and the palpable energy of Melvin Davis's 1965 jam "I Must Love You," the night unfolded into a memorable tapestry of emotions and music, a testament to the enduring power of connection and the bittersweet tang of farewells.

Have you ever been captivated by a tune so compelling that it demands your undivided attention? That's precisely what happened to me. Michael, gliding effortlessly towards me, was not just skating; he was performing the lyrics of the song with a passion that felt like it was just for me. Extending his hand, he beckoned me to join him on the rink. The crowd's gaze was fixed on us, their encouragement palpable. My shyness was no secret, and as my cheeks flushed with color, Michael persisted, skating in place, hand outstretched. My initial reluctance swiftly faded, and taking his hand, I found myself being drawn onto the rink with a grace that felt like a scene from a romantic film. His gesture of kissing my hand as we skated until the song's end was met with uproarious applause, whistles, and cheers. Normally, Sam would shine in the Solo Competition, but this evening, Michael was in his element, and Sam, opting not to overshadow his friend's moment, stepped back, allowing Michael the spotlight for the final round.

Michael's competition was John Tibbs, a member of the Black Stone Rangers, known for their formidable reputation across Joy Road. Their truce was simple: mutual respect ensured peace. Tibbs was a force on skates, yet his song choice for the solo skate, "My Baby Loves Me" by Martha and the Vandellas, though a hit, fell flat for the occasion. It seemed love was his theme for the night, but it missed the mark with the crowd, eager for a spectacle. When Michael took the floor, he chose "Michael the Lover" by the C.O.D.s, a selection that not only showcased his skating prowess but also narrated his own story through its lyrics. Our triumph was undeniable, sweeping first prize in all categories, with rewards ranging from cash to record vouchers, courtesy of Cookies record shop on Grand River.

The night didn't end with the competition. Amid a spontaneous snowball fight initiated by Ike, the playful battle was interrupted by the distant sound of music, a melody too familiar to ignore. It seemed to emanate from Tony Clark's house, though we knew he was away for basic training. The music, growing louder with our laughter, drew our attention to a shadowy figure approaching through the snow-lit night. To our astonishment, it was Tony Clark himself, uniformed and unscathed, surprising us all with his unexpected return. His mother was away, and there, in the snow, we shared a reunion filled with hugs, laughter, and stories—a perfect night under the backdrop of Livonia, Michigan's own Shades of Blue "Oh, How Happy" encapsulating the innocence and joy of our gathering.

The festivities continued on December 9, 1966, with a surprise birthday and farewell party for Sam at Cindy Carr's house. The Whitfield girls and I spent the day in preparation, creating an ambiance of warmth and nostalgia with Spanish peanuts, mints, potato chips, and pretzels. The basement, lit only by the soft glow of a red light, set the stage for an intimate gathering of the Whitfield gang, a celebration marked by genuine surprise and joy for Sam. We were taken aback to find Cheek among them, given it was a couples' gathering. They filed one after the other down the steep, narrow, wooden steps to the basement, ducking their heads as they went. The balloons and streamers hanging low from the ceiling were a challenge for all but Ike, given the height of the guys entering.

As Cheek took his final step onto the basement floor, The Spinner's badass 1966 jam "Truly Yours" began to play. Cheek, thrilled, leaped into the air, only to bang his head on the ceiling. On his way down, he burst several balloons, drawing all eyes to him. The room erupted in laughter; Cheek, mortified, felt his light skin flush red. Among the laughter, Michael's stood out to Cheek. He shot Michael a look that could kill, though he restrained himself, knowing Sam's fierce loyalty to Bo Rab would prompt a swift retaliation. Despite Cheek's glaring, Michael remained oblivious, head bowed.

Known as a Whitfield Boy, Cheek was labeled by Sam as a deceitful informant, unworthy of trust. He resided on Underwood, across from Dickey Bird and beside Anntionette Foster, another from Whitfield. Cheek, oversized and awkward for his age, was often dismissed as a lumbering fool with a frequently robbed paper route. His presence was sparse and, when around, he seldom spoke. Instead, he loomed, silently absorbing our exchanges. Tony Clark had warned us about Cheek long ago, describing him as a tell-all, always skulking in shadows or between houses.

My mother cautioned me against trusting those who are silent or avoid eye contact, claiming they're hiding something. Cheek embodied these warnings; his welcome was always lukewarm, his existence among us barely acknowledged. His demeanor was lackluster. Nevertheless, the party pressed on, feigned enjoyment masking our true feelings.

That night, we learned a dance named the rabbit—simple, cool, with a gentle hop. Yet beneath the surface, our hearts ached for Sam and Tony Clark. Sam had prepared us for his absence, advising against trouble, cautioning the girls against pregnancy, and stressing the importance of education. Sam imparted a life lesson for us to live by, demonstrating to the Whitfield Boys how to look after us in his absence. Though his words reached our ears, they fell on deaf hearts. He pulled me aside, urging me to heed Mama's advice and support her. He cautioned me to be wary, revealing his fight with Welton over me and the lingering threat of retaliation. With Donald Malone in hiding, my safety was compromised.

"I need you to be strong," he implored. His large, dark brown eyes brimmed with unshed tears, his voice thick with emotion. Embracing me, Sam's hug was a fortress of love, so tight I could sense his fear transferring from his heart through his shirt to mine. His tears soaked into my blouse, a rare display of vulnerability I'd only seen once before—at his mother's funeral.

Sam was our rock, the elder brother we all wished we had. He left us with a solemn directive: to keep strong until his return. The evening was to culminate in a final dance, a farewell to Sam, before we headed home. Cindy Carr's mother dedicated a never-before-heard song to us, a fresh release by Lou Rawls titled "Love Is a Hurting Thing." She placed the record and ascended the stairs.

Post-dance, we embraced Sam, making a tearful vow not to weep. He promised to write once stationed. I was focused on his departure. The party's mood was buzzed, except for Michael, who was visibly intoxicated. Ike mentioned he'd been drinking since dawn, a detail overshadowed by the anniversary of his mother's death and the looming farewell to Sam.

The grief was palpable, shared between Mike's male friends and us girls, except for Cheek, who appeared almost relieved at Sam's draft. The snowy night's chill was supposed to sober Michael as Ike and I escorted him home. Discussion turned to gathering at Percy's—a known figure with questionable intentions but who was agreeable in demeanor.

The plan required us girls to gain entry, so I rang Percy's bell and feigned being locked out. Percy, eager to help a young girl in distress, fell for the ruse. As he turned to answer the call, we stormed in, laughter echoing as Percy, bewildered, suggested the girls could stay. His offer was met with uproarious laughter; Ike defiantly secured our right to stay by confining Percy in the closet.

The evening spiraled into joy—dancing, eating Percy's food, and sharing laughter. Then Cheek arrived, unexpected and unwelcome, his intentions clear. His presence shifted the atmosphere, inciting a confrontation with Michael, which quickly escalated. Cheek's advantage was his sobriety and size, making the fight uneven. His final act of aggression—hurling Michael down the stairwell—sparked fury among us.

The chaos that followed was a blur of motion and emotion. Our efforts to retaliate were frantic as we tended to Michael, condemning Cheek's cowardly escape. The evening's joy turned to dismay, underlined by the realization of Cheek's motives: jealousy and an inability to skate, a rite of passage in our circle. Sam's foresight had been accurate, his warnings a testament to the challenges we faced in his absence.

The day after the incident, we gathered at Pam's house to dissect the events. Michael's attempts to brace his fall had left his hand and leg injured, his face marred by a red, bruised patch, his pride deeply wounded. I reminded him of the words he once told me: "Vengeance is mine, saith the Lord. God will even the score." I convinced Michael there was no shame in being blindsided by a cowardly sucker punch—in my eyes, it didn't count. Yet, Michael vowed retribution, insisting he wouldn't rest until he had his turn at Cheek. Given a fair fight, I believed Michael could indeed match Cheek, despite the latter's intimidating stature of 6'3" and a bulky frame, much of which was fat.

December 23, 1966—two days before Christmas and two weeks following their altercation, Dickey Bird invited us over for a breakfast gathering, suggesting a 9:00 am meet-up after his mother left for work. A schoolteacher working overtime at the Board of Education, you wouldn't guess her profession from Dickey Bird's behavior. His home, maintained by both parents who worked tirelessly, was unlike any I had seen—carpeted floors, pristine furniture, and a custom- finished basement complete with a built-in bar. The house was a testament to their hard work, beautiful inside and out.

As the group trickled in, Bird served fried salami sandwiches and Nehi grape pop. I had already eaten, but joined the gathering in the basement where we played music and learned a new dance—the chicken scratch. While everyone else indulged, I abstained from drinking, having lost my taste for it.

The party swelled as more guests arrived, turning the once spacious house into a crowded scene. As Dickey Bird began ushering some out the side door, Cheek made an unnoticed entry through the front, slipping into the kitchen to observe the chaos. Spotting him, I quickly informed Ike, cautioning against alarming Michael and suggesting we plot our retaliation in silence, especially given Mrs. Thompson's hospitality.

We gathered discreetly in the basement, formulating our plan. The atmosphere was tense, everyone aware of the impending confrontation. The key was to ensure Michael didn't get hurt again and to avoid damaging the Thompsons' home. As Cheek lingered in the kitchen, we prepared ourselves mentally and physically for what was to come. This time, we would be ready.

The Confrontation

Before I could warn Dickey Bird of Cheek's presence, Junnie Humphries, embroiled in a longstanding feud with Cheek over deceitful tactics and stolen paper route customers, made his entrance. Standing face-to-face in the kitchen, tensions mounted, and a confrontation was imminent.

The roots of their dispute ran deep, exacerbated by Cheek's sabotage of Junnie's little brother Harold's job. What Cheek hadn't accounted for was Junnie's size and strength—comparable to his own—and his close friendship with Michael. It was as though divine intervention had sent an equalizer in the form of Junnie Humphries, home for the holidays from Michigan State University.

Regrettably, the confrontation escalated into a physical altercation right in Dickey Bird's kitchen. Cheek's typical response—to flee—was thwarted as Junnie landed a forceful blow to the back of his head, sending him sprawling to the carpet. The fight was brutal, and though there were half- hearted attempts to intervene, the sentiment was overwhelmingly against Cheek. Junnie's relentless assault left Cheek unrecognizable, a scene made all the more tragic by the destruction of Mrs. Thompson's crystal lamp and glass table.

Witnessed by Michael and the rest, the aftermath saw us assisting in the clean-up before dispersing. It wasn't long before the news of Cheek's defeat at the hands of Junnie Humphries spread like wildfire. Anntionette Foster and Brunella London approached us for confirmation, which we readily provided, marking the beginning of what seemed like open season on Cheek.

Dickey Bird was acutely aware of the trouble looming over him, and fear took a tight grip on his heart. Knowing him as I did, it was clear he'd resort to drastic measures to avoid his father's punishment.

By evening, news of Dickey Bird's arrest for attempting to steal a car spread through our circle. The winter that followed seemed to echo the melancholy of a 1966 Temptations hit, "Fading Away." It was as if everyone chose to keep a low profile, retreating into the shadows of our own lives.

Nina and George, on the other hand, found solace in each other, becoming inseparable. George's visits became a routine, enriching the evenings of Nina, her mother, Rickey, and me. Even Geri, who saw a spark in George, cautioned that his pace of life was too swift for Nina. Unbeknownst to Mama, their time away was spent reveling in the nightlife of the Twenty Grand, Phelps Lounge, and Baker's Keyboard Lounge. Their weekends painted a picturesque scene of picnics at Belle Isle, amusement rides at Edgewater Park, movie dates, and outings to Bo-Lo. George even introduced Nina to his mother, marking a serious milestone in their relationship.

At seventeen, George openly declared his love for Nina in Mama's presence, a bold move that led him to propose marriage in the same breath. Mama, caught off guard, acknowledged their affection but insisted on patience. She championed young love but knew well the folly of haste. She advised waiting, promising consideration only if both pursued their education to completion. Nina's tears that night spoke volumes of her dismay at Mama's response, yet her respect for Mama's wishes was unwavering.

After George's departure, Mama took the opportunity to impart wisdom to Nina. She held George in high esteem, acknowledging his upbringing as a courteous and clean young man by his mother. However, Mama stressed that good manners were but a foundation, insufficient if the principles of life were forsaken—like the commandment against stealing. She foresaw a challenging path for Nina, one divergent from the rosy future Nina imagined.

George, standing tall at 6'6", was undoubtedly bright and once harbored dreams of playing basketball for the Michigan State Spartans. Yet, external influences and a divergence of interests hinted at a troubled horizon. Mama's counsel was not of disdain for George but a desperate bid to shield Nina from a potential lifetime of heartache and despair.

Chapter 2

"All Goodbyes Ain't Gone"

April 10, 1967. We were in the process of moving from Joy Road and Whitfield to 5341 Bewick. The sentiment of sadness was palpable within me as I confronted the reality of leaving my friends behind. The looming solitude was a daunting prospect. It was during a fleeting eavesdrop that I overheard Geri confiding in Mama about the acquisition of a new residence situated on the East side of Detroit. The house boasted four bedrooms, two bathrooms, alongside a living room, dining room, and kitchen, complete with our very own front porch and a top balcony adorning the back. The onset of packing ensued shortly after. Unbeknownst to me, the extent of Mama's possessions was vast. Although none of the furniture could be considered new, it was still adequate.

The day designated for our move finally arrived. In a desperate bid for closure, I hastened to Pam's house, armed with my new address and a heavy heart, to bid farewell to everyone. It felt akin to the end of the world for me. Emotions ran high as tears were shed, embraces were exchanged, and promises to maintain contact were fervently made. I implored her to keep me informed of any upcoming gatherings. Regrettably, the opportunity to bid Michael and Ike goodbye was missed, as they were away shopping with their grandmother.

Despite my desire for a house, cohabitating with Geri was far from my wish. Mama, on the other hand, radiated excitement, a sentiment echoed by the rest of us. Ricky, especially, seemed eager for a fresh start, harboring hopes of forging new friendships. At times, his solitude appeared to eclipse even my own, exacerbated by the absence of our father. At thirteen, Ricky showed no signs of rebellion against Mama, yet a palpable distance from the family emerged, perhaps a testament to the difficulties of growing up surrounded predominantly by females. Our bond was evident through the time spent together, though he often escorted me home, motivated by a protective instinct he harbored towards me. Unknown to him, his concerns were not unfounded, for I had already been subjected to harm, a secret too burdensome to share even with him. His temperament was a blend of kindness and severity, poised to exact vengeance should he learn of my ordeal. The revelation would undoubtedly trigger a domino effect, culminating in dire consequences for our father.

Collectively, we embarked on the task of packing, eventually culminating in our relocation. That day, marked by decent weather, seemed to signify a new beginning, notably in the absence of Geri's presence. Her ownership of the house appeared to absolve her from any obligations, a stance she firmly embraced. As we journeyed towards Bewick, the sunshine seemed to escort us, leading to a neighborhood vibrant with the laughter of children and the verdant allure of well- kept lawns. The community was a testament to the collective pride of its black working-class residents.

Upon our arrival, we were greeted by curious onlookers of a similar age, who quickly transitioned from spectators to helpers, aiding in the unloading process. Their warm welcome extended beyond mere assistance, as they took it upon themselves to acquaint us with the neighborhood, fostering a sense of belonging and home. This camaraderie was further solidified when Mama pursued early school enrollment for us, marking the beginning of a tranquil phase.

Our father's realization of the indispensable role he played in our lives prompted him to invest more time at home. Geri's employment at the Main Post Office on Fort Street, alongside her relationship with Thomas, remained a peripheral aspect of our lives. Thomas, characterized by his distinctive attire and demeanor, failed to resonate with us, his presence in the house marked by a conspicuous silence towards us.

Meanwhile, Nina's romantic involvement with her new friend Leonard brought a semblance of joy and levity into our lives, his presence endearing him to Mama through his gestures and humor. This period was characterized by an outpouring of affection towards Mama, a stark contrast to Geri's indifferent demeanor.

The announcement of Matthew's impending visit stirred a wave of anticipation among us, a sentiment tempered by the eventual delay of his arrival. His journey by car, as opposed to flight, hinted at a desire for a semblance of normalcy amidst our lives marked by transitions and the undercurrents of familial dynamics.

Around three o'clock in the morning, I found myself asleep across my mother's bed, having waited for his arrival. The distant sound of conversation and the clattering of pots in the kitchen eventually awakened me. After washing my face and brushing my teeth, I descended the stairs, only to be met with a long-anticipated sight—he was finally home. His embrace was warm, and his kisses were reassuring. He complimented my growth to Mama and, in jest, instructed me to fetch Ricky before his playful threats of tickling overwhelmed me. Knowing my aversion to being tickled, especially around my neck, I eagerly complied, awakening my brother to partake in the joyous reunion.

Ricky's response to seeing Junior was heartfelt, reflecting the deep bond and missed moments between them. My father, overcome with emotion, wept at the sight, realizing that the boy he once knew had matured into a man with his own family. Matthew's gesture of pulling out his wallet, which I initially misinterpreted as an intention to provide financial support for Mama, was instead to share photos of his family. His wife Sylvia, a schoolteacher, and her son from a previous marriage, had become an integral part of Matthew's life—a family he embraced with all his heart. His tales of life in Fort Bragg, North Carolina, filled with scuba and skydiving adventures, captivated us until the early hours.

Matthew's invitation for Mama to visit and meet his new family ignited a spark of excitement. Despite his brief stay, the prospect of traveling to North Carolina was a welcome adventure, particularly for Mama, who cherished such opportunities. The trip was planned to include Rickey and me, although Rickey eventually decided to stay behind, seeking to glean wisdom from our father.

Our journey to Fayetteville was marred by an unsettling incident on the Greyhound bus, serving as a harsh reminder of the unpredictability of the world around us. The visit with Matthew and Sylvia proved to be strained, with Sylvia's noticeable avoidance of Mama suggesting a feeling of unwelcomeness, prompting an early departure from our side.

Despite the visit's unsettling conclusion, the beauty and tranquility of Fayetteville left a profound impression on me, standing in peaceful contrast to the civil unrest and cultural shifts occurring back home. The news of Dr. Martin Luther King's opposition to the Vietnam War and the haunting memories of Emmett Till's tragic fate served as stark reminders of the broader social and racial injustices plaguing our country.

Upon our return to Detroit, the bus journey became a moment of reflection, underscored by the soulful strains of The Temptations' "It's Growing" and contemplations of the sweeping changes through the nation. The resurgence of African American culture and identity, symbolized by the empowering lyrics of Curtis Mayfield's "We're a Winner" and the visible shifts in fashion and demeanor, was a source of pride and solidarity.

However, our homecoming was overshadowed by a sudden and terrifying development— Mama's loss of vision. The frantic rush to the hospital, the struggle to maintain composure, and the fervent hope for a remedy were overwhelming challenges. Amid the fear and uncertainty, my resolve to be strong for Mama was unwavering as we faced the daunting reality of her condition in the emergency room. The introduction to Doctor James Brown, who seemed familiar with Mama's case, offered a glimmer of hope amidst the gravity of our circumstances.

I sat quietly while Mama explained what had happened and how quickly it all unfolded. "I fell asleep on the bus coming home," she recounted, her voice a mixture of disbelief, sadness, and resignation. "And when I woke up, my eyesight was completely gone. Just like that. I couldn't see anything."

I reiterated for my mother, "The Greyhound bus pulled into the terminal, and I was getting the luggage down when Mama stretched her hand out to me and called my name, 'Pat.' She said, 'Take my hand. I can't see.' I couldn't believe it. I reached for her hand, led her off the bus, placed her in a cab, and we came here to Detroit Memorial Hospital. Then I called my sister Nina at work."

Dr. Brown, his patience wearing thin, interjected sharply. "You say this happened quickly, but in fact, you've known you were going blind all along, Mrs. Lee. When we met back in 1964, we discussed this. I explained that the tumor in your pituitary gland controls many functions in your body. Since it has gone untreated—I assume since I last saw you—it has likely grown, pressing on the optic nerve, and that's what caused you to lose your eyesight."

His gaze fixed firmly on Mama, he continued, "The only option at this point is to have surgery to remove the brain tumor."

I felt my legs weaken at his words—brain tumor—but I stood tall, beginning to pray silently. "God, give me strength." Just then, Nina walked in.

Dr. Brown's demeanor was cold, almost indifferent. "If you're not interested in the surgery, why bother coming?" he questioned, arrogance lacing his tone. He then turned to face Nina and me. "Your mother needs that tumor removed, but she refuses. Perhaps you could persuade her."

Nina and I exchanged a look of disbelief. If Mama said no, that was final. "It's not about trust," Nina responded firmly.

"Mama, can he guarantee you'll be okay?" I asked, my voice barely above a whisper.

"No, I can't," Dr. Brown admitted, "but your life is at risk without the operation. I'll admit you to the hospital today, and you can sign the papers in the morning."

Nina's voice was laced with skepticism. "What kind of surgery is this? Can you guarantee you'll remove the tumor?"

He hesitated, then said, "It's uncertain. Like shopping around—we have to explore our options."

"You want my mother to sign papers for you to perform exploratory surgery?" Nina retorted, incredulity written all over her face.

"Yes," he answered bluntly. "That's the only way we'll know how much, if any, of the tumor I can remove."

His urgency palpable, he added, "Look, Mrs. Lee, if you don't have this surgery, you're going to die."

Mama stood up, her voice steady and strong. "And so will you, Dr. Brown. Just keep living. God ain't told me nothing yet; my life is in His hands. It's all up to Him."

I sat quietly while Mama explained again what happened and how quickly it had occurred. "I fell asleep on the bus coming home," Mama said. "And when I woke up, my eyesight was gone. So, with that being said, I'm going to keep on trusting God." I could tell he didn't appreciate Mama standing up to him. Dr. Brown turned and walked away without saying goodbye.

My mother was devastated over the loss of her eyesight. I cannot imagine the hurt and pain she was going through. My heart was completely broken for her. I asked God why.

Nina and I led Mama out of the room. Through the stream of tears flowing from our eyes, we walked up the street to hail a cab home. On the way, Mama shared a story about the time she was crossing the street with my oldest sister, Joyce. She didn't see it coming—stepping off the curb, she was hit by a pickup truck. Joyce was only nine months old, knocked right out of her arms. Mama was placed in an ambulance, and she insisted that her baby had been in her arms when she was hit. The attendants immediately started to look for Joyce. They found her half a block up, still wrapped in her blanket. Mama said she and Joyce were examined and released. She had a huge knot in the center of her forehead for a long time.

It was "By the Grace of God" that Mama lived to tell that story.

June 1967

I was sporting an Afro that I braided up every night to help maintain its shape. Mama bought me some new clothes with a whole lot of funk and style. I was having the time of my life, enjoying the summer. The freedom was unbelievable. Most hot summer days were spent sitting on the porch, visiting with neighbors or greeting old and new friends who dropped by. Geri and Nina played pinochle, and I supplied music for everyone. It was a joyous time to be alive.

Rickey was starting to run with the wrong crowd. He got caught gambling, smoking weed, and shooting craps by my father, who decided to teach him a life lesson. "Always have honor in everything you do. I don't want you to live this kind of life," he told Rickey. "The day will come when you'll grow up to be a man. I might not be there, so I'm going to show you how to do it right."

So, he took Rickey under his wing. They started to hang out together, out at all hours of the night, dragging from one after-hour joint to another. Gambling parties on the North End were just a few of their stops. He wanted Rickey to see how people made their money and how they lived. "This is the kind of life you'll lead if you don't learn to use your head, stay in school, and propel your talents to another level." He warned Rickey extensively about using drugs, adding, "The choices you make today will affect your tomorrow."

Time moved forward, and Mama's condition worsened. She'd been seen by another doctor who said Mama's tumor was inoperable; all she could do was rely on the medicine for relief. The medication wasn't helping, and she spent less time at the doctor's and more time at home. She hadn't given up her trust in God—it was just that. Mama would just call His name out loud, "Jesus." I could tell at times it was hard for her to concentrate. It was most devastating for her to become totally dependent on others for almost everything. She struggled with accepting that she had lost her eyesight and that it might never return. I prayed that He wouldn't let her down, that He would somehow restore her sight.

Everyone in the house was affected by what happened to Mama, everyone but Geri. She had a heart made of steel; nothing could penetrate. My mother was a beautiful, wonderful woman whom I'd known all my life. How could this be happening to her? I thought to myself, knowing people more deserving. She was totally helpless and dependent. Maybe she felt that if she put her life in the hands of the doctors, she'd be turning her back on the Lord.

Although everyone was devastated by Mama's loss, they were still busy with their own lives. I remember feeling misplaced, unloved, and ignored. I just drifted away. Nobody understood; nobody had time for me. I had three sisters, and I couldn't talk to them about anything without being criticized or browbeaten. I was having a hard time dealing with it all. I spent a lot of time getting into trouble, doing silly things I shouldn't.

I reached a point in my life where I couldn't deal with it anymore. I didn't know what to do or where to go. The days I didn't spend at home, I spent at the Brazil's house, anybody's house—anywhere else. I just didn't want to be at home. So, I thought of going back and visiting the old gang on Whitfield Street. Tomorrow, I'll surprise everyone and show up first thing Saturday morning.

I washed my hair, braided it up, took a bath, and ironed my two-piece psychedelic bell-bottom pantsuit that I got from Atlantic Spartans. Saturday morning, I got up, took a bath, fixed my mother breakfast, gave her a kiss, and out the door I went. Nobody knew I was leaving. I looked back, and nobody even cared to ask where I was going.

I had ten dollars that Mama gave me, and I'd been saving it for a rainy day. I cut through the gangway, through the alley, and walked past Jack's Party Store on Moffett to catch the Cadillac bus downtown, then transfer. I must say, I was looking good in all those groovy, bright, vibrant colors. Purple, yellow, orange, green, fuchsia—all swirled together on my two-piece pantsuit and short top. My stomach was out; I wore my fuchsia sandals and purse.

Before I left the house, while I was getting dressed, I took a good look at my body and the transformation it was undergoing. I was developing beyond measure. I no longer had to stuff my bras with my sisters' nylons—I was holding my own. I never had to stuff my pants. I was tall—I didn't know how tall, only that I was taller than my mother. Oh man, did I get plenty of whistles, phone numbers, and flirts. I never let that go to my head. I had established my own self- confidence at an early age.

The only person I wanted to notice me was Michael Martin, and wouldn't you know it, he wasn't home. His grandmother had taken them to visit their father in prison—it was her son who had killed Mike's mother.

Diane Smith came to her door when she saw me knocking at Pam's. She told me about Michael and where they had gone. She also said that she didn't know where Pam and Pat were, only that they had had a big falling out with Mr. Gorman and they had left last night. The police were called, she said. She recounted that Mr. Gorman attacked Pam with a belt, and Pat hit him in the head with a heated iron. She creased Mr. Gorman's forehead, then they ran away.

We were trying to figure out where they could be when Diane said to me, "You know my cousin Welton, don't you?" I looked at her as if she were crazy. I never knew that Welton Smith was her cousin. I thought to myself, "Yes, don't you know what he did to me?"

I replied, "Yes."

"Well," she said, "he got killed last week."

I couldn't believe what had just come out of her mouth. It was like I couldn't hear the words any longer. I was watching her lips move.

Diane told the story. She said that Michael Gardner had given a party last weekend at his new apartment on Broad Street, off Joy Road. People came from everywhere. Wall to wall, brothers and sisters were enjoying themselves, grooving to the music.

Michael Gardner searched the crowded party looking for his girlfriend, but she was gone. Diane went on to say that Michael Gardner said he felt something was wrong; he got sick to his stomach when he noticed that Welton was missing too. Michael put the two together when he noticed the bathroom door was closed and locked shut. Immediately, he went to his bedroom, grabbed his gun, and kicked the bathroom door in to find Welton on top of his girlfriend on the bathroom floor, trying to rape her. When Welton saw the gun in Michael's hand, he got up off her.

With his pants still down around his knees, he tried to run, but it was too late. Michael Gardner aimed and pulled the trigger. He opened Welton's gut with a sawed-off shotgun. When the police came, they found Welton's body in two halves. Michael folded him like a cheap wallet. Diane said that Michael Gardner blew a hole right through Welton's stomach, and it went through his back, severing him almost in half.

Michael Gardner splattered Welton's black dirty ass all over the bathroom wall. Welton Smith is no more. They arrested Michael Gardner and released him early that morning. No charges would be filed against him.

Well, you could have gotten me up off the floor! That was truly music to my ears and a blessing from God. I thought to myself, "Vengeance shall be mine, saith the Lord." In my soul of souls, I was glad that Welton was dead. I'm glad that he couldn't hurt any more little girls. God had truly answered my prayers. One down and one to go. Donald Malone is still out there. I left Diane's house, stepping high. I really wanted to skip down the street, but I knew how to maintain myself.

Diane was one of my close girlfriends, but not close enough that she knew what her cousin did to me. So why should I show any emotions to her and reveal my hand? But what really adds a twist to this story is that Michael Gardner was Welton's first cousin on his mother's side.

Michael Gardner was raised around him, so he knew what kind of animal Welton was. As far as I'm concerned, Michael Gardner did everybody a solid. My eyes combed the street. I had to watch my own back today; the street was deserted.

I walked over to visit Corinthia Jackson. We had a lot to talk about, and I wanted to hear what she had to say. She expressed how lonely Whitfield had been since Sam left. I asked her without hesitation if she had heard about Welton, and she said, "Girl, that's old news. Welton got killed last week, and nobody went to his funeral but his family." She proceeded to tell the story. I wasn't interested in the story; I had heard it already. I was only interested in the truth. Welton Smith was dead. I wasn't raised to feel like it was alright to be glad that someone died. But on the flip side, maybe that only applies to good people.

I stayed at Corinthia's house that entire day, hoping to see Michael, Ike, or some of the old gang. We passed the time playing on the phone and calling Greg's Pizza on Livernois Avenue, placing orders, and sending the food to people we didn't know. We were on our knees, laughing at the amount of food we were able to send.

Corinthia placed an order at a phone number she didn't know, and a boy answered, and they began to talk. He wanted to know more about us, so she invited him over. She ran to get dressed, and I straightened up her house. We weren't worried about Corinthia's mother coming home.

There were three things I knew about her mother:

1. *She never came home, and if she did, it was with a different man.*
2. *There was never any food in the house.*
3. *She always jumped on Corinthia's and beat her up.*

I played records and learned a new dance called the Shing-A-Ling while we waited for her new company to show up. I started to feel somewhat nervous, so I insisted that we keep the door open while her company visited. Corinthia didn't know the reason for my sudden feelings. Well, finally, he did show up, and he was driving a lovely car. He got out with his friend, and they walked up and introduced themselves to us. Thomas Newson and his friend, Eric. But I called him Eric. Immediately, we all hit it off.

We were laughing, teasing, flirting, and playing around with each other like we were old friends. The four of us had fun. Eric held my hand,

and we stayed outside in the open, talking to them both for two hours. Corinthia learned promiscuity from her mother's behavior. And soon she and Thomas Newson were upstairs in her bedroom, taking care of business. I invited Eric into the house. We drank Kool Aid, sat, and talked quietly. I even tried to teach him how to bop and socialize (slow dance) because he said that he didn't know how to dance. We just spent time getting to know each other and doing the things that kids do. I came to find out that he was just as shy as I was.

After Thomas got what he came for, he was ready to leave. Eric and I laughed at Corinthia and Thomas. We teased them about what they were doing.

"Of course," Corinthia said, "I didn't do anything with him; we were just kissing."

Thomas turned around, and the look he gave Corinthia was different. I knew that Eric was a kind boy. I could tell that his mother had raised him well because my mother had raised me well with manners and respect, and that's what Eric showed me.

I was very comfortable with him. He asked me my age, and I told him that I was fifteen. He said, "You look younger than that. He chucked with that bashful smile. He stepped back and looked me up and down and said, "I mean, your face looks young."

He told me that he was seventeen and didn't have a girlfriend; he was looking for one. He said, "You are pretty, and I like you." I blushed when he said it. And so did he. Eric walked over towards me and reached for my hand. He looked me in the eye and said, "I'm going to call you OK." Then he kissed me on the cheek. Oh my, I thought I almost fainted. He was adorable and gentle, and he was nice.

It was love at first sight. The moment our eyes met, I knew, and so did Eric. We exchanged phone numbers, promising to keep in touch. As he stepped back, opening the door for me, I insisted on walking him out to his car. It was then, under the soft glow of the streetlamp, that I truly saw him. Eric was undeniably cute, his bashful smile only amplifying his charm. Towering over me, his brown, curly locks cascaded down to his shoulders, framing a face that radiated warmth. His voice, soft and soothing, drew me in as we stood there, lost in conversation. I knew, right then and there, I had fallen in love for the second time in my life.

Plans shifted unexpectedly. Thomas, having to drop Eric off on McDougall Street, offered me a ride home. My mother's stern advice echoed in my mind, warning against accepting rides from strangers. Yet, with Corinthia agreeing to accompany me, I felt reassured enough to accept. Eric and I nestled in the back seat, our conversation flowing effortlessly. Thomas navigated to my home without incident, where Eric, ever the gentleman, walked me to my doorstep. His kiss on my cheek left me elated, floating on my own cloud as he promised to call.

No sooner had Eric descended the six wooden steps than I found myself stepping into a living room bustling with familiar faces. Dickey Bird, Ike, Pat, Michael, Pam, and Chalk were all there, engaged in lively conversation with Mama. The day's surprises seemed endless. After exchanging a warm embrace with my mother, the rest of us huddled together, sharing hugs and kind words. Michael's compliment, "Wow, you look nice," sent a wave of warmth across my cheeks. "Thank you," I managed, my voice tinged with a blush.

With Mama heading to bed, I took to the kitchen, cooking hamburgers and French fries for the group. She had given them permission to stay the night, trusting us to respect her home. Later, gathered in the small bedroom, we ventured up to the top porch, a place of countless memories.

The night air carried a different weight as the group insisted on stepping outside, claiming they had something to tell me. Under the dim alley light, Michael pulled me into a hug, his voice heavy, "Welton got killed last week." My heart sank; the news was not new to me. "I know," I whispered back, "Diane and Corinthia told me. I've been in the hood today, looking for all of you."

Just then, my father approached, his presence immediately cutting short my conversation. He greeted everyone with a warm embrace and, with a tone of amusement, asked, "Guess how Dickey Bird found you?" He then shared a story from last month, when he and Rickey were at the north end, and he happened to mention where we lived.

"I'm glad you did," I responded.

Offering a gesture of hospitality, he presented Dickey Bird, Michael, and Ike with his favorite wine, Muscatel. They each took a sip directly from the bottle, quickly realizing it wasn't sufficient for all. Without hesitation, my father made his way back to Wonder's Market on Shoemaker Street to purchase a bottle of Ripple, a slight upgrade from our usual fare. My father had always been the epitome of cool in our eyes, preferring we drink at home under his watchful eye rather than risk the dangers of the streets.

However, he was a tad too late tonight. By the time he returned from the store, we had already slipped back out to the alley to finish our conversation about Welton. Dickey Bird said that the word on the street was that Welton had raped several little girls in the hood. The police were gathering information on a suspect. They didn't know who he was; the police even stopped Cheek for questioning. They passed the bottle to me first to do the honors. I poured some out for the brothers who are not here, then took a drink from the neck and passed the bottle.

We toasted to Welton's death, of course, then we buried him. We promised that we would never say his name again. With a separate toast, we honored all the brothers over in Vietnam. It didn't matter what nationality they were; all blood is the same color. We were in this sh*t together. We toasted to Dr. Martin Luther King, Muhammad Ali, President Kennedy, Malcolm X, Viola Liuzzo, Emmett Till, Mama, Sam, and Tony Clark.

After we toasted everybody, we sat on the porch and just talked. I was surprised to see Rickey take a joint out of his pocket when he walked up and handed it to Ike. He fired it up. I looked at Rickey, and he said, "Do you think you're the only one smoking?"

I didn't respond; I was sitting with my back to the alley. They passed the joint from one end of the back porch to the other but never passed it to me. Rickey looked at me and said, "I know more than you think I do." I didn't know what he was talking about; I hadn't done anything wrong. Everybody got cool, and I got a contact.

We laughed and rehearsed a new badass jam by Marvin Gaye and Tammi Terrell titled "Your Precious Love." I say it like that because they sang it like that! Believe it or not, I was tired. I'd had an exhausting day. I went and got in bed with my mother. Pat and Pam slept in the rollaway bed in the room with me. We said goodnight. After breakfast, I walked them to the corner bus stop, and they went home. I was glad, in a sense, because I needed time to process all the information from the day before.

With the exception of stealing a few kisses from my mother throughout the day, I stayed to myself, played music, and cried silently. I felt sad and torn apart inside. As glad as I was about Welton's demise, I still didn't feel the true satisfaction that maybe I should have felt.

This animal stole something that belonged to me. Something that was precious to me was my virginity. I can never, ever get it back, and I'm mad about it. It's a terrible thing to be violated and taken advantage of. It was up to me to decide the day and who I wanted to give myself to. He ruined it for me forever. I didn't want my first time to be remembered with brutal nightmares and thoughts of Welton and Donald rapping me. As glad as I was, there's still no closure to what I was going through. I was going to have to find a way to deal with it, but I didn't know how.

God is in charge, and I had to pray to him for peace. I know that he heard my cry and my prayers. He saw what happened to me, and he made it right.

June 1967

Nina brought her new boyfriend, Leonard, home around the same time I discovered a stray dog in the alley. This dog, with her grayish-brown coat mixed with white, mirrored my every step with four of her own. After following me to Jack's Market and back, I couldn't resist bringing her inside. Instantly, I felt a connection, and without a second thought, I decided she was mine. She had a feminine grace, and I named her Frisky. Giving Frisky a bath with Mama's bubble bath, combing her hair, and adorning her with barrettes became our bonding ritual. As I fed her on the back porch, I could hear Mama, Leonard, and Nina's laughter, their voices mingling in the small kitchen as Leonard regaled them with jokes. Leonard had a knack for making everyone laugh, a quality that endeared him to us ever since Nina introduced him to Mama the previous year.

Leonard was already like family, loved for his humor and kindness. It wasn't a surprise when talk of marriage began to surface, though Nina was only eighteen and Leonard nineteen. Mama's initial skepticism, rooted in their youth, was palpable during Leonard's bold proposal at the kitchen table. Yet, the love and sincerity in Nina and Leonard's plea won her over, especially after Leonard's promise to speak with her father.

The news of their engagement turned the day into one of celebration, with neighbors and friends stopping by, sharing our joy. It was a time of happiness, tinged with Mama's optimism despite her concerns about their youth.

In the first week of June, preparations for the wedding and familial introductions filled our days. Dinner invitations between the families showcased their culinary traditions, from my father's culinary skills to the Eddingtons' soul food feast, marking a union not just of Nina and Leonard but of our families. One month away.

The wedding was set for July 22, 1967, a date that promised to be a beautiful culmination of love and family. Meanwhile, I savored my freedom, indulging in late-night talks with friends and exploring the world beyond our home, even if it meant sneaking out. My curiosity about life's broader canvas was insatiable, a contrast to the familial bonds and traditions that tethered me to home.

I spent a considerable amount of time at the Brazil family's home on Hurlbut Street, which was just behind where I lived. Their house had become the go-to gathering spot for everyone in the neighborhood. Mr. and Mrs. Brazil were free-spirited individuals whose warm, welcoming nature drew a diverse crowd of friends; they were the kind who never met a stranger.

My brother and father, already well-acquainted with the neighborhood, reintroduced me to all the local kids, and before long, I was meeting them in droves. The Wynn family boasted sixteen children, while the Huff family had an astounding twenty-seven. With families of eight, nine, and ten children being common, there were always new faces to meet. Soon enough, we were all on a first-name basis. I spent time with those I liked and steered clear of those I didn't, finding myself in the company of a whole new class of peers. It was a game of survival, and my mission was clear from the start: to lead, not follow. These kids were seeking pleasures in life far beyond what I was used to, and growing up hard and fast was the norm.

I knew I had to step up my game to keep up. Thus, I claimed to be fifteen, the same age I had told Eric. The Brazils were known for their parties; either they were hosting, or people simply gathered at their place over the weekend. Most were welcome, including me. I had plans to attend one of their parties without letting my mother know. My brother and I made our way there, navigating through alleyways. On a corner, we passed four guys shooting craps under a streetlight. I hesitated, but my brother urged me on, and once we stepped into the light, he recognized them. Proudly, he introduced me as his baby sister, Pat.

Spunky, Gramps, Robert, Kenneth, and Nanny greeted me, and my brother boasted of my looks, eliciting affirmations from them. I squeezed his hand and whispered to him not to say such things. Just then, a boy stepped into the light, locking eyes with mine, which embarrassed me. He was surprised to learn I was Rick's sister, having seen me around before.

We made our way to the party, enveloped by the crowd. The adults congregated upstairs, while we, the younger ones, had our own space in the basement, lit by the soft glow of red lights. The atmosphere outside was predatory, with the guys lining up like wolves, watching as the girls, dressed in the latest fashions, entered the fray.

Knowing I needed to stand out, I chose not to flaunt my figure but to test my ability to attract attention in other ways. For the occasion, I wore a bright red tent dress straight from Lerner's Department Store in Detroit, complemented by perfect red ankle pump heels that made my legs look longer. My afro and big red wooden beaded earrings completed the look. I felt good, fresh, and, most importantly, like myself. The compliments I received boosted my confidence, proving I could lead and dare to be different. In Detroit, fashion wasn't just about what you wore; it was about attitude and style.

As the night wore on and the crowd thinned, Evan Brazil took on the role of DJ, playing hit after hit, keeping the remaining guests entertained and the vibe alive. He selected a track by Leon Heywood, and the smooth rhythms of "It's Got to Be Mellow" filled the room. Mae Bertha Wynn and I took to the floor for the first time, and immediately, it was clear we shared something special. She moved with a grace that matched, or perhaps even surpassed, my own. Our creative chemistry and the effortless way we invented new steps on the spot were perfectly synchronized. As we danced, the crowd stepped back to watch. A few girls rolled their eyes in envy, but their disapproval didn't dim my spirits.

Evan then dimmed the atmosphere further, replacing the white bulb with another red one, casting the room in a sultry glow. The music slowed, cooling the air with its vibes. Several guys approached me, seeking a dance, but I declined their offers. While I enjoyed a slow dance, a "Social," I was selective with my partners. I disliked the unwelcome advances and disrespect some boys displayed on the dance floor, having witnessed too many girls subjected to such behavior. I had vowed never to put myself in that position.

The moment Evan cued up a hit by the Miracles, 1967's "Swept for You Baby," everything changed. Robert approached me, gently touching my hand, and drew me onto the floor into an embrace that felt as if I belonged there. We moved together as the room watched on; our connection was undeniable.

Driven by the crowd's enthusiasm and the guys' eagerness to find their partners for the evening, Evan played four more soulful tracks in succession: "Tell Him" by Patti Drew, "Hypnotized" by Linda Jones, "Together" by The Intruders, and "Hey Love" by Little Stevie Wonder. From the first notes of "Swept for You Baby," I felt a bond with Robert that went beyond the dance floor. His grip on my hand, firm yet respectful, spoke volumes. Each song saw us drawing closer, his embrace tightening in a tender, protective manner. Resting my head against his chest, I could feel the steady beat of his heart, a rhythm that whispered promises of affection. Unbeknownst to us at that moment, the love that began to bloom would endure for over thirty-seven years.

This sensation was entirely different from what I had felt for Michael. This was more profound, more real—I could feel it deep within my soul.

After the party ended, my brother Rickey and Nanny had vanished. Rickey was supposed to walk me home. Instead, I found myself outside, chatting with others. Some of the girls were clearly upset with me, jealous because their boyfriends had spent the evening talking to me.

I wanted to make it clear that just because I spoke to everyone, it didn't mean I was interested in stealing anyone's boyfriend. After all, my heart had already chosen its favorite.

In the midst of these exchanges, Robert Howard came over and draped his jacket across my shoulders. Taking my hand in his, he offered to walk me home. We opted for the longer route, and along the way, he shared advice on navigating the complexities of our neighborhood, revealing that my brother had confided my age to him. My heart sank with embarrassment.

Robert admitted he was fourteen and a half, which surprised me given his mature height of at least 6'1" and his dark brown eyes that seemed to hide stories beyond his years. His hair, a sandy brown, was neatly styled, and his appearance was undeniably charming. I knew right then—it was love at first sight. Again.

As we approached my house, Robert shared that he didn't have a girlfriend and wasn't interested in the local girls. "They're too fast, not like you," he explained. Then, with a gentle lift of my chin, forcing me to meet his gaze, he asked if I would be his girlfriend. Overwhelmed and shy, I barely managed to whisper "yes." Around the side of the house, he kissed me—a perfect first kiss that left my lips tingling.

At my doorstep, he confessed that my brother hadn't actually disappeared; Rickey had given his blessing for Robert to walk me home. Stepping inside, I leaned against the door, afluttering with the realization that I was experiencing true love for the very first time. Again

Robert's affection and compliments soon made us the talk of the neighborhood; we were inseparable. He spoke to me of his family, sharing the sorrow of his oldest brother's recent passing with a vulnerability that drew me closer.

Robert, the youngest of four brothers, came from a family of long-standing marriages. His mother worked in Grosse Pointe, while his father was employed at the Chrysler assembly line. Everyone, including my family, was impressed by the upbringing that had shaped him into the respectful and tidy young man he was.

He sometimes arrived on his bicycle, dressed in crisply pressed khakis and a starched shirt, his cleanliness extending even to his well-kept toenails visible through his sandals. Our dates often included rides on his handlebars to buy ice cream cones or NE-HI grape pops, which we'd share with a single paper straw.

We shared countless kisses, stolen in moments of privacy away from the eyes of friends and family. He assured me of his intentions to wait until we were older, a promise that both comforted and honored me. Our relationship was one of pure and innocent love, visible to all who knew us, including our parents.

Wedding Day, July 22, 1967

The morning air was filled with palpable excitement as everyone bustled about the house, preparing for Nina's grand wedding day. The decision to host both the ceremony and reception at home lent an intimate and heartfelt touch to the occasion. Nina, in her radiant beauty, donned a flowing white dress complemented by an exquisite bridal veil that seemed to capture the essence of her joy.

Unexpectedly, the task of escorting Nina down the stairs fell upon Rickey, as our father was absent, having to leave abruptly to see about his elderly mother. Eileen, Geri, and I, despite our mismatched dresses, stood proudly as bridesmaids, embodying the vibrant spectrum of a rainbow. Geri was resplendent in a yellow and white formal dress; her appearance was so refined it was nearly a transformation. I chose Mama's hot pink dress that ended at the knees, paired perfectly with swing-back shoes. Eileen's dress was a vision in soft green, its neckline adorned with delicate pearls.

Mama wore a pastel violet two-piece summer suit, her elegance unmatched. Rickey, caught unprepared without a suit, decided on a royal blue shirt adorned with black pinstripes, complemented by black slacks and shoes—a look that, surprisingly, suited the occasion well.

With a sense of pride, Rickey led Nina down the stairs through the living room and into the dining room, where they would exchange vows. Nina was absolutely beautiful in her white flowing gown with a matching veil and bouquet of flowers. Leonard awaited, distinguished in a white tuxedo trimmed in double rows and accented with a rainbow cummerbund, reflecting the day's vibrancy.

The house, front porch, and back porch were brimming with guests—family, friends, and neighbors, some of whom Mama hadn't seen in years. Aunt Janie, alongside Big Mama and the Eddington family, wouldn't have missed this for the world. My father missed the wedding, but he returned home just in time for the reception.

A hush fell over the crowd as the minister began to recite the vows, weaving the couple's commitments into the air around us. When he pronounced them man and wife, and Leonard lifted Nina's veil, the emotion of the moment was overwhelming. Tears streamed down their faces, an echo of the joy and sentiment that filled the room, moving us all to tears.

Leonard's kiss sealed their union just as the crowd surged forward, everyone eager to offer their congratulations. Gifts, cards, homemade dishes, and bottles of liquor, beer, and wine were presented, along with ice—a thoughtful and practical contribution to the festivities.

As the celebration unfolded, I slipped away to change into something more comfortable. With shorts on, I rejoined the party, which was in full swing, the music setting the tone for a day that would stretch into the night. We danced and celebrated, embracing the joy of the occasion until exhaustion claimed us, marking the end of an unforgettable day.

Mama was exhausted too. Before drifting off to sleep, she shared that George had called, wanting to extend his congratulations upon hearing of Nina's impending marriage. It was a moment of vulnerability for Mama; she confessed her concerns about George, pondering whether denying their union had been a mistake. The memory of Nina's tears after her phone conversation with George weighed heavily on her. It was clear to Mama that the love between them endured.

"Mama would probably have given her blessing for them to marry," she mused, "if only George had shown some willingness to change."

Nina had confided in Mama too, revealing George's emotional plea over the phone. He was inconsolable, desperately begging her to reconsider, professing he couldn't bear a life without her.

July 23, 1967

The festivity from Nina's wedding lingered into the next day, with friends and family still milling about. I found solace on the front porch, lost in music from my portable record player, when the abrupt sound of a warning siren cut through the air. The siren blared relentlessly, a foreboding interruption to the day's calm.

Confusion turned to fear as neighbors emerged with news of a riot erupting on 12th Street. Reports of looting, violence, and a city in flames spread like wildfire. The community was in shock, grappling with the reality of a city under siege. Amidst this chaos, the ominous presence of the National Guard, with their commanding presence and armed directives, underscored the severity of the situation. Despite the danger, I remained on the porch, enveloped in my music, a defiant act of normalcy in the face of escalating turmoil.

The mood changed quickly. The brothers put down their drinks and joints and shifted their brains into survival mode. No one knew what was coming or what to expect. So, the brothers went home and strapped up. Some patrolled the areas to make sure families were okay.

Brothers that were never seen before re-entered their familiar surroundings and communities. The brothers took turns watching out. Some partied through the riot; others paid close attention to what was going on. They stood on the back porch, strapped down, and talked about the civil rights movement going on. At the same time, others played cards and ate.

They continued to party the entire weekend. Some brothers even stopped by my house the next day to check on us out of respect for my father. They thought he was still gone, and there was a house full of ladies there, including Geri's boyfriend, Thomas.

Someone in the house stood up and said that brothers and sisters were dying for the cause. "We're going to party and celebrate their lives." And we did that the entire weekend. Mama didn't seem to care if we had a house full of company. In fact, I think she enjoyed it.

12th Street, as Detroiters knew it, was crawling with drug pushers, pimps, prostitutes, addicts, thieves, number-runner snitches, and murderers. During the riot, the city was under a curfew from 9:00 a.m. until 6:00 p.m. I stayed pretty close to home, with the exception of hanging out in the back alley sipping on Boone's Farm apple wine with some friends, courtesy of Jack's Market after brothers broke the windows and stole it all.

After it was all said and done, those brothers burned down their own community. 12th Street would never be the same. Over a period of five days, forty-three people were killed, and 33 of them were Black. I wasn't surprised.

In the first week of August 1967, I got dressed like any other day; my clothes were starched and neatly pressed. I spent so much time outside that the hot sun bleached my hair to a light auburn. I was spotless as always, gliding through the alley and then the dirt-filled gangway, careful not to tarnish my white, polished tennis shoes. My destination was Jack's, intent on buying a pack of cigarettes—claiming they were for my father, who knew Mr. Jack well from his wine-selling days in the store.

Upon securing the cigarettes, I stepped out to find the street deserted, save for Emory Brazil standing on the corner. Being shy, I refrained from speaking. Yet, in his husky, raspy voice, he addressed me, "Hey, ain't you Pat Lee?"

"Yeah," I replied, a lump forming in my throat. "You're the new girl that lied on me," he accused.

Confused and defensive, I retorted, "No, I'm not. I don't even know you."

His approach became threatening, aggressive. "Yes, you did!" he shouted. "You told my mother that I tried to kiss you."

"I didn't," I insisted, my voice rising. "I didn't say that."

Our argument escalated quickly, voices climbing, until we were face-to-face, toe-to-toe, shouting at each other. "If you were a man, I'd kick a dent in your ass," he taunted, repeating it for emphasis.

His words struck a nerve. Offended and hurt, I labeled him a bully in my mind—a bully I was determined to confront. Turning on my heel, I warned him to stay put until I returned, hurling insults as I fled. My earlier concern for cleanliness forgotten, I charged through the gangway and alley, propelled by rage.

Bursting through the back door with such force it shook, I took the stairs three at a time to my mother's bedroom. There, hidden beneath her mattress, was a German Luger Beretta. Seizing the gun and its clip, tears began to stream down my face as memories of past grievances flooded in. Determined not to let anyone hurt me again, I raced downstairs, past my brother-in-law Leonard, who was nonchalantly drinking Kool-Aid in the kitchen.

Leonard attempted to intervene, grappling with me on the back porch as he tried to calm me down and coax the gun away. But my resolve was ironclad. I loaded the gun and darted back outside, Leonard in hot pursuit.

Seeing Emory still standing there, Leonard shouted a warning, but I was already in motion, gun raised. Emory took off just as Leonard tackled me, wresting the gun from my grip. He helped me to my feet, his concern evident as he brushed me off and inquired about the altercation.

Leonard, ever the protector, offered comforting words, reminding me that my worth wasn't tied to the name's others called me. His intervention felt like a divine grace, preventing a tragedy I would have regretted for a lifetime.

He escorted me home, and his words lingered in my mind as I sobbed in the bath, grappling with the enormity of what almost transpired. It wasn't truly Emory I wanted to harm but the pain I wished to end. Through tears and reflection, I realized the importance of Leonard's intervention and the grace that saved both Emory and me from irreversible consequences.

No one, not even Mama, found out what transpired that day—just Leonard, Emory, Robert, and I were privy to it. That evening, Emory arrived with Robert Howard, ready to share the day's events. Emory apologized, explaining that some girls had fabricated the story about him. Feeling remorseful, I too offered my apologies, and we hugged—a gesture marking the inception of a dependable friendship destined to endure a lifetime. For this, I am eternally grateful to God.

On occasion, I would accompany Mama on leisurely strolls to the Dairy Queen on E. Warren, indulging in our favorite treat—hand-packed strawberry ice cream. With Mama in high spirits, we engaged in light conversation, me describing the neighborhood's nuances and counting the houses from ours to the corner. Nearing home after our extended outing, I noticed a man with dark brown skin standing before our house, his back turned towards me. As we approached, his familiar smile sparked curiosity within me. Who could it be? His hairstyle appeared different, and my eagerness to identify him grew with each step. To my astonishment, it was Sam, and he had finally returned home. He sprinted towards us, lifting me off the ground in an exuberant embrace, exclaiming how much I'd grown and jesting about keeping an eye on me. We shared a hearty laugh, and he greeted Mama with unprecedented warmth.

We settled on the front porch, eager to catch up on lost time. The screen door swung open, and out walked Rickey, Michael, Ike, Dickey Bird, and Pam. Rickey and I had a sporadic relationship, so his presence was a surprise, especially given the rumors of his entanglements with Mae Bertha Wynn. Nonetheless, we congregated on the porch, keeping Mama company. Rickey strummed his guitar, leading us in song, while we indulged in gossip and shared laughter. Later, I prepared a hearty meal of spaghetti, and together, we basked in Mama's presence, cherishing the joy of simply being together.

Sam and I found a quiet spot behind the house. He wrapped me in a warm hug, a gesture of dap following, and said, "You know that Welton is dead, don't you?"

"Yeah," I responded, a mix of relief and sorrow in my voice.

"So, you know he can't ever bother you again. Just throw it out of your head." His attempt to reassure me was sincere, accompanied by another strong hug and dap. Internally, I wished it could be as easy as he made it sound to let go of the past.

Later, I found myself on the back porch with Michael, delving into conversations about what lay ahead. He revealed he was moving, destination unknown, and expressed a resolve to finish school. As the eldest, he felt a duty to support his grandmother and younger siblings. His grandmother, nearing seventy, depended on him. He promised to keep in touch once he knew more about their future whereabouts.

The ambiance shifted when Mae Bertha arrived with Emma Jean Foster in tow, igniting a spontaneous gathering. Sam, ever the charmer, resumed his playful antics with Emma Jean.

That year, 1967, was like living in a dream, my spirit buoyed by the melodies of love songs. "Groovin" by The Young Rascals, "Everybody Needs Love" by Gladys Knight and the Pips, "Make Me Yours" by Betty Swan, and "You're My Everything" by The Temptations became the anthems of Robert and me.

Yet, as time passed, Michael and I found ourselves drifting apart, our situation reminiscent of the 1964 hit by Carla Thomas, "Pick up the Pieces." While there was still an undeniable attraction, it was clear that we were searching for different things. I yearned for growth, for something more, and I was uncertain if Michael could be part of that journey.

When I wasn't spending time with Robert or chatting on the phone with Eric, I found companionship in Mae Bertha, Rickey's girlfriend. Our friendship blossomed rapidly; we shared countless days and nights together, becoming inseparable. She introduced me to an after-hours joint her father, Mr. Wynn, ran in the basement of their two-family flat, painted in shades of woodsy green and white. Robert had cautioned me early on about whom to trust—advice that resonated deeply in Mr. Wynn's establishment.

Mr. Wynn's business catered to anyone with a dollar, selling liquor, beer, and wine—or at least, that's what we thought we were buying. The shocking revelation that he had been tampering with the bottles, adding his own... unsavory ingredients, deeply disturbed me. Despite this, his basement was a hub of activity; at night, its jukebox played the latest hits and timeless blues that I quickly grew to love. It was here, amidst the rhythm and blues, that we lost ourselves in the music, dancing the night away to the Shin Ga Ling, the Pearl, and the Four Corners.

The place was a magnet for neighborhood kids and an assortment of characters, all drawn in by the promise of a wonderful time. They gambled, drank, played cards, got high, and indulged in all manners of revelry. Mr. Wynn also sold hot sausages, fish, and chicken dinners, but after learning about his dubious practices, I lost all appetite for his cooking. My mother always taught me the value of eating at home, a principle that I clung to even more tightly after my experiences at Mr. Wynn's.

She never expressed concern over my visits to Mae Bertha's house; she didn't know about the after-hours joint, blissfully unaware of the goings-on there. Little did she know, the place was a melting pot of the community's hidden vices, a corner of the world where the night never seemed to end. What Mama didn't know is that I was running the streets with some of the biggest hoes Detroit had to offer. I was running in several circles, accompanied by hoes of all ages. Girls from the West Side, East Side, North End, and Highland Park were present. Hoes that were fucking out of both draw legs. I took a nosedive head on, and I ventured into another world. Pimp's gamblers drug addicts and prostitutes had become my friends.

One girl tried to sway me to dance in a top-less bar. I didn't even consider it. No matter how hard I tried, I didn't fit in. I saw and learned a lot fast. My brain was absorbing like a sponge. I thank God for them because they taught me what I didn't want to be. I knew that I wasn't a hoe, and so I stopped running with hoes. For the time being,?

Mama taught all her kids to lead and not follow. And so, I applied this principle to my life.

I learned about older men at an early age. Her father, Mr. Wynn, had the same greedy look in his eye as Mr. Gorman did for me. He looked at me as if he had something on his mind, which made me uncomfortable. I always kept my arm across my breast when I passed him in the room.

Years later, I found out that my feelings were true; he had forced himself on his daughters. I was always a big girl for my age. Men often thought I was older than I was; I was passing. I was always found in places I shouldn't have been. And when you put yourself in that position, anything can happen.

After a night of pure fun and laughter, Rickey and Mae Bertha walked me home. I could hear Geri pitching a bitch from outside the door. She found out that I had a dog. This bitch was screaming and hollering at the top of her lungs. That mother fucker has to go. I have allergies, and that dog has to go. She threatened, "Either you get rid of it or I will." At first, I was at a loss for words. The fact that she would scream and holler at my mother and me like a fucking maniac in front of my friend was unbelievable to me. Geri ranted and put on a show the entire evening. It wasn't until she left for work that the house was quiet again.

The following day, after my bath, I came downstairs, and Robert was sitting on the front porch talking to Mama. I was surprised to see Robert so early.

Robert often came to sit and visit with my mother, even during the times I wasn't at home. Whenever I stayed out too late, Mama would send Robert to look for me. No matter where I was, he'd find me and ensure I returned home safely, often draping his jacket over my shoulders on cool nights. His protectiveness was a comforting presence in my life.

One early morning, Robert came by to inform me he was visiting a cousin on the west side and planned to stop by my house later that night. He wanted to have a private conversation, so I accompanied him back to his place, just nine houses down from mine. During our walk, he expressed his concern about me spending time at Zettie Wynn's joint. Specifically, he warned me to steer clear of Dennis Oaks, sometimes known as Brown—a tall, dark-skinned, skinny man notorious for preying on young girls. Robert's protective instinct was palpable as he urged me to avoid any trouble. Despite his warnings, a part of me felt invincible, believing I was mature enough to handle myself and whatever life threw my way.

Robert also shared that his brother, Ted, was graduating and that he, alongside their mother, was planning a surprise party for him. Ted, three years Robert's senior, was about to graduate from Cass Technical High School—a testament to his intelligence and dedication. His aspirations included pursuing an electronic degree at Rex Electronics School. Ted's commitment to his education was evident; he was always buried in books, attending extra classes, or visiting the Detroit Institute of Art. His reputation for seriousness and hard work was well-known throughout the neighborhood, garnering him respect and admiration.

However, the tranquility of our lives was often disrupted by Geri, who returned from work one morning in a familiar frenzy. "That damn dog's got to go!" she bellowed, citing her allergies as the reason the dog couldn't stay. In a bid to save Frisky, I protested, "Mama, I think Frisky's going to have puppies. She has nowhere else to go. Please, let her stay." But Geri was unmoved by my pleas. Her indifference to the feelings of others was a harsh reality I had come to accept. Her motto seemed to be, "To hell with everybody else," a sentiment that reflected her selfish nature.

Later that afternoon, I descended into the basement, where Frisky had made her home. I prided myself on keeping her space as tidy as she kept her fur, always gleaming with care. Frisky usually greeted me with joyful barks, but today, silence hung heavy in the air. My heart sank as I searched the dimly lit corners, finding no sign of her.

Panicked, I dashed outside, only to be met with a scene that rooted me to the spot in horror. Thomas and Geri were there, shoving Frisky headfirst into a potato sack—the kind you'd find at Eastern Market. Shock rendered me immobile, watching as they drove away, Frisky in tow. When the realization hit me, my legs moved of their own accord, chasing after the car in a futile attempt to save her. Geri turned to look at me, her smile a sharp knife to my heart as Thomas accelerated, disappearing down the block.

I walked back inside, defeated and heartbroken, laying my head in Mama's lap. "Why does she hate me so?" I sobbed. Mama's gentle voice offered little comfort, "Geri hates herself, baby. That's why she can't stand to see anyone else happy."

Geri and Thomas returned later, indifferent to the storm raging within me. I confronted them immediately, demanding to know Frisky's whereabouts. "Where is Frisky?" My voice broke with the weight of impending dread. Geri's response was a blow colder than the harshest winter: "We dropped your dog off the Belle Isle Bridge."

The world stopped. I struggled for breath, unable to grasp the cruelty of her admission. How could anyone possess such malice? Everything I ever loved; Geri seemed determined to obliterate. I tried to banish the thought, to find solace in the belief that Frisky was now safe in heaven, beyond Geri's reach. Yet, the pain lingered, a constant echo of loss.

Days turned into nights, and the ache in my heart refused to ebb. I sought answers once more, only to be met with Geri's dismissive silence, her actions reinforcing the wall she built between us. Geri's capacity to inflict pain seemed boundless, her indifference to my feelings a well she drew from effortlessly.

The Detroit Institute for the Blind had once offered Mama a seeing eye dog, a gesture of independence she desperately needed. However, the oppressive presence of Geri, whom we grimly nicknamed "Old Slave Master," made acceptance impossible. Instead, the Detroit Public Library became a beacon of support, offering recordings with headphones and Braille- transcribed records. They even proposed sending an instructor to teach Mama Braille, but her spirit, worn thin by years of struggle, couldn't muster the enthusiasm to learn. Despite her resistance, Mama knew she could rely on Ricky and me. We were her steadfast pillars, ensuring her needs were met with unwavering dedication.

Twice a month, Ricky or I would accompany Mama downtown to meet Aunt Janie. Wednesdays transformed the city; known as Ladies' Day, luxury theaters like the Adams, The Madison, Grand Circus Park, The Palm, and Fox discounted their tickets to $1.50, inviting women from all walks of life. From housewives in Ferndale to beauticians in Highland Park, diversity thrived in those queues. Some flaunted mink stoles and diamond-adorned hands, while others donned their Sunday best. Yet, what truly captured Mama's heart was the generosity of Awrey's Bakery, offering an endless supply of donuts, from plain to cream-filled, paired with free coffee. To Mama, these simple joys transcended the mundane, highlighting life's often overlooked beauties.

Mama clung to the belief that her sight, which flickered in and out, would one day stabilize. She claimed to see shapes and outlines, a testament to her faith that with God, all things were possible. Her optimism fueled my prayers, hoping for a miracle to restore her vision. To shield her from prying eyes, she wore sunglasses, hiding the discoloration that marked her struggle.

1967

It was a sunny day in 1967, and Mama and I were enjoying the warmth on our porch. I found joy in describing the vibrant day to her—the intricate shapes of the clouds, the lush green of the grass, and the dance of colorful butterflies that filled our front yard, a sight rarely seen today. The melody of Mr. Softee's ice cream truck jingled nearby, pulling me away to buy Mama her favorite treat: a small vanilla ice cream cone.

As I waited in line, basking in the sunlight, an unexpected sight shattered the peaceful moment. Eileen, my sister, arrived in a cab, her face marred by tears and bruises, evidence of a harrowing ordeal. I rushed to her aid, helping her and her children out of the cab, doing my best to shield Mama from the immediate shock. Inside, I assisted Eileen in cleaning her wounds, a silent promise hanging in the air that she had finally escaped Teddy's clutches.

Eileen's children, a girl of seven and a boy of five, bore the silent marks of trauma. Their eyes, wide and unsettled, mirrored the chaos they had unwittingly become a part of. I busied myself in the kitchen, fixing them sandwiches and pouring glasses of milk, trying to offer some semblance of normalcy as Eileen recounted the day's horrors to Mama.

The uneasy peace shattered when Teddy roared up to our house in his red 1964 convertible, barging in as if he owned the place. Eileen, who had always trembled at the sight of him, stood defiantly, a stark transformation from the woman we once knew. As Teddy and Eileen's argument escalated, the air thickened with tension, the children's cries mingling with Mama's distressed sobs. She had always said she'd do anything to protect her daughters, even if it meant turning her son-in-law away at gunpoint.

Mama's gun, a gift from my brother Matthew for her protection, was usually hidden under her mattress, but today, it was in her dress pocket—a premonition, perhaps. I clenched a hammer tightly, ready to defend my sister should Teddy dare to hit her with his fist.

Eileen's voice, fierce and unwavering, filled the room as she declared her refusal to return to a life of abuse. She denounced Teddy's manipulations, his family's lies, and her resolve echoed through the house, marking a declaration of her newfound strength. Teddy, visibly shaken by his loss of control, seethed with anger but hesitated, knowing well the consequences of his actions.

In a desperate bid for dominance, Teddy grabbed the children, attempting to drag them away. Eileen sprang into action, fighting back with a ferocity born of years of suppressed anger. I joined the fray, determined to rescue my niece and nephew from his grasp. Throughout the struggle, Mama's voice rang out, a command for Teddy to leave and never return. The click of the gun's safety echoed ominously in the room, a final warning.

Teddy, confronted with the collective resolve of our family, fled as quickly as he had arrived, his departure marking the end of Eileen's torment and the beginning of her journey toward liberation.

As night enveloped us, I found solace in the unity of our family, gathered together in a single bed—Eileen, her children, Mama, and I. The comfort of having my sister home, safe at last, was overwhelming. In this newfound peace, I hoped that, in time, I could share my own burdens with her, finding solace in her strength and the shared resilience of our family.

The next day, Teddy could be seen parading up and down the street, driving his car back and forth from one corner to the other like a damn fool. So, I took the kids inside the house for total protection. I knew he wasn't going to try anything; he could see Sam, Leonard, my father, and Rickey standing on the porch. He knew, in his dirty black heart, he'd have to wait to sneak up on her. What Teddy didn't know was that Sam was living with us, and he was home all the time. He'd been with us ever since he got his orders for 'Nam. Sam came home on leave and declared he wasn't going back to be killed. Being AWOL from the Army, Sam had to lay low, which meant he was home all day and night. We all knew Sam didn't want to go to jail, especially not for hurting anyone. But we also knew he would protect us at all costs, without hesitation.

Eileen stalled when it came time to enroll her children in school, fearing Teddy would follow her there; then he'd know where the children were and what time they got out. Without the money, her biggest fear was that her children would go missing. So, we all took turns watching the kids. On her own, Eileen got a full-time job working at the Post Office as a mail sorter. She initially rode to work with Geri and Thomas, but that arrangement was short-lived. She soon found her own way to work—the bus. Working long, hard hours, she paid rent to the Geri and saved enough to hire a lawyer and file for divorce. After Teddy was served his divorce papers, the threats worsened. Eileen called home on every break to ensure her kids were safe. The police, who called several times, expressed their inability to help. "The courts have to handle it," an officer said. As her court date approached, she reconsidered putting her kids in school. Time moved forward, and so did we.

The day Nina announced her pregnancy, Leonard was nowhere to be found—in fact, he'd been gone for several days. He, too, had been drafted into the Army. Mama watched her children's lives fall apart in front of her, feeling helpless yet not showing despair. She spoke of their future with certainty, instilling hope.

We were all happy for Nina.

Finally, Eileen gathered the courage to enroll the kids in a neighborhood school program. That morning, before leaving for work, she spoke privately with the principal, expressing her concerns about their father. *"It's possible he might come up here and try to take my kids. Please don't let them leave with anyone but the designated persons I've listed on their enrollment form."*

Months passed, and her day in court arrived. Tearfully, she told the judge how Teddy beat her and then forced himself on her. "It's mental cruelty," she wept. She recounted how he even threatened her blind mother. The judge, seemingly preoccupied, excused himself in the middle of her testimony. Sitting still in the witness chair, Eileen prayed silently, keenly observing the male chauvinist judge's distractions. Feeling defeated, knowing her case wasn't being taken seriously, she nevertheless felt a surge of determination. With her mother's strength flowing through her veins, she was more determined than ever. Despite the degrading questions and her lengthy testimony, Eileen was awarded sole custody of her children. Teddy and his family of horrors, furious, made threats and stormed out of the courtroom.

It was truly a day of celebration and praise to the good Lord above! I had to be on the lookout, so I watched the kids. Although I didn't go to court with her, she told me everything when she got home. As I listened, my heart swelled with gratitude to God for the peace and faith He had restored in her. Eileen's face was radiant, brimming with hope and promise, reminiscent of her days before the marriage. All she talked about were the good things ahead for her and her children. She planned to move out after the first of the New Year.

It was September, and her children were enrolled full-time in school. Someone always accompanied them to and from school; they were not allowed on the playground or anywhere alone. We all kept a tight hold on the kids. It pained me that we couldn't allow them the freedom to just be kids. Eileen, walking, catching the bus, and taking taxis, did her utmost to get her children to school and herself to work. Mama admired Eileen's strength and never missed a chance to tell her so.

November, one day before the school let out for Christmas break, is etched in my memory. Eileen ran home in hysteria. She'd gone to pick her children up from school, only to find her worst nightmare had come true. Her children were nowhere to be found. Speaking with the principal, she learned that a fire drill had been conducted that day, and all the children were taken outside. Somehow, during the head count, her children's absence went unnoticed. It wasn't until Eileen began crying and screaming through the halls that the principal realized her children were missing. We called the police and a cab to canvas the area, with neighbors and friends joining the search. Sam stayed at home with Mama, praying for their safe return.

After hours of searching, including a visit to her old house where we discovered Teddy had moved out, and inquiries at her sister-in-law's and mother-in-law's houses—all met with denials and lies—we returned home empty-handed. Teddy's mother coldly advised Eileen to move on with her life, but how could she? "How can I get on with my life without my children? They are my life," she asserted, refusing to let them see her cry.

We called the police again, providing more pictures and descriptions of the children. The officer promised to search but couldn't guarantee anything. If their father had taken them, there was still nothing they could do. In the days that followed, sadness seeped into my sister's life. She prayed incessantly for their return, never ceasing in her search. Throughout the holiday season, we prayed and mourned. I lit white candles for their return. The ordeal broke us down, one by one, day by day. Watching my sister waste away before my eyes was unbearable. Despite trying to be strong for her, the sight of her despair, and the unopened Christmas presents under the tree, overwhelmed us all.

Chapter 3

"All Hell Breaks Loose"

February 1968

Last night, Sam and I decided to catch the bus to the west side early in the morning to visit the old gang. Sam was eager to see his new son, bring Cindy some money, and visit his brothers and sisters. The plan was simple: we'd stop in the neighborhood, visit for a while, then split up. He would walk over to Cindy's, then meet me back on his old porch to catch the bus home. That was the plan.

When we got off the bus on Joy Road, we walked a block and turned the corner. It seemed like everyone was expecting us; they were all sitting on his old porch waiting, including Michael and Ike. It took them a minute to recognize Sam without his do-rag and leather jacket. Sam was in civilian clothes, his hair cut low. The old gang rushed up to us, giving plenty of love, daps, and hugs. Despite the cold, it didn't stop us from talking loud and laughing. They had many questions for Sam about the Army. Nobody knew but Sam and I that he was AWOL, so we kept it between us. Old habits die hard.

We spent several hours on the concrete porch, singing, dancing, talking, and reminiscing about the good old days. No one was really paying attention until Sam noticed a white government car pull up and started searching for an address. That's when I paid attention. From the porch, Sam saw three white men driving up the street—two in the front and one in the back. They stopped and pulled off, then stopped again, right in front of Sam's house. Dressed in Army uniforms, it was clear they meant business.

The three men exchanged papers, looked around, and talked among themselves for a minute inside the car. Then, realizing they had found the correct address, they stepped out. Shuffling papers from hand to hand, the officer stopped and stood there, his eyes canvassing the neighborhood. They looked up at the address, paused again, then looked directly at Sam before walking next door.

The two-family flats were closely nestled together, making it easy for sounds to travel between them. When the officer rang the doorbell and took a step back, the distinct sound of Mrs. Clark descending her stairs was unmistakable. As she opened the door, the officer, now with her full attention, introduced himself courteously, displaying his identification before stepping inside. From my vantage point on the porch, I observed them conversing in the cramped hallway while his colleagues, arms crossed, waited outside. One officer's gaze met ours again, but no words were exchanged before a faint scream, followed by a resounding boom, echoed from next door. My line of sight, hindered by my seated position, offered no clarity on the unfolding drama. Sam, opting for discretion, remained motionless, blending seamlessly into our assembled group.

The urgent dash of the officer from Mrs. Clark's home to instruct his colleagues to summon an ambulance was the prelude to a wave of emergency services arriving. With the street now awash with curious onlookers and the neighborhood's children, the air was thick with anticipation and dread. The hurried pace of first responders in and out of the residence hinted at the gravity of the situation. A collective gasp escaped us as Mrs. Clark, her visage obscured by a white sheet, was escorted to the waiting ambulance, which then departed with a mournful silence rather than its siren's blare.

The revelation of Mrs. Clark's demise, shared by her landlady who had overheard the tragic events, cast a somber shadow over us. The heartbreak of learning that both of her sons, Tony and Raymond Clark, had met their end in the same week—Tony in Vietnam and Raymond in a motorcycle accident—left us reeling in disbelief. The community's sorrow was palpable as we gathered on the porch, enveloped in a profound silence punctuated only by the occasional sob.

Determined to honor Tony's memory, Ike proposed a night of remembrance at Orchard Gardens' skating party. The evening's somber tone was momentarily lifted by our visit to Cindy and her son, Pablo, whose cherubic presence offered a brief respite from the day's gloom. Yet, the shadow of the day's events lingered, coloring our every interaction.

Our journey to the Garden, marked by a solemn toast to the Clark family, was a testament to the shared grief and solidarity of our community. Inside, the mood was one of communal mourning and tribute, as friends and strangers alike came together to honor Tony's legacy through music and shared memories. The night, fueled by the classics of the era and the spirit of togetherness, was a poignant homage to a life and family irrevocably changed by tragedy.

In moments of reflection and remembrance, we found a temporary solace, sharing stories and laughter as we paid tribute to Tony's indelible mark on our lives. His jovial claims of being "The Entertainer" brought a bittersweet smile to our faces, a reminder of the joy he brought to our lives, now contrasted with the stark reality of our loss. The night, filled with music, memories, and a collective yearning for the past, was a poignant reminder of the fragility of life and the enduring bonds that sustain us through our darkest hours.

March 1968

The death of Tony Clark and his family had shaken me to my core. A month had passed, yet the event clung to me, invading my dreams with nightmares, making me cry out in my sleep. The sensation of Welton and Donald's hands stifling my screams haunted me; each recollection was more vivid than the last. Just the other night, my tumultuous dreams awoke Mama. She roused me, her voice laced with concern, inquiring about my nightmare. I feigned forgetfulness, yet the truth was etched deep within me. That night's unrest had left me desperate for solace. It was Eric I turned to, my confidant for over a year, whose presence always brought me comfort. Our conversation meandered from music to friends, and he extended an invitation for a barbecue on the Fourth of July. In moments of solitude, when Robert was nowhere to be found, it was Eric's company that I sought.

As the fourth month since Eileen's children's disappearance waned, her anguish remained palpable. Consumed by worry and depression, she found solace in cigarettes, pacing endlessly. The mystery of her children's whereabouts was a relentless torment, visibly wearing her down. Eileen harbored deep fears for their safety, haunted by the knowledge of Teddy's violent temperament. The revelation of his prolonged commitment to a mental institution by his mother only compounded her dread. Teddy's resentment towards his mother's dominance and his inherited disdain for women painted a grim backdrop for Eileen's concerns for her daughter, Joyce.

Amid her despair, Eileen encountered Duncan Shepard, a newcomer from the West Indies, who, along with his son Roland, aimed to establish a grocery store chain. Duncan's affable nature and generosity provided a temporary respite from her turmoil. Despite his penchant for alcohol, which Eileen slowly began to share, his support was unwavering. He went as far as hiring a private investigator in the hopes of finding her children, a testament to his empathy towards her plight. Yet, for all the material comforts Duncan offered, the absence of her children left an irrevocable void in Eileen's life, one that not even her burgeoning relationship with Duncan or her escalating alcohol consumption could fill.

Tuesday, April 2, 1968. It was Robert's birthday and Marvin Gaye's. Unaware he was not home, I made my way to his house, engaging in casual conversation with his parents on the porch. Soon after, a money-green Electra 225 convertible with whitewall tires pulled up. Inside were Robert and Ted, unmistakably enjoying the attention their arrival demanded. Ted, with a wide smile, shared that the car was a graduation gift from his father. Complimenting the car, I exchanged birthday wishes with Robert, which led to a stolen kiss, only to be playfully interrupted by Ted. He hinted at plans to meet up at the Brazil's later that night, a gathering I was eager to join.

As evening fell, I walked through the gangway and we congregated at the Brazil's, with Robert and Ted making a notable entrance. The car became the center of admiration, a testament to Ted's accomplishments and the pride of the neighborhood. The night was filled with laughter, drinks, and endless conversations, eventually shifting to my porch, where the topics ranged from the war to life's many challenges. Unexpected reunions with long-lost friends offered moments of advice and reflection. Amid the festivity, Jackie Brazil, in a rare moment of sobriety, warned me against the perils of drugs and bad company, including his sister Evelyn, his words leaving a lasting impression.

The evening continued with music and socializing, despite my internal struggle. The sounds of Bobby and the Vancouvers, King Curtis, and Jerry Butler filled the air, momentarily lifting the somber mood that had shadowed me. However, Al Green's "Back Up Train" unraveled my composure, bringing my emotions to the surface. In the midst of laughter and chatter, only Jackie noticed the tears I could no longer conceal.

Jackie approached, his embrace warm and his words encouraging, urging me to find solace in Curtis Mayfield's "Keep On Pushing." He emphasized the song's universal message of perseverance against life's adversities. Insisting I listen closely to its lyrics, Jackie imparted a lesson on drawing strength from various sources: the music, my mother, and the hardships I faced. His parting advice was to allow myself a moment of vulnerability before joining him on the porch. Despite his youth and his own turbulent life, Jackie, the streetwise eldest son of the Brazil family, had a wisdom I aspired to. His recent actions and the complexities of his personal life did not overshadow the guidance he offered me. His courage, despite the looming threat of Vietnam and his fear of returning to the army, resonated deeply. Jackie's words were a beacon of hope, teaching me resilience in the face of life's challenges.

April 4, 1968, marked a day of unity and communal living in our home. With a house full of people, including family and friends, everyone contributed what they could, creating a harmonious environment under Mama's and Geri's management. This sense of family extended beyond blood, with each member contributing to the household's upkeep and sharing the burdens of life together. Our home was a safe haven for many, a testament to Mama's unwavering generosity.

The assassination of Dr. Martin Luther King Jr. on this very day shattered the peace of our household. Mama's anguished cry upon hearing the news on television brought us all to a standstill, united in shock and grief. The loss of such a monumental figure, who stood for justice and equality, left us in a profound state of mourning. The somber journey to the store reflected the weight of the tragedy, a moment that deeply impacted my view of our nation and its failure to protect its most visionary leaders.

1968 was unfolding as a year of significant emotional and societal upheaval, a year that promised to test the resilience and strength of all who lived through it, defining the transition from youth to adulthood in the most turbulent of times.

In the wake of Dr. Martin Luther King Jr.'s assassination, riots ignited across the United States, a testament to a collective grief and a resolute stand against a lifetime of injustice. It was a time when the air was thick with the themes of peace and love, conveyed through the soul-stirring lyrics of entertainers and musicians. Amidst this tumult, I found myself desperately trying to grasp at any semblance of peace, to replace my swirling thoughts with anything that could distract me from the pain. The world, despite its inherent beauty, seemed marred by unending suffering, compelling us all towards a pivotal transformation for survival.

In my quest for solace, music became my sanctuary, a source of strength and a beacon of hope. Songs like Jerry Butler's "Only the Strong Survive," Stevie Wonder's rendition of "Blowin' in the Wind," The Temptations' "Why Did She Have to Leave Me," and Brother to Brother's "I Guess That Don't Make Me a Loser" spoke to me, their messages resonating deep within my soul. Each melody, each lyric, served as a lifeline, guiding me through the darkest of times.

My interactions with Robert had become sparse, his time increasingly monopolized by Ted and his new car. Despite this, Robert's nightly calls were a constant, a reminder that not all connections had faded. Yet, as days turned into weeks, a profound sadness took hold, an unrelenting pressure that threatened to consume me. The emotional turmoil rendered me breathless, each moment filled with an overwhelming sense of despair and isolation.

Amidst this internal chaos, my familial relationships offered little reprieve. My sisters, preoccupied with their own lives, seldom sought my company, except when in need. A vivid memory of betrayal lingered, a time when Geri promised compensation for my help, only to renege laughingly. Such moments underscored a pervasive sense of alienation, the realization that my existence was of little consequence to those around me. My mother remained my sole beacon of unconditional love, yet even her presence could not dispel the profound loneliness that enveloped me.

Driven by a yearning for belonging, I found myself veering into dangerous territories, associating with individuals and indulging in activities that I knew were reckless. The nights were spent in a blur of escapades, each decision a desperate attempt to dull the ache within. My companions, each carrying their own burdens and stories, offered a semblance of acceptance, yet the risks were palpable. In my pursuit of relief, I disregarded the potential consequences, indifferent to the peril I was courting. All that mattered was the fleeting respite from the pain, a momentary distraction from a reality I could scarcely bear.

Corinthia's call marked the start of an adventurous day, as she proposed we visit Thomas and Eric, signaling her intentions to run away from home. Eric, who had previously met my mother and earned her approval with his manners and upbringing, was to accompany me on this visit. Despite my mother's caution about my young age, I hoped my actual age would remain a secret between us. Setting out from different sides of Detroit, Corinthia from the west and I from the east, we converged on the Vernor bus line, where Eric awaited us with a smile.

Despite my reluctance, Eric insisted on introducing me to his mother, who had always been cold to me over the phone. To my surprise, she appeared pleasant in person, despite the underlying tension. It must have been that Hill& Hill Kentucky Whiskey she was drinking. The day unfolded with simple joys, shared between Kool-Aid and music, until it was time to check on Corinthia's resolve about running away. However, we found her situation had taken a turn; Thomas, having gotten what he wanted, was ready to send her away due to prior commitments. Stranded without a bus home, Eric dismissed our idea of hitchhiking, instead offering refuge at his friend Peewee's house, where we were warmly welcomed. Peewee, a kind-hearted young woman with a youthful spirit, and two kids immediately felt like the big sister I'd always longed for. We shared our love for songs, particularly Jerry Butler's "Never Gonna Give You Up" and Joe Simon's "Just Enough to Keep Me Hanging On."

Our evening at Peewee's was filled with laughter and music. After getting to know her, we occasionally visited clubs and bars, like the night we went to Mr. Kelly's Lounge on Chene and Garfield to see Dion perform

"Love Makes the World Go Round" and dance to Cliff Noble's jam titled "The Horse." Despite my young age, I managed to blend in, drawn in by the allure of the live performance and the vibrant atmosphere. However, the night took an unexpected turn when I encountered Barbara Tidwell from the neighborhood, who offered me cocaine rolled up in a dollar bill. In that moment, the guidance and warnings of my mother, Jackie, and Robert echoed in my mind, steering me away from a path that could have led to my downfall. I firmly declined, a decision that marked a pivotal moment in my life and reaffirmed my resolve to stay true to my values. This encounter was a stark reminder of the dangers lurking in seemingly enticing opportunities, and by grace, I averted a potential catastrophe.

On May 1, 1968, our family was blessed with the arrival of a beautiful baby girl, whom Nina named after herself and affectionately nicknamed Tina. The joy of Tina's birth was a beacon of happiness for both sides of the family, eagerly welcoming the new addition. However, the marriage between Nina and Lynn had been waning, their once passionate love dimmed by life's trials, evident as Leonard brought them home from the hospital. Despite the transient jubilation at Tina's arrival, Nina and Lynn's relationship deteriorated further, eventually leading to their separation.

Nina's resilience in the face of adversity was underscored by her determination to support Tina and contribute to the household without resorting to welfare. Inspired by Senator Bobby Kennedy's message of self-reliance, which she encountered during his visit to Detroit, Nina took a job at a bar. Her hard work not only provided for Tina but also offered support to our mother. Meanwhile, I found myself taking on a nurturing role with Tina, surprised at my own capability to care for her. My bond with Tina grew, as she accompanied me everywhere, becoming like my own child.

As Nina acknowledged the finality of her separation from Lynn, who had long ceased to be a provider or a partner, she opened her heart to Eddie Kelly. Eddie, affectionately known as "Fast Eddie" for his James Brown impersonations, seamlessly integrated into our lives. His presence was a godsend, providing joy, support, and laughter, especially with his unpredictable James Brown performances that delighted us all. Eddie's kindness extended beyond mere gestures; he truly became a part of our family, treating Tina as if she were his own daughter.

Eddie's impact was profound, embodying the notion that individuals are sometimes placed in our lives for reasons beyond our immediate understanding. His relationship with Nina and Tina blossomed into a new family dynamic, one built on love, respect, and mutual support. Through Eddie, we were reminded of the power of kindness and the unexpected paths life can take us on, teaching us that love can indeed heal and bind us together in the most unforeseen circumstances.

On July 4, 1968, I found myself at a crossroads, fully aware of my youth yet eager to embrace the responsibilities of adulthood. My friends and I indulged in every teenage rebellion, save for one—I had not ventured into the realm of sexual relationships. Despite the pressure, my hesitation stemmed from a mix of fear and a deep-seated belief that I was not ready. Eric and I, spending ample time together, had grown close, yet he never pressured me; the push came from my peers, echoing the pervasive "everyone is doing it."

The holiday weekend became a backdrop for my pivotal moment with Eric, a step taken not out of readiness but perhaps out of curiosity, peer influence, or the search for closeness in a confusing time. This decision mirrored a parallel in my life, recalling Evelyn Brazil's secretive encounter, which resulted in a pregnancy shrouded in secrecy and denial, a scenario all too familiar in our community's whispered stories.

Amid these personal upheavals, Eddie Kelly's move into our home marked a new chapter. His presence brought stability and joy, transforming our household dynamics. With Eddie and the bustling household, life seemed full of laughter and camaraderie, offering a brief respite from the challenges outside our doors. Geri's absence, due to her demanding work schedule, was a relief to many, highlighting the complex dynamics within our family.

My mother's wisdom often served as a guide; her observations on cleanliness and character are a testament to her understanding of life's nuances. Yet, her reflections on George revealed a deeper insight into the sacrifices and compromises of adult relationships, acknowledging the complexities of love, provision, and personal fulfillment. This period of my life was marked by significant transitions, from the innocence of youth to the stark realities of adulthood, each experience etched with lessons on love, responsibility, and the intricate dance of growing up.

One year, one month, and six days after Nina married.

Wednesday, August 28, 1968

The sun peeped through the cracked window shades. I lay in Mama's bed, halfway asleep, when the thump at the downstairs door startled me. It woke me, but not completely. The door opened and closed, and I drifted back to sleep.

Unfolded as a day that would etch itself deeply into our collective memory, the morning's peace was shattered by an unexpected disturbance: a loud thump against the downstairs door that roused me from slumber in Mama's bed. The sound of the door opening and then closing lulled me back towards sleep, until Geri's anguished cry, "Oh God No," pierced the quiet, propelling the entire household into a state of alarm.

Her cries, laden with despair, brought everyone rushing downstairs, only to find Geri inconsolable, pointing tremblingly at the newspaper she clutched. The Detroit News bore three images that brought our world to a standstill: George Beaver, caught in a moment of desperate criminality, fleeing a credit union with a bag of money and a sawed-off shotgun in hand; the second, more harrowing image with his hands held up to surrender and the third captured his lifeless body on the street, the ill-gotten gains and weapon still clutched near his hands. George Beaver's life had ended in a violent confrontation with the Ferndale Police Department.

The shock of seeing someone we knew, someone connected to our lives through the intricate web of community and family, depicted in such a tragic tableau was overwhelming. It was a stark reminder of the thin line between the lives we lead and the choices that can abruptly alter their course. As the news spread through the house, a somber atmosphere enveloped us all, leaving us to grapple with the immediate shock and the lingering repercussions of George's actions.

The news of George Beaver's death, depicted so vividly in the newspaper, sent ripples of shock and sorrow through our household. The image of George, hands raised in what appeared to be surrender before being fatally shot, prompted an outcry among us. We had all harbored affection for him, making the reality of his violent end even harder to digest. My mother's disbelief and Geri's uncharacteristic display of emotion underscored the depth of our collective grief. It was a moment of profound sadness, marking a day of mourning that would linger in our memories.

Reflecting on the circumstances surrounding George's death, the notion that he might have been driven or influenced to a desperate act, possibly considering the explicit mention of his not wanting to live without Nina, added layers of tragedy to his passing. His recent pleas for Nina to leave Leonard and his final conversation with my mother hinted at a turmoil far deeper than we had understood.

Seven days after he had rekindled his plea for Nina's hand, we found ourselves attending his funeral, a somber procession led by sorrow and disbelief. The funeral at Swanson's on East Grand Boulevard was a stark farewell to a life cut tragically short. George's peaceful expression in death, contrasted with the evident grief of his family, particularly his mother and young siblings, painted a poignant picture of loss and the far-reaching consequences of his actions.

The aftermath of George's death revealed the manipulations and betrayals that had ensnared him. His accomplice Preston, 20 years his senior, confessed in court, admitting to coercing George into the robbery, shedding light on the pressures George faced. Preston's remorse and subsequent life sentence offered little consolation for the irreversible loss of George; a young life ended at just 19 years old. Our prayers extended to George's family, as we mourn with the void left by his absence.

Numb with disbelief, we drove in silence, tears marking our grief. I remember standing over his casket, relief washing over me as I looked at his peaceful face. His neck looked swollen, as if burdened with unsaid words. His mother sat in the front row, crying silently. He left behind a baby sister younger than me. His older brother, handcuffed, attended the funeral, his hands covered by a sweater.

What a sad day, especially for his mother. After the funeral, we left and seldom spoke of him, but whenever WJLB played "Share Your Love" by the Fantastic Four, I thought of George. He had bought and dearly paid for his ticket to ride; now he was free. I will never forget that day, and every time I hear that song, I will think of George Beaver.

1968 continued to unfold as a year marked by adversity and heartache. Nina's ongoing struggles, Ricky's increasing detachment, and the lingering pain of unresolved family crises underscored the challenges we faced.

The year's events, from the losses we mourned to the personal battles we endured, painted a complex portrait of life's fragility and the indomitable spirit required to navigate its tumultuous waters. Through it all, the memory of George Beaver, symbolized by the strains of life's temptations, would remain a haunting reminder of the cost of desperation and the enduring impact of loss.

Our home, much like Brazil's, had become a sanctuary for friends and family, a place where Mama believed it was better for us to gather under her watchful eye than out in the unpredictable streets. The basement became our safe haven, hosting Emory, Evelyn, Mae Bertha, Pearly Mae, Shirley Garth, Ozel, and others—a microcosm of teenage exploration and the clandestine activities we wouldn't dare speak of outside its walls. Among the secrets I kept was witnessing my brother snorting dope, a sight that shook me deeply, leading me to hope it was just a fleeting lapse in judgment.

Sneaking into the house after 12:00 midnight, I took a bath and laid down in the bed next to my mother. I always snuggled up close to her when we slept together. As I dozed off, I was awakened by my mother's hand touching and feeling my body. I tried to hide the enviable, but it was too late. My mother sat straight up in the bed and leaned over, and she felt my stomach again. "Pat," she cried out, "you're going to have a baby. I was shocked to my soul that she found out. I wasn't even sure. I answered, "No, Mam." "Yes, you are," she cried out. I can feel your stomach. There was no more denying it. I said yes, mam'. Afraid and confused about it all, Again, the shame and humiliation settled inside me and stayed there.

Mama grabbed me and hugged me. She let out a scream from the bowels of her soul. She began to rock back and forth with me in her arms. "God no," please, she cried—not my baby. I tried to comfort her, but she was beyond consolable.

I began to cry because I knew that I had hurt and disappointed my mother deeply. And for that, I was sorry. I was pregnant, and I was thirteen years old.

Later on, that day, it was a shame to come down the stairs because I knew the consequences I would have to face. I buried myself in Mama's room until I heard knocks at the door and footsteps on the porch. I listened and heard familiar voices accompanied by screams of excitement and laughter.

It was my big mama and some of their old friends from 15th Street. Mama called me to come down and join in the festivities. With my head bowled down, I made my entrance into the room. I wasn't treated any differently because Mama hadn't told anyone. She wasn't going to tell anyone outside of the family. With them, they bought all the food, right down to the grease, and they brought beer and drinks. After all the hugs and kisses, Big Mama fried fresh pickerel fish. She made coleslaw, fried okra, and smothered potatoes and onions. The music played, and they reminisced and had a good time. The house was rocking with blues. Mama was having fun laughing and talking. Although I could tell that it was weighing heavily on her, she called me over to her, and she hugged and kissed me. She said, "You are a child of the most-high God." "And I love you." Mama never badgered or demeaned me because I was pregnant. But believe me, she was in shock, and so was I.

The music continued on, but when they played Little Milton's 1966 "Feel So Bad," my mother got up and threw her hands in the air as if she had surrendered her life. She danced from one end of the house to the other. Big Mama threw the salt on the floor, and Mama did her dance with streams of tears flowing down her face. She was so hurt and it was my fault.

As time passed, my connection with Robert faded into a series of missed encounters and unreturned calls, until the whispers of his new life, including a girlfriend named Gracie, reached me. Amidst these personal drifts, I found moments of solace and purpose in helping Evelyn babysit her sister Marlene's children, offering support in their strained household, marked by Marlene's hard work and her husband's addiction to drugs and men.

Our lives, intertwined with friends embroiled in their own battles, painted a picture of a generation teetering on the edge of innocence and the harsh realities of the adult world. One serene night, I shared music and dance with Mama, which momentarily lifted the heaviness, a precious memory swiftly overshadowed by the events of life.

October 1968

The abrupt arrival of two men at our doorstep, dressed in white uniforms, knocked on the door and asked for my mother by her first name. Intent on taking Mama away under the guise of a nondescript "ride," they catapulted Nina and me into a nightmare. Their forceful escort of Mama, despite our desperate protests and physical attempts to intervene, was a moment of sheer terror and confusion. They grabbed her by the arm and lifted her out of the chair. "Where are you taking her?" we asked. Mama said to us, "Stop fighting. I'll go with them." "Who are you?" we continued to ask. The subsequent revelation, without our knowledge or consent, left us reeling. They escorted Mama to the protected station wagon, placed her in the back seat, and drove off with her. I ran behind the car with tears flooding my eyes I could not catch them. They took my mother away. I ran to Geri's room to find her standing in her bedroom doorway, listening to it all. She slammed the door in my face. The discovery that Geri and Thomas were behind her demise added a layer of betrayal to our grief. Back inside, Nina frantically called our brother Matthew but only managed to leave a message with his secretary. Holding on to each other, we cried, overwhelmed by helplessness.

The phone's ring sliced through our despair. All along, we hadn't been alone; Geri had been eavesdropping from behind another door. When I caught her eye, she simply shut it, leaving us in our misery. Geri and Thomas had committed our mother to a mental institution.

In the whirlwind of emotions and the scramble for answers, no one confirmed our worst fears, marking the beginning of a new chapter of uncertainty. This act, orchestrated in silence and executed with cold efficiency, underscored the fragile threads holding our family together, now frayed beyond recognition. The realization that our sanctuary had been invaded and our protector forcibly removed was a profound loss, one that would indelibly change the fabric of our lives forever.

In the wake of our mother's sudden and distressing commitment, Nina and I found ourselves confused with a profound sense of helplessness. The stark reality that there was little we could do, given our youth and lack of resources, left us feeling abandoned and isolated in our grief. Our older brother Matthew's response to Nina, when finally reached, only deepened our despair. His words, suggesting we move on as our mother had lived her life, felt like a betrayal, accentuating the void left by her absence.

Days turned into what seemed like weeks with no clear action to take. Nina and I, both too young and powerless, felt utterly helpless. When

Matthew finally returned Nina's calls, his words were a cold comfort: He hung up without saying another word. Even Eileen, living between both houses, was as lost as we were.

I often thought that if Sam, Eddie, Ricky, or even my father had been home, this would never have happened. Time blurred—the months since Mama's departure were too painful to count. Her absence was a constant ache; everyone else seemed to move on, but Nina, Poppi, Eddie, Ricky, and I kept her memory alive. We played her favorite music and huddled in her chair, enveloping ourselves in the remnants of her presence. At night, I clutched her pillow and her duster, sleeping in her gowns, to feel her close.

As days turned into months, the absence of our mother haunted me. The home once filled with her presence now echoed with the void of her absence. Attempts to keep her memory alive, through her favorite music or by embracing her belongings, offered scant comfort against the pain of her loss. During the night, the longing for her presence became almost unbearable, driving me to seek solace in her gowns, her pillow, anything that once was hers.

My escape from this pain increasingly found refuge in alcohol and vomiting and the company of friends like Emory and Mae Bertha, where temporary distractions from the grief were welcomed. The absence of any form of parental supervision or concern from those around me left me feeling neglected, fueling a reckless disregard for my well-being.

The collective mourning and anger towards Geri, the orchestrator of our mother's absence, united me with friends and family who shared our loss. Our grief morphed into disdain for Geri, to the point of harboring dark thoughts of retribution, thoughts that were never acted upon but underscored the depth of our anguish. I didn't know where she was or how she was doing, only that she was gone.

As days passed, I drifted, visiting friends like Emory and Mae Bertha and drinking more than ever. Nobody seemed to notice or care about my absence—I felt abandoned yet defiant. The love for my mother united us, her children, in silent grief. I loathed Geri intensely and clung to the belief that God would handle Geri in His own way.

Throughout this tumultuous period, I clung to the belief that divine justice would eventually address the wrongs committed by Geri. Despite the chaos that enveloped our lives, this belief in a higher power's intervention provided a glimmer of hope amid the despair. The journey through this dark chapter was marked by a desperate yearning for our mother's return, a testament to her enduring impact on our lives and the void her absence had created.

I was having recurring dreams. At times, my dreams felt like an assault on me. Sometimes, I could remember feeling sick inside, my stomach churning. The dreams always took me back to when we lived on Linsdale, and I attended Pattengill Elementary School.

The school was located at the intersection of Maplewood and Linsdale. I loved Pattengill; it was my favorite school, and my favorite teacher, Mrs. Baker, taught there. She was a medium-built, fair-skinned woman with vibrant red hair. The children always seemed to get on Mrs. Baker's last nerve, and when she felt herself losing control, she would often grab the children by their arms, ball up her fists, and punch them in the back. Oddly, this was so funny to me. Sometimes I laughed so hard that I would fall out of my chair. Although I knew Mrs. Baker was wrong, I could never help myself from laughing. She punched almost every kid in the room— except for me. She always gave me hugs and pennies for penny candy.

There was a penny candy store on Maplewood's corner. If you had even one penny, you could get two things. My favorite candies were banana splits, chum gum, and Tootsie Rolls. Pattengill had a playground, and often after school, my brother and I would go over to swing on the swings. These weren't like the swings you see today with leather straps; these were made of wood, and they were sturdy—at least I thought so.

Once, I bet my brother Ricky a nickel that I could go over the handlebars without falling out. And I did, falling flat on my face like a fool. I skinned my hands, elbows, and both knees. Instead of helping me up, my brother was laughing at me, just like the other kids. I was so embarrassed that I ran home and told my mama, who would always, when I hurt myself, clean it up, kiss it, put Vaseline on it, and make it feel better.

We lived in a four-family flat on Linsdale. Our apartment was upstairs on one side, and just below us was my sister Eileen's and her husband's home. It was a modest building, but the neighbors were congenial.

Two significant events marked my time at Pattengill Elementary. The first event was the assassination of President Kennedy. My teacher, Mrs. Baker, sent a message to the office. As I ascended the stairs, the normally bustling hallways fell silent, devoid of any sound. The principal halted everyone, asking us to bow our heads in prayer; the president had been shot and killed. Tears started to flow, including my own. I didn't know much about President Kennedy, only that he was regarded as a good and fair man who didn't deserve such a fate. That day, the school dismissed us early. When I got home, I lay across my mama's bed, but she wasn't there; she was working at a convalescent home.

Shortly after, I went outside to play with my jacks and ball, my favorite game next to bat and ball and hopscotch. Back in those days, it didn't take much to amuse us kids. That's when I noticed a white car circling the block. Initially, I didn't pay much attention, but it kept coming back, around and around. Finally, it stopped. A white man emerged, his face carrying a disturbing expression. He stood by the door, beckoning with his hand for me to come over. *No. I kept shaking my head.*

He then pulled out his private parts, exposed himself to me, and began walking towards me. Motioning me towards him. I was petrified and couldn't move anything other than my head. Finally, he walked so close to me that I could get a good look at his face. Nina saw this man coming towards me out of my sister's window. She immediately ran out of the house, grabbed me from behind, and drug me inside the doorway. She got his license plate number and called my mama and the police.

Somehow, after encountering that man, I never felt safe again. The nightmares continued to haunt me, each one vividly replaying my fears. Often, I would wake from these nightmares feeling a deep-rooted fear, but then I would see my mama next to me in bed. I would snuggle up close to her, and soon I'd fall asleep. Now that Mama was gone, those nightmares had morphed into harsh realities.

One morning, I rushed to the bathroom, but before I could reach it, I vomited all over myself. This was becoming more frequent; I was still in disbelief. and I didn't know what the hell was wrong with me except that I couldn't keep much down. Maybe this is a sign that I really am pregnant. And in denial. Nina and Eddie were planning a visit to see Mama in the hospital. I asked if I could come along. Nina seemed reluctant, but Eddie made me feel welcome.

The ride was long. I hadn't eaten in days and felt nauseous. We arrived at a massive building that looked like a castle, intimidating in its enormity.

Inside, I was both excited and terrified at the prospect of seeing Mama, unsure of her condition, what she would look like, or even if she would recognize me.

We navigated through long hallways, trailing behind Nina and Eddie. Some doors had bars on them, making it seem like a prison rather than a hospital. Finally, we reached her room. My throat tightened at the sight: there lay Mama—no sheets, no blanket, no pillow—just her, balled up in a fetal position on a bare mattress. The room was cold, and the walls were a stark mint green. I rushed to her side, climbing into bed to hug and kiss her. She responded, her voice uncertain, "Who is that?"

"It's me, mama, Pat," I reassured her, desperate for recognition.

"Pat?" she questioned, then, with a tender touch, "Of course, I remember you, dear heart. You're my baby girl." She caressed my face, hugged me, and kissed my hands, making my body feel as if it were seeing me with her touch.

Nina exited the room, perhaps upset at mama's condition. I questioned her about when she might come home and about who had placed her in that room, but she could only offer uncertain answers simply because she didn't know. Nina returned with the nurse that said your mother does not belong here. This place is for crazy people and she don't fit that description. Your Mother is just as sane as I am. She gave Nina some phone numbers with other information attached to help get mama released from that prison.

Before leaving, we sought clean sheets and blankets to make her more comfortable, we gave her a bathe and put lotion and Vaseline on her body and put socks on her feet, we put an extra gown on her body so that she would be warm. I begged the nurse to be kind to her and she assure me she would. We all love your mother here she said. We tried to help her stand, but she couldn't; her legs were beginning to contract.

We hugged and kissed, saying our tearful goodbyes. Nina promised Mama she'd come back for her. I apologized to Mama for everything. Except for her, no one knew about my pregnancy. My denial even surprised Eric, who harbored suspicions. I was in denial myself, despite the signs: tighter clothes, increased appetite, excessive sleep, frequent vomiting. I hid my pregnancy for as long as I could.

Robert had returned home, and with his visit came a confession. "I came back to take care of you," he said, his voice tinged with a regret that wasn't his to bear. "I heard through the grapevine that you were pregnant, and I'm sorry it's not mine." His words hung in the air, heavy with unfulfilled wishes. But the truth was, Robert and I had never been intimate; his longing was for a life that could never have been his.

As my body swelled with the new life within, the whispers grew louder until silence was no longer an option. At thirteen, I faced the stark reality of my pregnancy. Yet, I refused to bow my head in shame, bolstered by the courage my mother instilled in me.

I felt every movement, every hunger pang, and every vigorous kick from the boy, who was undeniably mine. I cradled my belly, rocking him gently—a private dance of mother and son.

To the song Soulful Strut. This bond was mine alone—a fierce and unwavering love.

Eddie became my sanctuary and my unexpected guardian. On days when the cupboards were empty, he would meet me at the bus stop, his presence a silent vow of support. Together, we'd walk to Wonders store, where he'd buy me food—simple acts of kindness that sustained me. "What will you do now?" he once asked as we walked to buy a pickle. "I don't know," I admitted, the future a vast unknown.

Eddie's generosity extended beyond meals; he provided for the baby, too, slipping me money for clothes in secret. But not everyone looked upon me with such kindness. Geri's disdain for me deepened; her disgust was palpable. Nina's jealousy festered; her hatred was fueled by Eddie's unwavering defense of me.

Once, Eddie bought Nina a 2-pound box of candy. When I asked for a piece, her eyes bore into me with loathing, and she denied me even a single morsel. Months later, while cleaning, I discovered the untouched box in Mama's buffet cabinet; the candy turned white with age—a bitter testament to Nina's meanness.

Eileen, now known as Charlie, was indifferent to the turmoil around her. Ricky's disappointment was evident, though not overwhelming. But it was Eric who bore the full brunt of the revelation. Upon learning of my pregnancy, he proposed marriage, his voice filled with promises and a future secured by his enlistment in the Navy. Despite the love I harbored for him, it wasn't enough to bind myself to him in matrimony. If only he had been more cautious, we could have avoided this predicament. I felt betrayed.

I blamed him, perhaps unfairly, for he was the experienced one, whereas I was wrong, but he was a child in the grand scheme of life. Protection, a concept foreign and inaccessible to women of my time, was his responsibility, and he had failed. My resentment towards Eric festered.

One day, fresh from my bath, I stood before my mother's mirror, confronted by the reality of my transformed form. My body, once familiar, now houses another life; its contours are alien to my young eyes. Uncertain of my terms and devoid of medical counsel, I was alone in my journey.

It was then that Geri burst in, her presence as unwelcome as her words. Six or seven months later, she repeatedly demanded the unthinkable— the end of my unborn child's life. Day after day, she brandished a bottle of pills, a concoction of Quinine and Bitter Apple, as if they were the solution to her 'problem.' But to me, they were poison, and her suggestion was madness to approach my baby.I refused, silently vowing to protect my child against her will and the cruelty of others. Nina, a silent witness to the exchange, chose to overlook the situation and even offer intervention. But my resolve was unshaken; I would care for my baby, with or without their support.

Chapter 4

"What Love Has Joined Together"

1969

I was now 14 years old and due to have my baby around the first week of April. Prior to me finding out my due date, Geri had reported me to the state. She said that since I refused to get rid of my baby, I should put it up for adoption.

One sunny day, two social workers came to the house. One introduced herself to me and explained her reason for being there. I didn't catch the name because I wasn't interested. The other lady just stood there, holding up the wall. The worker stated that she had some forms that she wanted me to fill out and sign. Both ladies were tall, one black and one white.

The white social worker insisted that I should put my baby up for adoption, emphasizing that I was a child myself and too young to take care of my baby. I expressed to her that my age had nothing to do with me loving him and wanting to raise him myself. This baby was mine, and I had no intention of giving him away. I was terrified of the unknown and unsure of my rights, but I stood my ground. If my baby and I were going down, we were going down together. He's mine alone; I made my bed, and

I knew I had to sleep in it. (Whenever I spoke of my baby, I always referred to him as if I knew it was a boy, and that's what I wanted.)

Mrs. Shimanski was her name, and she was persistent and rude. She never asked me what she could do to help, only wanting me to sign the papers. On the other hand, the black social worker, Mrs. Washington, offered to help. She told me that they didn't want to pressure me and to give it some thought. The thought of giving my child away never crossed my mind. There was nothing to think about. She told me that they would leave the papers with me if I changed my mind, but I knew that I wouldn't. Mrs. Washington told me that she would arrange for me to be seen and follow up with prenatal care at the clinic. Again, Geri had struck out. Mrs. Washington told me that she'd place my name on a list at Detroit Memorial Hospital and to call her if I needed anything or any help for my baby. "Call me," she said, "and I will make sure that you get guidance."

My feet were so swollen that I could hardly bend them to walk. I had a special craving for Argo Starch and toilet paper, and sometimes I'd even eat matches.

April 6, 1969

On April 6, 1969, I was sitting at Mrs. Brazil's table, playing cards with Mae Bertha, when these pains started. I didn't know what to expect any more than I understood what the pain meant. Mrs. Brazil noticed my discomfort and asked if I thought I was in labor. Uncertain, I just shrugged, prompting her to instruct Mae Bertha to walk me home.

Mae Bertha stayed with me for a while, hesitant to leave me alone, but eventually, she had to go. I was left by myself, with the pain originating in my lower back and radiating around both sides to the lower part of my stomach. Overwhelmed with fear, I began to sweat profusely. Barely able to walk, I laid across Mama's bed and started to cry, wrapping my hand around my stomach to try rocking my baby to sleep, hoping the pain would subside. It didn't. Desperate, I rubbed some of Mama's old green liniment across my stomach, hoping to alleviate the pain.

Several hours later, my sister, Eileen, arrived home. I told her how I was feeling, but she was more concerned with getting ready for a night out. As I endured unbearable pain, kneeling across the bed, I could hear her splashing water in the tub. Time seemed to blur as I felt like I was dying. She eventually called a cab, accompanied me to Detroit Memorial Hospital, and left me at the entrance without seeing me inside.

At the hospital, the pain escalated. The examination was excruciating. I was nervous and shaking, and the doctor instructed me to bear down as if I were trying to have a bowel movement. He noted that I hadn't dilated enough and advised the nurse to send me home. What is dilation? I left the hospital on foot, caught a bus on Gratiot, and the pain subsided slightly during the ride.

When I arrived home, the bars had closed. Walking those long blocks, the pain intensified this time, worse than before. again. Barely able to climb the stairs, I sat down at the bottom step, eventually dragging myself up to the porch. Finding no one at home, I lay down on the porch, trying to fall asleep. Around 4:00 a.m., my sister Eileen returned, high as most times. She barely acknowledged my presence as she staggered upstairs.

By 6:00 am, I was on my knees, crawling on the floor, and pulling at her sheets, desperately trying to wake her. Begging for her help, I cried out, "Eileen, please, help me." She eventually awoke, irritated and dismissive, and said she had to work in the morning, adding, "After this, don't bother me anymore."

She called a cab and dropped me off on Gratiot Street. I had to walk over to the hospital in labor. Once again, I was left by myself. The nurses wheeled me back upstairs, where the doctor examined me. Again, he stated I had not fully dilated, that my water hadn't broken, and accused me of wasting his time. They claimed there was no room for me; I had to go back home. I was placed in a wheelchair and wheeled back to the emergency room exit. I had to walk over to Gratiot to catch a bus back home.

As I waited there, I started to cry, overwhelmed by fatigue, sadness, and a profound sense of loneliness. I thought about how my mother, if she were here, would have helped me; I wouldn't have had to face this alone. Somebody should have helped me; as much as I loved my sister, she should have tried. In my despair, I quietly began to repeat the 23rd Psalm to myself. I went back home in labor and alone. I walked six blocks after the bus let me off. Finally, I made it home, and the streets were deserted with no one in sight. I lay down across Mama's bed, exhausted and with no direction. The pain was so bad that it felt like my baby was coming. I didn't know where or how.

April 8, 1969

I walked up to Shoemaker Street and waited for the bus, then I transferred to Gratiot, only to realize that he wasn't going downtown. He let me off on Burns and Gratiot. I was in so much pain that I laid down on the ground on the side of the brown brick church, and I started to drift in my mind. Back to Whitfield, and I heard God say to me, "Get Up," then I heard the song melody and lyrics play in my mind: "What love has joined together" by the Temptations. I heard God telling me to get up again. I struggled with holding my stomach to get up. I did. And when I got to the corner, the Gratiot bus was there almost waiting for me. I rode down to the hospital and I walked two blocks up. Still in labor…

It felt like a miracle when I looked up and saw Mrs. Washington passing through the hallway. She recognized me immediately and asked what had happened. I explained that I felt ready to have my baby but was being turned away because I hadn't dilated. Mrs. Washington understood the underlying issue—that I didn't have insurance, though she didn't mention it at the time (I found out later).

She asked about my sister, and I told her that she had dropped me off before heading to work. Actually, that was two days ago. "Where's your mama, little girl?" she asked. I never answered. Immediately taking action, Mrs. Washington escorted me back up to the maternity ward and spoke with the department administrator. They agreed to let me stay until I dilated.

Mrs. Washington left the ward before I was placed in a room. I overheard the nurses joking about the "Death Room"—a room so far down the hallway that if I needed help, it would take a long time for anyone to reach me. In that distant room, I had been in labor with my baby for four days.

The pain was so intense that I began to hallucinate, seeing things and conversing with people who weren't there. At one point, I even saw myself in a casket. Amidst the confusion, I prayed fervently to God, asking for protection and pleading not to let me die. My lips were painfully dry and cracked from dehydration, and I imagined myself standing before a waterfall, talking to my mother. The bed rails were raised, trapping me in bed, unable to move even for bathroom needs, forcing me to soil myself.

The nurses sporadically entered the room, lifting the covers to glance at me but never truly attending to my needs. They neither offered water nor changed the soiled linens. Once again, I felt utterly abandoned. On Thursday, April 10, 1969, at 2:49 p.m., the pain escalated to unbearable levels. I found myself screaming at the top of my lungs, writhing against the headboard as though in a wild rodeo.

Eventually, my sister, Nina, arrived. Upon seeing my condition, she immediately called for the doctor. I was quickly moved to the delivery room, where I begged them for relief from the excruciating pain. Two nurses turned me on my side, contorted my body, and administered an injection in my lower back. "Lay real still," they instructed as they positioned my legs in cold steel stirrups. A large mirror mounted on the wall reflected the unfolding scene, revealing aspects of the process that were unknown to me. Naively, I thought babies emerged naturally through the stomach, not the birth canal.

The shot provided the first real relief in hours. I inquired about the medication, and a nurse informed me it was a spinal block, advising me to remain still and not lift my head. My lower body numbed, rendering my legs sensationless. Despite the relief, anxiety overwhelmed me, and I repeatedly asked if I was going to die. The doctor reassured me I would not, but urged me to push as he was eager to leave for lunch. With great effort, I pushed until I heard my baby's cry. Eager to see him, I lifted my head only to be reprimanded and forced back down. However, the mirror revealed it was a boy, connected to me by the umbilical cord.

The doctor and nurse briefly held him up before placing him on my chest, then casually left the room to take their lunch break. Alone, I used a sheet to wrap my newborn son, checking and gently cleaning him as we lay there. He barely cried, seemingly content. My thoughts raced about his weight, possible names, and his appearance, which, from my limited view, resembled mine.

After their lunch, the nurses returned to clean me up and weigh my baby—7 pounds, 11 ounces, and 21 inches long. They moved us to a ward shared with four other women and took him to the nursery. Despite my immobility, I yearned to keep him by my side. Upon inquiring about his return, a kind nurse explained he needed a routine examination and asked if I wanted him circumcised. Unfamiliar with the term, she explained it involved removing the foreskin to prevent infections. Wanting the best for him, I agreed.

When they finally returned him, swaddled tightly in a white blanket, his appearance amused me; he looked like a little "choo-choo train," which became his nickname. A white hat adorned his head, his T-shirt was comically large, and a clamp secured his navel. Despite my limited ability to sit up, I adjusted my bed and began to unwrap him. He had big hands, big feet, skinny legs, little hair on his back, and, to my surprise, none on his head.

'God was he special, I thought, and he's all mine.' These were the emotions that surged through me as I kissed my newborn son, inhaled his scent, and peeked into his diaper, noticing his tender skin was red. I slipped him under the covers beside me, holding him close, grateful for the moments we could share. The nurses allowed me to keep him for extended periods, bringing bottles so I could feed him myself. They instructed me to let him drink 2 ounces of milk before burping him, a task I was already familiar with from caring for my niece.

Each time they came to take him away, I felt a pang of longing; I wanted him by my side constantly. Following the delivery, I was required to lay flat on my back for seven hours, without even the comfort of pillows. Despite this, my desire to see my son grew overwhelming. Dressed in a hospital robe and slippers, I started down the hallway, only to become lightheaded as darkness encroached upon my vision. I reached out, trying to stabilize myself, when I nearly fainted. Thankfully, the staff caught me just in time—fortunately so, as I was stitched up tightly and any fall could have been disastrous. They offered me a wheelchair, but my soreness made bending impossible, so they assisted me back to bed.

Soon after, a nurse entered my room. "Turn over," she demanded rudely as she reached for my arm. Her demeanor was far from gentle, making her seem the most unpleasant person I had ever encountered. She was ready with a shot, which she kept in a holster, and despite my inquiries, she simply repeated her command. Internally, I protested—I couldn't easily turn over due to the stitches—but eventually, I complied, and she administered an iron shot in both hips. The pain was unlike anything I had felt before, sharply etching into my memory.

The nurse explained that I was anemic and that my blood count was low, which necessitated the iron shots as per the doctor's orders. She added that if I had been taking prenatal vitamins, I might have avoided this ordeal. Her timing for this advice felt particularly ironic.

Day Two

I kept wondering when they were going to bring my baby. Today, I could get up because they wanted me to take a cyst bath. Exhaustion had taken over my body; it trembled, consumed by nerves and a touch of fear. Facing this alone was daunting. All night, I dreamt I was searching for my baby, but he was nowhere to be found. Perhaps that explained the shaking.

The nurse had said, "The sooner you take your bath, the sooner you can see your son." So, I followed her advice, crying through the ordeal, feeling mistreated. In my purse, I had brought a pair of socks and some other things for him. I dressed his tiny feet so he wouldn't be cold. He barely cried and didn't open his eyes, but he knew. He knew I was his mama and that we belonged to each other. Holding him close, I feared I might break him. "Thank you, God," I whispered, "for this beautiful little boy."

Just then, a woman entered. I recognized her but couldn't place where she was from. It hit me— Mrs. Schmanski, the social worker from the adoption agency. I sat up straight.

"Who gave you that baby?" she demanded. "You should not be allowed to see that baby. I have your signature on paper, and I'm here to take that child from you."

She stormed out, then back in, asserting, "That child has been signed up for adoption, and I'm here to take him."

"I never signed any papers, and you know it!" I countered. The room turned chaotic as she and the nurses tried to take him from my arms. I clutched him tighter.

"Call the police!" she screamed, thinking I'd back down.

"I don't give a damn who you call; this baby is mine, and I'm not going to separate from him," I shot back.

She showed the papers to the nurses. "That signature is not mine," I insisted. "My sister Geri signed those papers, trying to take my son away, just like she signed papers to send my mother to a mental institution at Ypsilanti State Hospital."

Tears and hysteria overwhelmed me. Mrs. Washington, overhearing the turmoil, intervened. "Even if she did sign those papers, she has the right to change her mind. This signature isn't hers, so why don't you leave before I call security to throw you out?"

Mrs. Schmanski retorted, "You haven't heard the last from me. You have no rights. You can't break a contract like that. There's a family waiting for this child, and they're going to be very disappointed. They can give him everything he needs, and you have nothing."

"I can give him love," I sobbed, defiant. "I'm his mother. I will provide for my son, you'll see. You'll see."

All the commotion had roused him from his sleep. Mrs. Washington, seeing his distress, sat beside him on the bed to offer some comfort.

"So that's why you never answered me when I asked about your mother?" She inquired gently.

"It's not exactly something you want to broadcast—that your mother was committed against her will to a mental state hospital, is it?" I replied, "The weight of the words is heavy in the air."

"No," she acknowledged with a nod.

"Thank you for your help," I managed to say, gratitude mingling with a thousand other emotions. "No problem," she responded, her presence a reassuring calm in the storm.

That afternoon, a woman entered my room with some papers for me to sign. Reluctant, I hesitated, not knowing what they entailed. She explained they were just for naming the baby, which was necessary for his birth certificate. Still skeptical, I feared she was there to swindle me out of my child. I refused to sign.

She seemed genuine enough, but my trust was thin. She carefully read the band on my arm and matched it to the baby's band on his foot, ensuring their correspondence. Then she asked what I wanted to name him. Requesting some time to think, I asked her to return later.

Angry at Eric, I was sure I wouldn't name my son after him. Nobody had cared for me during my pregnancy, so I decided on the name Edward, after Eddie Kelly.

During my three-day hospital stay, the only visitor was Aunt Janie. She brought fruit, spending the afternoon munching and complaining about her high blood pressure and missing her husband, Uncle Pete. All the while, I lay there, stitched up and miserable, listening to her go on about her problems. After her shows ended, she promptly left.

Upon discharge, the hospital gifted me a basket filled with cloth diapers, t-shirts, baby formula, and other necessities. They sent me home in a cab and offered the services of a visiting nurse, which I greatly appreciated. But I was hesitant.

Arriving home, I found everyone on the front porch playing pinochle. Eddie Kelly leapt up and helped me inside with my bags, bypassing the rest as if they were invisible. Upstairs, I unwrapped my baby, and soon everyone, except Geri, rushed up to see him. Eddie held him tightly, as proud as any uncle could be.

Upon asking his name, I told Eddie I had named my son after him. His face brightened, and his eyes welled with surprise and joy. Nina, feeling perhaps slighted, walked out. But I was too drained to care.

Me and my baby settled into Mama's bed. Almost daily, friends and the visiting nurse stopped by, each teaching me more about caring for my son. I quickly shed the pregnancy weight, regaining my figure, which didn't go unnoticed by my sisters. Their envy was palpable as they eyed me with disapproval.

Despite their feelings towards me, they always wanted to hold my son. I let them, but I kept vigilant. My independence was clear—I asked nothing from my sisters, and if they didn't like me, I believed they didn't like my son either. Each day was a new learning experience, and I embraced motherhood with pride and a newfound sassiness.

Isaac Hayes' music was taking the nation by storm with his unique psychedelic funk sound. His top album, "Hot Buttered Soul," was everywhere. Around this time, my sister Eileen brought home two new friends, Eddie C. and Roger. Eddie, a married man she was dating, seemed to hardly ever go home, puzzling me. They got along well, but I noticed his stinginess; they even split the cost of drinks, which seemed odd for a couple.

During this time, Eileen suddenly wanted me to hang out more. It wasn't out of sisterly love—I figured it had more to do with Roger,

Eddie's friend, who was about to receive a hefty sum from a settlement. But I liked him as a friend, not for his money. Roger was generous and had taken a liking to me. We spent a lot of time talking, and he seemed to understand the rough deal I got in life. He adored my son, whom he nicknamed "Chooch."

The day Roger got his settlement, he made a grand entrance. Pulling up in a brown car, wearing a cowboy hat adorned with an extravagant feather, he was flushed with cash—$27,000 to be exact. Blasting the Funkadelic's on his radio.

While Eddie seemed annoyed by not getting a share, perhaps to support his habits, Roger was generous with me, discreetly handing me money and insisting on taking us shopping.

Although he insisted on me accepting gifts for my son, I didn't want to feel obligated to him in any way, so I voiced my concerns. He reassured me, saying he genuinely wanted to help because he loved my baby and liked me. At the store, Roger encouraged me to pick whatever I wanted for me and my son. I focused on essentials for my baby, like powder, lotion, and diapers. Roger, going beyond, bought a stroller, a car seat, clothes, shoes, and more.

Every night, I washed my son's diapers and clothes by hand to ensure he was always clean, even if he wore the same outfits. Roger's generosity meant my son could be well cared for without compromise. "Thank you, Roger," I thought, grateful for his unexpected kindness.

Chapter 5

"Surprise Happy Birthday"

1970

Not much had changed from the years before. Mama was still institutionalized; memories of her were still kept safe in my heart. Eric's letters arrived sporadically, sometimes three or four in a single week, filled with professions of love for me and our son. Apologies for his absence when our son was born mingled with his pleas for pictures to see how the boy had grown. But how could I send pictures when I struggled to buy even a can of milk?

Eric's letters spoke of grand plans—what he was going to do, wanted to do—but never what he should do. Not once did they contain a dime for his son. My resentment toward him grew with each empty promise.

Survival became a daily challenge. I couldn't afford formula, so I crafted my own from pet milk and Karo syrup, following the nurse's instructions. Sterilizing bottles, cooling, and storing them became routine. My son grew, his smile a beacon of joy. He was my constant companion, along with Choo-Choo and Tina, the latter initially confused by her cousin's attention but soon reassured of my equal love.

As Choo-Choo's first birthday neared—actually, on the very day—I celebrated his growth and our bond. Eddie had given me some money for a modest celebration, a birthday cake. That morning, I bathed my son, dressed him warmly, and reveled in his delight at the warm bathwater cascading over his head. His chubby legs, still too soft to walk, kicked as he blew spit bubbles, a sight of pure innocence.

After caring for Tina, I briefly left them under Eddie's watch to order a birthday cake from Farmer Jacks. Promises of a quick return were sealed with a warm bottle of milk and a kiss.

On my way, cutting through the alley, a police car pulled up beside me. The officers asked who I was, and I told them. Their next words sent a chill down my spine. "We have a warrant for your arrest. Get in the car."

I panicked. "No, I won't get in the car. I was going to order my son a birthday cake," I pleaded, my voice trembling.

There were three police officers and just me. Feeling cornered, I asked, "Why are you taking me? What have I done?"

"Just shut up and get in the car," they barked back.

With no other choice, I got into the car, and they drove me down to a place I didn't recognize at the time but know now as the girls' youth home. I sat there, bewildered and scared, not understanding why I was there. All I wanted was to go home to be with my baby.

They took me into a room where the doctor came in and made me bend over while she looked up at my buttocks. He then laid me down on the table and inserted his fingers into my vagina. He handled me very roughly, like he was angry at me. Afterwards, they gave me a gown, what I called a prison gown. He put me in a room and made me sit there for several hours. I forget how long they then moved me to a floor with other girls who wore the same dress that I did and the same colors that I wore.

Upon my arrival at the youth home, they handed me a pillow and a blanket and instructed me to make up my bed. Desperate for answers, I cried out, "What have I done wrong? I need to get home to my baby!"

Their only reply was cold and dismissive. "Someone will take care of him," they said, as if that settled everything. They didn't understand—nobody could know my family like I did. Isolated and powerless, I was denied even the use of a phone. I had no way to find out how my baby was doing. I was certain he missed me terribly, and I worried incessantly about his well-being.

I languished in that youth home for three harrowing weeks. During that time, I felt as though I had died a silent death. I was unable to eat, unable to sleep, and it seemed like nobody cared.

It was there I met Eldoris Smith. She was a very dark-complected girl who revealed that she had been to the youth home more than once. Curious and concerned, I asked her why she was there. Tears welled up in her eyes as she confided in me, "My mom placed me here because she didn't want me to have any kids." She hesitated before adding, "It's a funny thing—I can't have kids anyway because my mom had me fixed."

At the time, I didn't understand what 'fixed' meant, but the horrifying truth became clear to me later. Eldoris explained that her mother had taken her to a clandestine clinic where a doctor performed a total hysterectomy on her without her consent. Throughout my own ordeal, witnessing the emotional scars Eldoris bore, I couldn't help but feel a deep, aching sympathy for her.

We had become friends; we had so much in common. She always talked about how much her mother hated her, and I always spoke of how much my sisters hated me. We exchanged phone numbers and promised to stay in touch if we ever got out.

Third Week

The social worker came in and told me that I had to get dressed for court. They gave me back the clothes that I came in with, and when I put them on, they were hanging off my body. We went inside the courtroom, and I stood before the judge.

He asked me, "Do you know why you had been put in the youth home?" I told him no. "It was for soliciting," he said, and I asked him what soliciting was.

I was careful not to anger him. He explained, "Geri had signed a document stating that you were a prostitute on the streets, and it is against the law for you to solicit your body."

I was too afraid to backtalk the judge for fear that he would not let me go home. He told me that he would release me only under the supervision of an adult. He asked me where my mom was, and I told him. Then he asked if there was anybody in the courtroom to stand up for me. I turned around, and I could barely see through my tears. Aunt Janie walked up, and alongside her was Nina.

The judge asked my aunt if she would take me into her custody. I could not return home without supervision.

After my release, all I could hear my aunt say was, "I couldn't do this when I got to her house."

Nina told me that when Geri had me placed in a youth home, she threw her and Tina out of the house as well. Nina didn't have a job, Eddie had been laid off, and Nina was also in the streets. Eileen had a nervous breakdown while I was gone, and all I was saying to myself was, where is my baby?

I caught the bus home and ran down the streets. I was running so fast that I tripped and fell. When I ran into the house, Geri was not there. I ran up the stairs, and my baby was standing up in his crib, laughing, smiling, and talking baby talk. I picked him up and held him so tight that I could hear him grunt. I kissed him all over and wouldn't put him down. I told him how much I loved him and how sorry I was that I wasn't there for him.

I only put him down long enough to pack up my things—that wasn't much—and left. I carried my son and the stroller down to the bus line. As I told you before, the blocks were very long. I caught the bus to my aunt's house, and I knew all day there that she was going to dog me. It was in her; it was her nature. Echoing in my mind as we left the courthouse, she said, "You better be here before it gets dark, or I'll have you locked back up and your baby taken away from you."

I went around back and knocked on her door. She came down and immediately started to chastise me, telling me that my baby couldn't walk on her floor because Mrs. Maggie, who lived downstairs, couldn't stand the noise. She said that if I walked in her house, I had to take off my shoes. I wasn't allowed to play the radio, I wasn't allowed to watch TV, I wasn't allowed in her refrigerator, and I could only eat and feed my child when she said so.

I had always been afraid of Aunt Janie's house because every time me and Mama would visit, she only spoke of the dead. Her house was dark green and dreary, and at night I made a pallet on the cold linoleum floor for me and my baby to sleep on. She kept her house extremely dark with no lights burning at all. Some nights, my bladder felt like it was going to burst, and I'd hold it until morning.

She was always up before the crack of dawn, and it seemed like that was the only time that I could fall asleep when I could see the light coming through the dark and dingy splintered window shades. One day, a social worker came to the house. She said she was there to see how I was doing. She asked me how I was doing and where I slept.

I was too afraid to tell the social worker how my aunt was treating me, for fear they could take my baby and separate us once again. Before I could open my mouth, Aunt Janie took the social worker into her bedroom where she slept and told them it was my room.

While they talked, my son needed his diaper changed. I took him to the bathroom, laid him across my lap, and changed him on the toilet where I sat. I was too afraid to walk hard on the floors or to move freely through the house.

I overheard the social worker say, "Now that Aunt Janie is your guardian, she can get a check and food stamps for you. The check will come in both hers and your name and should be used to take care of your son. The food stamps should be used for both of you to eat."

She asked me to sign a paper and then left. My aunt proceeded with her day as though nothing had happened. Tentatively, I asked her if I could go outside and sit on the porch.

"No," she said firmly. "You have to stay in the house because I don't want my church members to see a young girl like you with a baby."

Once in a great while, I managed to sneak my son out for a walk in his stroller. On this particular day, I saw my sister Eileen on her way to the bar.

"Come and go with me," she said eagerly. "I want you to meet some of my friends."

I hesitated, torn. I guess I never really faulted her for the way she treated me. Perhaps she had lived a sheltered life and was now trying to make up for lost time. So, I put my son's stroller in the back of the car, and we went up to the bar.

She introduced me to everyone who walked in, announcing proudly that she had raised me, how much she had done for me, and how much I owed her.

There at the bar, I met several people who seemed to genuinely care about me and my son. I don't know if they really cared or if I just felt the need for someone to show they cared for me. Among them was a guy who would become a dear friend to me—Lawrence Blackwell. He was a tall, brown, slender man, only 20 years old, living with his natural mother while his father lived downstairs with a different wife. He had only one sister, and they looked just alike.

I also met a lady named Margie Austin, and through her, little Dot. We had a lot of fun, and she gave me her phone number and address, telling me to call her sometime or just stop by. She lived on Wilkins.

These people were passing my baby around the bar from hand to hand. Everybody wanted to hold him; everybody wanted to kiss him. They bought him milk and suckers because there was a store across the street, and several of the men even gave him money. They thought he was so cute with his bald head; they took him outside in the stroller and pushed him up and down the streets. Although he wouldn't cry when he was away from me, he would always turn his head to make sure I was in sight. He was such a friendly baby that a stranger could walk away with him, which is why I kept my eyes on him at all times. Maybe I was somewhat overprotective, but he was all I had.

In spite of it all, Choo-Choo and I had a really good day at the bar. He had eaten until he was full, and I ate very little. I strolled my son back to Aunt Janie's house, making sure to get in before it got dark. Thank God, I made it.

It was Thursday—choir night—and you couldn't beat her to church. Aunt Janie's voice was like a whisper; she couldn't hit a note with a pencil and paper. Every Thursday and Sunday, she had to be at church, shouting, praying, whooping, and hollering, pestering God about a number of her men. My mama always said, "If you want to find a whore, go to church. That's where all the hoes are." Aunt Janie was a self-righteous bitch and God was going to make her pay for her wrong doing.

Several days had passed, and all I could do was sit on top of the sofa, making sure not to let my feet touch the ground and not to let my son crawl across the floor. We didn't want to disturb Miss Maggie.

One day, Lawrence knocked on the door. I wanted to get to the door before Aunt Janie, but as the saying goes, when in Rome, do as the Romans do. He asked if he could come up and see me, but she told him no.

"He can wait for you on the front porch, and I'll send you down," she declared.

I was so glad to have someone to talk to and looked forward to his visits. We took a walk down the street, and he pushed my baby in the stroller. We stopped at the party store where he bought him a sucker. We just walked around and talked about his problems and mine.

We walked over to his house on Pierce Street, a few blocks from Aunt Janie's. He introduced me to his family and his sister, and we went upstairs to talk and play cards. Choo-Choo had taken a nap, and I knew I couldn't stay long—what would Aunt Janie's neighbors think if I was seen with a baby?

Lawrence and I developed a very close relationship. When you saw him, you saw me. We were only friends, but it was a friendship that meant the world to me.

On this particular day, I gathered my courage and asked Aunt Janie if I could fry an egg for my son. She agreed but made sure to add, "Be sure to wash out the frying pan when you're done."

I bit back my anger. Bitch, you don't have to tell me about washing out a fucking frying pan. My mother was a clean woman, and she taught all her children the same. Nevertheless, I swallowed my pride and responded with a subdued, "Yes, ma'am," knowing my son needed to eat.

Unfortunately, he didn't want to eat all of his eggs. I couldn't tell if it was too early in the morning or if he just wasn't feeling hungry. When I went to scrape the leftovers into the wastebasket, Aunt Janie erupted. "Get that egg out of the garbage and feed it to him now!" she screamed at me.

I refused her, my voice elevated. "I'm not going to feed my child out of the garbage."

It wasn't that I liked her, but my mother had always taught me to respect my elders, no matter the circumstance, good or bad. But she was wrong, and I stood up for my baby and myself.

I've never been one to take orders well, especially not from someone like Aunt Janie—this dumbass, old, worn-out last-year hoe who had bragged about bedding every man from Detroit to Georgia and was proud of her accomplishments. Trying to love and respect her was a challenge; she made it exceptionally difficult with her insults and her backward ways. She'd call me out of my name and pull my hair, and I realized she probably did it out of jealousy—she didn't have much hair of her own. Every time she saw me, she spat out, "You red-headed heifer!"

My mind was made up, but I didn't say anything. My eyes filled with water, remembering how she mistreated me. I waited for her to leave to go and play her street numbers. She walked down the street and turned to the right, and I was on her heels, but I turned to the left. Never to live in her house again. I was fifteen years old and homeless with my baby.

The first night, I knew that I had bitten off more than I could chew. I strolled my baby up and down, trying to find shelter for us. With no money and my stomach growling with hunger, I brushed it aside and continued to seek a place to lay our heads.

On Chene Street, right down from Mr. Kelly's Lounge, where I had once partied with Pee Wee, was a string of grocery stores side by side. I waited in the park for them to close and sought shelter inside the stoop walkway. I pulled the wrought-iron door gate across the door for safety. I laid down on the concrete ground, fed my baby his baby food, and made a pallet on top of me. I let him sleep through the night with me checking on him for rats and other rodents. I was afraid and cold. I prayed for our protection and God's grace. Balled up like a knot, unable to stretch out my legs, I lay there in that position all night. Off and on, I tossed and turned, thinking about how I was going to get myself and my child to safety. My brain was weary with thoughts as I drifted in and out of sleep, recalling the day and other times.

I remember the day Aunt Janie dragged me to the corner store where she traded daily to sign my name on a check that was supposedly for me and my son. After I signed, she snatched the check from my hands, covering it so I couldn't see the amount. It was for $316.00. I counted the cash as they handed it back to her. She bought one box of Pampers for 99 cents and pocketed the rest.

At first, when I left, I didn't know where I was going or if I had a place to stay that night. All I knew was that I was fed up with being mistreated by Aunt Janie and everyone else. I felt less than a dog. Over and over, as I pushed my baby down the streets with everything we owned packed up in the back of his stroller, I dwelled on my misery. What kind of heart does she have to do this to me?

Although I worried about where we were going to go and where we would stay, I couldn't visualize anything; it felt like hitting a dead end. I had no money and no food, but somehow, I was determined. I believed that someone would help us. God would send an angel to help us.

I pushed my baby up Mack Avenue to the Majestic Bar, where my sister Eileen worked. She could see in my eyes that something was wrong, but she didn't really have time to delve into it. I shared with her how Aunt Janie had treated me, pouring out my feelings. She listened, sort of, but she was also working and didn't have much time to spare.

I sat there for quite some time, relieved that Aunt Janie didn't know where I was. That meant she couldn't come looking for me. After a while, my sister asked if I was hungry or wanted a drink. I declined; worry always interfered with my appetite. My only concern was how to feed my child and where we would stay that night.

Throughout the time I spent at the bar, my sister never once asked where I would be staying. She seemed more interested in introducing me to almost every man who walked in. Some of them might have been nice guys, but I wasn't looking for a man. I was trying to figure out how to take care of my baby.

When her shift ended, she called a cab and left me at the bar, telling me to come back the next day and sit with her during her shift. Thankfully, I knew my way around; my mom had taught me how to ride the buses and make connections from one point to another. I was also a good walker—a skill I'd learned from Pat, Pam, and Sam, with whom I used to walk to all the parties we ever attended.

Feeling very sorry for myself, I strolled my baby back down Mack Avenue towards Aunt Janie's house. I didn't want to swallow my pride, and a lump formed in my throat; I didn't want to go back. But it was getting dark, and my baby was tired and sleepy. All I wanted was his blanket and hats for his head.

When I reached Aunt Janie's house, I knocked on the door. I knew she heard me, but she wouldn't answer. Frustrated, I went downstairs to Miss Maggie's after knocking for what felt like an eternity. "Could you please call Aunt Janie and tell her I'm trying to get in?" I asked her.

Miss Maggie was always kind; she made me and my son feel welcome. I stood by the door, listening as she spoke to Aunt Janie on the phone. Aunt Janie told her to tell me she wasn't at home. Miss Maggie just shook her head—she wasn't supposed to relay Aunt Janie's exact words, but she did.

"She said she's not at home," Miss Maggie relayed with a sigh.

I thanked her for making the call, despite the disappointing news. Resigning myself to the situation, I put my baby back in the stroller and started walking. I was walking fast, driven by anger. This black bitch had my money—money that belonged to me and my baby. Thoughts swirled through my mind about where we could go, but I didn't even have a bus fare. I just kept walking. And one of my favorite jams that strengthened me for a hard time was singing in my head. Luther Ingrams, "Ain't That Lovin' You (For More Reasons Than One")" And I started to cry silently within myself. Warm tears flooded my eyes. I think back to the time when I got raped, the loss of my mother's eyesight, and the loss of my mother. But I felt inside that I had to take care of my son at all costs.

"Praise God." On the second night of being homeless, I ran into Lawrence Blackwell. Tears blurred my vision so much that I could hardly see his face. Thank God it was warm outside. My son was snug under his blanket, and I found a hat to put over his head.

When Lawrence saw me, he came over and hugged me. "Where are you going?" he asked.

I pretended like we were just out for an evening stroll, too ashamed to admit what my aunt had done. He invited me over to his house, and I was so relieved he did. His sister and his mom made me feel welcome.

In his sister's bedroom, we talked for hours. She shared the latest about her family, and I confided in her about the events of mine. We exchanged stories of hardship, finding solace in our shared struggles.

When she casually asked if I could stay the night, a wave of relief washed over me. I don't think she knew I was homeless with my baby. Perhaps she was just lonely and wanted some company. I agreed to stay and pretended to call my aunt for permission, weaving a little more dignity into my desperate situation.

Lawrence had to leave to meet his girlfriend at the bar. I seized the opportunity to ask if I could give my baby a bath and lay him down for the night. Josephine, who adored Choo-Choo, kissed him, held him, and helped give him a bath. I was always extra careful with him because, even at 16 months old, he wasn't walking yet. He wanted me to carry him everywhere. His head was still bald, and I made sure to keep it covered so he wouldn't catch a cold.

After putting my baby to sleep, Josephine offered me something to eat. I declined; the place didn't look too clean, and I wasn't really hungry—I just needed a place to stay. Thankfully, my baby had his own jar of baby food and his own spoon, which was good enough for me.

Morning arrived all too soon, and once again, I was on the move. Determined not to give Aunt Janie the satisfaction of seeing me wandering the streets with my baby, I left with Lawrence, heading in the opposite direction. He was pushing Choo-Choo's stroller.

One of his friends approached and asked him whose baby it was. "It's mine," he joked, keeping up his usual playful banter. I walked away because, for some reason, I felt something was wrong. Pat, he called me and said I want you to meet my best friend, Tyson. We've been friends since kindergarten. I waved my hand slightly and kept on walking. I didn't want to meet him. I didn't like him.

By now, Lawrence was well aware of what had happened; he even mentioned seeing my aunt at the cleaners. "I'd recognize her anywhere from your description," he said. Aunt Janie was a striking figure: very tall, dark-complexioned, with broad, prominent features. Her eyes were large and bucked, her lips full, and she was always adorned with purple lipstick. When she smiled, her pink gums were on full display. Her hands and feet were large, and she stood at 5 feet 9½ inches tall in her stocking feet—a stark contrast to my mother, who was a small, brown- framed woman with a voice like silk. Mama had elegance and style, a soft-spoken charisma, and was always a lady through and through.

Lawrence's voice broke into my thoughts: "Where are you going to go?"

Hell, I didn't know where to go or what to do. A haunting thought crossed my mind—if I went back over to Bewick, they might take my baby from me.

So, Lawrence and I walked back to the bar. It was the only place I could think to go. Along the way, I asked him if he knew where Wilkins Street was. I remembered Margie—a lady I'd met at the bar—who told me that if I ever needed anything, I was welcome at her house. Lawrence knew Margie quite well, and he guided me to her home. When we arrived, Margie wasn't there; she was at work at a nearby elementary school, where she worked as a teacher's aide. However, her mother, Ma'dear, was there. Everyone called her Ma'dear', a nickname that suited her sweet demeanor, which all my memories of her fondly reflected. She was a heavy-set, round, fair- skinned woman who, from the moment I met her, treated me like her own.

As we walked up, Ma 'dear was sitting on the front porch. She had tucked her dress between her legs and placed a bowl there, busily shelling crowder peas in her bare feet—a clear sign of her Southern roots.

"Come on up, honey, and make yourself at home," she called out with a warmth that reminded me of the last conversations I had with my mother.

She looked at my baby, asleep in my arms, and asked, "What's this baby here, a boy or a girl?"

"Hand me that big old baby," she said. Without waiting for my answer, she extended her arms out to hug him, taking him completely from me as she peppered his face with kisses. Go on inside and get you something to eat, she said. This woman had never seen me in life, and she was kind and loving to me.

I shared his nickname with her, and she invited me to sit down and help her with the peas after we ate. "I got a bushel of peas from the Eastern Market," she explained, a place I knew well. My mother had often taken me there; it was famous for its fresh produce, live poultry, beautiful flower shows, and most notably, their corned beef sandwiches.

We sat on the porch, talking and shelling peas, enveloped in a peace that had been foreign to me for too long.

Being with Ma'dear felt like old times; I felt so at home. As we sat on the porch, she shared stories of her ex-husband, labeling him a no-good bastard. "Don't trust men," she warned, "they'll break your heart and leave your belly full of babies." She recounted how he had cheated and left her for another woman when their children were still young. Her kids had loved their father deeply and were devastated by the separation.

"He comes around from time to time," she continued, "but the children suffered a great deal from the breakup."

Ma'dear had left Chattanooga, Tennessee, when she was a young woman. "I wasn't a bad- looking woman back then," she reminisced, "having a little bitty waistline and big, bold hips." Chattanooga was a small town where everyone knew her business, and she didn't want her children to suffer more than they already had, so she moved to Detroit.

She spoke candidly about the constant struggles with her children, the hard work of scrubbing white folks' floors, and the long, tiring hours spent standing, ironing, and cooking for someone else's family when she yearned to be home with her own. "I worked for almost nothing a day," she sighed.

As she spoke, she emphasized the importance of education. "Without education, you limit your abilities to function and are almost forced to stand still. In today's world, you wouldn't be able to hold down a decent job without it."

She shared that she was very young when she married her husband, Moses, and was already a mother of three—two boys and a girl—by then.

We had shelled peas for so long that it was starting to get dark. I was so comfortable in her company that I had forgotten my purpose for being there, until I looked up the street and saw Margie and Little Dot walking towards us. Margie's pace quickened when she noticed me. She wrapped her arms around me in a tight hug, pointing towards her mother and excitedly telling her, "This is the girl I was telling you about, Charlie's sister, with the baby. She's a good mother to her son."

They invited me inside, where I helped Ma'dear wash the peas and bag them for the freezer. We gathered at the dining room table, talking and gossiping like old friends. I felt as if I had known them all my life. Ma'dear invited me to stay and eat with her family again. I didn't realize how hungry I was until I finally relaxed and ate my share. We washed dishes and sat around the table, talking late into the night. Ma'dear never asked if I had a place to stay or when I was leaving. Instead, she asked me to comb her hair and braid it for her. As I combed her hair and scratched her scalp, she fell asleep. Soon after, we all fell asleep. The girls and I slept upstairs in two big beds. Margie had even given me one of her nightgowns to sleep in.

The next day was just like any other. We sat around and talked and drank Kool-Aid. Lawrence even came over to visit.

We would talk about Lawrence like he was nothing, and all he would do was laugh; he never defended himself. He knew he was outnumbered. Margie and Dot, much older than me, were grown women with two children each. If Margie were honest, that woman was about thirty years old. Dot was about thirty herself. They were twice my age and then some, but age didn't seem to matter—I could hold my own in conversations with them.

Eileen knew I was staying with Dot and Margie. Occasionally, we would go out to the bar at night to dance and drink our worries away. I felt comfortable leaving Choo-Choo with Ma'dear; he even slept in the same bed with her. Those women drank much more than I did, hustling drinks like pros, and I just watched them. My sister always sent us drinks, and we would dance like there was no tomorrow. There was this dance called football, and one night at the bar, Lawrence and I tore up the dance floor with it. Everyone in the bar stood to watch us—he was a fantastic dancer, but he had met his match in me. The women adored Lawrence; some would line up just for a chance to dance with him. That man was so full of himself, always talking about his dancing skills and having fun. Everybody, men and women, loved Lawrence; he was just that kind of guy. Everybody but one.

Eileen dropped a bomb one day; she told me that Aunt Janie had been asking for me, wanting to see me. Thankfully, she had the sense to tell her she didn't know where I was staying. I waited a couple of days before deciding to visit Aunt Janie's house.

She confronted me as soon as I arrived: "Where have you been?" "Just staying here and there," I replied nonchalantly.

She quickly moved on to her own concerns, warning me that if I didn't stay with her, the social worker would cut off the checks and food stamps she was receiving on my behalf. She rambled on about how she had tried to be a good sister to my mother and what a wonderful aunt she had been to me. I remembered how, when I was little, she would give us one nickel to split and tell us not to spend it "all in one place."

As I listened to her go on, she pulled out another check for me to sign. I hadn't realized that a whole two weeks had passed since I last saw her face. "You know the routine," she said as we walked to the store. She bought a box of Pampers for Choo-Choo and stuffed the rest of the money into her bosom. As we parted ways, she threatened, "If you even think about telling someone what I've done, they'll take your baby away." I'll make sure of that.

She stopped me and called me back, her tone shifting slightly. "Your brother Ricky wants you to get in touch with him. You have some mail at the house," she said. She instructed me not to open it but to bring it to her instead.

"Aunt Janie, I don't even have a bus fare to get there," I protested.

She reluctantly dug into her bosom and handed me a single dollar. "Here, take the bus," she said dismissively. "Your baby rides free, you know."

With nothing else to do and curious about who could be writing to me, I walked back up to Gratiot and caught the bus home to Bewick.

It was a beautiful day, and Choo-Choo and I were inseparable as we strolled down the long block of Bewick. I dreaded passing Robert Howard's house. Every time he saw me, he wanted to hug and kiss me, and I was not in the mood for his stuff today.

As I neared his house, hoping to slip by unnoticed, I saw him standing at the top window shirtless. I couldn't help but take a second look. Uh, he sure has a nice chest, I thought reluctantly. He spotted me and yelled, "Where the hell do you think you're going? Stop right there!" I kept walking, pretending not to hear him, but he persisted. "Stop!" he shouted. "I want to see my son."

It felt like his voice carried down the entire street. He dashed down the stairs, jumped off the porch, and ran towards me, enveloping me in a hug. Reluctantly, I hugged him back. He scooped Choo-Choo up from the stroller, showering him with kisses and rubbing his bald head. "Where have you been?" he asked, saying he knew what Geri had done to me. We chit-chatted all the way to my house, only eight houses away from Robert's.

My brother, Ricky, was sitting on the porch. He looked good. He jumped off the porch, hugged me tightly, and took Choo-Choo from Robert's arms, though Robert was reluctant to let him go. They had a friendly squabble over it. Ricky introduced me to his friend, Melvin. "Man, this is my sister Pat; Pat, this is Melvin," he said. We exchanged greetings; everything was good.

Ricky seemed different, but I couldn't pinpoint what had changed. I decided not to sit on the porch but stayed at the front of the house instead. Ricky ran inside and returned with my mail—it was a package. Eric had sent me some money, at last! My mom had always said not to count your money before you get it, so I unwrapped the package eagerly, only to find a little box inside. What the hell could this be? I wondered.

Inside the box? A set of wedding rings. Attached was a note from Eric, proclaiming his love. Frustration surged through me as I tore the box apart. This motherfucker didn't send any money for my son. All he could think about was marriage, not how I was living or if I had food for my baby. "Eric is such a stupid motherfucker," I vented to my brother. The anger was palpable; I could have kicked Eric ass myself.

Despite my anger, part of me felt a little special that he cared enough to propose. There might have been a card or something with the box; everyone who saw the rings oohed and aahed, commenting on how nice they were and how much they must have cost. But all I could think was how selfish he was—I couldn't feed these rings to my child.

Robert, upset by the whole scene, walked home. My brother and I decided to visit Brazil's, with Ricky insisting on carrying Choo-Choo. I glanced at my brother's hands—they looked swollen. Hmm, I thought, but dismissed it. While we sat talking, I had a flashback to when I saw dry blotches on my brother's neck, which he would scratch absentmindedly.

After a while, Ricky became restless and left with Nanny, Mae Bertha's brother. Left alone with Melvin, we struck up a conversation. Most men I met liked me because I respected myself, and Melvin quickly became a dear friend. As he shared his troubles with me, I had no idea the impact he would eventually have on my life.

I would call him occasionally, and during one of those calls, Melvin shared a story that would haunt me for the rest of my life. It was late at night, and his voice trembled over the phone as he recounted the chilling events. I couldn't help but cry as he spoke.

He told me about the time his stepfather was at home with his youngest brother, who was then just ten years old. Two men had broken into their house, robbed it, and murdered his stepfather right in front of his brother. The trauma of witnessing such a horrific act devastated his brother so deeply that it ultimately led him to take his own life. Melvin found him hanging in the hallway closet, a sight so dreadful that it seemed to forever echo in the silence of their home.

His mother turned to alcohol to numb her pain, and his oldest brother ended up in jail. Melvin often talked about how isolated he felt, overwhelmed by a consuming depression. Sometimes, he confessed that he too harbored thoughts of suicide.

We would spend hours on the phone, sometimes stretching from one month into the next. I found myself desperately trying to instill a will to live in him, grasping at straws and feeding him everything I knew about hope and God. Even after we hung up, my worries for him lingered, heavy and persistent.

Some days were better than others, but most of our conversations circled back to thoughts of suicide, a dark theme that shadowed our interactions yet brought us strangely closer in our shared understanding of despair.

Chapter 6

"Death All Around Me"

Several months had elapsed with little change from the preceding months. One day, as I was inside the house, I heard my sister Nina approach Margie's porch. Recognizing her voice instantly, I scooped up my baby, who was just learning to roll, not walk, and hurried outside. Nina's expression was laden with worry—a sentiment I shared despite our civil interactions.

She revealed her recent court visit aimed at securing our mother's release from the hospital. Social services had provided a checklist for Nina, including securing a stable residence, employment, a phone, and the ability to care for our mother as she once did for us. Nina inquired if I would consider moving in with her to assist in caring for our mother and Tina. Without hesitation, I agreed, ready to support her in any way needed.

Our conversation soon turned lighthearted as we reminisced about the past, discussing Geri's and the impact of her actions on us all. We also spoke of Charlie, who was still searching for her children. When I asked about Matthew, Nina indicated that she hadn't heard from him, only managing to leave messages with his secretary.

Nina then checked on my well-being and offered her help, which I declined, assuring her of my contentment. After embracing me and showing affection to Choo-Choo with a kiss and some money, she expressed her curiosity about my departure from Aunt Janie's house. I avoided the truth, simply stating my inability to continue living there with her. Everyone was scattered, and we had no knowledge of my father's whereabouts. Even if he knew what was going on.

When Nina asked how she could contact me if needed, I directed her to go through Margie, making her promise not to inform Aunt Janie of my whereabouts. Despite feeling integrated and cherished in my current residence, a sense of detachment from this family lingered—an emotion that nudged me toward independence.

Living with Ma'dear's extended family—which included Margie, her children, her brother Junior (whom I admittedly had a mild crush on), Little Dot and her children, and now Big Dot, Margie's cousin—highlighted my non-blood relationship and intensified my feelings of alienation. It was time for me to seek a new beginning, mindful of my mother's advice about maintaining healthy distances in relationships.

Ma 'dear and Margie had equipped me with survival skills and the fortitude to maintain dignity as a young woman. During a walk with Lawrence, I encountered my big mama, who disclosed her address should I ever need her help. Eventually, I relocated to Pulford Street to live with her, ensuring to keep in touch with Margie, Dot, and Big Dot. These connections had transformed into sisterly bonds, providing invaluable lessons I carry with me today.

Big Mama's house exuded an air of gloom, its interiors as dark and dingy as the somber colors that adorned its walls. Her primary pastime seemed to be sitting at the kitchen table, surrounded by flickering candles, casting spells or prayers on everyone she knew. This eerie ambiance often drove me to leave; the house's musty scent hitting you like a wall upon entering did little to make it feel like a home.

Despite the odd atmosphere, there was a certain charm to Big Mama's character. She was constantly doling out advice on how to raise my baby and didn't hold back on her opinions about Aunt Janie, whom she accused of being deceitful enough to steal my money and food stamps. Big Mama's hospitality seemed tinged with an agenda; she appeared to relish having fodder for gossip more than genuinely helping me.

Her manipulative streak extended to insisting that I confront Aunt Janie to reclaim my checks— checks Aunt Janie had gotten so adept at cashing that she no longer even required my signature. Big Mama's confrontations with Aunt Janie weren't rare; she frequently hurled insults over the phone, yet she always advised me to tread cautiously, her facial expressions hinting at the potential consequences of antagonizing Aunt Janie.

While Big Mama's welcome was always warm in words, the reality felt different. Her house never truly felt like a sanctuary to me. Eventually, my inability to retrieve my checks from Aunt Janie soured our relationship, and I found myself back on the streets. One chilly night, after a visit to Margie's, I sought refuge at Big Mama's. I saw her shadow flicker behind the curtain, but the door remained closed to me. Dejected, I returned to Ma 'dear's place, where I was always greeted with open arms and a genuine sense of belonging.

Nina had secured a modest one-bedroom apartment on the corner of Elmhurst and Tuxedo Street. She picked me up on the day she moved in, excited to start anew despite the cramped quarters. The kitchen was so small that a single turn took up all the space, and the term "furnished" was generously applied, as it only included a stove and a refrigerator—the freezer was barely large enough for a single chicken. The building wasn't much to look at, but it was clean and represented the best Nina could afford at the time.

She managed to find some used furniture, though the origins were a mystery to us. Nevertheless, Nina, Choo-Choo, Tina, and I made do in this tiny space as we awaited the social worker's inspection for our mother's arrival. Nina had also started dating a new boyfriend, Leroy Jeffries. He seemed decent enough, though I didn't know him well. My impressions of Leroy were limited, but two things were clear: he genuinely wanted to help Nina, and she, less invested, seemed to need him for his connections in real estate. Despite his past boasting of being a prime prizefighter, that he was. His stature hardly matched the tales—barely half Nina's height. But he was warm and generally a nice man.

Weeks later, Nina received word that the social worker would be visiting. Given the apartment's size, preparation was minimal—it took no more than five minutes to tidy up. The visit stretched for hours, with lengthy discussions at the kitchen table, while I watched over Tina and Choo-Choo. The kids, having not seen each other since they were infants, played joyfully, now old enough to run around and engage in their toddler antics. Choo-Choo, starting to speak, amusingly confused "da-da" with "ma-ma," much to my correction and his laughter.

They were making so much noise, and I was trying to hear what the social worker had to say about Mama. I heard Nina inform Mrs. Graham, the social worker, about her enrollment in nursing school and her intention to pursue a degree. She said I would be at home to watch Mama and that we would have a telephone installed in case she needed to call. They shook hands, and Mrs. Graham left there with a smile, telling Nina that she would be in touch by mail. We were both worried because we didn't know what the decision would be. Nina didn't have a lot going for her, but the potential was there.

About two weeks had passed when Nina came running down the hall, screaming and crying, holding the letter in her hand. She grabbed me and hugged me, showing me the letter. They had agreed to release my mother into Nina's custody. They would give Nina exactly one year to move out of the apartment, and they would conduct monetary inspections of Mama just until they felt she was stable. Well, this was good news to me—I was so excited; Mama was coming home at last. Nina could go and get her at any time.

Nina's friends Ronnie and Willie drove us up to Ypsilanti. It was Willie's car, so that meant that Nina and Ronnie had to sit in the back. Something so small. Willie had been over to the house several times before, and I'd seen how he'd look at me. He was always so eager to run to the store for me and often bought my baby milk, Tina candy, and stuff. Nina and Ronnie both knew that Willie liked me. I think Nina somewhat felt his attraction by the fact that a lot of men liked me. Plus, he was married.

I hadn't been with a man since I had been with Eric. It was raining out really bad that day, and to me, we just couldn't get there fast enough. It had been over a year since I had seen my mother. When we got there, the nurses had her all packed and ready to go. I ran over and gave her a big hug and a kiss. I took her hand and began escorting her out of the hospital prior to her official discharge. All the nurses ran over to hug and kiss Mama goodbye. She was having a difficult time walking, so one of the nurses offered Mama a wheelchair. I never stopped walking with her halfway down the hall—I was afraid they would change their minds. I kept feeling that before I got my mama outside and safely locked inside

Willie's car, they were going to run up and grab my mama out of my arms and say that there had been some sort of mix-up and make her stay at the hospital.

The first sign of relief I felt was when we drove off. I was finally able to breathe a little bit better. We had Mama in the car, and we were on our way home.

We just kind of chitchatted in the car, asking Mama how she felt and what most of her days consisted of. She revealed that she spent most of her time either lying in bed or confined to her room. She wasn't able to get up and wander about. Despite the nurses' apparent fondness for her, Mama's appearance revealed neglect, and the majority of her time was spent alone. I felt so sorry for her. Mama never deserved all the low-down, dirty, and unfair things that happened to her.

I could think of a lot of people that this could have happened to, but who am I to judge? I just wanted to make up for lost time. I wanted to sleep with my mother like we used to. I wanted to be able to wake up every morning, look in my mother's face, and ask her what she wanted for breakfast or even how she felt. It didn't matter; I just wanted her home. I wanted to be able to hug her, kiss her, and feel her hand enclosed in mine. I miss her touch and I wanted to introduce her to my baby. I would do whatever I could to make it up to her. As we drove down the freeway, I was thinking about all the things that I could do with my mother. How much time would we be able to spend together? So many things crossed my mind. Running interference was provided by Welton Smith and Donald Malone. Briefly…

So much time had passed between us. I was just relieved that she was out of the hospital. My mind drifted back to that day, wondering why Willie was driving so recklessly. Where did he need to be? That was so urgent. If he was pressed for time, he should've mentioned it—I would have taken a bus instead.

Memories of a past car accident surfaced. Mama was at the wheel then, barely able to see the man whose feet she accidentally ran over at the corner. It was clear she was losing her eyesight, but she refused to admit it. I thought to myself how fortunate that man was, spared from a worse fate by mere inches. Her driving, often a subject of our lighthearted comparisons to Mr. Magoo, wasn't so funny now.

As these thoughts occupied my mind, Willie hit a rain puddle on the I-94 freeway. He slammed on the brakes, sending the car spinning uncontrollably down the road. Panic overtook me, leaving me frozen, unsure whether to sh*t or go blind from sheer terror. All I wanted was to make it home safely, swearing never to set foot in Willie's car again.

Days blended into one another with Mama watching soap operas and game shows while I managed the household—cooking, cleaning, washing, and ironing. Nina, ever absent, spent her scarce free days partying in the streets. Despite the workload, I was thankful for a roof over my head but yearned for some personal time.

It's a challenging endeavor to strive to be your best when no one seems to notice. Only Mama and the kids seemed to appreciate my efforts. Trapped within the home's walls, Nina's controlling nature grew more apparent. She exerted her influence over not just my life but Mama's too, making us feel like prisoners in our own homes.

We had been living in Elmhurst for nearly six months. My only solace was the telephone, a lifeline to the outside world where I could catch up on gossip with old friends. Melvin and I would talk daily, sometimes multiple times. When Nina was around and the phone rang, her disdainful glares and eye rolls made her displeasure clear. She wanted to sever all my connections to the outside, controlling even the simplest aspects of my life. Company was forbidden, and my world was confined to the stretch between our house and the corner store— not out of concern for my safety but as a display of dominance.

As Mama used to say, "Teeth and tongue fall out."

This particular night, the guy who lived downstairs—whom I'd seen several times in the hallway while getting the mail—stopped by my door. We exchanged names; he told me where he lived, and he knew where I lived. Nothing special; you could tell he was trying to hit on me, but like I said, he was nothing special. Earlier that day, we stood and talked about the unbelievable deaths of Soul Singer Darrell Banks and Tammy Terrell. He was murdered shot in the neck on LaSalle Street.

One of my favorite jams by him is. "Just Because Your Love Is Gone".

He knocked at the door, and oh, by the way, did I tell you I wasn't allowed to answer the door? He asked my sister if I was there. She stood and blocked the doorway, then told him, "Just a minute." She always had an attitude, and she slammed the door in his face.

"Pat," she said in a really shitty tone, "somebody's at the door for you. I don't know who he is, but you tell him not to come here anymore." She said it loud enough so that he could hear it. I was embarrassed.

I told her I didn't like the way she talked to me and that I was tired of her demeaning manner. "I took it when I was young, and I'm not taking it anymore," I asserted. I believe if you give respect, you should get it."

We started to argue, our voices filling the whole apartment. Surprisingly, she couldn't whip my ass like she thought she could. I stood my ground. My mother started to scream, holler, and cry, and the kids were crying too. She wasn't going to let me go, and I wasn't going to let her go either. My mother jumped in between us and separated us. That's when we stopped fighting.

I was so upset that I ran out of the house, my nose bleeding—not from her whipping my ass, but because I was so goddamn mad, I suppose my blood pressure went up and I had a nosebleed. I had never had a nosebleed like that in my life. My nose bled for over an hour and a half. As I walked around the block to cool off, Bobby, the guy that came to the door, packed my neck with snow, trying to stop the bleeding. All during my walk, I kept thinking to myself how bad I felt for having fought with my sister, for cussing her out, and for calling her a bunch of bitches that were long overdue.

I kept playing this scene over and over in my mind. Although I felt that she could have won the bitch of the year award, I would have never told her that to her face. She was my older sister, and I loved her—apparently more than she loved me. I had been taught all my life to respect my elders. She wasn't much older than me, but the respect was there. I would always sacrifice my feelings for someone else, but this time I just couldn't take it anymore. She had no respect for me whatsoever.

And I wasn't going to just lay down and let her whip my ass.

She wanted to be able to whip my ass and talk about it; I guess she wanted me to be the first notch on her belt. As a matter of fact, years later, when I asked her about it, she never recalled the fight we had. Why? Because she wasn't in control of the situation.

Oh yeah, she remembered.

A lot of time had passed before I was even able to look into my sister's face. I was embarrassed about the fight we had, especially over my mother. I wanted to accept responsibility for all the actions, but something in me would not let me accept full blame. The only reason I was still in her house was because of my mother and my niece.

Plenty of hugs and kisses came from me, and I extended my love to my mother, Tina, and Choo- Choo. They were always kissing and hugging because that is what I demonstrated towards my son; therefore, they kissed and hugged all the time.

Nina always talked about how much she resented Lynn after he told her that he would quit his job before he paid any child support to her for Tina, and he did.

Suddenly, I heard Tina scream and start running out of the bathroom, holding her face, with Nina running and screaming behind her. Tina was hysterical. I thought Nina might have hit her, but I don't remember hearing a sound. I ran towards the crying as Tina was running out of the bathroom. I removed her hand from her face to see it laying open; I could see the flesh—blood was everywhere. Tina's face had been sliced open with a razor.

Nina said that she was arching her eyebrows, and when she relaxed her hand, Tina ran into the razor. Nina took Tina to the hospital, and I took care of her face the best that I could, being careful to change the bandages every day. I would clean the wound and put Vaseline on her face to make sure it would heal.

It seemed like tragedy was all around me. I remember hearing over the radio that Jimi Hendricks had died of an overdose, and the next month, Janice Joplin had also died of a drug overdose. It was a kind of eerie feeling to me that two people of their stature would die of a drug overdose. They had so much to live for. I loved them both. I felt sad and depressed. Off and on, I managed to bury my feelings in the bathroom, where I could get some time for myself to cry. This heaviness' would seep into my heart and stay there. I played this song for three days straight. Was it a warning of what was to come? "God Bless the Children by The Staple Singers.

On November 18, 1970, after hearing about the deaths of Jimi Hendricks and Janice Joplin, my girlfriend Emma Jean called me on the phone to tell me that one of Mrs. Brazil's children had been killed. She said, I guess so, something was happening over there. There are a lot of people on her front porch. My heart sank because I loved the entire family. I began to pray to God to let it not be true. Maybe they are having a party or something. I started shaking inside. Please, God, I prayed; don't let it be Emory. I asked Nina if I could go and see what happened if she would babysit. She said yes because she had to study for the nursing program she was in. I fed the kids and Mama and left there running. I just had to get out and see for myself. I was able to catch the bus over to Brazil's house.

All the while I rode the bus, I kept saying to myself that this couldn't be true. But when I got off the bus and was walking towards their house, the streets were filled with people, young and old. There was standing room only on the porch. I knew then that it was true. Something terrible had happened. I walked inside the house, and the first person I hugged was his mother. She was very hurt. Although she wasn't crying, you knew that it was there. Not only had her son been killed, but her sister, Aunt Geraldine, died the night before him. Within minutes at the same hospital, before she died, she told Mrs. Brazil that when she died, she was going to take one of her children with her. Little did she know that Jackie would soon be behind her; they died minutes apart. People from the close community were everywhere, setting up food, drinks, and comfort for the entire block.

I was afraid to ask what happened. She took me to the side and told me that Jackie had been murdered. I almost collapsed right there. "No God," I cried out. She comforted me in her arms, and she showed tremendous strength for others in her own grief. I couldn't stop crying.

When I heard about Jackie's death, I cried. I was devastated. I couldn't believe it. I loved him so much; he was like a big brother to me. I only remember how much I cried and how bad I felt for him and his family. Thank God Nina was at home, because I don't know how I would have been able to maintain myself if she wasn't.

He was 21 years old, too young to die. The way that I understood the story was that he owed the dope man some money—less than $200 for some penny caps. He had now been clean for several months. The dope man found out where Jackie's cousin lived and told him that if he didn't have Jackie there within 24 hours, he would kill his whole family. So, his cousin set him up.

His cousin R. Lewis told Jackie to meet him on Calvert and 12th Street on the west side of Detroit, and he would tell him what was going down—and what he heard through the grapevine. When Jackie got there, Lewis was inside the apartment building. Jackie walked inside, where he would meet his death. The small-time dope man had his boys tie him up with his hands and feet bound behind his back and shoot him in the back of his head at close range with a 357 Magnum. Execution style. Lewis said at the trial that Jackie had begged for his life, and from what I can understand, he also asked his mother for the money, and she refused to give it to him.

I know that many days went by in her life where she wished she had given him the money. She didn't even tell her husband that Jackie had called. But he told his mom specifically that he had 24 hours to live and that he would be dead in 24 hours—and he was. I guess she didn't believe him.

I was overcome with grief. Somehow, I just couldn't believe that Jackie was gone, that I would never see him again, and that we would never be able to spend time together as we did so many times before. We did a lot of devilment together. The funniest memory that I have of him was the night Mr. Brazil came home from work, parked his car, took his bath, and went to bed. Me, Jackie, and a couple of other kids stole his car, stole his liquor, and went joy riding. We laughed to ourselves; Jackie had burned all the gas out of his car and had a good time doing it. Jackie was a nice person who didn't deserve to die like he did. Gunned down like an animal. He was somebody's child.

Jackie always said that he "wasn't going to Viet Nam to get killed," but he stayed home and got killed anyway. I called Nina and asked if I could come home late, and she said yes because she didn't have to work. Nina was sympathetic about it all. So, I stayed there at Brazil's house. I had a few drinks, and we all reminisced about Jackie. I then took the speakers and placed them in the windows, and I played the Jazz Crusaders "1970 Jam and "Way Back Home" repeatedly for blocks around; that's all you could hear. Jackie's Funeral was held at Swansons on the Boulevard with standing room only.

Mama always said, "If you play with fire, you'll get burned." Several months had passed by, and I was still grieving over my friend when one night I decided that I wanted to go to the "Funkadelic Parliament Concert." I was a big fan of Bootsy Collins. He was a bad motherfucker, and I had all of his songs. A friend of my sister's, Eileen, wanted to take me out; we had met some time ago. Charles was trying to talk to me and had invited me to the concert. He was one ugly motherfucker.

I had finished all my housework and was more determined than ever to go to the concert. I told Nina that I was going, dressed in a green and white miniskirt dress, white patent leather go-go boots, and a white faux fur short jacket. I looked good; I was ready. It was extremely cold outside; we caught the bus. Can you imagine anyone taking the bus in the wintertime to Cobo Hall downtown, right off the riverfront, to see Funkadelic? I didn't really care; I just felt the need to get out. I could have dressed warmer, but who cares about warmth when you're trying to look cute?

Just before I left, the phone rang. I whispered to Nina, "Who is it?" She said it was Melvin. I had talked to Melvin three times that day, and all his conversations were long. So, in a quiet voice, I told her, "Tell him I wasn't here."

The concert was a blast, and I enjoyed myself thoroughly, completely ignoring my date. He kept talking to me so close to my face that I could smell his stinking breath—it smelled as if he had been smoking cigars through his ass. He was older than me, and I had never noticed before, but he had a bald spot-on top of his head. Although he was nice, polite, and treated me like a lady, I wasn't interested in him. I was grateful for his kindness, but I wasn't interested in pursuing a relationship with him.

He took me back home, and I was so exhilarated from the concert that it took me several hours to fall asleep. It felt like I had just closed my eyes when I heard a knock at the door. Nina had gone to work, so I asked, "Who is it?"

"Ricky," he said.

I opened the door. He walked in, hugged my mother, and kissed her on the head. He asked me if I had talked to Melvin.

I told him, "I talked to him the day before." He said, "Melvin is dead."

I remember backing up against the wall, searching for something to hold onto to prevent myself from falling.

I told him, "If you are lying…"

I just talked to Melvin. I spoke to him over the phone just yesterday."

His eyes filled with tears as he urged me to call Melvin's house if I didn't believe him. I hesitated, thinking that if Ricky was playing a joke on me, it was a cruel one.

I called Melvin's house because I wanted to prove him wrong. Melvin's mother answered the phone. I greeted her and identified myself.

She said in a very faint, lifeless voice, "I know who you are, you're Melvin's friend who calls him all the time."

Holding my breath, I asked to speak to Melvin. When she told me that Melvin was dead, that he had hanged himself in the basement and she had found a suicide note next to his body, my world stopped. Melvin Causey was 17 years old.

The news of Melvin's death devastated me. I couldn't help but blame myself for what had happened. If only I had answered the phone when he called, perhaps he would still be alive. Maybe I could have saved his life. All I could do was think of Melvin day and night. I felt so guilty and took full responsibility for his death. "Oh God, help me," I prayed this is all too much.

I was also very angry with Melvin. I thought it was a very selfish thing to do. How could he do this to me? I was only 15 years old. How was I supposed to handle this?

Again, I associated the shame and pain with my past. I remember promising myself that I would not go to the funeral, that I did not want to see him like that. However, my resolve wavered, and I decided to go and say my goodbyes. Feeling responsible for his death, I thought I should intervene with prayers and pray to God for him, and for our forgiveness.

I went to the funeral home after everyone else had left. A man opened the door and let me in. I don't know where I got the nerve, but I started walking down what seemed like an endless dark hallway. The only light was shining on Melvin. As I approached, I could hardly recognize the body. It wasn't until I was right up close to him that I knew for sure it was Melvin.

Standing there, I spoke to him. "Why?" I asked repeatedly. "Didn't you know that I loved you and cared about you like a brother? Of all the things for you to do, this was one thing you didn't have to do." My thoughts then turned to his family. "What about your poor mother? What about all the people you left behind, all the ones who loved you?" Tears fell from my eyes onto his. He looked so still and young. I kept thinking to myself that I saw him breathe, that it seemed like his chest was moving up and down. But it was just my imagination.

I sat down in the chair, half-expecting that this didn't really look like Melvin and maybe it wasn't him. Maybe soon he would walk through the door, or someone would wake me up and tell me this was all a bad joke. I bent my head over and started to cry when suddenly I heard a sound that seemed to come from Melvin. It was as if he was trying to speak. I immediately stood up, said my quick goodbyes, told him that I loved him, and ran out of the funeral home.

I made a promise to Melvin—and to myself—that from this point on in my life, I would make myself available and take the time for anyone and everyone. If they wanted to talk to me, I would listen. If I could do no more than listen, then that is what I would do.

I often thought of Melvin and what he might have been like if he had lived. Sometimes he weighed so heavily on my mind that I would force myself to try and forget him, along with the pain I was feeling. But on many days, he would resurface, and I would just have to cope.

My heart was numb with pain. On my suitcase record player, I played Sweet James leading the Fantastic Four, the 1967 jam "As Long as I Live, (I'll Live for You)."

Chapter 7

"All It Takes is One Time"

1971

Four months had come and gone since the death of Melvin Causey. Not much had changed in my life. I knew I had to get a grip. I was trying, with every fiber of my being, to understand why he would take his own life—a life bestowed upon him by the good Lord above.

Some days were better than others. My emotions were mixed. Didn't he understand my love for him? He wasn't the only one hurting; he wasn't alone in this world. I felt his pain and reached out to help.

It was my fault that Melvin now lay sleeping in his grave. My fault, because I hadn't taken his call. Anger towards Melvin seethed within me. I wanted to scold him, yet in the same breath, I longed to tell him how much I would miss him, how much he truly meant to me. How could he do this to me? How could he do this to himself?

I needed him to understand the impact of his actions. Suicide—what an ugly word, what a selfish act.

My sister Charlie had moved in. I was glad she was there when she was. But I was starting to feel like Cinderella. Not only was I cooking and cleaning for my previous family, but now we had a new addition. I wanted to get out of this mess. I wanted to go back to school. I kept a lot of my feelings to myself—the special things that I felt, the important things that I thought, I dared not share. Whenever I expressed myself about my dreams and ambitions, they would only shoot them down. So, I had learned how to build a wall around myself, within myself, to protect myself from those vicious animals I called sisters.

Every night, when Charlie came home, she had been drinking. She was popular at the bar and everyone loved her; she had that contagious personality.

I felt boxed in, like there was no way out. So, I would spend most of my free time imagining myself as someone else, totally separated from who I was. The only time that I would really come back down to earth were the times that I spent with Choo-Choo. He was now 18 months old, as fat as a butterball. He only had peach fuzz on his head. He still wasn't walking and would lay down on the floor, roll to the other side of the room, and pull himself up. He had four teeth, and every chance he got, he would bite me. I would pretend to cry, placing my hands over my eyes, and he would pull them down.

I would say, "Peek-a-boo," and he would start to laugh. He had a very sensitive side to him as a baby. He was able to say a few words, and at night I would kneel down with him on one side and Tina on the other, take his hands, and put them together. I taught him how to close his eyes, as if he were asleep, and how to pray. Although he wasn't able to repeat after me, his favorite part of the prayer was "Amen."

I also taught him how to sit at the table and eat his food. But before he ate, he would say, while folding his hands together, "Amen, Mama." He was a special little boy and gave me the strength to live. From a very young age, he knew to pray before he ate and to pray before he went to sleep. At night, I would read him stories and talk to him about God. He was my constant companion and a good listener. He'd lay there, drinking his bottle, paying full attention to his feet, with his hands wrapped around his toes.

I knew he was still young, and I believed that when a person has children, they should commit to raising them. Parents need to respect their children and themselves—children learn only what they are taught. Parents should constantly reinforce lessons. I would often observe my girlfriends' children standing at the table to eat, chewing with their mouths open, never being taught to appreciate their food—or anything else, for that matter.

I didn't want my son to be a product of his environment. Just because a person lacks material things, it doesn't excuse parents from overlooking the basics—like teaching their children manners, respect, and prayers. They were being raised without manners, like animals; they ran around with dirty diapers, and if they wore a T-shirt, it was likely filthy. Their hair uncombed, and when you spoke to them, they could only respond with "huh."

I knew then that I would devote all my time and energy to raising my son differently. Children represent who you are. Looking at my son, I knew right then that I didn't want him raised like that. So, I took time with him and taught him every day. We would repeat the same lessons until he learned, and he caught on quickly. After he mastered one thing, I would reinforce it while introducing something new. Often, I would reward him with kisses and hugs—he liked that.

I was constantly receiving letters from Eric filled with empty promises. Although I'd push my feelings aside, I really did love him. I suppose it was a mix of love, disappointment, and anger. In all his letters, he expressed how much he loved me and wanted us to be a family. I thought maybe I would see him again soon. He wrote that he was coming home soon and asked why I hadn't taken the baby over to his mother's.

I never told him why, but the reason was that I felt she didn't like me. So, how could she like my baby? I wasn't going to expose my child to someone who didn't like me. I heard through Pee Wee that Mrs. Florence (Eric's mother) claimed the baby wasn't his. I thought to myself, how could she know? She wasn't there the night he was conceived. But what Eric didn't know was that I did take my baby over there to see her, and she stopped me at the door, saying in a nasty tone, "That's not my son's baby." And I responded, "You don't ever have to worry about seeing him again, and if you do, he'll be looking down in your face." Then, I walked off her porch and over to Pee Wee's.

I don't know what she thought of me, and I didn't waste time trying to change her mind. You take it or leave it. I knew whose baby this was; he was mine, and that was all that mattered. Now, I was both mother and father. I was the one up at night when he was sick, the one feeding him the best I could, the one taking total care of Choo-Choo. Frankly, I didn't give a damn whether she claimed him as her grandson or not. She wasn't paying the bills, and I was not about to grovel for anything. This was the attitude I took then, and it's the attitude I hold now.

It had been a long, hard winter. Finally, spring was here. I knew that all the snow was gone, and it wasn't coming back because you could see the trees starting to bud, and each time the sun came out, it stayed longer and longer. I loved the sunshine. I wished I could go somewhere else and live where the sun would come out and stay all day, and I could feel it's warm rays upon my face.

Choo-Choo was now walking on his own, most of the time anyway. His hair was starting to fill in with light brown peach fuzz. I wanted to potty-train him, but I wasn't sure I knew how. I mean, with him being a boy and all, how was I going to teach this kid how to use the potty? Boy, did I have my work cut out for me. Tina was already potty-trained, thanks to me, so I was hoping that she could show him how to go to the pot. The days that I was able to get him to the pot were few and far between. He always had to have an audience, and if I left him in the bathroom to run and answer the phone, when I came back, he and the potty and whatever was in the potty would be either on his head or all over the bathroom floor. And he would take off running through the house with his butt out. I wouldn't spank him; I would just show him what he had done and what a mess he had made of himself. He was an easy-going kid; he would only laugh. He'd laugh at me as if I had made the mess. Tina was absolutely no help at all. So, I spent a lot of my days trying to potty-train my son.

One day the phone rang, and the voice on the other end sounded familiar. It was someone playing over the phone. When I continued to ask who it was and threatened to hang up if they didn't stop playing, the voice said, "It's me." I asked, "Me who?" and they replied, "Me, Eldoris."

"Oh my God," I exclaimed, "Where are you? Where are you staying? The phone number you gave me is out of order; I've been looking for you all over the place." We talked for a while, and she asked if she could come over. I said yes before I thought about it, but I was determined to see her. I hadn't seen her since the youth home.

She caught the bus to the apartment, and we spent the whole day together, laughing and talking. She didn't have too much to say about her mother, only that she still loved her and that she forgave her for what she had done. She was living outdoors, from hand to mouth. I offered her a place to live with us, but she flatly refused because she knew of my sister Nina. She didn't want to add to my problems and felt very bad for my mother. "Besides," she said, "I'll be alright. I've been out here a long time by myself, and I will survive. Don't worry about me; just take care of your baby and your mama, and God will take care of you."

We hugged, and Choo-Choo and I walked her to the bus stop. "Eldoris," I said, "promise me that you will keep in touch with me." She promised she would, and I gave her the address over on Bewick in case we were ever separated again.

When I got back to the house, Nina was getting dressed. She said that she was going to look at a house with Leroy Jefferies and asked if I minded staying home and babysitting. The only reason she was so polite was that she had company and tried to hide the way she treated me. I was glad when she left; there was peace in the house.

Well, Nina got the house on Freeland Street off Grand River. She was so excited, talking about how she was going to decorate, and she had bought new furniture. She said that the house had three bedrooms and that it was a blessing from God. She talked as if she was going to be a better person and learn how to treat her fellow man. We moved over to Freeland and the house was nice. Nina had furniture delivered the same day that we moved in.

The only things we took with us were in small boxes; we left everything behind that wasn't worth taking. Soon after we got settled in, Nina reverted to her usual behavior; the niceness didn't last long. She reminded everyone, including Mama, that this was her house and her brand- new furniture, and that we had to fall in line, so to speak. The only person allowed to sit on the furniture was Mama; everyone else had to sit on the floor. We had to walk with our hands in our pockets, careful not to touch the walls, and we had to take our shoes off when walking on her new carpet. She monitored our every move. If I walked into the kitchen, she would come and stand, watching and guarding the house like she was crazy. I was very careful not to let my son touch anything.

I had to get out. "Mama," I said to her, "I don't want to leave you here, but I just can't take it anymore. I have to go." She replied, "No, stay here with me. Who's going to take care of me when Nina's at work? We need you here." My heart sank. She was right—they needed my help.

So, I stayed. One day, a knock at the door revealed Eric standing outside. My brother Rickey had shown him where we lived. He tried to hug me, but I refused. He sat down to talk with my mother and asked about Choo-Choo. When he requested, I wake him from his nap, I declined, saying he'd be cranky and that Eric would have to wait until he woke up naturally.

Finally, after a while, as I kept glancing at the clock, I knew Nina would be home soon, and I couldn't have company, especially not with him sitting on her new furniture. So, I explained the situation to him and asked him to leave, promising to call him later. As I hurried him to the door, he grabbed my arm and said, "You know that I love you. Marry me, and I'll take you away from all this."

"Why should I marry you? All I want from you is help taking care of my son, the child you fathered. I don't need to marry you for that."

This fool had some nerve. "I don't want to marry him, Mama," I said. "Can you believe him?" "Yes," she replied, "I really do believe that he loves you. Just give him another chance."

And I did. And guess what? I listened to all the nonsense and lies he told me, and once again, I fell for it. It wasn't so much that I loved him; I was looking for a way out, and at that time, any route that seemed like an escape was the one I was going to take, not knowing that my sister had already made plans for me. The days of crying alone in the bathroom continued, and I had nightmares about Welton and Donald Malone.

Nina asked me to move out, knowing I had nowhere to go, but that was alright because I was back at Ma 'Dear's house, and they welcomed me with open arms. I started to see a young man Charlie introduced me to from the bar. Everyone called him Yogi. Man, was he nice to me and my son. He was compassionate and funny. We spent time together as friends, visiting Margie's house where he showed interest. Some nights, after putting our children to sleep in bed with Ma 'Dear, we'd walk to the Majestic Bar, cutting through alleys, partying with Lawrence, Charlie, Yogi, and everyone there, dancing all night and having fun. The attraction was obvious between us, and everyone teased us because they knew we liked each other. Yogi worked in construction, and on Fridays, he would give money to my son as a friend. I wouldn't accept it, but he would sneak fifties and hundreds into Choo-Choo's hand, who would then run away with it, pocketing it with a smile.

It had been a long time since I had seen Mama. I prayed that she was doing well; my constant prayers were with her and Tina. My father was back home, living with Nina. I knew they were being taken good care of because he loved them as much as I did. I was very sad to have to leave my mother and my niece. I felt myself sinking into a deep depression that I managed to suppress around friends.

After staying with Margie for a while, she asked me if I had my cycle that month. I told her that I couldn't remember—that I had so much on my mind and that I really didn't know. So, I made an appointment at the hospital. I started to pay closer attention to myself and noticed that my clothes were getting a little tight and that my breasts were tender. Every day until my appointment, Dot and Margie teased me. Margie had to work that particular day, so she sent Big Dot to the hospital with me because she didn't want me to go alone. Just before we left, the phone rang, and it was Aunt Janie. She wanted me to come over to her house; she wanted to talk to me. It was still early, and I agreed. When I got to her house, we sat at the kitchen table, and I held my baby tight, careful not to put him down so that he wouldn't disturb Miss Maggie, who lived downstairs.

For some reason, Aunt Janie was exceptionally nice to me that day. I thought maybe her conscience was eating her up. While sitting at her table, she began to talk about various events in her life. She mentioned the number of men she had been with, the hardships she faced, and how God had blessed my mother with seven children while she had none. I thought to myself, she's jealous; she's been jealous of my mother her whole life.

She tried to talk down about my mother in a way that made me very uncomfortable. My mother had always taught me to respect my elders, and I didn't want to confront Aunt Janie directly, but I did tell her that whatever differences she had with my mother, she should discuss them with her because they really had nothing to do with me. She could always find fault in her sister, her only living relative, yet she always failed to acknowledge her own shortcomings—everyone has them.

Choo-Choo was squirming around because he wasn't used to being confined to just one area, so she suggested that I put him down. "Put him down, honey," she said, "he's okay." I asked, "What about Miss Maggie?"

Now that he was walking, his shoes made noise, and he would run at every chance he got. "Oh, that's okay," she said, understanding because you're my niece. I thought to myself, this backward, no-good woman—when my son was brand new, I couldn't walk on the floor to fix him a bottle. And now that he was walking, it was okay to put him down.

Anyway, while I sat there listening to Aunt Janie go on about various events in my mother's life, I tuned her out. I was worried about the doctor's appointment. Surprisingly enough, Aunt Janie must have felt guilty. She reached into her pocket and gave me $153.00. "This is the check money that came to you this month," she said as I extended my hand to receive it. I felt guilty for having to take it, but then I thought about my son, and that made all the difference. In my 15 years of living in the world, I had never had $153.00. She owed my baby far more money than this, and I knew she was misusing my son's food stamps. She conversed with me as if I were a complete moron incapable of counting. Nevertheless, I accepted the money because I needed it for my son.

She offered me a bottle of pop, but I refused it; I was now feeling a little nauseous. She got up from the table to go to the refrigerator, and as I turned my head and looked at her, I couldn't help but feel sympathy for this ragged, old, hateful black face lady I called my aunt, who harbored such bitterness towards my mother. She had lived her whole life through someone else's dreams; she was old and alone, and I couldn't wish loneliness on my worst enemy. In spite of all she had done to me, I still loved her.

I got up to look for my baby; he was in the living room, playing with the dust balls that had accumulated under Aunt Janie's table. When I stayed with her, there was no dust on the floors. I asked her if I could wipe my baby's hands off while I dusted the dirt from the knees of his pants.

"Sure, baby," she said, "anything you want, you just help yourself." "No, thank you," I replied, "I just want to wipe his hands off."

She handed me a bag of cookies to give to my little one. I didn't want to hurt her feelings, so I accepted them. "I'll be going now, Aunt Janie."

She walked over, hugged, and kissed me. Initially, I stood firm, but quickly my heart softened, and I returned the affection. She walked me downstairs and to the front porch; I didn't have time to talk to her anymore. I had to strap my baby into his stroller and get back up to Margie's house so Dot and I could go to the doctor.

When I got back to Margie's house, the hospital had called and asked if I could come in for a later appointment, so Dot and I decided to walk up to Gratiot and go downtown shopping at Hudson's. Choo-Choo would normally take his nap from 1:00 to 3:00 PM, and when nap time came around, he would automatically fall asleep because I had trained him that way. While walking through Hudson's with my baby in his stroller, I was browsing for a snowsuit for him and wanted to have him fitted for a pair of shoes.

Although he was able to walk, he wasn't as stable and secure as I felt he should be. He cried a little bit, and I gave him his bottle. I bought him a light blue snowsuit with leggings and a cute little teddy bear. During the shopping trip, I noticed that he was asleep, but it wasn't a normal sleep. He appeared to be extremely tired.

I took the teddy bear out of the bag and fluffed it in his face to notice his skin had changed color, and he didn't respond. I tried to wake him up, then went around the other side and called his name. Again, he didn't respond. I grabbed him and pulled him forward, and his head dropped backward. His body was limp.

I started screaming his name and shaking him vigorously, but there was still no response. I then snatched him out of the stroller and began running through the store. I was trying to get to the escalator or the elevator to get outside to the main street. I was screaming, "My baby, my baby, help me—my baby!" His body had gone totally limp. I found an exit, ran down the stairs out onto the streets, and hailed a cab, still screaming, "My baby, help me, my baby!"

People had gathered around me to see what was wrong. I pushed my way through and got into the cab, hysterical by this time. His eyes were not moving, and it looked as though he was barely breathing. I put my hand to his nose to see if I could feel any air, then put my fingers in his mouth to check if he had choked on something. He was still breathing. I started to scream his name, telling him to wake up.

The cab driver then flagged down the police, and they gave me a personal escort to the emergency room at Receiving Hospital. I ran straight to the back of the emergency room, with his lifeless body in my arms. They then ripped his clothes off and started taking his vital signs. I was crying and pacing the floor; to me, they weren't moving fast enough. I went over to him and slapped him; there was still no movement. I slapped him again while screaming his name, but there was still no response.

The nurse and the doctor tried to shove me out of the room, but I told them I wasn't going anywhere. I asked them if he was going to die. They never answered me, and I started to pray, "Oh God, please don't let my baby die." I said, "He's all that I have in the world, and I'm sorry if I did anything wrong; punish me; just don't let my baby die." I took a firm stand and told them I wasn't going anywhere.

They then drew his blood and took it down to the lab. I sat there and watched my baby lay lifeless on the bed. I was crying; I could hardly see his face. I was stroking his head and rubbing his body, all the while talking to him, telling him how much I loved him and how much he meant to me. "Please don't die," I said to him over and over.

The doctor came in shortly after to ask me where I had been that day. I told him that I couldn't remember; he told me to calm down, take a deep breath, and think. I told him to calm down and make my baby feel better. I asked him again, "Is my baby going to die?"

It wasn't until he told me no that I was able to remember where I had been earlier that day. I told him that I had been over to my aunt's house, and he asked me if I had seizures—was I an epileptic? I told him no; that was my aunt Janie. He then told me that my son had taken an overdose of pills, and what was in his blood system were pills that an epileptic person takes.

They said they were going to pump his stomach, and I was asked to step out. I couldn't bear to see it, and I couldn't bear to step out. So, I stepped aside while they pulled the curtain. My body clenched every time I heard my son gagging. I told them not to hurt him, please; he was just a baby. They never responded to anything that I said. I wasn't looking for any sympathy or comfort from them, but only for my baby. After they finished, I was able to sit down with my baby and watch him sleep. The doctor said that he had to sleep it off. They were going to admit him to the hospital for overnight observation. They told me that I could go home and come back tomorrow, but again, I refused. I slept in the chair all night by his bed.

"God Works Miracles" "By the Grace of God my child was alive…"

Chapter 8

"There's Still Honor
in The Hood"

1971

Several months had passed, and I was now living back in the house on
Bewick. Geri saw me strolling my son down the street and asked me to
move back home and take care of the house, now that she had put everyone
out. It was as if nothing had ever happened. I agreed to live at the house
on Bewick, but only if Eldoris could live with me. I found Eldoris, who
had been living off Jefferson Avenue near Belle Isle. At first, she refused
to move in with me because of my sisters. But I assured her that we would
have the house to ourselves, and we could have fun—we would be grown
up and act like adults. Although we hadn't seen each other in a while,
our friendship was lasting. We had a good, solid relationship. I could tell
Eldoris all of my problems, and she could tell me hers. The good thing
about the house is that all Mama's furniture was still there, and we didn't
have to pay any rent or utilities. I thought to myself, this would get me off
the streets with my babies. I wondered if Geri had something going on;
I couldn't speculate about the future. I wasn't trying to get caught up in
a trick bag. I knew how to duck if I saw trouble coming my way. Hell, I

really didn't have any other choice. I was going to take it for what it was worth. Because I was homeless.

Thank You, God…

My brother Ricky came by the house to pick up some clothes that he had left in his room; it was the first time he met Eldoris. I introduced them, and after we spent the day together, she was head over heels in love with him. I knew my brother, and all I felt in my heart was that all he wanted from her was a good time. No more, no less, but I promised myself that whatever developed between them, I would stay out of it because I loved them both. One thing she found so attractive about my brother was that he was light-complected. She said to me, "Honey, I like a light-skinned man." They started to spend time together.

Eldoris was very faithful; whenever she left, she always made sure she returned before dark. She knew that I was afraid to be in the house alone and that my time was near. She knew that I was expecting another baby, and I didn't want to be left alone. I didn't know if I could carry my baby to full term, and I didn't want to take the chance. Rickey stayed in the house with me and Eldoris. He seemed to be so angry with me at times, and at other times, he seemed to love me. I didn't understand what was going on with him until one evening when I walked around to Mae Bertha's house. I asked for him, and they said he wasn't there. Her body language told me a different story. I knew he was there by the way Bertha positioned herself in front of the bathroom door. I asked for him again; Bertha said he wasn't there. She knew that I knew she was lying. So, she came clean. I walked towards the bathroom door and pulled it open to see my brother sitting on the toilet with the seat down, a needle stuck in his arm. Blood was backing up in the needle. I screamed, and he told me to get the fuck out of the bathroom. I told him no, and I approached him, and he became violent. I started crying and ran out of the bathroom.

Later that evening, he came over to the house. He didn't know that I had told Eldoris what I had seen. Eldoris told me that she knew my brother was using drugs. I was totally devastated and afraid for him as well as for myself. I remembered the blotches on his neck and put two and two together, figuring out what he was doing. All night I lay awake, worrying and wondering about my brother. He could get killed, or he could kill himself. My brother was not a junkie, I told myself. I was so angry with him because he didn't have to do this. If anything happened to him, my mother would only blame herself. How many people knew? Did my family know? Could we get him some help? Whenever I tried to talk to him, he would only deny it or get so angry that I felt as though he wanted to fight me. He was so far gone that he had stopped looking like himself; he wouldn't comb his hair or change his clothes. He went from one dope house to another.

Suddenly, all the friends that I had held dear, I found myself saddened and upset with. I found out through the grapevine that not only was my brother using, but also Nanny, Emory, Evelyn, and her twin brother Evan, Robert, his brother Ted, Kenneth, Bird, and Jennie Lawson, Pickles, Frank Arnold, Elaine, Sam, Pee-Wee, Dickey Bird, Lynn (Nina's husband), and Roger just to name a few. Most of the kids that I met and grew up with on Bewick had started to use drugs.

Jackie had also used before he was murdered; he snorted mixed jive. Evelyn had abandoned her son, and I was changing his diapers and giving him baths to help Mrs. Brazil while she was out on the streets.

As time moved on, I caught Evelyn in the Brazil bathroom sharing a needle with Elaine Moore, one of the prettiest girls in Detroit. They shared a needle; Evelyn was shooting up in the neck, Elaine had already shot up in the hand. "Man," I said to myself, "they're all getting high. They all ran in separate cliques; they were all in their own individual hells… Although they were all junkies, there was loyalty in the hood. Not one of them was robbing or stealing. Most of them worked or hustled for their habit.

I asked my brother how he got involved in drugs. He told me he first started to smoke marijuana, then moved from marijuana to snorting scag (girl), then he started to snort (boy). Girl had quinine in it, and that's what caused the blotches on his neck. It was all starting to make sense now—his nodding off when I thought he was asleep, his scratching his neck from the reaction to the drugs. "Got damn it," I said to myself, "what am I going to do?" This was the same little boy that I used to shoot marbles with, the same brother who had played with me, protected me, comforted me. I cried about it then but laughed about it later—I think I was in shock because there's nothing funny about using drugs. I wanted my old brother back, but I didn't know what to do. I could no longer reach him. I was too embarrassed to talk to anyone, and those that I talked to had the same problem I did; their family members were doing the same thing.

Robert was so strung out in the summer of 1967 that his parents allowed him to stay with his cousins on the west side, not knowing that they were the ones who turned him out.

I couldn't get angry with Eldoris, although I did walk around the house for a couple of days not talking to her because I felt she should have told me. When I confronted her, she started to cry. These were real tears of sadness. "How could I tell you," She said, "when he asked me not to? I didn't want to hurt you, and I didn't want to betray him. I didn't want to hurt your family." She also told me in the same breath that my sister Geri had been giving him money he used to get high—to keep him off the streets. Geri pretended not to know. "My God," I said to myself, "this would kill my mother if she knew," so I kept it to myself. But I was glad she gave me money…

I was now about six months pregnant. The shape of my body seemed to whisper secrets only a mother could discern—I was sure it was a boy. My belly had grown large, round, and full, stretching the limits of my favorite dresses. My hips had spread accommodatingly, my nose had broadened, and my skin had taken on a curious shade of bright yellow. Life pulsed visibly within me.

Occasionally, Yogi would visit, his presence now sporadic and uneasy. He remained oblivious to the fact that I still conversed with the same old friends—those who had overheard him adamantly deny paternity. "That baby isn't mine," he had declared to them, a statement that echoed bitterly in my mind. The shame of his lies hung heavily around him; he had been unmasked not only about his age but also about a hidden life—a wife and six children tucked away from view. His friends teased him, and in his desperation, he shifted the blame onto me.

Despite the chaos, I was resolute. I would own up to what happened between us. I would raise my baby and move on, I affirmed silently, a fierce determination steeling my resolve. There was no love lost between Yogi and me, and perhaps that was for the best. Amid the ruins of our relationship, I found a silver lining—the precious gift of life from God growing inside me.

Amidst it all, Eric's unwavering support was a bomb. He still wanted to marry me, despite knowing the child wasn't his. I remembered a small but telling gesture: once, he had bought a single can of Similac milk for a mere fifty-three cents—a modest contribution, but it spoke volumes of his intentions.

I wasn't going to impose myself or my son on him. Eric's kindness was enough to sustain my hopes, but not enough to entangle our lives beyond what was necessary.

He was a veteran with commendable benefits, dutifully sending an allotment check to his mother each month. Yet, when it came to his own son, his provisions fell markedly short. He believed he held the upper hand, thinking his proposal of marriage would coerce me into dependency. His logic was simple: marry him, and he would take care of everything. My response, however, was fierce and unyielding. "No," I told him flatly, because I knew that he wasn't strong enough to raise a family and resist the temptations that were out there.

I vowed, the resolve etching itself deep within my heart.

These men needed to understand a simple, brutal truth of life: the very child you neglect might one day be the only one willing to bring you a glass of water. Mama always had her sayings, and one stuck with me more than others: "If you dig one-hole, dig two, 'cause you might just fall into one of them." It was a warning about the repercussions of how you treat others.

Eric had moved back in with his mother, trapped once more under her watchful, controlling gaze. In fact, all his brothers had ended up back home, some of them barely scraping by, their lives reduced to shambles.

Charlie, ever the fleeting shadow in our lives, would drop by occasionally just to change her underwear—her visits were so brief, you'd miss her if you blinked. She spent her days running to the bar with her girlfriend, Lee. It was Lee who introduced Charlie to Little Junior Canaday, a local blues singer with talent that belied his modest fame. Through Junior, Charlie met his brother, and soon, the four of them were inseparable. When you saw one, the others were never far behind. Despite her outward indifference, rarely speaking of her children, I knew they remained in her heart. She was just drowning her sorrows, one drink at a time.

Despite the impending arrival of my second child, I was still ensnared in bureaucratic limbo, unable to secure public assistance for my baby. The checks, now increased, continued to be sent to Aunt Janie's house under her name. The social worker believed I still resided there, and the only time we communicated was when it was time to answer her routine questions.

My attempts at finding a job had been thwarted repeatedly; every time I managed to get close, the inevitable question of my age arose. "Come back when you turn 18," they would say, a recurring rejection that stung each time.

However, food was one less worry. Eddie Kelly, ever the unexpected benefactor, would sometimes drop by with groceries and even slip me some money for Choo-Choo.

And Eldoris, with her mysterious trips that ended with her pockets full of cash, always reassured me, "Don't worry about it. I'm going to take care of you."

Resources were scant for my new baby; I relied on the clothes I had saved from Choo-Choo's infancy and my old maternity wear. Lacking a washing machine, I washed all our clothes by hand in the bathtub, my hands raw and blood red from wringing them out. Yet, I took pride in their cleanliness, hanging them neatly on the line to dry, folding them with care—some items still looked nearly new.

In my solitude, I taught myself the essentials of survival: cooking and cleaning. My repertoire slowly expanded to include turnip greens, candied sweet potatoes, Jiffy cornbread, and fried pork chops. Occasionally, I baked a cake, delighting Choo-Choo, who eagerly licked the icing off the spoon and the bowl. He was growing, robust and joyous, barely toddling around.

Each day, I taught him—to speak, to eat, to pray, and to embrace the virtues of being a good boy. He was blossoming into a fine young man, a son anyone would be proud to call their own.

As my due date drew near, the days began to stretch interminably. I continuously played Aretha Franklin's "Spanish Harlem" until the 45-record turned white.

On the morning of July 12th, 1971, discomfort turned sharply into agony. My feet were so swollen that walking was a challenge, and the pains that began in my stomach and back around nine in the morning were initially bearable but soon intensified mercilessly. The waves of pain came hard and fast, leaving me gasping for breath, overwhelmed by the fierce throes of labor. Eldoris summoned the young man that lived across the street from us. He speeded down Gratiot Avenue until the police pulled us over, then they escorted us to Detroit Memorial Hospital

Finally, in the delivery room, I gave birth to a baby boy. He was bald, his skin mirroring my mother's complexion, and he looked just like her.

Placed on my stomach, he contentedly sucked his thumb, his fingers spread across his jaw—a habit he must have developed in the womb, as he promptly returned his thumb to his mouth after the nurse pulled it away.

After being cleaned up, he was weighed: six pounds, twelve ounces, and nineteen inches long. Born at 12:53 PM on a Monday, he was adorably wrinkled, like a little bucket of chitlins. My heart swelled with love and pride as I held him. I loved him so much.

The nurses allowed me to keep him beside me. I meticulously counted his fingers and toes, examined his tiny body, then wrapped him up and nestled him under the covers with me. Tears flowed silently as I lay there, overwhelmed by the reality of having borne two sons with seemingly no one to care for but me. It was a moment of self-pity, a longing for someone else's presence.

Yet, I was not alone. God's love enveloped me, unconditional and steadfast. I made no grand promises to myself, only a commitment to be the best mother I could. Inspired by my own mother, who raised seven children on her own, I believed I could raise two. I vowed to teach my children fairness and love, just as I had already begun with Choo-Choo.

In the midst of my reflections, I had almost forgotten about Eldoris and Choo-Choo waiting outside. Suddenly, I heard the nurse announce to Eldoris, "It's a boy!" Her ecstatic cries filled the corridor. "I'm a father, I'm a grandmother!" she shouted, her joy mirroring my own.

Exhausted beyond measure, I finally succumbed to sleep, my body and heart both spent from the profound events of the day.

After returning from the hospital, exhaustion and sickness still clung to me. My breasts had swollen painfully, resembling overinflated balloons. Uncertain and overwhelmed, I had Eldoris call the hospital for advice. The nurse revealed that the doctor had forgotten to prescribe a shot to reduce my milk production. Instead, they offered pills, but the very thought of venturing out was inconceivable; stitches hindered every step, and transportation was a luxury we lacked.

In desperation, I bound my chest tightly, trying to mitigate the discomfort. Lying down became an impossibility; the milk seemed to shift within me, intensifying the pain and pushing against my skin. Tears were my only release from the relentless ache.

As word of my new baby spread, old friends began to stop by, including Yogi. Their faces showed a mix of curiosity and concern as they peered at my son. Heeding Ma 'Dear's old wisdom, I let them look but not touch, especially the women, for fear of the 'strains' they might pass on during their menstrual cycles. Some brought gifts; others came empty-handed. I didn't care; only that they came.

One tumultuous night, my sobs broke the stillness, drawing Eldoris to my side. She checked me for fever, noting my trembling body. She pleaded with me to return to the hospital, but I resisted, fearful they might separate me from my newborn. Instead, she sought help nearby, returning with Mrs. Wynn from around the corner.

Without a word to me, Mrs. Wynn rummaged through our cupboards, fetched a saucepan, and mixed a concoction from a brown bottle. Her remedy was pungent, but I was past caring. She instructed me to lift my gown, then gently applied the warm liquid to my breasts, massaging downward as the milk began to flow, offering me a semblance of relief. She advised me to use camphorated oil similarly in the future, covering my chest with a towel afterward. Finally, sleep overtook me, the first in what felt like an eternity.

Gratitude for Mrs. Wynn swelled within me, but my physical pain restrained any show of affection. Feeding my son was a struggle; he was spirited and demanding, disrupting my nights.

In the midst of recovery, Nina visited. It had been ages since we fell out. We talked about everything except the sore subjects. She updated me on Mama but avoided mentioning Tina. Nina, ever the show-off, boasted about her new car—a sharp, steel-gray Oldsmobile with gray leather interiors. Despite our history, she doted on my baby during her visit, even asking to take him home. I refused, fearing the breakup more than doubting her intentions.

She managed to convince me to let Choo-Choo go with her for a short while, promising a Friday return. However, when Friday passed without his return, panic set in. A call to Nina only offered excuses for long work hours. When Mama put Choo-Choo on the phone, his words were a mix of reassurance and a child's oblivious contentment. "Um hum, I'm a good boy, and I miss you, but I don't want to come home yet." His innocent and sincere words prompted me to agree to another week, despite the ache in my heart.

At three weeks old, my baby Andre was blossoming into a delightfully chubby infant, his skin still wrinkled like a ten-pound bucket of chitlins. After each bath, I would gently apply Vaseline, and sometimes I'd carefully peel the flaking skin. He hardly minded, just gazing up at me with patient, trusting eyes as I tended to him.

Nina finally brought Choo-Choo back home, and in a moment of maternal weakness, I allowed her to take Andre for what was supposed to be just one night. However, I soon learned that she and Charlie had grown overly fond of him, taking turns caring for him. Nina had even bestowed upon him the nickname "Pork-Chop," a sign of her deepening affection. She had affectionately called Choo-Choo "Fat Boy" as well. Her care was evident; she extended his stay to four days, much longer than we had agreed.

Meanwhile, I was swiftly regaining my pre-pregnancy figure, shrinking back to my usual size 9. My stomach flattened, and my hips seemed more pronounced than ever. It was the era of "hot pants," and every girl seemed to flaunt them. Driven by my newfound confidence and Eldoris's indulgence, I acquired a pair for myself. I felt good—my children were thriving and always looked spotless, and I was starting to feel attractive again.

One sunny day, filled with this fresh sense of well-being, Eldoris, the children, and I decided to take a leisurely stroll to Dairy Queen. The day promised simple pleasures—a momentary escape from the complexities of our lives—as we looked forward to the sweet, creamy delights awaiting us.

Returning home from our stroll to Dairy Queen, we found the telephone man from Michigan Bell waiting on the porch. He had come to install a telephone, a gift from Geri, I presumed. Nevertheless, I was grateful; it meant I could now speak with my mother without having to trek to Mrs. Brazil's house. As soon as the phone was installed, I eagerly dialed my mother's number to share our new connection. Our conversations became a daily ritual, sometimes spanning several calls a day. She seemed in good health and well settled.

Occasionally, Eldoris and I would take the bus to visit Mama, but whether we could see her depended on Nina's whims. At times, Mama seemed like a prisoner in her own home, cut off from the friends she cherished because Nina insisted on controlling everything, including all of Mama's possessions and our childhood memories encapsulated in photographs.

During a rare moment of leniency from Nina, she allowed us inside. My father, always the cook, filled the house with inviting aromas. That day, Nina was in high spirits and left us in the house while she went shopping. I seized the moment to shower Tina with affection, playfully wrestling her to the ground and smothering her with kisses. Nina was good to Tina, assuming the role of both mother and father just like I did to my own.

After a brief visit, we kissed my mother and father' goodbye, eager to return home before dark. My days were a whirlwind of activity, centered around the children or my own needs. One significant day, I took the kids with me to Kettering High School to meet with a counselor, Mrs. Griffin. Her warm welcome was a balm to my soul. She listened intently as I recounted my recent challenges and pulled up my records, outlining what I needed to do to graduate.

"I can't attend school full-time," I explained, citing my responsibilities at home with two young children. Understanding my situation, she provided me with textbooks and assignments to complete at home, allowing me to earn credits towards graduation.

Nights were my only respite for study, often cut short by the needs of my baby. The task was daunting, and sleep was scarce, but my resolve to graduate never waned. "What example would I set for my children if I didn't finish school?" I often pondered, determined to ensure they would not face the same struggles.

Eldoris, lost in her youthful pursuits, rarely grasped the gravity of my educational goals. I couldn't rely on her consistently, understanding she was not bound by the same responsibilities. Nevertheless, I grabbed every possible moment to advance my studies, driven by a fierce desire to create a better future for my children. Each page I turned was a step closer to the independence and stability I so desperately sought.

🙛🙚

One weekend, Nina and Charlie dropped by, brimming with excitement about a local gathering. "There's going to be a party down at the bar," Charlie enthused, "and all our old friends might be there. We're going to party our asses off." The idea tantalized me; I could almost taste the freedom and laughter. Yet, as fate would have it, I was once again babysitter-less. I only trusted Eldoris with my children, and she was gone.

Understanding my predicament, Nina offered a solution. "I'll watch the kids for you," she said, generously freeing me to attend the event. We managed to steal away for a brief stint at the celebration. I reunited with familiar faces—Margie, Dot, Lawrence, and a few others. Despite the jovial atmosphere, a nagging unease tugged at me. I didn't belong there; my heart was elsewhere, at home with my children.

Thus, I excused myself early and hopped on a bus to Nina's. Intent on retrieving my little ones, I was halted by her advice. "It's too late," Nina cautioned. "Just stay here tonight with them. Sleep on the floor, and we'll all leave together at 5:30 in the morning." Her words left no room for negotiation, nor did I wish to impose further by sleeping elsewhere in her house. Reluctantly, I agreed, comforted by the thought that responsibility beckons unwavering commitment.

The dawn of the next day marked a return to our routine. I bathed my babies, their skin warm and clean, dressing them up as if they were little dolls. With not much else to do in our quiet corner of the world, I decided on a walk to the Dairy Queen, a treat in mind for my young ones. My baby, still so small, reacted comically to a dab of ice cream on his tongue, his face scrunching delightfully. That day, Eldoris joined us, and together, we enjoyed our banana split on the outdoor seats, basking in simple, familial joy.

Chapter 9

"Thank God for Willie"

Eldoris was always so intrigued by light-skinned men; their complexion really didn't seem to matter. All the way home we argued. "If it wasn't for you, we could have had a ride home," she said. All I kept telling her was that I didn't know this man who offered us a ride and that I really didn't feel he was trustworthy, even though he lived right down the street from me.

"That's what's wrong with you," she said. "Since Eric has done to you what he's done, you don't feel like you can trust any man."

And I told her that Eric had nothing to do with it, that I wasn't overly excited about riding with this man. That she didn't know Eric and she didn't have anything to say about him. That our friendship was one thing, but my relationship with Eric was none of her damn business.

We had the biggest falling out. She didn't speak to me, and I didn't speak to her. While walking home, we had to pass by this same man's house, and he was just sitting on his porch with his brother. He whistled as we walked by, and I think she knew and was pissed off because he was whistling at me and not her. Frankly, I didn't care. I kept stepping.

That day Aunt Janie called and told me to come over to the house; that my check was there, and she had my food stamps. I caught the bus to

Aunt Janie's house with my kids. Thank God I had the stroller. When I got there, Aunt Janie wasn't home. I specifically told her what time I would be there. I stood outside so long that it was starting to rain, and it was getting cool out. I had spent my last dollar catching the bus to her house, and this woman didn't have the decency to be home when I got there. My babies were hungry, and I knew from past experience to pack my children a lunch. My baby had plenty of bottles, but I couldn't get back home, so I walked over to Margie's house, who always greeted me with open arms.

I told her what had happened, and she understood. It was too late for us to catch the bus home, so we stayed at her house. I called and called until finally that evening, she answered the phone. "Oh baby," she said, "Auntie forgot. I forgot you were coming."

I asked her if I could come over and get my money, my stamps, and a few baby clothes that I had left there that belonged to Choo-Choo. "Yes," she said, "I'll see you tomorrow."

I walked over to her house the next day, where she hugged and kissed my baby Andre, whom she'd seen for the first time. She told me that he looked just like her papa, and I countered that I felt he resembled my mother. However, she never changed the subject; she continued raving about how he looked like her Papa.

"Whatever," I said to myself. I had to go; I was ready to return home. I didn't have any clean clothes and needed to check on the house. She gave me $70 of my check money and $100 in food stamps. "That's all you need to feed your kids because I'm keeping the rest," she said.

I just looked at her and shook my head. "You know," she said, "if that worker finds out you're not staying here, they will cut your check off, and if they find out that you are not taking care of your kids properly, they will take them from you." I fought back, insisting that I take good care of my kids. And I could take better care of them if you would give me what's mine…

She always beat me with the same stick. "Old bitch," I said to myself.

"I'll be glad when you die." But later on, I asked God to forgive me. I didn't mean it. I just felt like a dog; I had these two children and no help, and the help that the state was giving me, Aunt Janie took. It wasn't that she needed my money—she was drawing disability from her husband who stayed married to her for only one week. After he discovered what kind of person she was, he walked off and left her and never looked back.

Uncle Pete was a small, stocky man who smoked cigars. He used to come to town on the weekends to gamble and visit. Uncle Pete was a professional gambler—and he was good. Mama said that Uncle Pete, Matthew her first husband, and her brother Robert were all good friends. They ran together; they did everything together. Uncle Pete would say that he must have been drunk when he married Aunt Janie. He claimed that he never loved her; in fact, he never even liked her.

He'd visit my mom, whom he lovingly called 'sis', every time he came to Detroit. He would stop at the corner store and buy groceries for my mother to cook—grits, bacon, broom sausage made right here in Detroit, eggs, milk, and plenty of butter. He always had Mama make him homemade biscuits. He was a short, wide, dark-complexioned man who smoked fat, stinky cigars. His voice was raspy from all the liquor he drank. He sported a Fyodor hat and wore Florsheim shoes. He was always dressed in a three-piece suit with a pimp chain that carried the only thing his father left him before he died—a pocket watch that played music.

He insisted on my mother cooking breakfast for all of us, as we'd gather around the table to listen to stories from their past. Things that happened to them way back when foretold their future. He often spoke of the loving relationship that he had with my mother's brother, Robert, before he was murdered by his best friend Robert Johnson. Uncle Pete told the story of my Uncle Robert, who as a tailor by trade, laughed about the night he lost all his money in a poker game. And the next day, my Uncle Robert took the green felt off a pool table, made a three-piece suit, and pawned it the next day.

As a matter of fact, the first time I ever decided to smoke was the day I took his cigar that he left in the ashtray and smoked it—and that was the beginning of my end because Mama whipped my butt, not too bad, because I was high off the smoke and she felt sorry for me.

He spoke about my cousin Billy, who was living in the house with Aunt Janie; she told everybody that Billy was her natural son. For years, I believed it until my mother revealed that Billy was actually my mother's brother's son, whom Aunt Janie found crawling across his dead mother's body after she had died from a stroke. They placed him in a home, and Aunt Janie went and took him out, attempting to raise him on her own. No wonder, I said to myself, why Billy hates her like he does. Sometimes, when I was there, she would talk to him and try to appease him, and he would just ignore her, walk into his room, and slam the door. I understood why; this was Aunt Janie's big secret. She wanted everyone to believe that Billy was her natural son—a shameful secret that would embarrass her if it ever got out. All her neighbors and choir members thought he belonged to her. I wanted to just broadcast her business to everyone who knew her; I just wanted to do something to hurt her like she had hurt me.

After cashing the check at the store, she handed me $70 and $100 in food stamps, instructing me that I had to spend the food stamps in the store because she traded with them. How in the world could I spend the food stamps in the store and catch the bus home with my two children? I needed the $70 so badly because my son was outgrowing his shoes, and he had been complaining that his feet hurt. All the shoes that I had bought him were cheap, and he needed shoes with an arch in them. So, I spent the food stamps in the store, and now I had two babies, a stroller, and six bags to carry on the bus.

When the bus arrived, I had to put my babies on the bus along with the stroller, step back down off the bus, and put the bags on one by one. I felt so ashamed, and everybody was looking at me. I thank God for the bus driver and this man, who was just a passenger on the bus, because they came to help me with my bags. The bus driver asked, "Are those your babies?" I told him yes. He said, "They sure are pretty. You're a young girl, and you look like you take good care of your kids." I thanked him for the compliment and for being so kind to help me with my bags. "No problem," he said, "you just take care of those kids. I don't mind helping a person when I see that they are trying to help themselves."

Soon thereafter, it was time for me to get off the bus. The driver pulled up and helped me get my children off the bus, then went back for my bags and set them out on the sidewalk. How in the world was I going to get my bags home with my babies? Then, a little boy came up the street, and I asked him if he would stand there and watch my bags while I took my babies home to get help. I knew that Eldoris was there because she had been out all night; more than likely, she was at home asleep. I offered him a dollar and promised him two if my bags were there when I returned.

I took my babies into the house and asked Eldoris to come down to the corner to help me bring the bags home. She left with me; we went back down to the corner, only to find two of my bags gone and the boy nowhere in sight. All I could do was cry.

Eldoris had both babies, and I was struggling to carry all four bags, constantly looking over my shoulder for that little son of a bitch who had stolen my children's food. My heart was just broken. Not only had I spent close to $100 in a neighborhood store where your money doesn't stretch far, but now I had also lost my children's food. I took two bags across the street at one time. As I was bending down to rearrange the contents of one bag that had split open, I looked up to hear a horn blowing. Guess who? It was the guy in the white Cadillac who had offered me a ride at the Dairy Queen that I had refused.

"Let me help you," he said, offering a ride home. I told him, "No, that's okay, I would make it." But he insisted. Eldoris insisted. Choo-Choo was holding his weenie—he had to go to the bathroom. So, now I had to accept a ride home from this guy that I didn't want to. There was something about him that I didn't like.

He got out of the car, grabbed my bags, and put them in my trunk. I then reached for my baby to get him out of Eldoris's arms and grabbed Choo-Choo's hand to get in the back seat. When he pushed the seat back, he told me to get in the front. Eldoris had all but stepped over me to get in the front, but it was evident that he wanted her to ride in the back. She played it off, but she knew that I saw it.

He took us home, popped the trunk, and helped me with my groceries. I thanked him and told him I appreciated it. I offered him $5.00 because I didn't want to be obligated to him. I figured

$5.00 was enough to pay anybody for a ride from one corner to the other. He refused. "That's okay; you don't owe me anything," he said. "Anytime you need my help, I just live right down the street. Twelve houses from you. You come on down, and I'll be glad to help."

"Thank you," I said, and as I was getting out of his car, I could feel his eyes on my body.

Eldoris put the groceries away while I fed my baby a warm bottle and Choo-Choo a nice sandwich, a bowl of soup, and a glass of milk, and put them both down for a nap. I just wanted a few minutes to get my brain together. After resting for a while, I washed my kids' clothes and hung them out to dry.

I didn't have too much to say to Eldoris. The house was rather quiet; she knew that I was pissed off with her because she had gotten slack with her housework. The sink was full of dishes; the floor needed to be swept; things needed to be put in place. I didn't say anything to her; I just washed the dishes and swept the floor. I did mention to her my other bags of groceries that were missing. She threatened to catch the little boy and beat his ass. I told her no; maybe he needed it more than me, and that was his reason for stealing it. "God knows why."

Later that evening, Willie called. He said he had gotten my number from Nina and wanted to know how I was doing; he knew I had another baby. "If it's okay, I'd like to come by and see Choo-Choo and my new baby."

"Sure," I said, "it's okay." I told him he better get there before they go to sleep because I put them down at about 8:00 p.m. When he arrived, me and Choo-Choo were up on the floor dancing, something we did almost every night before bed. Willie came over and loved my new baby. I told him what a terrible day I had had and all the bad things that were happening to me with Aunt Janie and all. I told him I couldn't visit with him for very long because I had to feed my baby and give them both a bath. I always had to read Choo-Choo a book and help him say his prayers.

"That's okay," he said. "I will wait and help you."

"Okay," I said. I ran Choo-Choo's bath water and bathed André in the face bowl. I put Vaseline all over his body, dressed him in warm pajamas, and gave him a warm bottle. After burping him, I put him down for the night. I gave Choo-Choo his bath, and Willie asked me if he could help.

"Sure," I said. He told me he didn't have any children of his own and that his wife couldn't have any. He wanted to be a family man. So, I watched him while he bathed Choo-Choo. Afterwards, I dried him off, lotioned his body, and made him use the potty, only to find he had already done that in the water. I kneeled down with my son, and we said our prayers. He could put his hands together by himself and had memorized his prayers pretty well. His favorite part was 'Amen.' Choo-Choo and Andre slept in the same bed with me. I sat on the side of the bed and read him a story. Soon he was fast asleep. I kissed him on the head, told him I loved him, and pulled the covers up tight. Andre had already fallen asleep, so I took him downstairs with me to the living room, where I could keep an eye on him.

Willie went back upstairs to use the bathroom. He came back down and went to the store. He bought a six-pack of beer. I didn't drink then, but I was damn sure going to have a beer now. We just talked about what had happened that day. He gave me some advice on turning Aunt Janie in.

I walked him to the door, and he kissed me on the head and told me he loved me. "You're a fine lady," he said, "and you have two beautiful boys. Take care of them."

I asked Eldoris to keep an eye on Andre while I took a bath and got ready for bed. When I pulled the covers back to get into the bed, there were two $100 bills under Choo-Choo's pillow. I sat straight up in bed and screamed Eldoris's name.

"Whose money is this?" I asked.

"Sush," she said, "lower your voice. You'll wake up the kids." "Is this your money?" I asked her. "No," she replied. "Where did it come from?" "I don't know," she answered.

Then it hit me. When Willie went to the bathroom, he must have laid it under Choo-Choo's pillow. My eyes filled with water. I now had $270.00, and I lay there thinking of what I could buy my children with this money. I wanted to call and thank Willie, but I couldn't because he had a wife, and she would answer the phone.

Willie had always been a kind, tender man, mismatched with his wife. I was so grateful to him.

God worked a miracle through Willie. The next day, I got up, bathed my kids, dressed them warmly, and took them downtown to Hudson's for shopping. In the shoe store, I told the salesman that I wanted Choo-Choo fitted for a good pair of shoes.

"He can have Buster Browns," the salesman told me, "But nothing can be done about his flat feet." Underneath my breath I said how do you know you're not a podiatrist you just sell shoes.

I remembered telling Eric that he needed a better pair of shoes. If he bought them you did. Choo-Choo first started walking. I felt like crying, seeing my son's feet level with the floor. He doesn't have an arch. "That son-of-a-bitch," I muttered to myself. "He could help me with this boy, but he won't." And I'll never ask him for help either. This is my son and I shouldn't have to ask. Then a thought struck me—damn, I still had the wedding rings. I'd keep them for hard times.

I didn't take any chances on the weather, so I bought my baby a snowsuit and, for Choo-Choo, a coat with a hat, mittens, and a scarf. I bought André some clothes, T-shirts, and socks. If you shop in the basement of Hudson's, you could save money. They always had nice clothes at a reasonable price. I didn't buy anything for myself; I wasn't worried about myself; only my kids were important. I kept $100.00 to live on.

I was feeling good about being their mother and providing for them, when I returned home, Yogi was there. He wanted to see the baby. I let him; not too many words were passed between us. I unwrapped my baby, and he looked at me, smiled, and said, "That's my baby, alright. I'll be back to see you," he said, and he handed me three hundred dollars. I tried to give it back, and he said, "I want you to use it for the kids." He leaned down and kissed me on the forehead, and he whispered to me, "He's beautiful, just like you." He looked back at me, and he said, "I never doubted your word, despite what you heard people say. I hope that it will be my last time looking into his black face."

I knew I was doing the best I could to take care of my children. Eldoris, however, had gotten to the point where each time she left the house, she stayed out longer and longer. Sometimes, I'd come home, and the food I bought for my babies would just disappear. When I confronted her about it, she admitted that Ricky had been coming by to change clothes and eat when I wasn't there. Well, that's cool if he's hungry.

"I was shocked that you didn't tell me," I said, feeling betrayed.

"I didn't feel it was my place," she replied, her answer catching me off guard. Immediately, I sensed she had a hidden agenda for not telling me. Eldoris knew I wanted to see my brother. I disagreed with her, but I took what she said in stride. Perhaps I was just utterly disappointed in my brother, angry at him—as he probably was with me. He had so much potential; he was bright and intelligent. To me, he had taken two steps back—one with drugs and two with Eldoris.

Eldoris was the type of person to live and let live; she lived only for today. If she had been a different person, maybe she could have encouraged him to leave the drugs alone. But she only wanted Ricky in any way she could have him. Hell, most of the time that she spent away from home, I wondered if she was using drugs. I had no evidence, but I knew she was doing something. Mama always said, "If you look for something, you'll find it." Eldoris was really confused about who she was and where she belonged; like me, she didn't seem to fit anywhere.

Whenever she'd drink, which was quite often, she would only cry about her mother. She said that her mother told her that she never loved her and that she wanted her to leave her house. I never understood Eldoris's mother and I, tried as much as I could to avoid her, but I did meet her on one occasion—a day I'll never forget.

Eldoris and I went over to her mother's house. Eldoris just wanted to pop in, say hello, see how her mother was doing, and see if there was anything she needed help with. She stopped us both at the door. Eldoris went inside, leaving me on the porch. Honestly, I didn't mind. I was used to that kind of treatment from Aunt Janie's antics, but then Ms. Smith, Eldoris's mother, came to the screen door. She stuck her head out and spoke to me in a manner that made me very uncomfortable.

"Oh, you can come in," she apologized. "Ah, Eldoris knows that I don't like strangers at my house."

I just told her, "No thank you, I'm fine on the porch," because I didn't want to be somewhere I wasn't welcomed. She just let the screen door slam as she went back inside. She had a really dismissive, nonchalant attitude. Eldoris had once told me her mother never liked light-skinned people. So, I felt like the reason she treated me the way she did was because of my color. The same dog that bit her ran the hell out of me. I decided that was the last time I ever wanted to see that lady.

Before it was over, Eldoris and her mom got into a fight over her love. Eldoris only wanted her mother's love, which to me seemed so simple and unselfish. But you have to feel and know love in order to give it. You could hear her mother screaming and calling Eldoris a bunch of black

bitches, telling her how much she hated her, wishing she was dead, and not to come back over to her house ever again.

I knew that if Eldoris didn't hurry up and come out, her mother was going to jump on her—she was as big as a two-family flat and could overpower Eldoris easily. I walked off the porch and started back towards the bus stop, walking slowly, looking back for Eldoris to catch up. I wanted to spare her feelings; I guess I didn't want Eldoris to know that I heard what her mother said to her. I was embarrassed and hurt for her.

"What a hateful lady," I said to myself. "One day she's going to regret the way she treated her."

Fall of 1971

Not much had changed from one month to the next. I was still reading my books, trying to prepare myself to get back to school. Damn, this was such a struggle for me. I was so behind but determined to catch up. Meanwhile, Eldoris seemed to be hitting the bottle more than she should. Whenever I'd talk to her about it, trying to explain the danger she was heading for, we'd always end up arguing.

It had been some time since I had seen my brother Ricky. I often wondered where he was, how he was, and if he was okay. Occasionally, I'd run into Robert, who was singing the same old sad songs. He wasn't on drugs; someone had misled me, but he was lying to himself. I noticed Geri was starting to come over to the house as much as three times a week. She wouldn't stay very long; thank God for that—just long enough to patrol the house. I felt like she was up to something, but what? I didn't know. Whenever she came, Eldoris would always move out of her way; I didn't know if it was out of fear or plain old dislike.

This particular day, I was outside raking leaves on a beautiful day. Glancing down the street, I saw Eric walking up. "Goddammit," I muttered to myself, "what the hell does he want?" I couldn't run inside and close the door because he had seen me. The closer he got, the faster he started to walk.

When he finally reached me, I never stopped what I was doing; I just continued to rake the leaves. I had raked a big pile, and every time I would get it neatly piled, Choo-Choo would dive in and roll around, splashing leaves everywhere. I'd holler at him to stop, but he would only laugh. While I listened to WJLB play Freda Payne's badass jam "Bring the Boys Home," Eric walked up and picked Choo-Choo out of the pile of leaves, started kissing him all over, hugging him, and explaining that he was his father. "How much I've missed you, and what a big boy you're growing up to be," he said to Choo-Choo.

I kept my eyes on my task, raking the leaves and seething internally. "This motherfucker is full of shit," I thought. "Put my baby down," I finally said aloud, "and you are not his father. You made him, but you are not his father."

He wouldn't put him down, so I threw the rake on the ground and walked over, snatching Choo- Choo out of his arms. Eric didn't say anything. He just looked at me with those same sad, selfish eyes, as if wondering, "What did I do wrong?"

"Can I talk to you?" he said. "I really need to talk to you."

I hesitated for a minute. Although I was mad as hell at him, I was glad to see him, and I still loved him. We went inside to talk while I fixed the kids' lunch. He played with the baby, occasionally sneaking into the kitchen to kiss me behind my ear. I'd push him away.

"Don't start any shit, and there won't be nothing," I'd say to him. "Whatcha mean? I ain't starting no shit; I missed you," he'd reply.

Ignoring him, I took Choo-Choo upstairs and washed his face and hands to get him ready for lunch. Today, he would have grilled cheese sandwiches, a nice warm bowl of soup, and a glass of milk. I offered Eric something to eat. "Mama said if you feed someone, God will feed you."

After I put Choo-Choo down for his nap, his brother was just waking up. I washed his face and hands while heating his baby food on the stove. Andre was so greedy; if he smelled food, he would wake up. So, I fed him. He ate both jars of baby food. I gave him a warm bottle, thinking he was going to go back to sleep, but no, he wanted to play.

Eric was very patient, and I kept telling him he could leave when he wanted to. I guess he really didn't have any choice; he kept watching me and complimenting me on what a good mother I was.

"Don't you wish you could say that for yourself?" I said it to him sharply.

"Pat," he said, "you know that I love you, and I'll do anything to help you. You look like you're doing pretty well for yourself."

I told him that I was and that I didn't need him for anything. "Look, if you came over here to upset me, you came to the wrong person. And I heard you have a girlfriend anyway. You can't upset me anymore."

"No, I didn't come over here to upset you," he said. "I was just thinking about you, and I talked to your mother. She told me where you were."

"Why won't you marry me?" he asked suddenly.

"Why should I? You are irresponsible, and you drink a lot, so I've been told. I don't need you around to encourage my kids. Marriage is sacred and forever," I told him. "What are you going to teach them when they get older? Besides, your mother will not allow it."

His eyes filled with water, looking down at the ground. Before I knew it, the argument had started. "I was raising a hundred dollars' worth of hell. I raised so much hell with him that day that I felt shamed. But he deserved it because, again, I don't have to marry you for you to help me with your son. These are my kids. I don't ask you for anything, and you don't offer anything, so let's leave it like that. I didn't try to trick you, and I damn sure didn't ask you to marry me—and that's more than I can say for a lot of girls that I know. Since your son has been in the world, you've only bought him one can of Similac milk that cost 57 cents. You should be ashamed of yourself, and don't you ever in your life tell my son that you're his father because you're not. I'm their father and mother. And if you're done talking to me, you can get the hell out of my house."

Well, he left, alright. I peeked out the window to see which way he went, only to find this son of a bitch sitting on the porch. And I didn't make it any better; I laid down on the couch and took a nap with my baby, only to wake up and find my brother Ricky and Eric standing over me, laughing and talking. Eric was telling my brother how much he loved me and how much he wanted to marry me.

"Girl, don't do him like this," my brother Ricky said. "You know the man loves you; why don't you just marry him and get it over with?"

I told Ricky, "Since you love him so much, why don't you marry him and get it over with?"

I got up off the couch, took my baby upstairs, and laid him in bed because he was still sleeping. I went back downstairs, and eventually, I acted cordially towards him. I listened to what he had to say, which to me was a bunch of nonsense. He had been looking for a job, and there were no jobs out there. If he couldn't find one, he might end up enlisting again in the Navy. So, after a while, we were all laughing and talking—me, Ricky, Eldoris, and Eric. He stayed for a long time.

We reminisced about our old friends and talked about Peewee and his brother Tony. Ricky and I talked about Melvin and what a tragedy it was. We just enjoyed each other's company; it was a real peaceful evening.

We never finished raking the leaves.

Months had passed, and I was receiving letters from Eric at least twice a week. He was stationed on the U.S.S. Roosevelt. Sometimes, he sent pictures of himself and often wrote about how happy he would be if I became his wife. He always asked about Choo-Choo and the baby, always wanting me to send him pictures. He had re-enlisted in the Navy for three more years. "Things are going to be different this time," he wrote in all his letters. "I'm going to do right and not pressure you into marriage." Yet, despite all these promises, he never enclosed any money for his son. *Was this son of a bitch stupid?* I had real feelings for Eric, but something within me couldn't fully commit because of how he treated my son.

After the last night I saw him, I explained my circumstances, so he knew I was only in this house on borrowed time. I could understand if I was in a different situation and asking for all of his money, but goddammit, he could have given me $5.00 a week—that's only $20.00 a month— what a small price to pay for your son.

At one point, things got so hard for me that Roger came by when I was down to my last can of milk for my baby. He drove me to the pawn shop, where I asked him to pawn the wedding rings Eric had given me. I was underage, and I had never done this in my life. When the man asked how much time I needed before coming back for the rings, I told him he could keep them; I would sell them to him. He gave me $50.00, and I was too glad to get it. It felt like I had just dropped a load.

Eric, with all his lies, bullshit, and promises that things would get better, just give him one more chance to prove himself as a man. Shit, he didn't have to prove anything to me because I knew what he was all about.

The pawn shop we went to was called Sam's, located on Gratiot and Mt. Elliot, right around the corner from Margie's. Roger D. seemed to be having a streak of bad luck. He didn't know that I knew he was shooting drugs. As bad as it seemed for him, I still trusted him; he would always be a friend to me. I offered him $10.00 for gas, but he refused, telling me, "No, that's okay, you need it for the babies."

I insisted, but he kept refusing, pushing my hand away. "You don't have to take me back home," I told him. "You can drop me off at Margie's, and I'll stay the night with her, catch up on gossip, see who's doing what to whom, and kill some time." He gave me his phone number and told me to call him when I was ready to go home. As I got out of the car, I left the $10.00 on the seat.

I went over to Margie's house, where we laughed and talked. We played Bid Whist. Lawrence came over, and Big Dot and Little Dot were there too. Pretty soon, the house was filled with people. We played records and partied half the night. We played our favorite song by William Bell repeatedly—the one that me and Lawrence loved.

The next day, we sat around, rolling each other's hair and painting our nails, doing nothing. But we had so much fun together; we had that type of chemistry about us. Ma 'Dear knew we were up to something, but what she didn't know was that we had planned to sneak out to the bar that night. Charlene was having a birthday party at the Majestic.

I'd given Choo-Choo his bath, fixed his dinner, and said his prayers with him. I'd bathed Andre, fed him his dinner, given him a warm bottle, and burped him. Whenever we were over to Ma 'Dear's, my kids always had to sleep with her. That's the way she wanted it.

We snuck out the back door and hauled ass up Gratiot; there were five of us, cleaner than the Board of Health and looking good.

Chapter 10

"A Whole New Type of Animal"

Soon after we arrived, we managed to snag a seat. The place was packed; it was standing room only, and that little hole in the wall would jump all week long. After settling in for a few minutes, someone asked me to dance. I was very picky; the man had to have a clean look about him, especially his hands. And don't try to hold me really tight.

There was this one guy, Joe Dorsey, who came into the bar from time to time. I would always look forward to seeing him. I'd point him out to Dot and Margie, whispering, "Girl, he is so fine."

"Yeah," Margie would reply, "but you know he's a married man." "Yeah, that's what I heard." I don't want him; he's just fine.

The funny thing about him was that every time I saw him, it was from a distance. He would just stand on the side, leaning against the wall, sipping his drink out of a straw. We always managed to make eye contact throughout the night, especially when I was out on the floor dancing. Sometimes, I would dance through three or four records. When Tyrone Davis "Turn Back the Hands of Time" came on the jukebox, we all screamed because that was the jam.

Charlie was working at the bar that night, but it was hard to see her through all the people. Finally, she made it over to my table. Although her face appeared somewhat bloated, she was still looking good. She was always a sassy dresser. We couldn't really talk because of the music.

We were having a real good time, but I was starting to miss my children and was ready to leave. Dot was waiting for some man to pick her up, so we waited. During the wait, I had Lawrence Walk me to the phone booth, where I called Ma 'Dear to check on my children. She assured me everything was alright and told me to go enjoy myself. "I'll see you when you get here," she said. I felt relieved after talking to her. We walked back over to the bar, and that's when Lawrence grabbed my hand, holding it tight and refusing to let it go.

"Pat," he said, pulling me towards him. I resisted his advances. "Lawrence, don't," I insisted.

"Look, I know that I've been drinking," he admitted, "but I can't hold it in any longer. I love you. I don't care how many kids you have. And fuck Yogi. Shit, a lot of people right now think that Choo-Choo is mine and the new baby because we spend so much time together and people saw me pushing him in the stroller. Let me take care of you."

"Lawrence, don't do this, please," I pleaded.

Then he started to force himself on me, and we struggled. "Lawrence, don't do this." I pushed him away, but he kept trying to kiss me.

"I don't just want to go to bed with you," he said. "I love you. I always have and always will," he declared, holding me tight.

"Lawrence, let me go," I said. "You're drunk."

"I may be drunk," he replied, "but I know how I feel about you." "Let me go," I demanded, struggling to free myself.

"No, not until you kiss me," he insisted.

Lawrence finally let my arms go, realizing he was holding them too tight. "You are hurting me," I said.

"So? You are hurting me," he retorted.

"God damn it, Lawrence, turn me loose. I yelled, then started to push back. Eventually, he let me go. And when I broke free from his embrace, I felt a cold wind pass by the side of my face. I was somewhat offended, but not enough to end my undying love for him.

Nobody really noticed I was missing; they were too drunk and caught up in their own fun. I didn't tell the others what had happened with

Lawrence outside. All I kept thinking to myself was why he would want to ruin our relationship. We were like brothers and sisters; at least that's what I thought. This hurt me because I loved him so much, and I didn't want to be at odds with him.

All night, I wondered, Why now? The more I thought about it, the more I couldn't understand. Old feelings started to surface again. I had flashbacks and then pushed my drink away from me. Hell, I wasn't going to drink it anyway. I learned a long time ago that when you leave a drink on the table and come back, you should order another one.

Dot and Margie were drunk. Margie hugged up in the corner with some strange guy, while Dot was checking her watch.

"Let's go," I said. "Are you all ready to go yet? The bar is getting ready to close. Let's get the hell out of here."

"Yeah," they replied, "we are going to the bathroom, and we'll meet you by the door."

"Okay," I said. "I'm going over here to talk to Charlie before we go," I said, pushing my way through the crowd.

When I finally got to her, Charlie looked into my face. "What's wrong with you?" she asked.

"Nothing," I said to her. That asshole," I added, pointing my finger towards Lawrence. "Tried to go with me," I said with tears streaming down my face.

"Oh girl," she replied, oblivious to my distress, "shit, I thought he was trying to hurt you or something."

"Shit, you know that guy's always thinking that we want to give them some.," she added nonchalantly. She laughed.

I looked at her with disappointment and walked away, muttering under my breath, "I'll never be the way you are, stupid bitch."

"What did you say?" she called after me.

I looked up at her and repeated, "Nothing."

"Girl, what's a little bit of pussy to share among friends?" she laughed, trivializing the situation. "Shit, I do it all the time," she laughed. I knew she had that kind of sense of humor.

Still, I left there disappointed. It wasn't funny at the time.

"See you later, Charlie," I said, and I walked away, meeting Margie and Dot outside the bar. "Come on, we got a ride," so we jumped in the back seat.

"Where are we going?" I inquired.

"Shit, you ain't driving, so shut the fuck up and ride," Dot retorted. They all started to laugh. "Fuck you," I said to Dot. "You don't tell me what to say."

"Shit, I just asked you a question. What the fuck is wrong with you? Don't try to act funny with me, cause, I don't give a big rat's ass about no motherfucking car. I've been walking all my life, bitch. Who the fuck are you trying to impress?"

"All right, girl, I was just playing with you," Dot said, trying to lighten the mood. "Well, don't play with me like that," I said firmly.

"We're going over to Dot and Etta's shrimp shack up on Gratiot," she explained.

"Well, tell me, cause I ain't in no hurry to ride anywhere with no strange motherfucker," I retorted.

"Girl, I said I was just playing with you," she reassured, sidling up under the arm of a brand-new acquaintance she had just met.

"And after we leave Dot and Etta's," she continued, "we're going to the after-hour joint." "I'm not going to anybody's after-hour joint," I declared firmly.

"I'm going home, or to your house, rather, to be with my kids. I've been gone long enough," I said. Dot scoffed, "I forgot you're such a goodie two shoes." Then she and Margie started laughing.

"It ain't about being no goodie two shoes," I retorted, "it's about taking care of my children. I don't know what your intentions are, but I do what I have to do, bitch. Look, I don't know what's wrong with you all, but you can let me out. I can walk back to your house, pick up my kids, and go home."

"You can't go home tonight," Dot declared. "Yes, I can," I insisted.

"Girl, we're going to the after-hour joint, and that's the end of that." "Yeah, well, we'll see, 'cause I'm not going to anybody's joint tonight."

Big Dot chimed in, "When we get to the shrimp shack, we'll get out and walk home, Pat. Don't worry, 'cause I ain't going to no joint either. I got a baby to look after myself," she said in her southern voice. "I got to get this ass home and lay it down, mm-hmm. I want to check on my baby too, so I'll Walk with you."

Just as we pulled up into the shrimp shack to get out and order, we all went inside—everyone but Dot and this strange man. They were hugged so tight that you couldn't tell them apart. Our backs were turned, and all we heard was a holler, "Oh God, help me!" Dot screamed.

We all ran outside when Dot's boyfriend, Charles, was beating her up. He must have followed us in his car when we left the bar. When we ran outside, her head was underneath his arm, like Jim Brown holding his football, coming out of the backfield. He ran her head into the brick wall and knocked her out cold. And the strange motherfucker she was all hugged up with totally disappeared. He hauled his ass down Gratiot, running off and leaving his car.

We ran inside the shack to get some help, but Dot didn't want us to call the police. She said that she was okay, that it was her fault, that she would be alright, and that she was used to Charles beating her up. After Charles got through kicking Dot's ass, she got down off her high horses. We wiped the blood from her head and knees, and she wasn't talking big sh*t anymore.

As we all had to walk home, I felt sorry for Dot. She was the kind of person who would throw away her old doll when she got a new one. She is the kind of person who would burn the bridge behind her, forgetting that she may one day need to cross that bridge again. She didn't have as much as I did, materially; her ass was just as raggedy as mine. But she was more than willing to sell her soul to the devil for the things she wanted, willing to do almost anything, stepping on and over anyone that got in her way to live the fast life of luxury and leisure, to be a kept woman at any given price. She was a hustler, and she was pretty.

Again, I felt very sorry for Dot, needing to keep all sympathy for myself, but I couldn't help but share. She was on a path of destruction, a road that she paved for herself.

We stayed up half the night laughing and talking about the party at the bar. Margie was talking about some guy she met there when suddenly there was a knock at the back door.

"Get the door, Pat," everyone said.

"And bring me some Kool-Aid on your way back up," Margie added.

"Fuck you, bitch," I retorted playfully. That's how we talked to each other when we were just joking around.

"Get off your big ass and get it yourself," I said. But I was going to get it for her anyway. As I poured the Kool-Aid, I asked, "Who is it?"

"Lawrence," he replied.

So, I opened the door. "Pat, I'm sorry, okay? Please forgive me. I don't know what happened," he stammered.

"Yeah, well, I do," I said, pointing my finger at him. "Don't ever put your hands on me like that again, grabbing my breast like you did."

"Okay," he said quietly. "I just came to apologize to you. I'm sorry." "I'll accept your apology," I said.

He asked, "Can we still be friends?" "Yeah, we can still be friends," I affirmed.

He asked me for a hug, and I did. I couldn't stay mad at him for long. Another cold wind passed across the side of my face.

"Alright, I'm going home now 'cause I got a hangover," he announced. "Okay, see you later," I replied.

As soon as I lay down, it was time to get up and look after my children. Ma 'dear was at work, and everybody was still sleeping, so I fed all the kids and got them all dressed.

Pretty soon, Eldoris came by to check up on me, to let me know that she would be gone for a few days, and not to worry about her if she didn't come home.

"That she was with some friends and she would see me later," she reassured me, but expressed concern. "I was worried about you; I thought something had happened."

I told her how Lawrence had tried to attack me and how Dot tried to confront me when we got in the car.

She told me, "Dot is not your friend, but I knew better anyone that was close to me, Eldoris, would find fault in them."

"You are young yet and have a lot to learn. People that you think are your friends despise and hate you. So be careful. I don't want to have to come over here and kick ass about you," she half- joked.

We laughed and hugged. "You old b*tch," she said, laughing. "You know that I love you. Get the kids ready and go home, because these people don't really care about you. Yes, they do, as I said. Eldoris said, "You saw how they treated you last night; let that be a lesson to you. Now go home." Dot said that she was only trying to show me how bitches would treat me in the streets if I got careless watch, you own back, she said. I knew, without a shadow of a doubt, that Dot and Margie loved me. Unconditional. They were teaching me street games.

"El," I said, "don't go to your friends' house. Go home with me." I felt like I might not see Eldoris again.

"No, bitch, I'm partying this weekend," she said, and I've got me a new man. You should try getting one," she joked, and we both laughed. "I'll see you in a few days."

Whenever she left, I never knew if she was coming back. I always felt such uncertainty about her. Nevertheless, I packed up and caught the bus home. For the first time, I felt that I had worn out my welcome. I was uncomfortable with what had transpired between us and the words that were said, and I knew that Margie and Dot were very close, and somehow, I felt their loyalty to each other.

Margie made me promise to come back by for the holiday—Memorial Day—for a barbecue in the backyard.

"Okay, now you take care of those kids, and I'll see you later," Margie said. We hugged and said our goodbyes, as always, and I was on my way.

While riding the bus home, hoping to get there before dark, I thought about what Eldoris had said. After getting off the bus and walking home through the gangway, Gramps ran over to me.

"Where have you been? Don't you know what's happened?" he exclaimed. "No," I replied, puzzled. "What happened?"

"Somebody broke into your house, stole everything, and set it on fire," he said gravely. "What?" I gasped.

I started to run towards the house, my children in tow, screaming, "Where is Eldoris?" "Pat," Gramps called after me, "don't go over there; you don't know all that's happened."

His voice faded away as I ran towards the house, only to see the sky filled with smoke and the house I once called home completely burned to the ground. People stood everywhere; fire trucks were parked in the front yards.

"My God, what am I going to do now?" I sobbed, holding my children close.

Geri had given all the necessary information to the fire chief. She stated that she lived there and was away at work when this happened. The house was totaled. I couldn't get any answers from her about Eldoris, only that she wasn't in the fire.

As the fire department packed up to leave, I just sat down on the curb with my two babies, shaking my head in disbelief. When I finally got up to walk towards Geri to see if any of my belongings had been saved or how all of this had happened—just some answers as to what I was to do now that all my children's things had burned in the fire—Geri turned and walked away. She pulled off in her car, leaving me sitting on the curb with my two babies.

Several hours had passed, and I was still trying to make some sense of what had happened. What to do? Where to go from here? I couldn't catch the bus anywhere except to ride the bus line all night. Through my tears, I tried to see my way down the street when a white Cadillac pulled up and started to blow his horn, asking if I needed some help. He had seen the fire.

"Hey," he said, "I've got to go to work, and you can fix your children something to eat and lay them down for the night. I work at midnight, so I won't be at home anyway. My brother Richard is home, but he won't bother you, I promise." You can use the phone until you figure it out.

So, I trusted him—it was the biggest mistake of my life.

He said that I could sleep in his bed with my children if I wanted and made me feel welcome in the kitchen. I made them a pallet on the sofa with some sheets Richard had given me out of the linen closet. I didn't trust the sheets because they looked soiled and dingy, so I laid my son's receiving blankets on top of the sheets and sat up all night, watching over my children, dozing off and on. I didn't want anything to happen to us, so I was very careful about what I said and did. I was between a rock and a hard place. I was determine not to lose my kids.

Richard could see that I was uncomfortable with him being there. He kept pacing the floors, back and forth, until eventually he left and told me that I was safe to stay there and that he would see me in the morning.

It was already after midnight, and I prayed that we would be alright and that God would watch over and protect us from any danger or harm. "God, please send your angels to protect us," I said to myself over and over all night. I knew not to call Aunt Janie because she was asleep.

"Lord, what am I going to do? Please show me what to do. I'm scared. God, please help me." The next morning, I got up and cleaned the bathroom so I could use it.

The bedroom door, which the man had offered to me, was closed, so I assumed he had come home and was asleep. Richard came back and I asked if I could give my children a sponge bath and fix them something to eat, as I had brought food with me. It was early morning.

"It's okay," he said. He also agreed when I asked if I could call my aunt Janie. "Yeah, be my guest," he said, turning on the television for Choo-Choo. I waited then

I dialed her number. "Hello, Aunt Janie," I said. "Yes, baby," she responded.

❧ ❧

I started to cry. "Aunt Janie, the house burned down last night, and I don't have any money and nowhere to stay with my children."

"Where are you now?" she asked.

"I'm at this man's house. He offered me a place to stay last night with my children. Could we come and stay with you, please? We won't get in the way, please, Aunt Janie. I don't have anywhere to go with my children."

"Baby, I wish I could let you stay with me, but you know I don't have any room, and Miss Maggie… Well, you know, it's not like you have a new baby and all. Your babies are knee babies."

"Aunt Janie, please, we'll sleep on the floor, and I'll sit on the porch outside every day until it's time to come in."

"And then what will my neighbors say? What will they think?" she replied. Tears were rolling down my face. "Aunt Janie, please don't call the worker.

"What do you mean, your worker? She ain't your worker; she's my worker, and she can't do anything to help you. And if she finds out that you ran away from home, she'll take your children from you; do you want that?"

"No, ma'am," I said.

"Then you better get your ass somewhere and sit down, you hear me?" "Yes, ma'am," I replied. "Now this man that you're staying with, let me speak to him."

"But I don't—"

"Girl, put him on the phone. RIGHT NOW, DO YOU HEAR ME?" she insisted.

I put the phone down to go get Richard to wake up his brother to talk to her when I turned around and saw him standing there. Listening

"I'm sorry," I said, "but my aunt wants to talk to you." "Okay," he said.

He took the phone. They started talking, and he was mostly listening, responding with "huh" and "uh-huh, yes," and occasionally speaking. "It's okay with me. Yeah, yeah, well, my address is 0000 Bewick between Warren and Shoemaker, and the phone number here is 571-0068. You can call back here if you want to."

"Here, your aunt wants to talk to you again. She's a sweet lady," he said, handing me the phone. "Hello," I said.

"Look," Aunt Janie started, "he said that you could stay there with him and work babysitting his two little girls until I find you a place to stay. You stay put, or I'll have you locked up and take your children from you. Do you hear me? Now I will pay him rent for you to stay there. And you can work off the rest. Now, that's the best that I can do right now. I have the phone number and address, and I'll send the worker and the police over there to take your children if you don't stay put. Do you understand me, young lady? I'm tired of hearing from you, and I had to use your checks this month to help Billy pay for a hot water heater. And I won't look for anything next month either because I have to pay for my glasses. Now get your fast ass somewhere, sit down, and be thankful that somebody wants to help you."

She hung up the phone.

I was so upset that my children started to cry.

"Hey," he said, "it's not so bad. You can stay here with your children, and you can babysit my two little girls. You'll like them. You can cook and clean up the house, and I'll buy all the food. Kind of an even trade—you scratch my back and I'll scratch yours, okay?"

I never answered him. I only listened to what he said.

"Oh, and your Aunt Janie told me about your situation and that you're only 16 years old. I thought you were older. You really look older... never mind," he said.

A couple of months had gone by, and I was adjusting to my new situation. I was afraid to anger Aunt Janie and make waves because Geri had locked me up, and so I believed that Aunt Janie would do the same.

The man had been very kind to me and my children at first. He had taken us shopping with his girls. What he claimed was the money Aunt Janie gave him for us to stay there. He even gave me the money that was left over after spending. My sons and I were sleeping in the bedroom; André had his baby bed that I had managed to salvage from the fire. I washed it down, gave it a fresh coat of paint, and it looked like new. I let it air out, and thankfully, it didn't smell. Choo-choo shared a bed with me, although I wasn't able to go anywhere without him playfully threatening to tell Aunt Janie about me. Despite this, I was managing pretty well. His girls really liked me, and one of them was only 6 years younger than me.

I had my own bedroom, and his girls had their bedrooms. Their father had a bedroom upstairs. He worked afternoons and would return in the early morning. There was very little interaction between me and their father. Most days I'd have the children, and we were gone.

After their bath and breakfast, I'd take all the kids out. Always in the downtown area. We walked up Woodward Avenue to Grand Circus Park. I'd buy them popcorn at Otto's, right next to Flamming Emeralds. "His girls, they loved me. They clung to me like my own. Asking me not to ever leave them. Stay with us forever, they'd say. We love you. I couldn't help but feel their need for love and acceptance in their space. So, I returned the favor. I stretch my arms out and hug and kiss those babies every day. I made sure my trips would take up the entire day, so when we all returned to the house, they'd be tired, and he'd be gone.

He didn't know, but every time he gave me money, I saved it. I hid the jar. Sometimes, the man would come in drunk, tracking mud all over the floors that I had just mopped. I would hear him come in at all hours of the night, making noise in the kitchen with pots and pans. Sometimes he would come over to the couch where I had fallen asleep, fully clothed, and ask me to get up and heat him something to eat. That's when I started crushing glass. It wasn't because I liked him; I was trying to gain some leverage over him. He appeared to be a wolf in sheep's clothing. Every time he got drunk, he would look me over and ask me if I was sure I was only 16 years old.

"Yes," I would tell him. Every time he asked, "You are really mature and good to look at," he would say.

Sometimes he and Richard would sit and talk in another language, something like Pig Latin or code words, but I didn't really pay any attention to what they were saying because it seemed stupid for two older men to be sitting there pretending as if they had graduated from college with a foreign language degree. Dumb Mother Fuckers. I was busy hanging curtains and painting his children's bedroom. I took very good care of his girls. And I was planning my escape.

Sometimes Richard would do little things to help me out. I knew he was not trustworthy he was only loyal to those who bought the drinks. I called Aunt Janie every day to see if she was any closer to finding me a place to stay. Always, she said, I'm still looking."

One day, the man drove up just as I was outside getting his mail and looking for a letter from Aunt Janie. He drove up really fast and told me to hurry up and get inside. Then he ran over to the telephone and called Aunt Janie. When I asked what was wrong, he hung up the phone, turned to me, and slapped me so hard with the back of his hand that I fell across the coffee table.

I grabbed my face, which felt like it had been split in half, and tried to get up off the floor when he stood over me.

"You will never disobey me anymore. Your Aunt Janie said that you needed your ass whipped, and I'm just the man to do it. I'm in charge now. Get the fuck out of here and fix me something to eat," he dominant and flexed his arms. The big bad man he was…

I got up off the floor, my body was shaking so bad. Blood was dripping down my face as I tried to fix his food. I stopped to go into the bathroom to wipe my face, but he ran in after me, grabbed me by the back of my head, and slammed me down on the floor.

I could hear him shouting at me. "Bitch, did you hear what I said? When I tell you to jump, you better ask me how high. Don't fuck with me."

I don't know how much time had passed before I realized what was going on. I pulled myself up off the floor, holding onto the bathtub for support. I felt so weak. I peeped out the door, listening for any sounds of life from my children, who were sitting at the table eating. Thank God they were okay. I eased the door shut quietly to look at myself and clean up when I almost slipped in the blood on the floor. There was so much blood that I couldn't believe it all came from my little body—I only weighed 98 lbs. My hands were trembling so badly that I could hardly hold the cloth to my face.

When I looked at myself in the mirror, I started to cry very quietly, careful not to frighten my kids. I looked like a monster. My face was cut around my eye, the swelling had started, the inside of my mouth was cut and chewed up, and blood was gushing out from where it had been cut.

"Oh my God," I whispered, "please help me," as I cleaned myself up.

I felt myself getting sick to my stomach and started throwing up. I ran to the face bowl, filled it with warm water, and got myself cleaned up. My head was hurting, and my ribs felt like they had been broken. My primary concern was for my children's safety. I didn't want my kids to get hurt.

I was careful not to upset him as he lay on the couch watching television, drinking his drink.

With his gun laying across his lap, he put the gun on my son's head. I ran to him and straddled my body over Choo-Choo.

"And you better not pick up the telephone either, 'cause I got it bugged, and I can tell if you pick it up. If you so much as touch the phone, it'll send a signal to my little black box, and you know what that means," he said, balling up his enormous fist and threatening me.

"Nobody loves you; nobody even cares about you," he continued. "If they loved you so much, why did they leave you outside when the house burned down? Your auntie said that you were hard-headed and didn't want to listen to her, and now she doesn't even love you. You think you're too good for me, don't you?" he said. "Well, when I get through with you, you'll be begging for mercy." Help me, God. I prayed to myself.

As he grabbed his keys and walked out the door, I stood there watching, waiting for him to leave. He then opened the door and stuck his head back in. "Oh yeah, and I know where your mama lives, on Freeland off Grand River in a corner house, and I know what time your sisters go to work. Your mother's blind, and she'll never know what hits her if you leave this door. Do I make myself clear?"

I nodded my head and said, "Yes," paralyzed with fear.

I knew that I would do whatever he said to protect my children. Several weeks had passed, each one heavier with the dread of the days to come. The beatings worsened; my face resembled potted meat, my eyes were black and blue, and the whites of my eyes had turned blood red, making it impossible to distinguish the colors.

I would soak my face in cold water every chance I got, trying to keep the swelling down. However, if he caught me taking care of myself, he would erupt in anger, taunting me with words like, "Nobody loves you.

If they did, why don't they come and get you?" I had lost all contact with my family. Eldoris never came back, and nobody even looked for me. The block was empty because everyone was strung out on drugs. His words resonated in my head—he was right—nobody looked for me.

All the free time I had was spent with my children; his had gone home. I had no contact with the outside world. Several times I'd wanted to use the phone but was paralyzed with fear. What if he caught me? I never knew when he'd be home because he was always around now. He had Richard and Rayfield, his two grown, stupid brothers, sitting on the front porch when he was gone. The man controlled them with bottles of wine; they were winos. I watched their pattern every day, planning my escape. After they would get drunk, they would start an argument with each other, talking loudly and drawing attention to only themselves.

I was being held prisoner against my will. He boarded up the house and every window.

My nerves were shot; I was constantly vomiting and had picked up the old habits—smoking cigarettes. I couldn't stand to be around him; there was something sick about this man.

I kept on crushing glass. It took me days to do it. I broke a pop bottle in half, and I placed one half inside a sock that I doubled. And I beat it down with a shoe heel until I got it broken all the way down. I started to crush it into fine, glittery pieces, then I put it inside a pot of chili for him to eat.

As time moved forward, his underwear was soiled. I noticed that when he stepped out of his pants and dropped them on the floor in the bathroom for everyone to see. Inside, there was plenty of bright red blood.

It must have worked. He didn't die like I wanted, but he was in a lot of pain. He almost never bathed, and I once overheard him telling Richard that their mother used to bathe him in something red, like blood. He never brushed his teeth. Sometimes, when he would stretch his arms out, I would jump—a reaction I was all too familiar with.

"Why are you jumping, honey?" he would say.

I knew that I had to survive in order for my children to live. He had rigged the bottom back door with some kind of trap, and the top back door was nailed shut with large two-by-fours. He had all the windows boarded up and nailed shut. He also housed a full-grown female German

Shepherd living in the basement that he never fed. There was no way out for me. Or so he thought…

He threatened me, promising that he would hurt me badly and cut up my kids to feed them to the dog if I tried to leave. He and Aunt Janie had become the best of friends. One day, she called and asked to speak to me. She inquired about how I was getting along and suggested I should be happy that I had someone to care about me and my children. And she again threatened me, "Stay there and watch over his kids, or I'll have you locked up and have your children taken away from you."

I knew that, then she encouraged him to beat me and try to break my spirit by beating me. She said that I think too much of myself. I couldn't tell her everything because he was standing in the doorway, listening to the conversation. But as soon as I thought it, she confirmed it: "Yeah, I told him to beat your ass like Henry did mine, and it'll make you a better woman like it did me. I thank God for those ass whippings Henry gave me. God rest his soul; he sure was a good man. "There's nothing wrong with a man whipping your ass when you get out of line." I whispered.

He's nothing to me.

I just laid the phone down while she was still talking and walked away.

Around 6:00 that same evening, he told me his friends were going to have a barbecue on the front porch. "I want you to behave yourself, alright?"

"Yeah," I said quickly, careful not to provoke him slapping me.

I always found something else to do when he was around. I spent a lot of time coloring with Choo-Choo in his coloring books, teaching him about his numbers. Choo-Choo was a bright two- year-old; he could count to ten on his fingers and knew his nose, ears, and toes. He was astute enough to sense something was wrong with his mama. He always rubbed my face with his little hands.

As I looked at my children and wept with sadness, I knew I would never forgive myself if anything happened to them. He seemed to resent the love I showed my sons, so I would close the doors when I put them to bed at night, when we kneeled down to pray, or whenever I gave them their baths, holding them very close to me. I stopped sleeping on the couch and moved into the bedroom with my children to protect them, ensuring that if he tried to hurt them, he would have to kill me first. His children had gone home to their mother.

Later that day, he returned from the store with liquor and beer, cartons of cigarettes, charcoal, and all the ingredients for a barbecue. As I pondered all kinds of ways to escape, I realized this would be the first time anyone had visited him at the house. If I was careful, I could get away. Maybe his friend had a wife I could ask for help. I thought to myself that if I had the chance, I would run like hell.

While sitting on the side of Choo-Choo's bed, my mother's voice spoke to me so crystal-clear inside of my heart. She said, "When your head is in the lion's mouth, tread easy."

Chapter 11

"Game Changer"

———————————————————

Labor Day had come and gone, and my only respite was being friends with Martha and Willie Bronner, a couple who lived directly across the street. The man seemed to trust Martha and allowed her to visit his house, although she rarely did. When she did come over, I looked forward to seeing her. She'd often send her daughter, who looked to be around ten years old, to borrow things like sugar, flour, and milk.

One day, Martha borrowed some money from me to prevent the gas man from cutting off their service. I loaned her the money from my savings jar but made her promise to repay me because it was meant for my children. Martha and her husband appeared to be just getting by. They had eight young children; she looked old enough to be their grandmother, and he looked old enough to be their great-grandfather. Willie was a retired auto worker who had been injured on the job. He had one foot in the grave and the other on a block of ice. When I first met them, I thought Martha was Willie's daughter—not that she looked so young, but because he was so old. Martha claimed to be in her late forties, though I would have said late fifties with a zero behind it. Willie was so old that they had stopped counting.

I really confided in Martha; she always seemed so willing to listen to my problems and led me to believe she would help me. She knew about the beatings; the fresh bruises all over my body were evidence enough. I thought she was my friend. Little did I know, she was telling him everything I confided in her, even about the money I loaned her.

Martha once told me she had been a striptease dancer and that Willie had been her manager before they married. I implored Martha not to let him know that I had any money and to wait until he was not around to pay me back because if he discovered I was saving money, he would beat me up. She knew I was deathly afraid of him, and my biggest fear of him was about to come true.

I remember one Friday evening. I was in the dining room, feeding my children, when he came in. He went upstairs and then came running back down the stairs. He was screaming and hollering at me, accusing me of using the phone.

"I hadn't used the phone!" he was yelling. I was so afraid of him. Suddenly, he hauled off and slapped me so hard that I fell out of the chair.

Choo-Choo started to cry and ran over to me, crying out, "Mama-Mama." As Choo-Choo was coming over to me, I was reaching out for him, trying to shield him from the day's horror, when he hit me with his fist and knocked me back down to the floor.

Somehow—I don't know how—I managed to run with my children. I needed to lock them up in the bedroom. I just threw them inside and closed the door. When he hit me with his fist again, so hard that my head hit the door and knocked a hole in it, I ran into the dining room. I was telling

Choo-Choo to close the door and stay in the room when he grabbed me and started to beat me— relentlessly, in my face and head with his fist. I fought back but didn't have no win.

I was crying and trying to get away from him, but he was like a madman. "Oh God," I cried out loud, "he's trying to kill me; help me, please."

I tried fighting back, but I had no chance; it only made it worse. "You want to fight me, huh?" he taunted. "You want to fight me?" He just grabbed me by the collar and kept beating me with his fist until my body went numb. I could no longer feel anything.

He then threw me onto the couch and ran upstairs. "Bitch, I'm gonna kill you," he kept shouting. "I know you used the phone; who did you call?"

"Nobody," I said. "I didn't touch the phone." "Please," I cried, and Richard ran in.

"Hurt you?" he mocked as he ran back down the stairs. "You'll know not to mess with me when I get through with you." I tried nervously to open the door and grab my kids.

My babies were crying in the bedroom. Choo-Choo stuck his head out of the door, and I shook my head at him, signaling not to come out. He started to cry even louder when he saw my face and head covered with blood.

He ran back down the stairs with a gun—a shotgun—and pointed it at my head. "See, bitch, this is what I'll do to you if you ever lie to me."

"Now tell me who you called. Was it your mother? Because you know I will kill her, don't you?" He was holding the gun to my head and pulling the trigger. Click.

My whole life just flashed before my eyes.

All I could do was sit there and cry. My whole body shook uncontrollably as he held the gun to my head, engaging in a horrifying game of Russian roulette. He'd put bullets in, pull the trigger, take them out, and pull the trigger again.

My babies were crying. They had been crying for so long now that they were starting to cough and choke. "Please, can I go see my kids? Please," I begged him.

"Yeah, and don't you try to run 'cause I'll blow the back of your head off, bitch," he said coldly.

I could hardly see through the blood dripping into my eyes. Somehow, I managed to quiet the kids and tried to get them to lay down, but they wouldn't stay in the room.

"Bring those little bastards in here, so I can show them what a real man is supposed to do when a bitch like you gets out of line," he said.

"Please don't hurt them," I pleaded, holding my children in my arms. "Please, they're only babies. Don't hurt them; I'll do anything you say." He pulled the gun on my children.

"You're gonna do what I say anyway. Now, bitch, get down on your knees and beg. Beg me, bitch, not to kill your motherfucking ass, like the dog you are."

Trembling, I got down on my hands and knees and begged him not to kill us. Each time I tried to rise, he would press the gun to the back of my head and pull the trigger.

Finally, he let me rise from the floor. He forced me to sit on the couch next to my children, then he went down to the basement and stayed for hours.

He issued one last warning: "Don't move. If I hear you walking across the floor, I will come back upstairs and finish the job I started."

I sat on the couch, too afraid to move. Eventually, I heard him come up the stairs and go into the bathroom. The sound of the shower running filled the air, a sound I rarely heard him make. He quickly dressed and walked out the door. My vision was blurred, but I could feel the warm sunlight rays creeping through the blowing flakes of snow. As I listened to the sound of his car driving off, and the door lock for the first time in my life, I understood my mother's pain and what it was like to be blind.

Gathering my strength, I stood and felt my way to the bathroom. Splashing water on my face, I tried to reduce the swelling. The kids were still asleep on the couch. My movements were restricted as I peeled off my clothes; my arms and legs barely responded, my face was so swollen it looked like minced meat, and my eyes swollen shut. I used my fingers to pry them open. I did my best to sponge off my body. I've got to get away from here.

Carefully, I turned the faucet down low, straining my ears for any sign of his return. I placed my blood-soaked clothes in a brown paper bag to dispose of them in the kitchen trash. Then I eased the bag outside to the backyard, where the garbage was kept. Looking around at the house the windows and the dog's location, planning my escape. As I approached the bin, I saw Mr. Brazil coming my way. Pretending not to see him, I held my head down, dropped the clothes inside the can, and turned around quickly to avoid any contact.

"Pat," he called out to me, "what the hell happened to you?"

I kept my head lowered, too ashamed to let him see my face. "Nothing," I lied. "I ran into a door."

"Ah, door, my ass; it looks like you were beaten with the door. What is that negro doing to you over there? Come here so I can see you."

"It's nothing," I said as I walked towards him, my hand up, trying to hide my face. "I'll be alright."

"That's a goddamn shame," he said, moving my hand away from my face. "Does your mother know where you are?"

I hesitated. "No, sir, she doesn't. Please don't tell her." I'm going to get away from him you'll see.

"Okay, okay," he reassured me, "don't upset yourself any more than you have to. I won't tell." "I don't want her to know what's happened to me," I admitted. "She'll only worry."

"That goddamn nigger needs somebody to put their foot up his ass really good; that'll stop his monkey ass."

Mr. Brazil had his own special way with words. I could barely smile, as I always did whenever I heard him talk. He was a southern man from Little Rock, Arkansas, his voice thick with accent.

"Here," he said, extending a bottle of liquor towards me, "take this. You need it more than I do. Anyways, I got another bottle in the house."

We laughed together. "I was just walking back here, checking out my garden," he explained. Mr. Brazil was known for growing the best vegetables in the neighborhood. Reflecting on it now, I believe Mr. Brazil essentially had a community garden. He gave it all away, yet nobody but him could work in his fields.

"Well," he said, "you take you a good stiff drink of McNaughton's Scotch, pick up a frying pan, bust that son-of-a-bitch in his head, and haul your ass outta there. You understand me?"

"Yes," I said, "but you promise me you won't tell, please." I was embarrassed by the situation I was in. And I didn't want to get anyone else involved because he threatened me with a gun.

And I didn't know how that would play out.

"Yeah, and promise me that you won't let that dirty motherfucker kill you either," he said as he turned to walk away.

"I promise, as soon as I figure out a way without getting my children hurt."

I hurried back into the house to look after my kids when I heard a car pull up. My heart skipped several beats—it was the man.

That day, the telephone rang more than ever before. I knew he was trying to trap me into answering it, but I didn't dare.

Later that evening, I had two drinks. I was so nervous and upset that I could hardly hold the glass steady. Choo-Choo wanted me to read his favorite story, "The Gingerbread Man," something I always did at night before putting him to bed. He didn't understand that my eyes were swollen shut; I could hardly see out of them. Choo-Choo absolutely loved the Gingerbread Man. He especially loved the part when the gingerbread man popped out of the oven and ran away from the old lady and the old man. I'd read the story to him so many times that I knew it by heart. So, I let him hold the book in his little hands and pretended to read to him.

Finally, we all dozed off to sleep.

I was awakened by the large shadow of him standing over me, pouring the bottle of liquor all over my face and body. In my eyes, I cannot see. I rolled over on top of my kids to protect them. Blinded by the alcohol, I started to wipe my eyes and search the room with my hands in the air.

The room reeked of alcohol; the sheets were soaking wet. I knew he was going to set me on fire and burn us alive.

"You wanna drink, bitch? You wanna drink? I'll give you a drink!" he screamed. You been out this house.

He started striking matches and throwing them at me. I could feel the matches as they landed on my body, scrambling across the bed in total darkness. The sound of him tearing matches from the book was terrifying, but that wasn't all I heard. As he threw the matches, I heard a faint whisper ("whoo, whoo")—as if someone else was in the room with us, blowing the matches out.

That was God.

"He was going to burn me and my children alive." But God saved my life; all the matches he threw at me went out. He became discouraged and left me alone.

I lay there until I could hear him crawl back into his hole. I got up, felt my way into the bathroom, and splashed my eyes with warm water, trying to get them to open. Before getting back into bed, I got down on my hands and knees and thanked the Lord for saving my life. I asked him to protect me and to help me get out of there alive.

"Show me, Lord, what to do," I prayed silently. A couple of weeks had passed, and the beating got worse. His brothers knew, but he didn't want anyone to know what he had done to me. I was sixteen, and he was forty-one.

He forced me to have his way with me because I wouldn't give in to him. When his mother visited, I had never heard him mention her but once before. She was a short, fat woman with brown skin. Her hair, tinted reddish-brown to mask the years, couldn't hide the wiry gray hairs that jutted out under her chin, noticeable like a sore thumb. It was the first time I'd seen a woman with facial hair. She introduced herself as Pauline Collins and spoke nostalgically about her days as a young mother and how her husband had left her when their children were just babies. He had thought she was feeding him her menstrual blood in his food, a story she recounted with a laugh. The more she spoke, the more I believed she might actually be as unhinged as he thought.

I treated her with the utmost courtesy, waiting on her hand and foot—I was too afraid to do otherwise. I fixed her something to eat while he stayed close by, listening intently to every word exchanged between us.

"Do you remember the red water I used to bathe you in?" she asked him suddenly. His eyes were filled with such intense hatred that it sent chills down my spine.

"Yeah, I remember," he muttered.

She snickered. "Your father thought it was blood too," and she threw her head back in a hearty laugh.

Her son, now 41 and the oldest of five siblings—who all seemed to have different fathers— looked on silently. "You remember sleeping with me in that big bed upstairs? Boy, the things we used to do under the covers," she reminisced. "We had so much fun; he was so frisky back then. He'll hardly let me touch him now. But, oh, when his father wasn't around, I could have my way with him." In my mind I pretended not to understand what she was saying.

"Why don't you keep your big mouth shut, Pauline?" he screamed at her. "Get your coat; you're going home now."

"I ain't going nowhere," she retorted. "Not until I'm good and damn ready to go."

He walked over and slammed his fist on the table so hard that it split. The violence of the action terrified me, and I ran into the bedroom with the kids, assuming my usual position of keeping out of sight. Earlier that day, I'd been hanging curtains, trying silently unhinging the nails from the plywood on the windows. Climbing back onto the chair, I could hear their argument escalating, the tension thickening like fog.

I didn't care about getting acquainted with her; she would never be anything to me other than his mother. But I knew once she left, he would unleash all his frustrations on me. So, I played along, eagerly leaving the room to busy myself with anything else. I kept listening.

Driven by desperation, I threw myself through the double glass window, landing outside on the ground. For a moment, I thought I had blacked out. Pauline waddled over to look down at me. I wasn't seriously hurt—just another bruise to add to the collection—but I lay there, hoping someone would call an ambulance or take me to the hospital so we could escape.

"Are you alright?" she asked. I only moaned and whispered for her help. She called out for him. "Take her to the hospital!"

"For what?" he replied dismissively.

"Come on, honey, I'll take you," she offered. "You stay here and watch the kids."

My plan had backfired. I pretended to revive and asked my children to take them with me. When he said no, they would stay here with me. Suddenly, I got better. She ain't going to any hospital, nowhere anyway, he said. Come on, honey, she said your kids would be alright. Just then Martha walked across the street, and she intercepted herself into the conversation. And she assured me that she would take care of them for me.

I couldn't leave without them. I was scared because I knew what a dirty b*tch she had been to me. You promise me that you will take care of my kids. Yes, I promise. I'll stay here if you like.

"Oh God," I whispered to myself, "please don't let him hurt them while I'm gone. Maybe I've done more harm than good." All through the day, I could only pray for my children. At the hospital, the doctor examined me thoroughly. He noted fresh bruises across my body and face.

"How did these get here?" he asked, his voice flat. Then, without waiting for my response, he requested some urine. "You were probably doing something you had no business doing," he remarked casually.

"I didn't do anything," I retorted, rolling my swollen eyes. He simply looked at me and walked away. He was so slow in his procedures that after a couple of hours, I asked to be released so I could return to my kids.

"Yeah, that's what you better be doing now that you're going to have another baby," he said nonchalantly.

"What?" I was shocked. "A baby?"

"Go home and be good to your husband."

"I'm not married," I snapped, frustration boiling over. "And I would appreciate it if you kept your insults and comments to yourself."

He frowned, clearly displeased. "No wonder you're getting your ass beat at home. Don't give him any more problems, even though you probably deserve much more."

"Fuck you," I muttered under my breath, feeling like the bottom had dropped out of my stomach. "You're six weeks along. You'll have to follow up with prenatal care," he stated flatly as he left.

His mother, who had overheard everything from the hallway, didn't speak a word to me on the drive back. As soon as we entered his house, she blurted out that I was pregnant, suggesting he should be happy and that we should try to get along.

"This crazy bitch," I thought furiously. "Try and get along? I don't even know this motherfucker."

He looked at me with murder in his eyes. "You're pregnant? How did you get pregnant? I never touched you," he accused. Cause he didn't want anyone to know what he had done to me.

He raised his hand to slap me, but his mother intervened. "Not in front of me," she commanded. "Take me home first."

"Get your coat on, now!" he yelled at her, demanding the keys. "Pauline, give me my keys!"

He rushed her out the door and into the car. As soon as I heard the car pull off, I frantically called for a cab. "Please send a cab to 0000 Bewick between Warren and Shoemaker. The porch light is on. Hurry, please," I pleaded into the phone.

After hanging up, I grabbed the money I had hidden in a jar, scooped up Choo-Choo, and wrapped Andre in a blanket. I dressed Choo-Choo quickly, and we waited anxiously by the door. Pacing, I prayed the cab would arrive first. He didn't have far to drive to drop off his mother.

As I tried to open the fence, which he had locked, Choo-Choo started to cry. Just then, the cab pulled up. I jumped over the fence, landing awkwardly on my butt with Andre still in my arms. The cab driver was slow to help. Frustrated, I threw my baby into the cab and ran back to lift Choo-Choo over the fence.

We were in the middle of the snowy street when I saw him driving towards us. He pulled up behind the cab, jumped out, and ran towards me.

"In the cab, screaming, I pleaded with the driver, "Please, pull off! He's going to kill me; help me; please call the police!"

He grabbed the cab door, yanking it. "Stop this motherfucking cab now!" he demanded.

The cab slowed to a stop, and the driver, laughing cruelly, pulled me from the cab. "If he's going to kill you, he's not going to do it in here."

I grabbed my babies and started running down towards the blowing snow, the only light reflecting from the streetlamps. He tackled me from behind. I screamed, crying, "Help me, somebody, please help me! Oh my God, he's trying to kill me."

As I tried to get up, he threw me to the ground again, punching me in the face and dragging me by the collar down to the porch. Desperately clawing and crying for my life, he kept hitting and smashing my head against the stairs. He lifted me and threw me into the wooden fence, breaking it down.

"My babies, my babies!" I screamed. "God, please help my babies."

"I'll help your babies, you bitch," he screamed. He stepped over the remnants of the fence and picked up my children, who were screaming and crying in the street. As I tried to get up, he kicked me in the side. I fell, protecting my unborn child, with my hands over my stomach.

He dragged me back into the house by my hair and locked the door. As I tried to run, he punched me so hard that I was thrown into the next room. The kids were hysterical. I begged Choo-Choo, "Don't stand there and watch him kill me. Take your brother into the room. Get out of here."

Choo-Choo screamed to me, "Run, Mama, as fast as you can, like the gingerbread man."

I was desperately trying to get away from him when I slipped and fell. He started to kick and stomp me all over my face, my hands, and my side. "How are you gonna be pregnant, bitch? I haven't ever screwed you. You stupid bitch, who's baby, is it?" he kept shouting.

Just then, the police knocked at the door. "Open up," they commanded. "Come on, open up."

He wiped my blood from his hands and walked to the door. Before opening it, he turned to me, his voice low and menacing. "You shut your mouth; do you understand?" I nodded, paralyzed with fear. I knew the police would take my children from me.

He opened the door, and a police officer inquired, "Is there a problem here?" "No, there isn't," he replied smoothly.

"Well, what's going on?" the officer pressed. "Someone called and said they heard a woman screaming."

"I'm having an argument with my girlfriend. Can't a man have an argument in his own house without somebody calling the police? Look, we'll keep it down."

His partner, standing by the door, chimed in, "Look, man, I don't care about your beating your old lady's ass. It's not my business; just keep it down."

"Yeah, I will," he replied. They both laughed, wished each other a good evening, and never once did they ask to speak to or even see me.

He walked back to the room, where I lay still on the floor. "You disgust me. I hate you. You're just like all other women. I spent my hard-earned money on you, and look what you've done to me. You think your Aunt Janie's been sending money here for you and your bastard babies."

"I let you stay here because I feel sorry for you. Your aunt is a no-good bitch," he said. Finally, something we agreed on, though for vastly different reasons. "She takes your checks and food stamps and never sends you one penny. I've been taking care of you all this time."

"She sent one fifty-dollar bill," I whispered.

"Why don't you let me go?" I pleaded. "Please, just let me go, and I'll pay you back all the money that I owe you."

"Shut up!" he shouted. "Are you crazy? I can't let you go just like that. Somebody's gonna pay. You, Pauline, and your black-ass aunt."

He walked over to me, anger flaring in his eyes. "Somebody's going to pay, starting with you." He raised his foot and kicked me in the face. "Now do you fucking understand? If you ever try to leave here, you will pay. Now get the fuck up and clean this house. Better yet, get down on your hands and knees like the dog you are and clean this house."

My being pregnant didn't seem to stop the beatings. In fact they increase he was trying to kill my baby because he didn't want people to know what he was doing to me, I was in a state of mind where I could no longer help myself and free myself from the mental and physical bondage that had been placed upon me. The burden was more than I could bear. The circles under my eyes had grown very dark, and my voice had dropped in volume. The only life left in me was that which was growing inside my body.

Thanksgiving was just a week away. It is my favorite holiday of the year. I love Thanksgiving more than my own birthday. I learned to appreciate Thanksgiving at a very young age, understanding the true meaning of it. I wanted to teach my children as they grow what my mama taught me: that we should give thanks for all that God has done for us, no matter how small or how big. All blessings come from God.

Mama said to never look down on people less fortunate than we are, for all that we have are true blessings from the Lord. She told us to never judge a person, for God will judge you in the same manner as you judge others. But not to practice these teachings only at Thanksgiving time, but to always remember in your heart to live them.

Thanksgiving was always a modest affair in my mother's house, but it was filled with love, and that made the lack of trimmings inconsequential.

He insisted on taking me to the market for groceries alone, claiming it was "insurance" to ensure I wouldn't talk or try to escape. I did what he said; fearful he would harm my children if I didn't. I was relieved they were asleep, which made it easier for me to hurry out before they awoke. I loaded all the groceries into the trunk of his car without his help, and then carried them inside. They were heavy, and my stomach was starting to hurt. I stayed as far away from him as possible, always praying he would leave the house and never return—wishing death upon him.

After putting the groceries away, I prepared lunch for my sons and read them a story. Andre had developed a new cough, so I gave him cough syrup, baby aspirin, and plenty of fluids. He entered the room to check on us, and upon seeing me holding and rocking my children, he abruptly left and slammed the door.

He got into his car and drove off but brothers were pacing around on the porch and walking around the outside of the house trying. A wave of relief washed over me as I watched him disappear down the road. My nerves were shot. Andre fell asleep in my arms shortly after, so I laid him down for another nap. Choo-Choo and I then went into the kitchen to cook dinner.

"Mama," Choo-Choo said while rubbing my stomach, "what's wrong? You sick?"

"No, sweetheart," I replied, trying to reassure him. "Mama's going to have another baby, and he will be a baby just like your brother André. And I will love him just as much as I love you."

"Ok," he said, but then I bent down to kiss him, and a sharp pain struck the lower part of my stomach. I groaned in agony, and Choo-Choo started to cry.

"Mama, don't die, please," he pleaded.

"Baby, Mama's not going to die. My stomach is just hurting, and I'm going to sit down with you for a little while," I assured him, trying to calm his fears. "Now, stop crying. I'm going to be alright. Would you like to color in your coloring book that I just bought for you?"

"Yes, ma'am," he sniffled.

"Ok, let's go get it," I said. We retrieved the book and crayons, and I explained the pictures to him as we settled down at the table. As he colored, I started on dinner.

I was still learning to cook, but my children were my most appreciative patrons. They always ate all their food. Today's menu was fried chicken, mashed potatoes, green peas, canned biscuits, and pan gravy. Well, so much for the gravy—I burned it.

After he finished coloring, Choo-Choo asked if he could go outside. "After you colored that page so nicely, stay inside the lines just as I taught you," I noted. Though I was reluctant to let him go, I bundled him up in his snowsuit, hat, and mittens and told him to stay on the porch and play. For a few seconds. Richard and Rayfield were standing guard on the porch.

I nervously peeked out the window every few minutes to check on Choo-Choo playing outside. Abruptly, he drove up, stormed into the house, and cornered me with his face inches from mine. "What the hell are you doing walking up on me so close that we could kiss?" His voice was laced with fury.

I froze, too afraid to speak, fearing any word might provoke him further.

"Bitch," he seethed, "what the fuck do you think you're doing?" My mouth hung open, but no words came out.

"Oh, you a smart bitch," he mocked before slapping me so hard I stumbled towards the stove. My hand knocked the pan of gravy off the floor. As I tried to break my fall, he punched me in the stomach. Collapsing, I lay there gasping for air, clutching my stomach.

Then he took his foot and stood on top of my face, smashing it into the floor. "Now you get that boy inside my house," he commanded. "Get up," he barked, "and do what I tell you."

Still grasping for air and trying to pull myself up, I held onto the oven door rail, but it gave out, and I fell again. I crawled to the dining room table and pulled myself up on a chair, wiping the tears from my already blackened eyes. My mind was made up I'm going to kill this mother fucker tonight. My second thought was then they will take my children for sure.

"Bitch, get up and get that boy inside this house, or do you want me to get him?"

"No," I managed to say, and I stood up shakily. I walked to the door and called Choo-Choo inside. Richard ran inside to see the commotion then he left and stayed on the porch patrolling the outside.

Later that evening, after putting the kids to bed, I longed for a bath to soak my body and try to reduce some of the swelling. I never dared to take a bath while he was in the house. I sat on the side of my children's bed, waiting and praying for him to leave. Suddenly, he burst into my room.

"Take off your clothes," he ordered. "Why?" I asked, my voice barely a whisper.

He advanced towards me; his fist drawn back. "Don't you ever question me. Take off your clothes," he demanded.

Trembling, I stood and walked towards the bathroom, my hands shaking so badly that I could hardly manage the buttons. "Oh God, please," I whispered. "Please, God, don't let this happen to me again."

As I was pulling my shirt over my head, my arms came down, and he was standing there. "Oh God, please," I repeated, terror overwhelming me.

"You're gonna need more than God," he sneered, "when I get through with you."

Chapter 12

"The Gloves Are Off"

As I undressed in front of this man holding his gun, I felt sick to the stomach. He was looking at me all over, like something good to eat. I took off my shirt and sat down on top of the toilet seat to take my pants down. "Now give them to me," he said, walking towards me with a sick, perverted look on his face. I handed him the clothes before he got too close to me, covering myself with my hands. I had never undressed in front of a man in my life. When Eric and I were together, I asked him to turn off the lights. I was too embarrassed and ashamed. I felt humiliated, like a piece of meat at the meat market.

"Stand up," he said to me, "let me see what I'm buying every month." "I couldn't."

"Get up, bitch," he said. "Don't make me come get you," so I stood up with my arms crossed over my body to hide from him.

"Are you sure you're only 16? You have the body of a grown woman," he said. "Turn around and let me see the rest of you," I hesitated then I turned around slowly.

"Goddamn, you have a nice body," he said. "Hey man, come here and look at this fresh young meat; she's fresh," he said.

I didn't even know that there was someone else in the house.

He said, "Jim, man. Come and see this." It'll make your dick hard even though you can't keep it up for long."

His friend walked into the bathroom and said, "Man, don't do this to her; give her back her clothes." I started to cry in shame. He then turned around and walked away.

"Here," he said, "put this on," and he handed me a bag from the Federal Department store. "I want to see you in these from now on," he said as he turned and walked away.

He said, "It'll be easier to get to that."

I put the duster on; it was an old flower cotton print in brown and green with two pockets and no sleeves. Although the price tag was still on, it looked older than his mother.

"Come on, man, take me home," his friend said. "I don't like to see any woman mistreated. Whatever you have on your mind that you like to do, you'll have to do it alone."

He walked back in the bathroom and said, "Now that's what I like; do something with your hair," grabbing my hair from the front and snatching it backwards and putting it in a ponytail.

"Yeah, a ponytail."

My hair at that time was shoulder-length and naturally red. I always kept it pressed with a warm comb. It neat. So, I put it in a ponytail off my face, and now I'm starting to look like someone's old grandmother.

"Oh yeah," he said, "before you go and start looking for your clothes. I threw them away in the garbage. If you're going to be my woman, you're going to have to start dressing like it."

He walked out the door, and I followed behind him, looking out the front room window. As soon as he left, I ran to the closet, where I kept my few clothes still folded in a paper bag. He had thrown away all my clothes, including my underwear. There were only three duster dresses and three pairs of underwear lying on the bed. Bloomers that look like his mother could fit. I was smart enough to leave things just as they were pretending not to notice that all of my clothes were gone. I started my bath water and walked to the kitchen to get the salt. When the pain started in my stomach again, I held my stomach and poured the salt into the water. As I took off my clothes, I pulled my panties down; they had blood in them. Light pink blood: "Oh my God, please do not let me lose my baby." I prayed.

Chapter 13

"Survival Kill or Be Killed"

As I lay beside my children, I could see the rain thump against the window—big, bold drops of rain, strong and determined as they fell from the sky. They pushed their way through the gusty wind, yet somehow weakened and were discouraged as they reached their destiny.

I missed my mama and just wanted to put my arms around her and hold her real tight one more time. I wanted to tell her how much I loved her and how much she really meant to me. I wanted her forgiveness for any pain or hardship I had ever caused her. I wanted only to remember the happier times we had shared together, though they were far and few between.

I remembered those red patent leather shoes I wanted so badly when I was just 6 years old. I cried a river of tears over those shoes when Mama said no., I didn't understand then, as I do now, that she wasn't being mean to me, but only that she couldn't afford them. All I knew at the time was that I wanted them. They were the prettiest shoes I'd ever seen in my six years on this earth. They were so bright and shiny that when I picked them up, I could see my face in the shoe. There was a small pump heel, made just for a girl my age, with a matching red strap to go across the top of the foot, and there were red buttons on each side of the shoe.

"Man, they were really something special, made just for me," I would think to myself.

Mama had gone out shopping without me. I didn't understand why she left me behind; I figured that she was tired of me worrying her to death about those shoes. That was very rare for Mama to leave me behind. I cried, but I stayed anyway.

When she returned, I had hurt my foot playing around with the other children on the block. We jumped from porch to porch, and there was a large opening on the sides of all the porches on Elmhurst Street. When it was my turn to jump, I got scared. But I did it anyway. I didn't want the kids to laugh and tease me because I was afraid to jump. And I landed on top of a large nail that was sticking out of a board, and I ran the nail straight through my foot. I screamed for my mama, who wasn't home, and so my father came running down the stairs, picked me up off the ground, and pulled the nail from my foot.

My father carried me upstairs and put a piece of salt pork on my foot, he said, to draw out the poison. Well, when Mama came home, we told her what happened, and I told Mama that I could no longer walk and that my foot had poison in it.

And Mama said she had a surprise for me and to close my eyes. When I opened them, she handed me a pair of red patent leather shoes, just like the ones I'd seen in the window store downtown. I put them on, hugged and kissed my mama, and ran down the stairs to play with my friends.

Gosh, I felt so special.

As a four-year-old, when Mama returned from her shopping trips to the Goodwill store, she always brought treasures. On one occasion, she gifted me a white linen dress adorned with bright red apples in the pockets. That dress held a special place in my heart, cherished by everyone in the family. I clung to it until I turned twelve.

But one day, Geri, rummaging through Mama's dresser drawers, discovered it and disposed of it with casual indifference. It was as simple as that.

As I lay there, memories flooded back, transporting me to our time on Mandalay Street, where I embarked on my kindergarten journey. Each day, Mama walked me to school, and at midday, she returned to collect me. Those walks were filled with chatter about my day—reciting the alphabet, dabbling in watercolors, and singing songs. "I'm a Little Teapot" was my favorite, and Mama indulged my enthusiasm.

We'd sing together, "I'm a little teapot, short and stout. Here is my handle; here is my spout." and all the children eagerly awaited their turn to mimic the teapot's motions. One afternoon, I eagerly asked my teacher when it would be my turn, unable to contain my excitement.

She promised, "Tomorrow, it will be your turn." That night, anticipation kept me restless.

The following day, the children gathered around me in a circle, hands clasped, swaying as they sang the familiar tune. I mimicked the teapot's stance, hand on hip, the other raised, ready to tip myself over. But just then, Geri entered the room, delivering news that I had to leave immediately.

And just like that, the moment slipped away, leaving me yearning for the simple joy of being a teapot among friends.

The teacher pleaded with Geri to allow me to finish my turn. "Please, Geri, let me finish," I begged, desperation creeping into my voice. But she ignored my pleas, gripping my arm tightly with her sharp, witch-like nails.

I broke free from her grasp and dashed back to the circle, determined to reclaim my moment as the teapot. Yet Geri followed, whispering threats in my ear, her words a venomous reminder of the power she held over me. She knew my secret—my lingering attachment to a baby bottle— and she wielded it like a weapon.

In that moment, I couldn't comprehend why she harbored such animosity toward me. But it didn't matter. I never got the chance to be a teapot again; life's currents swept me away before my turn could come around once more.

The humiliation clung to me like a heavy cloak, weighing me down even as I tried to move forward. Seeking solace, I found myself standing at the kitchen sink, lost in memories that felt as fresh as yesterday.

Then, like a beacon cutting through the darkness, my mother's voice echoed in my mind, offering words of comfort and wisdom. "Never walk with your head down," she would say. "Hold it high; look people in the eye. You have nothing to be ashamed of. You are somebody. You are my child. And I love you."

Her words were a balm to my wounded spirit, restoring my confidence and reminding me of my worth. With her love as my guiding light, I faced the world anew, ready to hold my head high and embrace the person I was meant to be.

And then it was torn down again. He started raping me…*over and over again.*

March 1972

All the holidays had somehow passed me by. It was now March 1972. My body and brain were overwhelmed with worry and suffering. My mental state was that of a walking zombie. Like a robot, programmed. There was no more fight left in me. He no longer saw me as a threat.

Therefore, I was able to run to the store when I ran out of small items. He knew that I would come right back because he always made me leave my kids. Andre was eight months old and able to pull himself up. In his crib, I made sure that the children always played in their room and made as little noise as possible.

Andre was running a fever, and I was all out of baby aspirins, so I asked him if I could go to the store and get some. The store was only two blocks away, and it wouldn't take long to run to the store. Choo-choo was still sleeping so I hurried up and ran all the way. The streets were clear of any friends left. The kind of friends that would gladly kill him and rescue me from all harm.

When I left, André was asleep, and when I returned, I could hear my baby screaming and hollering to the top of his lungs. He had been crying so long that he could hardly catch his breath. I ran up the porch stairs and into the house, where Andre was standing up in his crib, holding on to the railing. Tears were streaming down his little face, and I went over to comfort him and dry his tears, only to notice that he had a handprint across his face that was so deeply embedded that I could still see the fingerprints.

I picked my baby up, took him to the bathroom, and put a cool towel on his face to stop the swelling. Choo choo now awake he slept through it all thank God. The three of us started to cry as we heard the front door slam. He walked out. It was the first sign of relief we'd had in a long time. He wouldn't leave until his simple brothers showed up. After getting the children settled down, I had some time to myself. I never told anyone until this day what happened to André. And for the past 24 years of my life, I've carried around shame and guilt. He was a helpless child who had done no wrong to anyone.

As I sat on the couch, gazing out the window at the children playing outdoors, I observed people simply being themselves. I reached down inside and found "COURAGE" and I said to myself that I would no longer let this man do anything else to me. I would do everything possible to keep him off my ass. Every time I escaped, he would find me, snatch my children out of my arms, and throw them in the back seat of his car. Forcing me to return to his dark dungeon. Seven times I escaped and every time he would find me.

My mindset had changed. It was Kill or be Killed, plain and simple… I'm responsible for my children's safety. It is up to me to protect them. And, got dammit, that's what I'm going to do.

NO OTHER MOTHER FUCKER IS GOING TO HIT MY CHILD…

I needed a plan to escape again, fearing for my mother's safety. Determination surged within me, driving me to action. I had earned his trust, a fragile thread I would now exploit. "Grin and bear it," I whispered to myself, steeling my resolve.

Careful not to arouse suspicion, I penned a letter to the Department of Social Services, detailing Aunt Janie's abuse and our dire circumstances. With stealth, I located their address in the phone book, avoiding the risk of a traced call. Spotting a young boy playing nearby, between the houses, I slipped my letter to him out the side crack of the boarded-up window along with a dollar, take it straight to the mailbox, and dropped it in. Shuu, I whispered, don't tell anybody it's a secret.

Martha's sudden visit soon after raised suspicions. We played the charade of friendship as she inquired about my well-being. Seizing the opportunity, I asked about the money she owed me, cautioning her to wait until he was absent. Her assurances of friendship only fueled my trust.

In Martha, I confided my sorrows, seeking solace in her kindness. She offered her home as a sanctuary, a refuge from his violence.Tears welled in my eyes as she spoke with compassion, urging me to seek help from my family. But fear paralyzed me; the thought of his wrath sent shivers down my spine. I was afraid of losing my children, afraid of the state taking my baby from me, afraid of Aunt Janie's threats, and afraid for my mother.

Reluctantly, I shared my family's phone numbers with Martha, pleading for her aid. With promises to call on my behalf, she departed, leaving behind a glimmer of hope. Yet, the days stretched into months, with no word from Martha Bronner and uncertainty tightening its grip around my heart. A lie ain't nothing for a nigger to tell....

A lesson learned about friendship

It was now the last day of May, and I had grown very tired. My stomach was a lot smaller than when I carried my other sons. A reflection of horror and humiliation was on my face. I could no longer look myself in the eye. I was sitting outside on the porch with the children and accompanied by his watch dog brothers when he got out of his car. Strutting across the street like a peacock, he walked into Martha's house. It was just about dusk. I got up and went inside to give the boys a bath and get them ready for bed. They fell asleep while I was reading them a story. I went back onto the porch, looking at every car that rode down the street, praying that one, just one, would stop to get me. But they all rode past. I looked up to see Martha and him walking out of her house towards where I was sitting. My heart almost stopped beating. I got so nervous that I couldn't sit still. I ran but walked into the house. When I heard the screen door slam, I ran into the kitchen, fumbling around, pretending not to notice them.

I then grabbed myself a small kitchen knife and eased it into my pocket. Martha called out to me. "Pat," she said, "I'm sorry that it took me so long to pay back the money I borrowed from you."

"Here, sweetie," she said, holding her hand out, with the money rolled up inside. As I turned to walk towards her, I was shaking uncontrollably. She laid the money on the table and said, "I'm sorry, I forgot that you told me not to mention the money in front of him. I hope I didn't start any confusion." It all happened so fast; he then slapped me, and I fell across the kitchen table.

"You lying bitch," he said to me, "I'll kill you."

Martha hurried towards the door and yelled out to me, "I tried to call your family, like you asked me to, but the phone number's been changed."

"Help me!" I hollered, running towards the door where Martha was standing, "He's going to kill me."

And Martha ran out and slammed the door behind her. He grabbed me from behind and swung me into the next room, where I broke my fall by grabbing onto the dining room table. The room was dark, and the only light shining was from the kitchen. He cut off the light, and I drew the knife from my pocket.

"Come on, motherfucker, I'll kill you!" I said.

He laughed at me and pushed the table into my stomach, and the knife fell out of my hand as I fell and hit the floor. He ran over to me and started to beat me in the face and head with his fists. I again started to fight back, and it made him even angrier. He beat me and stomped me with his steel-toe work boots. I don't know how I got off the floor. I ran outside, screaming for help. The neighbors went inside their houses and closed their doors. I ran around the back of the house where the dog was barking, picked up a tree branch, and stood on the back side of the house when he came around. I hit that mother fucker across the face so hard that he drew blood; he grabbed me, threw me to the ground, and started kicking me all over. I covered my stomach, balling up into a knot. He was trying to kill my baby.

I crawled to get away from him, towards the backyard fence. It was dark, and I couldn't see the blood pouring down into my eyes.

"You wanna fight me, bitch?" he said to me in rage. "You wanna fight, bitch? I got something for you."

He took off and ran back to the house. I could hear him. "Oh God," I thought to myself, and I screamed, "my children! Oh God, my kids!" I started running back down towards the alley. When he jumped out and choked me from behind, I couldn't breathe; the weight from his body was that of a yoke. I started to collapse down to the ground, gasping for air. He beat me until I could no longer feel the blows; I was limp and numb with pain. He then ripped off my dress and raped me right there in the alley. The more I tried to fight, the more excited he became. Savage mother fucker. So, I lay there still, in the alley. It started to rain so hard that it washed the blood from my body down into the drain. He looked up at the sky and got off me.

Walking into the house and locking the door, I couldn't get to my kids. I ran across the street, house to house, beating on doors and holding my stomach in pain. I could barely walk; blood was dripping on my feet—I'd been beaten out of my shoes. My hair was snatched a loose and standing on top of my head. I cried out for help.

"Somebody help me, please, my children!"

He came outside with his shotgun and told me he would blow my head clean off my shoulders if I didn't stop waking his neighbors. He then grabbed me and threw me down the flight of stairs, kicking me in the face. Through the blood, I could see Martha look out her window; she pulled the shades down as he dragged me across the street. My hands were together, and I prayed. He beat me in the head with his enormous fists, trying to separate my hands, but I wouldn't let go.

June 4, 1972. Four days later, he made me go with him and another couple to Belle Isle Park to see a big attraction called the Giant Slide. Everybody was on the slide, and Choo-Choo wanted to go. So, I took him and André up a long flight of stairs. And my eyes searched the grounds for anyone I knew. They'd place a potato sack underneath you, give you a push, and you'd slide down. But not me; I came down standing up. Everyone was looking at my badly beaten body. My face carried the heel print from his work boot. I needed to see a doctor. My stomach had been hurting for the past four days, so I laid down in bed. I didn't feel good and wanted to lay back down. How I made it up the giant slide three times, I don't know. But I did. Whenever I would walk away to go to the bathroom or anywhere, he would stand guard over my son or son's holding them hostage.

After the giant slide, he wanted to go to the drive-in with this couple. I was afraid to say anything different. I didn't know or care what was showing at the movies. I kept feeling this pressure on my bladder, like I had to go to the bathroom. After going to the bathroom for the third time, I saw blood in my panties. When I got back to the car, he slapped me because I had been gone so long. I didn't even flinch. He hated that. I told him that I was in labor, and he said to me, "Well, you'll just have to hold it until the movie's over."

He drove me to the hospital and warned me that if I told anyone what happened, he would kill my children. I was to say I had been in a car accident if anyone asked. Desperate to protect my children, I agreed to his terms. Jim his friend mentioned that he and his girlfriend would be living at the man's house until they found a place of their own. His girlfriend said that she would keep an eye on my children. She touched my hand reassuringly. She knew the circumstances, but she didn't say anything because Jim was the man's good friend. I was afraid, so I asked her if she would promise to take care of my kids, and she said I'd stay there until you came back, and I would take care of your kids. Please don't let anyone take them from you. I promise, don't worry.

But I couldn't help but worry because she was a complete stranger.

Before I left, I bent down to kiss my sleeping children, whispering a prayer for their safety. Fear gnawed at me as I leaned on the car for support; he sped off, nearly hitting me. At the hospital, a nurse immediately wheeled me to the delivery room.

As I was changing, Dr. Hodari entered. "My name is Doctor Hodari. What happened to you?" he asked.

I hesitated, pulling the covers over my body.

"Don't do that," he insisted, gently pulling the covers away. "Who did this to you? Your husband?"

"No," I said, shaking my head. "I'm not married."

"Nurse, get Dr. Veba right now," he called out before turning back to me. "Who did this to you?" "I was in a car accident," I lied.

"Like hell you were, more like a train wreck," he retorted. "Are you in labor?" "I think so," I murmured.

"Get me her chart," he shouted to the nurse. "When is your baby due? Have you had prenatal care?"

"No," I admitted. "Because he wouldn't let me come to the clinic."

"So, you're telling me someone did this to you?" "No, it was a car accident," I repeated.

"Lay down and let me examine you," he instructed. After a moment, he added, "You're dilated." "I am?" I asked, surprised.

"Yes, and it won't be long now," he said, his voice softening. "But I'm not hurting at all, just mild cramping," I told him.

He placed his hand on my leg, his tone compassionate. "Haven't you been hurt enough?" God spared me the pain.

As the nurse brought in my chart, Dr. Hodari reassured me, "Relax; I'm going to get you some help. Do you have other children?"

"Yes, two boys," I responded. "Where are they now?" he probed.

"With that person who did this to you?" I dropped my head. "No, they're with my mother," I corrected quietly.

I could hear them whispering outside my door, demanding a complete update on my file to determine the whereabouts of my other children.

"There don't appear to be any broken bones," Dr. Hodari eventually said. "However, I can't be sure until after I've delivered your baby. Then, I'll order an X-ray."

"You know it's not going to do any good if you don't tell me who did this to you," he pressed. "I can't," I whispered, fear evident in my voice. "He'll kill my children."

"Who will kill your children? Where are they?" he asked urgently.

"I can't tell you," I pleaded. "Please don't ask. Do you understand that we're trying to help you?"

"Do you understand that I'm trying to keep my children alive?" I replied, desperation coloring every word.

"I said, 'Would you be willing to talk to someone else about this?'" she asked. I never answered her because I knew they would take my children once the state was involved.

"I don't want to upset you," she continued. "I'm just trying to help."

"I understand," I replied, appreciating her concern. With so much on my mind, I felt like I was going crazy. The thoughts of my children being with him and two total strangers were overwhelming. I wondered why I wasn't having hard labor like I did with my other children. Was my baby alright? I always felt him kicking, which I thought was a good sign.

I managed to go to the bathroom alone, without any help from the nurse, which was a small victory. I asked if I could use the phone to check on my children. I called his house and asked if the kids were alright. Jim's girlfriend answered.

"They dropped her off with the kids to go fishing. The children are asleep, so don't worry," she assured me. "I won't let anything happen to them. Although I know what's happening to you, don't talk now; you never know who's listening in.

God, I felt a sign of relief. "Thank you," I said to her. She introduced herself as Jackie Rivers and mentioned she was listed in the phone book. And true enough, she was—I looked it up.

Shortly thereafter, I delivered a five-pound, four-and-a-half-ounce baby boy at 2:06 PM on a Sunday afternoon. I chewed gum and had no complications during delivery. Everyone was kind to me. My baby was the smallest of my other two; he could fit in the palms of your hands. His head was covered with black hair that fit like a cap. His hands and feet were very large and long. He was so tiny, cute, and all mine. I loved him.

At feeding time, all the other babies would take a bottle, but he wouldn't. The doctors were concerned about his refusal to eat. That whole day after he was born, he did not take a bottle. The nurse came in to tell me that if he didn't eat, they might have to force-feed him through an IV. I was upset; I didn't understand what was wrong.

By Monday morning, my baby had lost a pound. He cried a lot, and when he wasn't crying, he wanted to sleep. I sat up on the side of the bed and held him in my arms. Nurse Pinkey showed me how to force-feed my son another way, by placing my fingertip over the nipple and milking it into his mouth. She held him while I washed my hands.

When Mrs. Washington walked into the room, she was the hospital social worker and an old friend.

"She said she wanted to talk to me after feeding time." I agreed. I fed him two ounces, burping him in between, but he threw it all up. He cried like he was in pain. I held him and rocked him until he fell asleep. Nurse Pinkey came back to get him because the pediatric doctors wanted to see him downstairs.

"Can I go with him?" I asked.

She smiled at me and said, "I don't think so. He'll be fine."

Mrs. Washington walked in with my lunch tray, which I thanked her for but quickly lost interest in. I had no appetite, so I lit a cigarette and stood by the window, looking out.

"So, Patricia," she began, her tone serious, "tell me what happened to you. How did you get here?" "I went into labor," I said simply.

"You know what I mean," she pressed. "We go too far back for this."

Reaching into her hospital jacket pocket, she pulled out a cigarette. "Tell me what happened," she insisted.

She lit her cigarette and sat down on the bed. "I can see that someone has been beating up on you, and I want to prevent this from happening to you again."

"First, she said, 'Tell me, are your children alright?'" "I'm praying to God that they are," I said. "Who's keeping them?" she asked, referring to the person who did this to me.

"Yes," I said, "and he may kill them if I tell them what happened."

"Girl, are you crazy?" she exclaimed. "Why did you leave your children with that maniac?" "I didn't leave them with him. He wouldn't let me take them with me," I explained.

"Do you promise not to tell anyone, at least until I get my children out of there?" I asked her earnestly.

Safely," I added. "Yes," she agreed.

I told her what happened, from the beginning to the end. She said, "I'm going to see what I can do to help you. Have you gone to the police?"

"For what?" I retorted. "They know he beat me up. And they did nothing to help me. They'll take my children away from me. Do you understand?" I asked her. I'm too young to have my children, and my aunt is my guardian, and she has the will to take my children from me.

"You're right," she said. "If they find out…"

"I'm going to drop by the house to see if they're alright, pretending not to know your circumstances," she said, "just to make sure they're okay."

"No," I said so loudly that it woke up my roommate's baby. "You can't. Then he'll know I told you."

"Listen," she said, "haven't I always helped you?" I nodded my head, yes. "Don't you want to know if they're alright?" she pressed.

"Yes," I admitted.

"Then trust me. Will you do that?" she asked and leaned over to hug and kiss me on the cheek.

That was the first sign of kindness from anyone in a long time. "Now, I'm going over there right now, on my lunch break. I'll take a friend with me; this way, he'll think twice before harming those kids. Like a safety net," she explained.

So, I wrote down the address and his name and gave them to her. "Now don't worry, I'll be right back."

And she walked out. All I could do was pray that everything went okay. After she walked out, Aunt Janie walked in, saying that she had to call the house to find out I was in the hospital, and she came to see how I was doing. She took some papers out of her purse.

"Just sign your name," she said. I refused. She looked shocked.

"I'm going to have to call your worker," she threatened, "and tell them everything if you don't. I'll have your children away."

"Well, let them take them," I said to her, "because I'm not signing a damn thing. And furthermore," I said, "Get the hell out of my room, and don't ever come near me again."

She jumped up off my bed, looked at me with her big bulging eyes, and said, "That's why he beats your ass like he does." And that's why I told him where you were all those times. Yeah, well you won't get that chance anymore. I said.

I stood up and walked towards her.

"No," I said to Aunt Janie, "the reason he beats my ass is because of you."

She stormed out, leaving her umbrella behind. So, I grabbed it, hurried to the door, and threw it down the hallway, muttering "you bitch" under my breath. I splashed my face with cool water to calm down and walked back to the doorway. I saw Nurse Pinkey, and she said, "He is still being seen by the doctors."

"Was he crying?" I asked.

"When I saw him, he was still asleep," she said. "I will bring him to you as soon as the doctors finish running tests."

At 3:35 PM, Nurse Pinkey entered, cradling my baby, already asleep and snug in his blanket. "Is he alright?" I asked, taking him anxiously. "He's losing weight quite rapidly," she said. "He's already lost another ounce. The doctors will be in to see you. Let's wake him up and see if he'll eat for you."

"Is he going to die?" I whispered.

"Oh, honey," she said, placing a comforting hand on my shoulder. "I certainly hope not."

"I love him so much," I confessed, tears welling. "Even before he was born, I loved him. I tried to protect him."

"I know, honey," she said softly. "All you can do is pray."

As I watched my baby sleep, I silently prayed for my children. I begged God for guidance and forgiveness. I felt unworthy of His love, but I pleaded for mercy and for the strength to be a good mother.

◈◈

Mrs. Washington entered my room, her expression solemn. Fear gripped me until she spoke. "The kids are fine," she assured me. Relief washed over me. "Where were they?"

"A lady answered the door," she explained. "She had your youngest child in her arms. I told her I was from the hospital on a routine check."

"Did she believe you?"

"Yes," Mrs. Washington nodded. "Your son was inside, eating a sandwich. The house was clean. I didn't stay long. No one else seemed to be home."

"Did you ask about her?"

"Yes," Mrs. Washington replied. "She said she was keeping the kids for a friend in labor. I left my card with her."

"That's a relief," I said. "The kids are okay."

"I found out enough about her," Mrs. Washington added. "But I'll keep an eye on things." "Thank you," I said, embracing her. "I'll never forget this."

"Don't thank me yet," she warned. "I haven't done anything."

"You checked on my children," I insisted. "That means everything to us."

"You're worth saving," Mrs. Washington said, though her expression was troubled. "But I won't involve the authorities. I'll find another way to help you."

After she left, I fed my baby, though he took only an ounce of milk.

God Answers Prayers

I tossed and turned all night, pacing between the nursery and my room, smoking cigarettes one after another. Thoughts swirled in my mind until I finally lay down around five o'clock in the morning, only to be awakened by a nurse drawing my blood. After she pricked my arm, sleep eluded me, so I rose, tidied my bed, and took a sponge bath and shower. The swelling in my face was receding; my body seemed to be on the mend.

By 7:00 AM, they were bringing the babies. I stood in the doorway, eagerly awaiting my son's arrival. But the nurse informed me I had to be in bed before I could receive him. Rushing back to bed, I complied. Everyone else seemed to be getting their babies, but not me. All the babies were feeding except mine. I buzzed the nurse, but there was no response. Panicking, I leaped out of bed, forgetting about the stitches in my buttocks, and hurt myself. I dashed to the nurses' station, searching for Nurse Pinky, but she was nowhere to be found. Frantically, I asked anyone I could find about my baby's whereabouts, but they all seemed oblivious to my presence.

I raced to the nursery, tears streaming down my face. He wasn't there. All the other babies were with their mothers. "Oh God," I whispered, the dread settling in. I hurried back to my room, my stomach churning with grief. I couldn't comprehend anything except that my baby might be dead. A hollow ache gnawed at the depths of my soul. I sprinted, desperate for answers, when a nurse informed me that I couldn't be on the floor while the babies were being attended to. She grabbed my arm to guide me back, but I recoiled. "Don't touch me," I snapped, running back to the nurses' station.

Nurse Pinky appeared and enveloped me in a hug. "Where's my baby?" I demanded, trying to break free from her embrace. She wrapped an arm around my waist, guiding me toward the room. "You need to lie down," she said softly. "The doctor will be in to talk to you."

"I can't," I protested. "Where is my baby?"

"I can't tell you anything," she replied gently, leading me back to the room. "I can't sit down," I cried. "Is my baby dead?"

Chapter 14

"By the Grace of God"

The doctors walked in, and Nurse Pinky walked out. One doctor sat down on the side of my bed; the other remained standing.

"We have some good news and some bad news," one said. "Is my baby alright? Is he alive?" I asked.

The doctor said, "What would give you any indication that he wasn't?"

"Because they brought everybody else's baby but mine. If he's alright, where is he?" I said. "Your baby should be back in the nursery by now," he said.

"But I looked everywhere for him, and I couldn't find him. I started crying. I asked everyone about him, and nobody told me anything," I said.

"Your baby is very sick. We think that he may have a problem with his stomach. He doesn't digest his food like he's supposed to. We have to study the tests we ran on him today. Also, have you noticed a yellow tint to your baby's complexion?"

"No," I said. "I hadn't noticed anything other than him not wanting to eat." "He has jaundice. His eyes and hands are yellow."

"Is that why he's been vomiting?" I said.

"That we don't know yet," he said. "We're going to check it out."

"Then," I said, "I've heard of yellow jaundice, but I never knew much about it. How did he get it?"

"I'm not sure," he said. "Sometimes it's contracted from other babies. We're going to do two things here. One, we're going to put your baby in isolation, away from the other babies, and start him on antibiotics. Two, we're going to change his formula and see if he can keep it down."

"You're going to put my baby in isolation, by himself?" I said.

"Yes," he said. "For forty-eight hours, as a safeguard period, to see how he responds to the treatment. If jaundice is not caught in time, it will attack the liver and other vital organs. It is contagious and dangerous if not treated properly. We are also concerned about his rapid weight loss."

"Hi, I'm Doctor Morgan," he said, butting in. "And I'll also be treating your son," he said, extending his hand out for me to shake. "We'd like to get him stabilized before sending him home. You'll probably be discharged tomorrow, but your baby will have to remain in the hospital for a few more days. You can come and visit him whenever you want to."

"I'm not leaving my baby in the hospital," I said. "When I leave, I'm taking him with me."

"Well, he's under five pounds, and we can't discharge him until he's at least five pounds. If you decide to take him home, you'll have to sign a consent form releasing the hospital from any responsibility. But we still have another day or two before we see if he's improving," he said. "I'll arrange for you to have special feeding hours with your son, and we'll take it from there. Do you have any questions for me?" Doctor Morgan said.

"Yes," I said. "Is my baby going to die?"

"I can't answer that," he said. "It depends on how he responds to the treatment. Anything's possible. I'm sorry," he said. I have a lump in my throat. "Can I see my baby?" I asked.

"Let us get him ready," he said, "and I'll send the nurse for you."

The night of June 6, 1972. I had a special feeding time with my son. When I walked into the room, he was just lying there, staring into space. I walked over to him and picked him up. I held him very close to me, in my arms. I didn't say anything to him at first. I just held on to him, rocking him in my arms. I felt like crying, but I knew it wasn't the time.

I looked at his face. He somehow reminded me of a weeping willow, softly fighting his way through the mean wind that blows no good. In front of my son, I knew then that I had to stand up with my son and be the backbone that my mother was to me. I had to face the world as she did, with courage.

He was a beautiful little boy with a sad look in his eyes. To the world, don't mean shit if you don't have the courage to live. I started talking to him and said, "I love you very much, and I'm proud of you. You're a real trooper. That means you're a fighter, a strong little boy. You may feel that nobody loves you or cares that you've arrived, but that's just not true. We waited a long time for you, your brothers, and me to get here. And I speak as your mother on behalf of your brothers; the wait was well worth it. You're probably thinking that things were pretty bad for you on the inside. So, why would you want to come into this world and stay? Well, the answer to that question, my dear, is obvious. We love you, and God loves you, and my life would never be the same without you. Please stay with me," I said to him. "And I promise you that I will never let anyone else hurt you again. I will do everything in my power to protect you."

As he lay there looking up at me, as though he understood my every word, his eyes, as well as mine, filled with water, and the tears rolled down his face. He understood. That evening, he drank an ounce of milk and didn't throw it up. I walked to my room, lay down in bed, and dreamed of the time I first met God. I was just 7 years old. And in this dream, I relived my experiences with God all over again. I remember listening to God chastise me, and I begged for his forgiveness for what was to come. From that day forward, I developed a relationship with him, and I accepted him as my lord and savior, whom I shall not fear.

June 7, 1972: The nurses came into my room to wake me up, but I was already awake, sitting on the side of my bed. Doctor Hodari had ordered X-rays and other tests for me. So, I knew that I wasn't going home that day. Before taking me down to the X-ray, I asked if the nurse would stop me from going to the nursery to see my baby. As always, he was sleeping. I wanted to talk with Dr. Hodari to see if I could breastfeed. I knew I had to wait until after the tests came back. After lunch, I walked to the nursery, where I ran into Mrs. Washington.

"I was down to your room looking for you; how are you feeling?" she said. "Pretty good," I said, "just a little sore."

"I read your baby's chart," she said, "and he'll be fine. Just pray to God; He knows what to do."

As we turned to walk away from the nursery, "I've been working on your case diligently," she said. "I've written letters to everyone involved and some letters to those I want to get involved with. She paused. "I'm going to get to the bottom of this. And I know I'm in for a fight. My coworker, Mrs. Shimanski, is also working on the case."

"She knows we have to protect those children, so she'll be very careful in what she says and who she talks to."

"God bless you," I said to her. "He already has," she said.

"Oh yeah," she said as she turned to walk away, "when are you getting out of here?" "I don't know," I said.

"Well, we're going to pay your kids another visit," she said. "Don't worry. I'll be careful." Throwing up her hand and waving goodbye.

I walked back to my room, where I waited for Dr. Hodari to come. Finally, after waiting for three hours, he walked in.

"Yes, my dear," he said to me.

"Dr. Hodari," I said, "can I breastfeed my son?"

"No," he said to me. "It would be a wonderful idea, but your body has been through too much trauma, and I wouldn't recommend it."

"What is trauma?" I said to him.

"All of these beatings that you've been through. It's too much," he said, holding his head down in shame. He was embarrassed for me and for myself.

s "We looked at your test results and X-rays and found no broken bones this time. However, you have anemia. Do you understand what that means?"

"Yes," I answered.

"Good," he said, "then we are going to start treatment today." "Okay," I said, "do you know when I'll be able to go home?"

"Yes," he said, "maybe tomorrow you can go home. I'll write a prescription for you and have the nurse set up your return visit."

"Thank you," I said to him. "You're welcome," he said.

I lit a cigarette and picked up the phone. "Hello," Jackie answered. "Hello," I said. "It's me, Pat. Can you talk?" "Yes," she said. "How are you doing?"

"Fine," she said, "everything is fine." "Is he standing around?" I asked. "Yep, right here," she said.

"Don't tell him I'm on the phone. Can you answer one more question?"
"Huh, huh," she mumbled.

"Are my kids alright?" I said.

"Yes, it is a beautiful day outside," she said. "A beautiful day.

Day 4. I've been up since the crack of dawn, taking my bath and standing by the nursery window, waiting for my baby to wake up for his feeding. While standing there, Nurse Pinky threw up her hand to me, waving from inside the nursery. I could read her lips as she said, 'I've got something good to tell you, but you got to go back to bed.' Waving her hand to me, I'll be down. So, I waited in my room, and it wasn't long before she walked in with my baby in her arms.

"The doctor said that he no longer has to be isolated and that you can feed him right here from your room."

"That's wonderful," I said to her, eagerly taking him from her arms. "Now he can feel that closeness from me that he needs."

"He is still underweight," she said. "I weighed him this morning, and he is well under five pounds, and that's what he'll need to weigh before you can take him home."

"How much does he weigh?" I said to her.

"Not enough," she said. "How much is not enough?" I said, "He weighs only four pounds and two ounces, and that's not enough for him to leave yet. If you leave today, you'll have to come and visit him here," she said.

"I can't," I said to Nurse Pinky. "If I leave, I'll have to take him with me. There's just no way I'm leaving him here, not without me."

"You can't take him, sweetie," she said.

"I'm taking my son home with me," I said.

"Well, you'll have to sign him out of here, releasing the hospital from any responsibilities," she said. "Yes, I said; they told me."

"Well, we don't even know if you're going home today anyway," she said. "What's his name? No one's been here for me to name him."

I said, "Let me go and call downstairs and find out why."

She said that after staying gone for several hours, a lady walked in and said that she was there to get his name for the birth certificate. So, I asked her if I could have until this afternoon to think of one. She was agreeable and apologetic for being so late. "We've never had so many babies born at one time," she said. "I'll leave the papers here for you to sign." The doctors came in and asked me not to sign him out, but that I was free to come and see him whenever I wanted to. But I told him I prayed over it and was trusting the Lord with this decision. I was afraid, but every day I walked in faith. I signed him out.

I named him Terrance, and he was small enough to sleep inside the dresser drawer, and when I wasn't holding him, that's where he slept. His older brother seemed to like him; André didn't seem to care. They were both babies, and they were only eleven months apart. I now had two, both in diapers, both on a bottle, both not walking. He cried all the time. I would cut his formula with water twice so that he was able to keep it down. I also put cod liver oil in his formula and gave him a small dose of Father John's or Scott's emulsion every other day. He was on baby vitamins, and after the third week, I started to spoon-feed him baby cereal. At first, like his formula, he wouldn't take it, but I continued to force-feed him, day in and day out, watching him very closely.

Terrance had his days and nights mixed up. And I had a hard time trying to put him on schedule with his brothers. Terrance was just as unhappy as everyone else in the house, and it showed. I felt like I was walking on eggshells, afraid if the baby cried too much or too loud, I would get the shit beat out of me. I was so busy with the kids that I always had something to do for them. Most of my time was spent in the bathtub, washing their clothes by hand, using only bar soap. My back would ache so bad sometimes that I could hardly walk. Most times, I would forget to take my vitamins or even remember to take care of myself. As I look back now, I know that I didn't care or love me, only because nobody loved or cared about me. I blamed myself for everything that had gone wrong in my seventeen years in this world. Therefore, I became self-sacrificing and self-destructive. I found comfort in Tyrone Davis song "Without you in my life" I was in a dark funk. I was able to draw strength and pass it on to my baby: encouraging him to live..

The lyrics spoke volumes to me. I played it over and over on his HI- FI when he wasn't home.

This had been a bad day for me; my left eye jumped all day long. I could feel the tension building in the house. As I tried to stay out of his way, I took the kids into the room and closed the door. I could hear him breathing outside of the door while he stood there listening to the conversation that I was having with my children.

Finally, he left the house, and I could breathe. I had been looking for a wind-up radio clock that had once belonged to Choo-Choo. I noticed that whenever Terrance heard music, he would go to sleep, and whenever I would turn the radio down or off, he'd wake up. This little radio that I was looking for played the melody "The Mouse Ran Up the Clock," and it showed pictures of the little mouse as it turned around. I found the clock hidden behind some towels in the buffet. I didn't think anything of it; I just thought that Choo-Choo threw it inside the drawer until I found a picture of my mother wrapped in a piece of paper underneath the clock. Her address and phone number were on it. As I looked further, I could see where she had tried to write me a letter. It looked like a child's scribble at first, until I recognized the handwriting of my mother. There was no letter inside, just the envelope. I continued to look further into the drawer when I found an envelope addressed to me. It had been opened, and inside were four checks with my name on them. I put them back in a hurry, not knowing when he was coming home. I looked out of the window to see him walking up the walkway. I grabbed the radio off the table and put it back as well. I ran into the bedroom and eased the door shut. I heard him walk in and go into the kitchen and open up a beer. Shivers overcame my body as he opened the bedroom door and looked in.

I was terrified of him.

"What do you think you're doing?" he said. "Nothing," I said to him.

"Why are you sitting here in this hot bedroom with your kids, acting like you're scared to come out? Do you know it's 95 degrees outside?" he said. "You're always sitting somewhere with those fucking kids. Don't you think they get sick of you fucking with them all the time?" He yelled.

"No," I said. Standing up to him… Because my mind was made up to kill him.

"Well, what do you know?" He said this as he walked out of the room and slammed the door.

I heard him answer the phone and say, "Yeah, I'll be ready to go fishing around six o'clock this evening, but I've gotta do something first."

I ran to the door to make sure that he left, then I went to the buffet cabinet and got the checks. I took them out and put the envelope back. I hid them inside the diaper bag. I had no intention of packing anything. I was playing it cool. I found my jar where I had stashed $55.40. I took it out, put it in with the checks, and put the diaper bag back on the bedroom shelf. It was 3:35pm, and I went into the kitchen to fix the kids a snack. I woke them up to feed them. I sponged their faces and hands off and sat them at the table to eat vegetable soup and grilled cheese sandwiches. They were eating so slowly, and I kept watching the clock and listening for him to come in.

I wanted to feed the baby his bottle before he came back because of his crying. The way I was sitting at the dining room table, I could see him if he came in. At 5:50 p.m., his car pulled up, and he walked in the door. The baby had just woken up and was crying, as most babies do when they first wake up. I was trying to quiet him down when he said to me, "Hand him to me. I'll quiet the little motherfucker down." As he tried to reach for my baby, I pulled back, and he slapped me with the back of his hand. I huddled my body over my baby to break the fall.

He knocked me down again and hovered his body over top of me, daring me to get up. He began beating me in the head and face with his fist. I was bloody. This savage mother fucker beat me with that belt all over my body—my back, hands, and face. There's blood everywhere. I was huddled down on my knees, backed down in a corner. He beat me across my back until my skin split open. Someone heard my cry; someone heard me calling for help; they called the police. He had knocked me out. When I came, he was on top of me, still punching me in the head.

He hit me so hard that my nose started bleeding. Choo-Choo ran out of the room and over to him with his fists bawled up, punching him and crying. "Leave my mama alone." I remember partially seeing him with something down by his side. And he slapped me across the face with it. I grabbed my face and went down.

We struggled when he swung the big black leather belt towards Choo-Choo, and I grabbed it.

He then turned away from me and lunged towards Choo-Choo again, as I turned and lunged towards him to protect my son with my baby in my arms. He turned towards me and hit me so hard with his fist that I fell on the dining room table. I scrambled up off the floor, running towards Choo-Choo to take him into the room, telling him to stay in there and not to come out. All of the children were crying by this time, as I ran out of the door and slammed it inside for safety. He was coming behind me, grabbed me, and threw me to the floor as he started to kick and stomp me in the hallway. I tried to crawl to the telephone for help when he snatched it out of my hand and hit me in the head with it. I was laying up under the dining room table, trying to see my way off the floor, when Choo-Choo came to the door, screaming and crying again.

"Leave my mama alone." I got up to run to the door when he came from behind and hit me in the back of my head with his fist. All I could remember from that point on was him taking his belt off, folding it over, and saying as he stood over me, "You need somebody to beat your ass."

He started to savagely beat me with the belt across my face, my breasts, and my arms. As I crawled to get up off the floor, I couldn't. He then kicked me with his boots in the back of my head. I fell forward on my face. I was grabbing and clawing the walls, trying to stand up to get my balance, but I kept slipping and falling back down in my own blood. I was screaming and gurgling with blood in my throat, "Somebody help me; call the police; he's trying to kill me." As I crawled on my hands and knees towards my bedroom door, I made it to the open window and pulled myself up where I could see the children and people standing outside the front door.

"Help me, please; he's trying to kill me." He then hit me so hard with the belt that it wrapped around my neck like a whip and pulled me down. I was wedged in the corner of the wall, balled up in a fetal position. I huddled myself as he stood up over me, beating me like the big bad man he was. I could hear my skin being ripped apart from my body.

He beat me so long that I passed out. And when I came, he was still standing over me, beating me. I heard my savior come. God sent the ambulance; I heard the siren and saw the flashing lights reflecting on the bedroom wall. He ran like the coward he was to close the door. But they were already inside. They pushed their way through and started working on me immediately. As they placed me on the stretcher and took me out, I cried to them, "Get my kids, get my kids; they're in the bedroom."

"The diaper bag, please get the diaper bag." I tried to get off the stretcher to grab my kids and the diaper bag, but the ambulance attendant said, "Tell me where it is, and I will get it." They placed all three of my children in the ambulance with me, along with the diaper bag. As we drove away from the house, I looked out the window to see him standing on the porch, next to the belt that he had hung out to dry. He hung the belt on the porch plant hanger for all to see. The big bad man he was.

"It's all over but the shouting."

I don't even remember my trip down to the hospital. I've tried so often to recall, but I can only remember a feeling of safety and freedom. I was rushed off the stretcher and into Henry Ford Hospital's emergency room, where I was greeted by a host of doctors and nurses working on me, trying to save my life. I was in and out of consciousness as they asked me many questions about what happened. They wanted to know my name. They wanted to know my next of kin. I gave them Nina's information. I wanted to go to sleep, but every time I dozed off, they would ask me another question or say to me, "No, honey, you can't go to sleep; you have head trauma. We're trying to see where the blood is coming from."

I remember asking my kids, and someone said that they were alright, sitting in the playroom, and that they called the pantry to get them something to eat and my baby a bottle. I remember saying to them, "I have three sons; are they all here with me?" and the nurse said yes.

"Please watch my children," I said. "Don't let him get to them."

"Nobody's going to get your kids," the doctor told me. "We're waiting for the social worker to come." "Is there someone you want us to call for you?" the nurse asked.

"Yes, please call Mrs. Washington at Detroit Memorial Hospital," I said to her, my words slurring. "Tell her my name and that my kids are here and what happened to me; ask her to come.

She's a friend, please."

"I will pass this information on right away," she said. "Thank you," I said in a whisper.

I was then turned over onto my side while someone held my bloody head, which had no feeling in it, in their hands while someone else placed a collar on my neck. The nurses asked me if I could undress myself, and I told them yes, I thought so. I pushed my way up off the bed, with their help, to get in a sitting position to undress myself. Looking down at the buttons on my shirt, I noticed my hands were cut up and had dried blood all over them.

I wasn't able to close them; they were swollen so bad they looked like the hands of a veteran junkie. For a moment, I hung my head down low, in shame and despair. I started to cry—a cry out loud that shook my soul.

When the nurse reached out to me with a warm smile and said, "That's okay, I'll help you," She tried to, but she couldn't get my shirt off, and they had to cut the shirt off my body; the blood had dried and stuck to my back. They called for someone to take pictures of me over and over again.

I don't know how much time had elapsed, but when I regained full consciousness, I was on my way back from the X-ray. My hand had an IV in it, and they had pumped blood from my stomach. I was feeling like hell, inside and out. Although I cried over what had happened,

I was determined not to let it get me all the way down. It was my cross to bear, and no matter how heavy the weight, I had to carry it. Jesus carried his. In no way am I comparing myself to him; I'm just saying who am I not to suffer, for Jesus, who was without sin, suffered and died for the sins of the world. This was another obstacle that I was not going to let stand in my way. I knew that I would be forced to live with the haunting memories of the days gone by, but I was so grateful to God for sparing not only my life but my children's lives as well. I was alive, and I had a lot to be thankful for. I still had a chance. The road that I would choose to travel would have to be carefully hand-picked.

There was still some fight left in me, buried deep below. I just wanted to find peace and solitude with myself and let the healing begin.

With that thought in mind, I wanted to be with my kids, and I did just that. The nurses put me and my kids in touch with each other. I hugged and kissed every last one of them. We were placed in a room together with two beds and a cot to sleep on, but I put all my kids in bed with me, and we stayed there all night. The nurses checked on me throughout the night and offered to help me with my kids. The nurses tried to feed my baby, but he wouldn't take the bottle from anyone else but me. He wasn't crying, but I knew that he hadn't eaten. So, I sat up on the side of the bed, barely able to use my hands. I picked Terrance up in my arms and asked Choo-Choo to get his bottle out of the diaper bag. "Please, baby," I said to him. "I need your help now, okay?" He looked up at me with his pretty brown eyes and said, "Yes, mama." He was a polite little boy, and with his help, I held the bottle by the nipple with my fingertips under the water and warmed it, and Choo-Choo held the bottle in his baby brother's mouth, and we fed him together.

I was up and down that whole night, reliving the day before. It played like a tape recording inside my brain, over and over. By the time morning came, the children were sleeping peacefully, and I was tired and sore. I felt worn out; the swelling had set in, and I looked like hell. A hospital social worker came in to talk to me. I told her that I didn't want to talk in front of the kids. I was hoping they wouldn't remember, but I didn't want to refresh their memories in case they had. So, we stepped out into the hallway to talk, and I remember not being able to relax myself. I was really jittery and nervous, looking around for him to walk up at any time. I was looking for a place to hide. Mrs. Martin, the social worker, noticed my uneasiness and told me to relax, saying that he couldn't find me here. But I knew that was a lie being told. If a person was so full of hate that he wanted you dead, it wouldn't be hard to find me. I had a gut feeling—the same feeling I had when I first laid eyes on him—only this time it made me vomit. I was shaking so badly that Mrs. Martin had to call the nurse to help me. They spoke words of comfort, but it didn't help; the feeling was there.

Mrs. Martin said that she would arrange for me to get an apartment in the infamous Jeffries Projects, the slum of slums. I didn't know which was worse: the Jeffries Projects or the Brewster Projects. In my opinion— which is just like an asshole, since everybody's got one—they were both a half-step up from the alley. But again, who was I? That day, I was discharged from the hospital with the understanding that I was to go over to the housing office at Jeffries Projects the next day. "Be there at 8:00am sharp," Mrs. Martin had said to me, "or you may not get that apartment. You know there's a long waiting list, and you really got lucky."

I just looked at her and said, "Thank you." I knew what I was in store for. I was given a night's stay at the Rio Grande Motel down on West Grand Blvd. and Linwood, a motel that specialized in everything from drugs to prostitution and plenty of roaches. I had to take my chances. I had also been given an emergency furniture voucher to take to any furniture store that would accept it.

The value was worth two hundred and fifty dollars, and it was listed in order to buy three beds, a kitchen table and four chairs, or a stove and refrigerator. Thank God the apartment came with a stove and refrigerator, because I was already up shit's creek without a paddle.

Mrs. Martin had also given me transportation in a cab down to the motel—no further than that was written on the order. So, what was I going to do for food for my kids? I persuaded the cab driver to take me over to the Chene grocery store, where Aunt Janie had been cashing my checks, to cash the checks that I had in the diaper bag. The cab driver was a nice old man and said to me that he had daughters my age and that he would want someone to help them if they ever needed it. I took my children inside the store with me as everyone looked at me like I was a monster. I tried to hide my face and hands, but I couldn't. My body was so stiff that I could hardly walk, let alone bend down to get the food off the shelves for my kids. The man who owned the store didn't hesitate to cash all four of my checks for me, and I told him that I had been beaten up and that my aunt Janie was responsible for the beatings.

He just shook his head in shame for me and told his son to help me to the cab with my bags. He didn't even take out a check-cashing fee. I don't know if he was just being nice or was distracted by the way I looked. On my way out of the store, I walked right upon Aunt Janie, who I couldn't see well as my vision was limited in both my eyes, and she didn't even recognize me. On my way back to the motel, I put my money in my shoe like my mother had always told me to do. And I had the driver take me to Virley Coulter's furniture store on Chene and Gratiot. I gave him the voucher, picked everything out, and he said that he would deliver everything tomorrow. He and his brother saw me all beat up.

My eyes hurt me so badly that I could hardly see out of them. I wanted to close them but was afraid they wouldn't open again. It was a long ride back, and the kids had fallen asleep from the ride. I offered to pay the driver more for the trip and a five-dollar tip, but he would not accept it. "You need that money for your kids to eat with," he said, and he offered to come back and take me to the Jeffries Projects the next day. "Only if you let me pay you," I said. "You got a deal," he replied. "I'll see you at 7:00." "Thank you," I said to him. I was barely able to get inside the motel with the kids and two bags. The cab driver once again offered his help, but he wasn't able to; you could tell he was just being kind. "I'll make it," I said to him. "Thank you anyway. I'll see you tomorrow.

"Tomorrow didn't come fast enough. The doors slammed all night; people were in and out, back and forth, as I watched, afraid for my safety. I was so, and once again I sat up, watching over my children with one eye on them and the other on the rats and roaches that were taking over the room, peeking out the window, afraid to look.

Chapter 15

"God Gave Me a Second Wind"

Time passed in 1973.

Finally, I thought I got away from him… or so I thought. I was 17 and lived in the Jeffries Project on Gibson Street with my three sons. Terrance was my baby boy, and he wasn't walking yet; he was still in a stroller. I took my children out for a walk before their nap. When we returned to the 10th floor, I pushed the front door shut, but it didn't catch and lock.

I went to push it shut, and the man pushed the door open with such force that it scared my baby.

Terrance started to cry. I ran for Terrance, and the man ran for me. He grabbed me, and we started to fight. He turned me loose and went for my sons. I jumped on his back, and he threw me to the floor.

He grabbed me and started to beat me throughout the small apartment. He was dragging me like a mop across the floor. He kept going for my kids, and I kept fighting him. He hit me so hard in the stomach that I dropped to my knees. He grabbed me and dragged me into the bathroom, and he slammed my head against the toilet bowl. He stood up over me and held my head underwater. Flushing the toilet profusely. His hands kept slipping from all the blood that was coming from my head. I was losing consciousness. My head was submerged in water. I heard my mama calling my name from afar." Pat, Pat" Thank you, Lord! Somehow, I caught a second wind with my arms stretched out like a bird in flight. I was able to catch that mother fucker in between his legs, and I clamped down. He hollered like a BITCH. The BITCH he was.

He turned me loose. Before I could catch my breath, he grabbed me, threw me into the living room, and straddled me. With both knees, he had my arms pinned down. I was trying to fight him and breathe at the same time. He was unzipping his pants, sitting in my chest, trying to force his penis into my mouth. What the fuck is this? In my mind, I said, I bit down and kept my mouth shut. We struggled. I couldn't see him; I felt his hand movement. He did what he set out to do. He masturbated in my face. I continued to fight when some man heard me screaming for my life. Someone heard the whole ordeal. Thank you, God, I said in my mind. He shouted up to him. Leave that girl alone. If you want to fight, fight a man.

"You son of a bitch."

And he got up off me and ran like the punk-ass coward that he was. I have never seen him or his two little girls again. My Prayer for him was this…I ask God to burn him up alive and let me live to see it on the news, or let him live with longsuffering wanting to die and can't.

Vengeance is mine. Romans: 12-19

July 22, 1973

I made up my mind to leave—not because of the man; God had other plans for him.

But because I wanted to make a better life for my son's. Thinking only of their future, what would they become if I raised them in the projects? What kind of mother would I be if I didn't try to give them a better life? "Nothing beats a failure but a try."

I had sold the little furniture that I owned in my apartment to a married couple who owned their own party store on Detroit's west side. Although the furniture wasn't new, it had been well kept. I was only asking for two hundred and fifty dollars for everything. The husband dropped his head in shame when he heard his wife offer me one hundred and twenty-five dollars, with a promise to mail me the remaining balance once I got settled.

I was so desperate to get out of there that I accepted the money. I stayed up all night thinking, dreaming, and praying, getting things ready for our trip to a new life. I gave my children a bath along with dinner. I read them a book, we said our prayers, and when they fell asleep, I washed their clothes—socks and underwear—by hand. I hung them on the oven stove until they dried. At the crack of dawn, I was still ironing creases into their pants. I brushed their teeth, gave them breakfast, put their new jackets on, and called a cab.

I packed peanut butter and jelly sandwiches, boiled eggs, bologna sandwiches, cheese crackers, fresh fruit, coloring books, crayons, and games for them to play with. I called Amtrak Train Station and priced a one-way ticket to San Jose, California. Worst come to worst; I could always come back to this hellhole. Nothing beats a failure but a try, and I knew I had to do just that— try. I had to try and give them a better life. My children were the right ages to ride free, which was a blessing. I was seventeen years old with three babies—one clinging to my hip, one in my arm, and one in my hand. I left Detroit with $38.00 in my pocket. Not knowing what life challenges had to offer or what I would have to face, I knew that I had to try. How many uphill battles I would have to fight didn't matter to me. But what did matter was that any other situation had to be better than the one I was in. I was committed and determined.

Early that morning, the same cab driver drove us to the train station on Michigan Avenue. It was a dark, misty morning, with the sun trying to peek out behind the cloudy sky that surrounded the Motor City. I was still shaken up and afraid that he was somewhere lurking around or that Aunt Janie had called the police on me. But I was not going to let it steal my joy of wanting a new life for my children and of wanting to see them grow up into fine young men who would make any mother proud to call them her sons. I was going to enjoy this ride. I never wanted to forget the feeling of being free.

As I looked at the city that I was leaving behind, a place that I had called home, I no longer felt welcome. The living conditions for the poor were in serious trouble; housing was in the slums of the city. The school system wasn't productive enough if you just happened to live on the wrong side of town. There was so much heartache and bad memories for me that I wanted out. I had had my share of Detroit. I started to cry tears of relief. For the moment, it felt good. I turned and looked over at my sons, who sat quietly sleeping. My eyes were so flooded with tears that they streamed down my face and rolled down my neck. A 1972 song came to my heart by the Just Brothers: "Things Will Be Better Tomorrow."

I knew that God would take care of us as He had in the past. I cracked my window to smell the fresh air, hearing the sound of water bouncing from the tires of the cab as we rode down the cobblestone street. This street was here when my mother and her family first arrived in Detroit back in 1926. All the Black people that came here from the South rode on the very same train tracks. Parts of the Underground Railroad that led many slaves to freedom were now located in Greektown, in downtown Detroit. The church that actually housed and fed the newly freed slaves was still standing. The tracks and the church can still be seen on Monroe Street.

Michigan Avenue is one of the few streets left bearing Detroit's trademark. Approaching Trumbell Street off I-94, we rode right past the Tiger Stadium. Eager Detroit fans were starting to form a line to buy tickets for the next Tigers game.

A few more blocks, and we were there. I paid the driver and hurried inside. I figured if he was going to attack me again, he would have to do it there. Being the coward that he was, I didn't see it happening. So, I relaxed. I could feel the burdens lifting from my shoulders as we boarded the train. I could feel the freshness of my new life with us. I could envision their future.

We moved to San Jose, California.

We sat near the front entrance, in plain sight to be seen. After being there for around thirty minutes, it was time to board. Together, we held hands and walked through the train. The porters helped us on, locked the doors, and we pulled away. I took the first two seats facing each other so the kids could have plenty of room to stretch out and play.

The further away we got, the more I relaxed. What I like about the train is that you can get up and walk around. We went to the dining car and had a hot lunch. I was determined to get at least one hot meal in them a day until we got there. It was three days and two nights of travel. We spent our days looking out the window, coloring, playing Old Maid, and eating.

There were two male porters that worked the train; they both took a special liking to my sons. Every time we'd go to the dining car, they would give them free food, milk, and desserts. I would refuse for fear they would get into trouble, but they would insist. I thanked them repeatedly. "God made a way for my children to eat."

At night, at least one of them would come to our seats and bring sandwiches, cookies, and milk.

Brother Benjamin was a Muslim. He invited us to visit the temple in San Francisco once I got settled in. A former professional football player before a knee injury ended his career, he was tall, brown-skinned, strong, and good-looking. The other brother, Brother Preston, was also devoted to the Nation of Islam. We talked about Malcolm X and Detroit. I told him about the day I saw Malcolm X in Detroit, standing on Linwood Street near West Chicago, delivering one of his many speeches. We were on the Joy Rd. bus line with Mama, not knowing that she was taking us to see this famous man who was making history right before our eyes. We blended into the streets, filled with Black people from everywhere. It was early 1963. Brother Preston was single, not as good-looking, but still very nice. He also invited me out to the temple and even offered me a ride, which was good because I couldn't drive.

I had survived my last night on the train, feeling mixed and uncertain about it all—hesitant and anxious. The third morning was an easy one; the children seemed a bit restless but were well- behaved. That allowed me some time to myself, which I didn't often get. I sat back to enjoy the ride and scenery, starting to reminisce about the past, thinking about my old friends like Emory,

Sam, Robert Howard, Jackie and Lawrence. I thought of Melvin and wondered if he would ever forgive me for not being there. Did he make it to heaven? I felt a sadness in my heart for Melvin; I wished to God that I had done more to save him.

We were about twelve hours from San Jose, and the ride was getting longer. Finally, we stopped in Albuquerque, New Mexico. We could get off the train; our stop was a fifty-five-minute layover, which was good enough for me. I took the kids outside. Vendors were lined up, selling everything from tacos to blankets. I'd never seen anything like it. It was exciting. This was right up my alley; since I'd never had a taco, we decided to try one, and let me tell you, it quickly became one of my favorite foods. The outing had done the kids some good, and my hip was worn out from carrying my baby, who was getting to be a big boy now.

After we re-boarded the train, I washed their faces and hands, put lotion on them, brushed their teeth, and put them down for a nap. Occasionally, I'd smoke a cigarette, so I did, right inside the bathroom. It made me dizzy, so I staggered my way back to my seat. Between the train shifting from side to side and the old cigarette, I started to drift out of consciousness. In my dream, I could feel him beating and kicking me. I was reliving the rape attack by all three men. I was running with my children. I woke myself up; my children were fast asleep. I asked another mother to please keep an eye on my kids while I went to the bathroom to cry and splash some water on my face. I was constantly reliving the bad things in my past. I couldn't tell anyone; I had to keep it to myself. I had to maintain the wall that I had built within myself.

At 5:20 pm, we arrived in what I thought was San Jose, but to my surprise, I was a long way from there. I asked Brother Benjamin, and he said, "You're in Oakland, California, and the next train leaving for San Jose is in the morning." That meant that we would have to stay all night in the train station, and I was down to eighteen dollars. I grabbed my things and got off the train, looking up at the mountains and mountains of beautiful bliss. The sky was cloudy and thick, and the air was different from Michigan. I'd never seen anything more beautiful in my life. We walked, and I paused to look up at the beautiful sky that God had created. It looked as if God took his paintbrush out and hand-painted the sky. My eyes filled with water. Thank You God.

Well, we took a seat outside the terminal, and I asked the cab driver how far it was to San Jose. His reply was, "Lady, San Jose is at least an hour ride from here, and that's gonna cost you a lot of money"—money that I didn't have. I gathered the kids to walk inside the terminal when I saw Brother Benjamin and Brother Preston; they were off duty. They knew the situation at hand and offered to drive me to San Jose because they lived there. I was hesitant for two reasons: one, I didn't know them—they could kill me and my children; and two, I didn't have anywhere to go.

I looked over at my kids, thinking to myself that I could be placing them in harm's way. On the other hand, I knew that I had to trust someone to help me. So, I prayed silently, asking the Lord to take care of us because I'd made a stupid mistake in the past. We all piled into the small, light-brown car. I was prepared to fight them if they tried anything. They reassured me that they meant no harm to us. "We can't leave you in Oakland; it's no place for a woman and kids," they said. I sat in the front seat, holding my baby tight. Brother Ben was telling me about San Jose and where to get some help for my children. He asked me where I was going, and I told him that I didn't know. I asked him to take me to a shelter; did he know of any?

He quickly replied that he did. The ride seemed longer than the cab driver had said, and I was starting to get anxious. "What if they tried something? How would I get my children out?" I thought to myself. It was getting dark, and we were still stuck in traffic. I didn't know where I was headed. Then, we pulled up in front of a beautiful brown brick building, and he said, "This is called Brandon House; it's a shelter for women and children. They will help you here." They opened the doors and helped me out with my children and bags. They gave me their phone numbers and plenty of hugs; they wished us well. "Goodbye, my sister," they said. "Call us when you get yourself straight, and we'll go to the temple."

I looked around me, then stepped up to ring the doorbell. A woman was approaching the door. She was tall and brown-skinned, maybe in her mid-fifties. Through the window, I could see her approaching. She opened the door and greeted us with a warm smile. She reached down to help me with my kids and held my baby throughout the entire interview. She introduced herself as Mrs. Brown, the head honcho there. She had the kitchen assistant cook us something to eat and then show us around. The shelter was beautiful, clean, and warm, with plenty of room in each room. There was a laundry room and a recreation room with carpet on the floor. A playground and plenty of books to read—it was like being in heaven. "Thank you, God," I said to myself. "Thank you, Mrs. Brown." She hugged and kissed me and my children and bade me a good night. She was getting off work, and I was going to give my kids a shower. They'd never had a shower before, and neither had I.

I'd never taken a shower before because the houses we lived in had only bathtubs and no showers. We had our own private bathroom; some of us had private baths, others had to share. I was so happy—it had been a long time since I'd felt that way. After putting the children to bed, I used the payphone to call my mother. I hadn't spoken to her in several days. She was surprised to learn that I had moved to California and urged me to be careful. She wanted my phone number and the address where I was staying.

I went to the kitchen and asked the assistant for information to give to my mother. During our call, Mama asked about the kids and why I had left Detroit without telling anyone. I dared not lie to her, so I bent the truth a bit. I told her I wanted to give them a better life. "But you're so young," she said, "and I worry about you." I assured her that I was fine and that I would call her in a few days, and I told her not to worry about us. I said I loved you, and we hung up. Nina called right back and she asked me how we were doing. She also told me that Mrs. Washington called her and told her what happened to me and what he did to me. Then she said that she got her shot gun and went over to his house on Bewick. She said that she knocked on the door with it, and called for him to come out. Repeatedly she called and begged for him to come out and he didn't. Because he is a coward. When she turned to leave Nina said that she saw the belt hanging from the porch.

I returned to my room and went into the bathroom to pray. I asked God for wisdom and guidance, to lead me and not let me fail. Then, I crawled into bed and slept for twelve hours.

At breakfast, I met some other mothers. They explained how the social worker would help me find my own place, provide me with insurance and food stamps, and even pay for me to go back to school. Mr. Martinez, the social worker assigned to Brandon House, visited the home on Tuesdays and Thursdays. Since it was Saturday, I was told to sit back and relax for the weekend. Supervision was minimal on weekends; only the cook was in.

After breakfast, I asked the kitchen aide if I could help clean the kitchen. "Sure," she said. That turned out to be the best decision I had made in my life because it started a conversation with her. She introduced herself as Laura Person, the head cook at the shelter, working there part- time. A trained electrician, she had been with General Electric for nineteen years and had lived in San Jose for the past thirty. Originally from Tuskegee, Alabama, she told me how she had worked hard scrubbing floors at night to put herself through school. She had to provide for her son as a single parent.

"Why do you think I gravitated towards you?" she asked. "I recognize strength when I see it." She told me that she worked at the shelter to help young women like me. We talked and shared stories, and she invited me to her apartment for a party over the weekend. Initially, I declined because of the kids, but she insisted they were welcome, adding that I needed to get out and meet people if I were to live here. We were developing the friendship I desperately needed.

Over the weekend, I played with the kids, read them books, watched TV, took naps, and let them play as much as they wanted. There was something in me that wanted to express myself without any hidden feelings. When Tuesday morning arrived, Mr. Frank Martinez did just what the other mothers said he would. I told him I was seventeen and a half, turning eighteen in October. He said I needed to be eighteen now or have a guardian. Mrs. Brown, who sat in on the interview, stepped out into the hallway with Mr. Martinez. When they returned, he said he would sign me up and cautioned me not to tell a soul because he could lose his job, as he had a family of six depending on him. Eagerly, I agreed and signed the papers. He said he would be back to take me to the office to help me find an apartment.

"Thank you," I said, barely believing my luck. I felt a deep sense of gratitude. A week later, I received a food stamp card and a letter stating we were entitled to receive Medicaid and cash assistance. The very next day, I received my first check for four hundred and fifty-seven dollars and forty-one cents. I thanked the Lord again. Laura offered to take me to open a bank account and get a state ID. I put two hundred dollars in the bank and offered her gas money for taking me around. She refused but suggested we go for Chinese food instead, and she insisted on paying the bill.

The only time I'd seen cars like hers was in Detroit—Laura drove a pristine 1964 cream-colored Thunderbird. "I don't need any money," she said. "Use that money for your children and yourself." Then she took me shopping, showing me around and pointing out everything I needed to know.

I spent two hundred and fifty dollars on clothes, shoes, and underwear for the kids and bought some new clothes for myself. I was thankful to God because I could buy inexpensive but nice clothes for the kids. I no longer had to worry about buying boots, mittens, coats, hats, or warm clothing.

Again, Laura invited me to her house for the weekend, and this time, I accepted.

"Good," she said. "I'll pick you up tomorrow." I was built like a brick shithouse, so I knew that whatever I wore, I would look good in it. I'm confident about the way I look—not vain, but confident. My face had healed from all the beatings, and I was back to looking good. But I really wanted a whole new look. The people of San Jose were laid-back and relaxed; their clothing and choice of styles were funky. Being from Detroit, I liked that. I've always been good at creating my own style. Making something from nothing—that was me.

I called Mama to share the good news about my new friend, Laura Person. I even gave Mama Laura's number and address to ease her worries. That Friday night, to my surprise, Laura sent her son Winston to pick me up. I was a bit hesitant when he called out my name, explaining that his mother had asked him to pick us up. Standing at 6'5", he was a good-looking brother and truly his mother's son—they bore a striking resemblance. He knew all about me from his mother. "I'm not going to hurt you," he assured me. "You're safe with me." He helped me and the kids into the car, and as we drove off, I noticed his glances at my thick thighs. He stopped at the Dairy Queen to buy the kids ice cream, and I made sure they stayed clean. Throughout the ride, he kept checking me out, and I did the same.

He shared that he was impressed by how I was raising and providing for my kids, and the fact that I was from Detroit only piqued his interest further. He was a kind-hearted, tender, and warm man who held much respect for his mother. He mentioned he was single, without kids, and was a student at Hayward College in Palo Alto, majoring in computer science. "Wow," I thought to myself, "I wish I could go to college."

When we arrived at the apartment he shared with his mother on the weekends, he opened the car door for me and took Shawn (Choo-Choo) and Andre by the hand. "So, how old are your boys?" he asked. I replied, "Terrance is thirteen months, Andre is two, and Shawn is four."

"Three knuckleheads, that's nice," he commented.

He observed me carrying my baby on my hip and walked behind us. Laura made me feel warm and welcome in her apartment, introducing me to everyone and sharing where I was from. She adored my boys, commenting on how well-behaved they were and that they prayed at night and blessed their food. The traditional values resonated with everyone, as they all recognized I was raised them right—which was how I could instill good values in my children that would follow them throughout their lives.

Laura handled the kids' dinner and made up the beds. After I gave them a bath, they fell fast asleep. She exuded Southern hospitality, reminiscent of the folks back home. When Detroiters threw a party, you knew it was a real party. She served fried catfish, coleslaw, smothered potatoes with onions, succotash with okra, dirty rice, sliced tomatoes with scallions, spaghetti, and fried chicken. There was all the beer and liquor one could drink, and plenty of Al Green's records like "Here I am" ("Come and Take Me") played in the background.

I didn't drink, and neither did she, but when she hit the dance floor, swinging her big hips and throwing her head from side to side, you'd think she had been drinking. Laura looked good for her age, whatever that was. Winston, her only child, was twenty-two. After a while, Winston asked me to take a ride with him. I hesitated, reluctant to leave my children behind. Laura overheard us and quickly offered to babysit. She even had a crib in her apartment for my baby.

"Girl," she said, "lots of my friends have kids, and I love children, especially yours. Go ahead; they'll be fine."

Convinced that she was no threat to my children, I trusted her, and we left. Winston introduced me to a friend of his, a girl named Jackie, who also had big hips like mine. We all went to a new club called The Living Room, where I met several of his partners, including Mrs. Brown's son, Lonnie. They were all as tall or taller than him.

He introduced me to his friends, who tried to strike up conversations with me, but Winston promptly informed them that I was off-limits. Jackie was left sitting alone at the table because she didn't dance. The atmosphere shifted dramatically when his close friend T.C. Everett walked in—it was as if a celebrity had entered. The club erupted into a frenzy. We partied hard; I let my hair down, we clowned around, I danced, and we had a few drinks, including Jackie, who, along with everyone else, had more than their share. We partied into the wee hours of the morning. Even though T.C. was with Jackie, his eyes kept wandering over to me. Every slow song that played, Winston was the first to ask me to dance, holding me close and flirting in a friendly manner. The connection between Winston and me was undeniable.

We left the club in separate cars. He safely returned me back to the apartment, and I thanked him for a wonderful time. He didn't know how much it meant to me to get out like that. We retired to our respective rooms. All of Laura's guests had left; the place was clean, and the children were still asleep. It felt great to be around people who knew how to enjoy themselves.

❧❧

I wriggled out of my new jeans, which fit like a glove, slipped into my nightgown, and fell fast asleep. The next morning, I was up before everyone else. After taking my shower and getting dressed, I went downstairs and waited for the house to wake up. Even the kids were sleeping late. Downstairs, I found a note addressed to me from Winston. It read, 'Hey, I had to go back to school for exams. I'll be thinking about you this week. Think about me. My heart felt something for you last night; did you feel something for me? Peace, Winston.' I didn't dare show the note to Laura; I wasn't sure how she'd react, and I didn't want to jeopardize my friendship with her.

❧❧

Later, Laura took me and the kids to the flea market, out to lunch, and to meet more of her friends. She mingled with her supervisors and coworkers, people who were living their best lives—Black and Hispanic individuals who drove new cars, had bank accounts, nice furniture, and a steady income, and it showed.

I spent the week with Mr. Martinez looking for apartments. At work, Laura called me into the kitchen. "Move over there where I'm at; I can get you an apartment where I live," she suggested. Her apartment was stunning, with snow-white furniture, wall-to-wall carpet, new appliances, cable TV, and a master bedroom with a king-sized bed—no rats or roaches. "Do you want to move there?" she asked. "Yes," I replied, "but I don't know if I can afford it." "Sure, you can," she assured me. Two days later, she was taking me to fill out my application for a two-bedroom apartment. I could move in right away; the manager was her friend. "I've been helping my family for years," she said.

Social services covered the security deposit and the first month's rent for me. The San Juan Batista apartments were absolutely beautiful. My rent was only $79.00 a month, including heat. "God is good," I thought, realizing I was on my way.

The apartments' rent was based on the head of the household's family income. With housing priced so high in California, many affordable housing options were available to help prevent families from becoming homeless. I didn't understand all the details yet, but I was learning. On August 2, 1973, I got my keys to move in. I hugged Mrs. Brown and Mr. Martinez, thanking them both from the bottom of my heart for their help. I was leaving Brandon House for good. I prayed to God that I would never have to return. "Take care of those children," Mrs. Brown said as she waved goodbye, "they're all you have."

Mr. Martinez would continue to be my social worker since I was moving into his district. Winston told Jackie about my move, and she came to visit almost as soon as I had settled in. I was glad to see her. Together, we explored the newly painted apartment. Laura had to leave for work, but she left me in a beautiful home. It boasted wall-to-wall new carpet, a large bathroom with a shower, and two spacious bedrooms. The kitchen featured all new appliances, and cream- colored drapes framed the rooms. The children ran from room to room, delighted by the ample sunlight flooding in. Until I could afford beds, we could sleep on the floor—a situation Jackie quickly offered to remedy by helping me get utilities and other necessities set up like a phone.

August 17, 1973: Paul Williams' Death

I was standing in the kitchen, baking sugar cookies, and listening to Gladys Knight and the Pips "Midnight Train to Georgia" on the radio. A flash bulletin came through: Paul Williams, lead singer and founder of the Temptations, was found dead. Apparently, he committed suicide. Found with a self-inflicted gunshot wound to the head in his car parked near 14th Street and West Grand Blvd. in Detroit, Paul was 34 years old. He is survived by his wife and six children. Paul was best known for his outstanding live version of the song "Don't Look Back." He'll be deeply missed. To my knees, I fell; it almost took the wind out of me. I couldn't believe what I was hearing. The man who encouraged me to live, who literally saved my life through his music, supposedly committed suicide. Immediately, I felt the loss as if I'd lost an old, dear friend. He was someone I could connect to through his music, someone who returned my love and never asked for anything in return. Their music made me not want to give up. Someone who helped guide me through life had lost his own. The Temptations were always there when I needed them.

I cried until my eyes and my nose were red. I called home to talk to a couple of my friends who said the radio stations were blowing Paul Williams and the Temptations up. They were playing all their old hits. It was a sad day at MOTOWN.

His funeral is scheduled for August 24. His death is under investigation.

On the Labor Day weekend of 1973, I received my check along with three hundred dollars in food stamps. I paid a prorated rent of $17.00 and managed to put $100.00 in the bank. Jackie drove me to buy bunk beds for the kids and an almost-new yellow kitchen table with matching chairs. It was pretty. I also enrolled the boys in Head Start and daycare right on the apartment complex premises. They attended for free due to my income. Jackie, however, seemed a bit jealous. She had a little boy and lived with her mother, Roselee, who struggled with alcoholism. Unlike me, Jackie wasn't receiving much support, for whatever reason possibly because she lived with her mother. I was not my business and I left it like that. I was grateful for the available opportunities.

By Christmas of 1973, my apartment had become the local hangout. Winston, Jackie, and T.C. were frequent visitors. We played music, danced, drank, and smoked cigarettes. They even spent Christmas and New Year's with me. Not having any furniture didn't seem to matter. I cooked a huge meal—turkey, dressing, candied yams, chitlins, greens, string beans, white potatoes, cranberry sauce, macaroni and cheese, giblet gravy, rolls and butter, sweet potato pie, apple pie, and Waldorf salad from my mother's recipe. I was still learning how to cook, but I tried. The children had a tree, plenty of toys, clothes, and food. Fresh fruit and candy were abundant. The weather was spectacular, around 85 degrees, allowing the children to play outside in shorts and T-shirts—a stark contrast to the dressed-up Christmases back home.

I sent Mama one hundred dollars for Christmas. She protested, claiming I couldn't afford it and didn't need to send her money. I insisted she keep it, wanting to give her more but lacking the means. Laura insisted that the children spend the night with her, so I agreed. Me, Winston, Jackie, and T.C. rang in the New Year together. First, we went out and returned before midnight. Some friends from the club followed us home but soon left. The four of us always stuck together, spending our time talking, laughing, and just enjoying each other's company. We drank a wine called Wolf 'n Son from an old-time dark green jug with a hook; you'd hold it over your shoulder and take a swig.

Winston didn't like T.C. spending so much time at my apartment. He had to go to school, and

T.C. would visit me almost every other day. But nothing was going on; sometimes he'd show up with Jackie, other times he showed up alone. But Winston was truly his partner. T.C. would hit on me, but he knew that nothing was happening. I'd been celibate since I'd been there. I liked Winston, but that was it. I was focused on my children, and he knew it. My children came first under any circumstances. The holidays were over; it was time to get back down to business. I met several acquaintances over there who always invited me to coffee. I was looking into going back to school, but it was too far away without a car. So, I took a part-time job at the daycare center, making $1.75 an hour. I was popular and had made many friends, mostly men.

February 21, 1974 here

I was still sleeping on the floor. I wanted the kids to have new beds, I had furnished my apartment with furniture from Goodwill. That day, Laura came by and asked me to accompany her to the flea market. Upon our arrival, I browsed around but found what I wanted was too expensive—a king-size bed adorned with big red roses in perfect condition. Laura was on the other side of the store. Silently, I told God how much I desired that bed, laying my hands on it and claiming it in His name. After the market, Laura dropped me off at home.

Around 7:30 PM that same evening, my doorbell rang as I was getting my children out of the tub. Peering through the peephole, I saw nothing; my eyes leveled with the sky as we lived upstairs. Opening the door, I was stunned to find the king-size bed and frame on my doorstep. I couldn't believe it. Stepping out, I looked around—nothing. "Where did it come from?" I cried, "Who sent this to me?" It couldn't have been Laura; she hadn't seen me praying in the store. How did they know my address? It felt like a gift from God. The kids and I dragged it inside, and I immediately called Laura to see if she had bought this magnificent bed for me; she said no. The next day, T.C. came by and put it up for me. Winston didn't like that. "He has no business in your bedroom," he said, grabbing me by the waist and throwing me onto the unmade bed. He kissed me with passion and desire, making my knees buckle. "I've been wanting to kiss you since I met you." Behind the kiss and the miracle, I was totally baffled. God worked in my life. Next I had to learn how to drive and get a car, as I was too dependent on others for transportation.

Saturday Morning

My phone rang; it was Mama. She wanted to talk to me about my father. I listened to what she had to say and remembered what she had told me about him before. She gave me some names if I wanted to try and locate him. Frankly, I didn't give a damn about him. He had demonstrated that he didn't give a damn about me. Later that day, I thought about it.

Chapter 16

"Time Stood Still: 1974"

After lunch, I put the boys down for a nap and picked up the phone to call for information. He wasn't listed in Akron, Ohio, but his sister Annie was. She shared everything about herself in a friendly manner and spoke of my so-called father as if he were something special. According to her, he made a strong impression on his sister. She mentioned he no longer lived in Akron; the last she heard was that he was living with his family in California. Annie revealed that he seldom kept in touch, for reasons she knew but didn't disclose. She described his life as secretive, as though he had something to hide. Annie recalled my visit as a baby with my mother to see my father in Akron.

Annie was long-winded, and I was eager to end the call, especially when I noticed Winston at the door. I excused myself to let him in and gave Annie my name and number just in case he was interested. Unbeknownst to me, two weeks later, I received a call from a Spanish-speaking man named Ralph. He had gotten my number from Annie; he was a friend of my father, Johnny Chatman. Ralph gave me a post office box address in Anchorage, Alaska, suggesting I write to him. He relayed that my father wanted to hear from me. After hanging up, I shared the news with Laura, and Winston, overhearing, seemed excited for me.

"Where the hell is Alaska? I know it's cold there," I mused aloud. I penned a letter, and about a week later, he called. We spoke about his life; he revealed that he had been living in Alaska for the past twelve years. He shared his phone number and encouraged me to call him collect sometime. He began writing to me, sending pictures. In his letters, he detailed his relationship with his ex-wife and the five children born after me, who lived in Milpitas, California, not far from where I resided. After their breakup, he had driven his mobile home to Anchorage. The letters included pictures of him and his current partner, Clara, who, from the pictures, seemed to have a horse-like face. His letters made it clear—it must be the money. He was a tall, distinguished-looking man with a character-filled face, clearly my biological father. Yet, he could never replace my stepfather, the man who helped raise me and was always there.

I knew I wasn't going to like him. There was something hidden in his eyes; he looked mean, stern, yet friendly. It wasn't about his bragging about his job, his accomplishments, or how much money he had. My gut told me differently. I knew for a fact that this S.O.B. had never provided for me and never given my mother a penny for my upbringing. Hell, he never even looked for me. My mother had recounted his violent behavior when drunk; he threatened her and all her children one night, prompting her to move out that same night. He wasn't going to help with me if he couldn't have her. Despite an apology letter he wrote her, I had no respect for him. How did he think that made me feel? Knowing the hardships my mother endured trying to raise and provide for me—the nights without food, sometimes without shoes or basic necessities. It all made me sick to my stomach. His voice seemed more empathetic, at least trying to smooth things over. "There's some lying being told here," I said to myself.

He portrayed himself as the doting dad who did no wrong. I wasn't buying that. In May of 1974, he invited me and the boys to visit him and Clara in Alaska. "I'll buy your tickets," he said. In the same breath, I thought to myself that it would be the only way I'd go. I told Laura, and she told everyone else. Excited for me, Laura believed in family; she wanted me to get the chance to meet my father and hear his side of the story.

May 21, 1974

Laura drove us to the airport in San Francisco. The scenery was breathtaking—the streets were hilly, and the blue sky was surrounded by mountains. We traveled across the Golden Gate Bridge, which seemed to be the choice of transportation, along with the well-maintained street cars, bright red and beautiful.

I was a constant worrier; I was afraid to fly. Between praying, packing, and worrying about flying, I didn't get any sleep and was dead tired. I didn't know how long I would stay, so Laura agreed to collect my mail, pay my rent, and check on my apartment. She said I could pay her back when I returned. I had paid my rent for two months before leaving. We hugged and kissed and said our goodbyes; her constant reassurance really helped, but deep down, I was scared to death of flying.

I'd never been on an airplane before. Laura stayed behind in the terminal, waving and telling me to call her. I waved back, again wondering if I'd made the right choice. I hadn't told Mama, wanting to wait until I got there. As we took off, I held onto the chair so tight that the fabric began to lift from the frame. I felt knots in my stomach. After we stabilized in the air, I unbuckled myself just long enough to help the kids stretch their legs. The stewardess gave them crayons, coloring books, and juice. What she didn't know was that I never traveled any distance with my children without packing them a full lunch with snacks and activities—something I learned from my mother. We thanked her.

Trying to relax, I sat back, thinking about the night before when Winston showed up at my door and confessed his feelings for me. He asked me to call him and not stay gone too long. He hugged and kissed me, telling me to kiss the boys for him. My thoughts were interrupted when the stewardess began serving a nice, full lunch with beverages. I asked for a shot of Tequila with very little water to help settle me down and lit a cigarette. Looking at me with all those children, I guess they thought I was of age to drink. The flight was four hours long, and the only time I moved from my seat was to take the boys to the bathroom. They took a nap. Except to blink, I never closed my eyes.

After lunch, I took out my ticket to make sure it had a return flight on it. It did. "Well, if nothing else, I can always say that we lived in

Anchorage, Alaska," I murmured to myself. We arrived safely and exited the plane, walking into the terminal, where I saw him waiting to greet me. So, I thought, and then he called out to me, "Cherry."

I said to myself, "Who the hell is Cherry?" This M.F. doesn't even know my name. I was offended, and he could see it in my face. It was plain to see that this man was my father. I looked like him, and I didn't like that. He said to me, "You look just like your mother, Mildred, and you have her pretty moles too." I smiled and extended my hand to shake his. Clara walked over and gave me and the boys a warm greeting. She was nice.

Surprisingly, the weather in Alaska was nice—slightly dark and dreary, but cool. After an early dinner, Clara and he took us to their place. We sat and talked, but he offered no real excuse for his past actions, and I didn't ask. Clara showed me around their nice, big, plush home, equipped with all the amenities one could ever want. They also told me about a three-bedroom trailer set aside for me to stay in. It was away from their home but not too far, ready with everything I needed, he said.

The first night, we stayed with him. The following morning, he drove us around the wilderness town with very little sunlight. My heart told me I wouldn't stay long. He then took us to the trailer; it was nice, clean, and warm. He didn't linger, just long enough to say he had been there. Clara was at work. I cooked lunch for the kids, turned on the old color television set, and flipped through the channels to find nothing of interest, so I put the boys down for their daily nap and went outside to look around. All I could see was a mist of smoke or steam coming from the mountaintop, big brown trees that stood still, and I could feel the dampness in the air—I didn't like that. There was plenty of wilderness, and it made me feel very sad inside. "I want my mama," I thought for a brief minute as I felt her presence. "I'm going inside to call her," I said to myself.

I hadn't ventured very far when a young white woman, older than me, came outside half-naked and introduced herself. I wasn't looking to make any new friends. Instantly, my gut told me not to trust her, and I didn't waver—I didn't trust her at all, not because she was white, but because she offered too much information about herself. I was tired, I didn't feel like talking to anyone except my mother, and I wasn't in the mood to hear anyone's problems. She talked about her sex life—things I knew nothing about—and her "bad twin boys" always misbehaving. She said she didn't have a life and wanted out of her marriage to her husband, who worked long hours on the pipeline. "I get lonely," she said. I didn't know what the hell she was referring to; I just wanted her to go back home and stay there.

I called my mother, who was surprised to know that I had traveled all the way there. She asked if I wanted to stay. "No, ma'am," I said. I hadn't made up my mind when I was going to leave, but the next day came and went, and before I knew it, I'd been in Anchorage for almost four months. It was exciting for those who liked to fish and hunt. Shawn, five years old now, made a new friend, Carl, an Eskimo boy four years older than him. Nevertheless, I'd baked cookies and brownies for them; he was good company for the kids. I found myself sitting in the house all the time, with nothing to do but perfect my cooking skills.

Anchorage was getting ready to see the last of me. On September 28, 1974, I called Johnny to ask him to take me to the store to buy groceries. I planned to tell him then that I was ready to go back to San Jose. When we were about to pull off, the lily-white woman next door came outside in her cut-off shorts and half-cut shirt, practically naked. Quickly, I covered my son's eyes with my hands. "Are you going to put on some clothes?" I asked. She ignored my question and asked Johnny for a ride to the store. "No," she replied, "I'm already dressed," and she hopped in the front seat. From where I was sitting, I could see him looking at her thighs; they were deep in conversation as if I weren't even there. He dropped me off at the store, and I shopped with the money Clara had given me for food.

Clara had insisted I take $300.00. I had $350 in food stamps saved, but I couldn't use them there. If nothing else, I could feed my babies when we get back. I didn't buy much because my mind was made up to leave in a few days. I was amazed that there were no taxes on anything. We shopped and walked outside to get in the car, and they were gone. The town was small, so we started to walk around and sightsee. As we approached the post office and passed the local hardware store, something caught my eye. Fear took over when I looked up and saw a huge white polar bear hunched over, paws and all, his teeth showing. It scared me to death. He looked to be 14 feet tall.

I took off running, with Terrance in my arms having left the kids behind momentarily. I turned around to see them running too. It dawned on me that the bear wasn't moving. I turned around, realizing that it was stuffed. My heart was in my throat. I could taste blood. The kids and I laughed, but nevertheless, it was a frightening experience for me. We walked up a few more blocks when we saw a large crowd of people, some in uniforms, others in regular clothes. I wondered about the commotion when I looked up and saw a full-grown moose with full-grown antlers. "Oh my God," I said, "where did he come from?" I was scared to death again. "Do they just wander around like this?" I cried out. "Yes," someone from the crowd said. "Sometimes they just walk the streets." "Shit," I said to myself, "I'm getting the hell out of here. I'm from the city; I can't go through this." I had never seen anything that big in my entire life. Someone yelled that the moose had come down from the mountains and was eating out of the cemetery. They were trying to block the streets off and get him to go back up into the mountains.

I increased my pace, but I was still unable to find them. Then, all of a sudden, they came from behind a building. I never said anything; I just got in the car. She was trying to fix her clothes, but I could see that what she had on was twisted; her shirt was on backward, and her hair was a mess. The car smelled; I dropped the window. He hurried up and dropped us off; she gave him her phone number, told him to call her, and ran inside.

Later that evening, there was a blackout throughout Anchorage. I was cooking dinner for the kids. I felt through the house for my children and gathered them on the couch. I searched for a flashlight and candles. The menu changed; I made peanut butter and jelly sandwiches instead. All of a sudden, someone started beating on my door like the police. "Who is it?" I asked. "It's Mike from next door. I got my gun. Where's the motherfucker that lives here? He tried to rape my wife." "That's not true," I said. "Open this fucking door; I'll kill him." Between his ranting and raving, I couldn't get a word in. "I'll kill that black motherfucker; I'll teach him to put his black hands on my wife." I was trembling. I called Johnny on the phone to tell him what was going on over there—that her husband was threatening me and the kids.

Well, Johnny told me to handle it and hung up the phone. I couldn't believe it. I went back to the door to tell the man that no one was here but me and my children. He continued to threaten to break in. My kids were crying, and I was scared, but I was ready to fight him if he broke in. My first instinct was to protect my kids. I'd armed myself with a butcher knife. I was prepared to do everything in my power to stop him. I told him that I was calling the police. When I went to the phone to call the police, it was dead. I didn't panic and didn't tell him any different; I pretended to be talking to them on the phone. Pretty soon, things quieted down; he was gone. The house was dark, and the phone line was dead. I was afraid, not knowing what to expect. I held my children close to me and prayed for God to protect us.

Andre and Terrance were fast asleep; I laid them down on the couch. Shawn stayed up with me. I was too afraid to move when I heard something at my back door. Something in my gut told me not to make any noise. I told Shawn to be quiet, placing my index finger on my lips. I eased up and tiptoed to the kitchen. I slowly eased the curtain on the back door and looked out. Oh God, I nearly lost my mind with fear. It was a black bear rummaging through my garbage. My mama used to say, "I didn't know whether to shit or go blind." I eased back to the couch with my finger over my mouth, signaling to Shawn not to make any noise. We huddled together and stayed very quiet. "God, please help us," I prayed. Please keep us safe." I was shaken all over with fear.

The bear was out there for about fifteen or twenty minutes, then he left. Shortly thereafter, the lights came on, and the phone line was restored. I didn't hesitate; I called American Airlines and booked my flight for the same morning. It was 12:40 AM. That was too much going on for me in one day.

I called Johnny around 1:37 AM, telling him to be there in the morning to take us to the airport. I thanked him and hung up. He called back, but I didn't answer.

The morning, we were scheduled to leave, I was holding Terance in my arms, standing him up on the kitchen table with the front door open, looking out for Johnny. I let Terrance go, and he started to walk across the table. Surprised, I realized he was walking. I put him down on the floor, and he started to take off. "It's about time," I told him. "You're two now."

We clapped our hands and cheered him on. Well, that was short-lived. I had to carry him to the car. I didn't say much to Johnny, and when we got to ourselves, I tried to give Clara back her money. She wouldn't take it. "God Blessings"… Again, I said thanks. At 9:20 AM, we boarded the plane. I waved my hand goodbye and never looked back. We both knew that I would never see him again.

On my flight back to the Bay Area, I tried to relax. I hid it well; I was very upset inside, and I was having flashbacks of the trauma that consumed me. Had. If it weren't for the love of my children, I don't know where I would be. I refused breakfast and continued thinking back about the time I spent in Anchorage. I experienced many violent dreams and nightmares from my past. I slept in bed with my sons for the duration while in Alaska. Laura had to work, so she had Winston pick me up from the airport. We had a nice flight back, though I was still scared. He gave me my keys, carried my luggage, and walked us in. He played around with the boys for a while, then he left. I gave the boys a bath, lunch, and put them down for a nap. I cleaned the apartment. I opened the windows to let the fresh air in. I mopped floors, washed clothes, unpacked, cooked dinner, and swept the wall-to-wall carpet.

I didn't have a vacuum cleaner. Before I wore myself out, I called Mama. I talked to Nina and Rickey. He informed me of the latest gossip and said that everyone from the neighborhood sent their love. He also said that Mama wasn't doing as well as she had said; she didn't want me to worry. I asked them both if they thought I should come home. "Not yet," they said, "she's just feeling a little sad." "Well, you let me know," I said, "and I'll leave for home in the morning. I've got some money saved." God blessed me through Clara.

I got in bed with my sons and took a nap.

Things settled down and were getting back to normal. I enrolled Shawn in half-day kindergarten; he was brave and independent and wanted to go. I cried the whole day because I had to leave my baby at school. "Don't cry, Mama," he said to me. "I'll be alright." Andre was back in daycare; I spent my time learning how to cook. Mexican food, soul food, and Chinese food, and I was teaching myself how to bake cakes and pies from scratch. My time was mine again. I spent the days praying, cooking, cleaning, mopping, washing, ironing, reading books, and reading the newspaper. I was looking through the paper when I spotted an ad for a car for sale for one hundred dollars.

Well, I asked Steward, who was my neighbor. Steward was seventy years old and a friendly man. He'd run neighborhood people around San Jose, only charging them for gas money. He wouldn't take my money;

instead, he'd ask me to buy him a drink and play him some blues. "Shit! That was right up my alley."

He drove me and another neighbor who could drive to see the car. Being from Detroit, you'd think I'd know better, but I didn't really know what I was looking at. It was a 1955 Ford, a turquoise and white hoop-dee. Sharp as hell, inside and out. I paid the lady one hundred dollars, and Deborah drove it back for me. She parked it in the driveway behind my building.

And when we got back, we went to his apartment and celebrated my new independence. He played "Z.Z. Hill "It Ain't No Use" for me on his new Hi-Fi stereo.

I told Laura, and she encouraged me to learn how to drive. She took me to transfer the title. I couldn't afford insurance, and it wasn't mandatory at the time. I was afraid of and highly intimidated by this beautiful car. There was no one there to help me; I knew that I had to do this for myself. So, at night, I'd stand and look out of my bedroom window down at this car.

I prayed for strength. One evening, I grabbed the keys, locked my apartment up, and went downstairs to practice driving. Up and down the long, spacious driveway, I drove. I mimicked the people I knew who could drive. Laura came by; she showed me how to use the turn signals. I learned how to park and back up. Every night after I put the boys to sleep, I'd go downstairs and practice driving until I gained more self-confidence. Several months later, I was driving myself and the kids around. I was scheduled to take my driving test. I did well, except for when I dropped the tester off and ran over the big cinder block in the parking lot. He laughed, and so did

I. I passed my driver's test anyway. I got my driver's license. Now I could go back to school and take my children on family outings. I was proud of myself.

Pretty soon, we were everywhere. Up and down the road we went. Everyone loved my car, and they all told me that I didn't know what I had. "This car is a classic," they'd say. On weekends, we'd go to White Hill Park. I let the kids play while I learned how to play dominoes. We went to the museum, church, skating, picnics, fairs, and flea markets. You name it, and we went. I was determined.

The people in San Jose were laid back, as if nothing bothered them. The atmosphere was easy, and quiet like a like a Sunday morning." It was the ending of 1974, and I was still looking for a new look. I didn't wear makeup; I never felt like I had anything to cover up. My skin is smooth, light, and olive-toned.

But I did wear lipstick, eyebrow pencil under my eyes, and mascara. My mental state was sad and blue. I felt so bad inside. I couldn't wait for the kids to go to bed at night so I could cry without interruption. I was good at keeping my feelings to myself, hiding them within myself, careful not to show them on my face. I learned this from the streets—if Detroiters didn't teach you anything else, they taught you that living life in the streets is a valuable life lesson. Take it with you.

I was still haunted by past memories of the many beatings I endured, encouraged by Aunt Janie, and nightmares of being raped by Welton Smith and Donald Malone. It was truly affecting my life and state of mind, but I was dealing with it the best I could. I often wondered where Donald Malone was. Loathing for him was still in my heart. I was waiting for God to kill them all. All of that had hurt me.

Chapter 17

"It's All Over, but the Shouting"

On this day, the kids were in school, and I went to the beauty parlor to get something done to my hair. My hair was auburn in color and shoulder-length. I hadn't been to a beauty parlor since my mother took me back in 1964. Being poor, Black folks did their own hair.

She had the beautician press and curl my hair. Except for her burning me around my ears more than once with the hot comb, my hair did turn out nice. But this day was different. I wanted some freedom and expression; I wanted to be free from my past that tried to hold me down. I was inhibited, and I was coming out. I pressed forward, and I came out with a Quo Vadis haircut. I decided to have her cut it all off. I can't explain the freedom I felt, along with the sharp new look. My confidence soared, and I was looking good.

I had V points on both sides and a W cut in the back. I felt empowered, just like Samson in the Bible.

I wore large hoop earrings to enhance my new style. It was different, and I looked good. People would stare at me and compliment me. The kids looked as if they couldn't believe what I had done, but I was still mama;

they grew to love it. I had a size 40" hip, a 24-inch hourglass waistline, and a 34B cup—anyone could plainly see that I was all women. My new haircut truly enhanced the two beautiful moles on my face—one on my nose and the other above my lip. These trademark moles were inherited throughout my whole family from my mother.

Jackie and I stood outside her apartment talking when a car drove up. It startled me at first—a quick reflection of my past. It was none other than Brother Preston selling bean pies. We were excited to see one another; we hugged, and he invited me out to the temple in San Francisco. That Saturday, he picked us up, and we drove to hear the Honorable Elijah Muhammad speak. I didn't know or understand who he was, only that he was the leader of the Nation of Islam for Black people.

I also knew that Malcolm X had been a brother to the nation before his assassination on February 21, 1965. They didn't eat pork, drink, smoke, or party. They didn't believe in Jesus, and I did. They had strict rules set by him to live by. I hadn't seen so many Black people gathered in one spot since Mama took us to see and hear Martin Luther King Jr.'s speech in downtown Detroit on Woodward Avenue in 1963.

Babies were not allowed inside; they were cared for by the older sisters in the nursery. I kept my children with me. It was an enlightening experience for us. We visited the temple several times, and Brother Preston tried with all his might to convert me. But I wasn't interested in my life being limited and controlled by a man who didn't practice what he preached. I continued to support the nation by buying bean pies and reading the magazine they offered, but that was it.

I enrolled myself in school. I dropped my children off in the morning and went to school. It was hard at first, but I knew that only the strong survive, like Jerry Butler said in his song. Songs like that would give me courage and strength to continue on.

I hit the floor at 5:00 a.m. every morning, and it was nonstop from there. I went to school three days a week and studied until the early morning. Finally, I would be able to get myself together and get off-state assistance. I was embarrassed by my current situation and wanted more out of life for my children. They deserved a chance, and I planned to give it to them. I had to lead by example and set standards and goals for my children to live by.

My secret passion was to become a firefighter. I wanted to help save lives. I spent my weekends solely with my children, teaching them valuable life lessons—how not to steal, to be honest, and to avoid anything that could land them in prison. I told them never to use drugs, alcohol, or ride in stolen cars. "Education is your way out," I would say.

I turned the music up loud and taught them how to dance and skate. Considering myself a good dancer, I wanted to extend the favor to my kids. We did the bop and the twist; I showed them the mashed potatoes; we social; (slow dance) we did the jerk and the calypso; and I taught them how to do the stroll. My main focus was on my children and their happiness. It was a fun time for them.

I introduced them to various music from the past, including their heritage—Motown music. They were exposed to various languages; they were becoming bilingual. They played with children from different cultures, and they were being taught to speak Spanish in school. I was teaching myself how to perfect mouth-watering desserts, including homemade ice cream and rich-tasting custard. Most of all, they were happy. And if they were happy, I was happy.

November 2, 1974

On this particular day, the kids and I were coming from the movies. I didn't have much money left, so I packed the kids' corned beef sandwiches, potato chips, cookies, candy, and bottles of juice. We saw Mary Poppins, starring Julie Andrews and Dick Van Dyke. Afterwards, we decided on pizza and a salad for dinner.

We took our seats, and I placed our order. I noticed a guy looking at me; he worked there. When our food was ready, he walked it over, and instead of one pizza, he brought two fully loaded. My children and I thanked him; he went back to get our salad and pop. After dinner, we went up to pay the check, and he refused my money. I pressed my way to pay the bill, and he said the pizza was on him. I thanked him, and as I turned to walk away, he asked me out on a date. He said he'd be punching out in a few minutes and wanted to talk to me; he asked if I would wait for him. He gave the kids ice cream, and we sat down. He came out and introduced himself as Greg, and I introduced myself as Patricia—I dropped "Pat" when I left Detroit.

We engaged in a lot of small talk. He was nice-looking and seemed friendly, but he wasn't for me. And I told him that I was only interested in making friends right now. He said he understood. "So where are you from?" he asked. I told him. He said he was born in Youngstown, Ohio, but was raised in Akron, Ohio; he had three sisters and a baby brother. He told me that his father and mother separated, and he moved out. He mentioned his father's name was Johnny, and I told him I just came back from meeting my father in Alaska, named Johnny. When I said that, he looked at me really strangely. "That's my father," he said, pulling out his wallet and taking out a picture of Johnny Chatman, and we both said it together, "That's my father."

We paused to catch our breath, then I looked at him real good, and yes, we did look alike. I drove him home; he wanted me to meet the other children. They said he never mentioned me to them, but his wife, sitting in the chair, said she knew about me before they married. She wasn't very friendly to me at all. And I didn't make it any better.

1974

Nina called me late one night. She said that Mama wasn't doing well—not that any one particular thing was the matter; she just wasn't herself. Nina explained that she needed someone to help her care for Mama while she worked. Mama was at home during the day with Tina.

"Come home as soon as possible," she said. I didn't hesitate. I called Amtrak, checked the schedule, and made reservations. I started packing that night. I packed up the kitchen, linen closet, and what little clothes we had. What I couldn't take with me, I gave away. I gave Sister Cole all of my food—God knows she needed it. Sister Cole, a single mother of ten children,

I was sure to keep my collection of wood that I had purchased from one of my many visits to the flea market and various second-hand stores. My favorite of all was the hand-carved face that hung on my apartment wall. I had to give up my apartment to another family. I opened a post office box and gave the key to Laura. I notified Mr. Martinez to close my case. Mr. Martinez said that I was entitled to keep my current check and food stamps. I was grateful. Before I left, I shopped for coats, boots, hats, gloves, and warm clothing for us.

San Jose was unable to accommodate our needs. The stores Laura and I went to had nothing in stock to compare with the cold winters in Michigan. I bought what I could with the little money I had. I would buy the rest when we got to Canton Township, Michigan. I had never heard of Canton, Michigan, but Nina said that it was thirty miles from Detroit. I didn't care where it was; I was going home to see about my mother at all costs.

Two nights before I left, Laura asked to keep the boys. I really didn't want them to go, but I said yes. I was feeling somewhat anxious about getting home to my mother. I could feel that my mother needed me. "God," I prayed silently, "please take care of my mother; don't let anything happen to her. She's a good person, and she loves you very much. In Jesus' name, I pray this prayer, Amen." I stood in Laura's bathroom and prayed this prayer while she was getting the kids situated. Laura had a telephone in her bathroom. I picked it up and called my mother; she answered.

"Hello," she said.

"Mama, how are you?" Just hearing her sweet voice made me want to cry. I choked back the tears; I didn't want her to hear me crying.

"Mama, it's me, Pat."

"Baby, I know your voice, cause you're mine. I carried you in my stomach. A mother knows all her children."

"Hi Mama, how are you feeling?"

"I'm feeling a lot better; I have my good and bad days," she replied. "Are you hurting anywhere?" I asked.

"No," she said.

"Well, Mama, I'll be home this Friday, and you'll feel better. I'll take care of you." "You will?" she said in her playful baby voice.

"Yes, ma'am, I will." I could hear her voice perk up. "Baby, I'm fine; I feel better already," she said.

"I love you, Mama," I said.

"I love you too, baby," she replied. We hung up. I tried to dry my eyes so my children couldn't see that I'd been crying. I went in to kiss them goodnight and to remind them to say their prayers before going to bed. They were excited to be staying.

I told Laura about the phone call that I made. I laid fifteen dollars on the table. "If it costs more than that, let me know." Laura didn't say anything. I told her that I had to get back and finish packing. I was almost done. "I'll be here first thing in the morning to pick up the boys," she said. "OK."

I was feeling kind of lonely and blue inside as I proceeded to walk home. An unfamiliar car pulled up and started to slowly follow me. The man inside the car started to whistle. I ignored it but paid attention to what was going on. The car stopped, and I could hear the car door open, and someone stepped out, closing the door behind them. I turned around, and it was Winston and his partner, Freddie Holmes.

"Winston said that Jackie, T.C., Bitsy, and some other friends that I met since I was here were all waiting for me at the club." They wanted to give me a going-away party. I told him that I didn't want to go, but he insisted. So, I told him to give me one hour to get ready. I hurried and turned the radio on in my bathroom. I'm trying to feel better about my mother. Trusting God to help her.

I wore my well-fitted blue jeans with brass buttons down the sides of the legs and my off-white beaded V-cut sleeveless top that was tied in the back. The beads were lined around the cup and the bottom edge.

I also wore my patchwork leather platform shoes. My costume jewelry included large brass and wooden bracelets, coordinated with big hoop earrings. I was looking and smelling good, and I knew it. Disco was in. The clothes and shoes reflected the pure, uncut funk. The time period that fit like a glove.

Winston picked me up and complimented me on how nice I looked and how good I smelled. I was trying to make myself feel better. I'd just hung up from talking to my mama. I was missing her really badly. I pressed on through. The Manhattans, Dazz Band, The Commodores, The Bee Gees, Chaka Khan, Ohio Players Jam "Heaven Must Be Like This "and Brick were jamming on the charts. I'd never seen a disco ball that big—it lit up the floor, and we partied non-stop until 2:00 AM. I hugged and kissed everyone goodbye. I promised to call, and told them that I hope to come back and we exchanged phone numbers.

Two days later, we boarded the train in Oakland. I thanked Laura, and we hugged. She told me to keep in touch with her. Almost as soon as we boarded the train, I noticed a girl who favored Burnella London, my girlfriend in Detroit. We went to school together, and our children were born around the same time. I expressed how much she looked like my friend. I introduced myself to her, and she told me her name.

(Let's just say she told me her name was Carmen.) We instantly bonded and became inseparable. She helped me with the kids, although she didn't have any of her own. She said that she was going to visit her brother in New York and that she was running away from a boyfriend who physically abused her and tried to kill her. I was amazed at how much she looked, talked, and made gestures with her hands like Burnella. We got along well, like old friends. I felt like I really knew her. On day three, we arrived in Chicago. We exchanged phone numbers along with hugs and kisses. We promised to call one another; we parted ways.

Nina picked us up from the train station, and I couldn't wait to see my mother. Nina talked about how much the boys had grown and that she missed us. She said that she would take me to the new Meijer's to shop for coats for the kids. I hugged and kissed my mother so much that her cheeks were turning red.

We talked, and I reassured her that things would be better for her and Tina now that I was home. I promised to help Nina take care of them. That evening, Nina cooked fried chicken, mashed potatoes, fried corn, biscuits, and a side salad. We made our pallet on the floor. Although I knew I couldn't stay there sleeping on the floor for long, a few days wouldn't hurt.

The second day I was in town, I called my old friends from the neighborhood to let them know I was back. They were glad to hear it. I called Anntionette Foster and asked her how everyone was doing. She dropped a bombshell—Burnella London had been killed. I couldn't believe it. She went on to say that Burnella's husband, Ollie, whom nobody liked, had killed her. Everyone had begged Burnella not to marry him. Anntionette recounted that they had held her funeral yesterday morning while I was still on the train.

Anntionette explained that Ollie, Burnella's husband, had been carrying a snub-nosed thirty- eight because he'd gotten robbed at his job at Chrysler's Plant. She said that Burnella had overslept, falling asleep on the couch and forgetting to pick him up from work. Ollie came home mad and upset. An argument ensued, and he pulled out his gun and shot her in the head, between the eyes, at close range. Burnella fell dead between the bunk beds in front of their two little girls, aged two and four. He was out of jail before Burnella's body was released from the morgue. Ollie claimed he didn't mean to kill her, but we all knew better. The judge ruled it an accident. Burnella was nineteen years old and three months pregnant. I started to cry; the pain resurfaced she was one of my very best friends. I was in shock.

I thought about the girl I met on the train. I dropped the phone and ran to get my purse. I scrambled for her name and phone number in my wallet. It wasn't there. I put her number in a place that only I could find. It wasn't there either. I'd even forgotten what she told me her name was.

I told Anntionette about the train ride and the girl I met. We both agreed that it must have been Burnella's spirit I rode the train with—that she was coming to see me one last time because everyone else made it to her funeral but me. I was devastated. I cried off and on all day. I didn't tell the kids what happened to Burnella. I asked them if they remembered the girl on the train. Shawn and Andre both said they heard me talking, but they never saw anyone. That gave me a haunting, eerie feeling.

I tried to dismiss the memory of the train ride, but it lingered in the back of my mind. A few days turned into a month, and it was cold outside. Nina still hadn't taken me to the store. I found myself feeling like a prisoner in her house. She had changed. I was always home, not allowed to leave or even open the door. The only time I could use the phone was when she wasn't home. Nina monitored everything I did and everything we ate. I could buy my own food if she would just take me to the store. We weren't allowed to sit on her furniture. I couldn't use the telephone because calling Detroit was considered a toll call, and that cost money that I didn't have. Everything was spread far apart; there wasn't any transportation in the rural area. I certainly couldn't afford the cab fare. The money that I came with was gone.

All I had on me was twenty cents—not even a whole quarter. Even the money I held onto for their coats was gone; I used it to make phone calls. All we had were lightweight jackets and sneakers. I thanked God because I remembered packing away their mittens, hats, and scarves, but we needed more than what we had to survive. During the day, I would clean, cook, wash, iron, give baths, comb hair, vacuum, mop, sweep—you name it, I did it. I was on call twenty-four- seven, and I was tired. In between all of that, I would walk up to the gas station, pay the phone, and make calls to various apartments and projects in Detroit. Social Service wouldn't give me any money or food stamps because I didn't have an address. Nina said that I couldn't use hers for Section 8.

The waiting list was five years long. Mother Waddles Perpetual Mission said they would assist me with beds if they still had them when I was ready to move. Focus Hope, a program run by Father Cunningham, offered no financial assistance. They would only commit to providing commodities—powdered eggs, powdered milk, and the lowest grade of canned meat you could imagine.

After I put everyone down for a nap, I'd Walk on foot to the nearest apartment buildings, putting in applications. I wanted to stay close to my mother. I was denied because I would only be receiving welfare, and they didn't accept welfare recipients. They didn't want your black ass out there anyway. Nina got lucky; she and two other families might have been the only blacks out there.

At night, I'd lay down with all that life had offered me that day and rehash everything that had happened. My deeply hurt feelings made me grow stronger inside. I was filling up with emotion, but I had learned on the streets that you have to put that to work for you. Don't get sidetracked by your emotions. Keep them in check; they can be controlled. I had to stay focused. I didn't have time to cry. I had to provide for my kids. I had to find them a clean, decent place to live, even though they said I couldn't. I made sure that I made myself remember how it made me feel. "God bless the child that's got his own."

I'd been insulted, belittled, demeaned, and humiliated my whole life, and that made me more determined to have what you said I couldn't have. It was clear to see that I wasn't going to be able to live near my mother in this upscale neighborhood or the surrounding areas.—and the white folks surely weren't going to let your black ass live in their cities to expose their hoods. All things come to an end, in due time!

Nina would come home from work in a huff. She was always angry, with a nasty attitude, checking to see how much was eaten, who sat on the couch, and which glasses were used that day. "Hell, I could buy my own food if she would just take me to the store," I muttered under my breath. I still had food stamps. I couldn't take it anymore.

Nina had grown into a beautiful young woman, light-skinned, and she sported Mama's trademark too—big brown moles on her face and cheeks. Standing at 5'9" in her stocking feet, her small frame was built nicely. She was totally independent and worked very hard to get everything she had. Nina didn't wait for anything or anyone to help her. She was a go-getter type of woman. I was proud of her.

Michigan's local TV channels 2, 4, 7, 9, and 20 had been reporting a weather advisory for the entire viewing area. A severe snowstorm was coming. All counties, get prepared. A bad blizzard—a winter storm—was on the way. I'd been hearing this report all day. The storm was scheduled for tonight, causing a constant interruption for Mama. She loved listening to The Bill Kennedy Show broadcast live from Ontario, Canada, at 1:00 PM, Monday through Friday. Bill hosted the show, which played old movies she liked—Jean Harlow, Clark Gable, and Randolph Scott—and you had Mama's attention.

It was snowing hard and steady that whole day, already below zero. After the delicious meatloaf dinner I cooked, I gave the children and Mama a bath and put the kids down for bed that evening. Mama insisted on staying up. How do I tell my grown mother to go to bed? I didn't.

Around 11:30 PM, Nina walked through the door, and all hell broke loose. She started looking for something, anything, to start an argument. I tried to ignore her, but it's hard when someone is talking to you and treating you like a dog. I continued to mind my own business.

When she went upstairs and pulled Tina out of bed, she started to whip her for some foolish reason. I got tired of hearing her cry, so I spoke up for Tina, and we got into a bad argument. We were screaming at each other, standing toe to toe. The argument upset my mother; she was crying and yelling at us to stop before we came to blows. Neither one of us was backing down.

"This is my goddamn child," Nina yelled, "and you don't tell me what to do with her!" I stood between her and Tina with my hand stretched out to protect her. By this time, Mama was crying and trying to find her way to stop us from fighting. We ignored Mama's pleas for us to stop. I was raised to respect my older sisters, but tonight was a different story. I stood my ground, and she knew it. There was nothing separating us but space and opportunity.

I didn't want to fight my sister, but if she hit me, there would be a fight. Nina started storming through the house in pure anger, and she told me to get out. "Take your kids and get out of my house."

My mother screamed at her, "You dirty low-down cow, don't you put that girl out with her kids. It's dark outside; she doesn't have anywhere to go."

"Nina!" Mama cried, "How could you put her out? They don't have any coats. That's your sister!"

"She ain't sh*t to me," Nina snapped. "She ain't nothing to me. Just get your motherfucking ass out of my house."

"Fuck you, bitch," I retorted. "I'm getting out of your house." I heard Nina say this as she walked away from me and stood in the kitchen. She lit a Kool menthol cigarette, almost setting her shoulder-length, sandy red hair on fire. I caught a glimpse of her. My back was turned; I was putting my kids' clothes on, and I said to my mother, "Mama, I want to apologize to you for fighting and cursing over you. I was raised better than that; please forgive me."

"Don't go," Mama said, reaching out for my hand. I reached back and kissed her hand and said, "Mama, I've got to go; she put me out."

Nina, Mama pleaded, "Please don't do this; she's got the kids." I heard my mother cry in a different tone that night.

"Don't worry about me; I'll make it," I reassured her.

"Pat," my mother cried out, tears lacing her voice, "please don't go."

"Don't worry, Mama, I'll be okay." Despite my words, the situation didn't improve. I picked up my children and left. Nina continued to scream, "Get out!" as I walked away.

On the way out, I heard my mother call Nina a dirty bitch. Nina slammed the door behind us. "Get the hell out!" she screamed. It was 12:45 AM. I was mad enough to go back and confront her—not for me, but for the position she had put my children in. Yet, on the flip side, these were my kids; I'm their mother, responsible for their well-being. They depended on me to make things right. That night, I became a woman. I could feel something festering inside of me.

I'm spinning these thoughts fast in my mind, not wanting to upset my mother any more than I already had. Nina and I were both Scorpios.

We both knew, "You got to bring ass, to get ass." She was just as game as I was. Tears streamed down my face, not knowing what lay ahead.

My babies were wet, cold, and crying.

I grabbed their little hands and held on tight. The blizzard snow was so thick that I couldn't see it in front of me. My tears froze on my face. I had no money to make a phone call, nowhere to go, and I didn't know anybody in the area. We were thirty miles from Detroit.

"Where are we going, Mama?" they asked.

"I don't know, but we're getting the hell away from her," I said. "God, please help us." I started to pray. "Help us, Lord; I don't know what to do." I was feeling my way through the snowy blizzard. My hands and feet were so cold, I couldn't feel them. My face was numb; I knew how my children felt. I couldn't tell if we were walking in the street against traffic or where the underdeveloped sidewalk was.

"God," I pleaded, "please don't let us freeze to death out here."

We continued to hike through the snow, blinded by the blowing wind, walking into traffic on the side curb of the I-94 freeway. Suddenly, out of nowhere, a white man stopped his truck, got out, and helped put my children into his truck. I was so cold that I could hardly bend my body, but I managed to get in.

"I feel sorry for you and your kids," he said. "Let me help you. Do you live around here?" "No," I replied, "my sister threw me out."

"With your children?" he asked, incredulous. "Yes," I said. "Wow," he muttered. "Can I take you somewhere around here?"

Moving with the flow, he merged onto the freeway. "I don't know anyone around here," I said. "I'm from Detroit."

"Then I'll take you to Detroit. Can you find some help there?" he offered.

I hesitated. "It's late. I don't have any money and nowhere to go at this time of morning." "Well, let's go and see if someone will help you with your kids."

The truck was warm, and the long ride gave us time to dry off. He took me to the fire department on McGraw Street. He helped me out with my children and handed me a fifty-dollar bill. I refused, but he insisted, pressing it in my hand and saying he wouldn't be able to sleep if I didn't accept it. I told him I couldn't pay him back.

"He said God would look after him for looking out for me." He was an angel." He hugged us and left. I couldn't thank him enough. He was gone as quickly as he appeared, leaving no trace in the snow or tracks of ever being there. At 2:42 AM, embarrassed, I explained to the Fire Chief what happened, and he said he would have someone drive me to the Cass Corridor Shelter on Cass Street and Third. I knew from past experience the reputation of Cass Corridor. I had no other choice. He gave the kids some hot chocolate and donuts; I thanked him, and we left. After I registered with the shelter, we got a room for one night only. It was Friday. The drug dealers, tricksters, and pimps were turning in from a hard night's work. I didn't sleep; I dried the kids' clothes on the radiator and tore phone numbers out of the telephone book. At 7:00 a.m., they put everyone out of the shelter.

With my kids in tow, we headed to White Castle on Woodward and bought them burgers and milk for breakfast. Afterward, On Monday I made a phone call to the Department of Social Services at 640 Temple. The intake worker asked us to come in. We caught the Woodward bus, transferred to the Grand River bus line, and walked over six blocks. The line for help was so long that it met us at the outside door. Both black and white poor people were standing outside in the cold, waiting on the concrete steps for assistance.

Around 11:30 AM, we finally made our way inside. I sat my children down and went to stand in another line just to sign up to be seen. At noon, the workers went to lunch. They returned at 1:00 PM and started calling our names by 2:10 PM. We were called back into the office of an older, heavy-set black woman who listened very carefully to my story. The only things she could offer were a bus ticket, an emergency food voucher for Olde King Kole supermarket, a furniture voucher for beds, and a kitchen table with four chairs—redeemable at the local Salvation Army, St. Vincent de Paul, or any other Goodwill store that would accept it. She mentioned that the state would pay for us to stay two nights at the Rio Grande Motel on West Grand Blvd. and Linwood, across the street from Northwestern High School, where The Temptations and various other Motown artists had graduated. I was familiar with the roach motel. She couldn't give me any money because I didn't have an address. However, she promised that if I found a place to live, she would pay a deposit of $125 for me.

"Where do we go after Monday? Where do we stay?" I asked.

"I don't know. I've done all I could," she replied. "I'll call the motel and tell them you're coming."

I thanked her, and we went back out to wait for my name to be called. At 5:00 PM, they finally called me. I walked to the glass window; the inside shade was drawn well below eye level. I was given four bus tickets, four transfers, a food voucher for $65, and a furniture order for $119. We left there, walking to hail a cab on the Grand River.

I thanked God that we didn't have far to go. I had the driver take me to the motel first to register and get my key. I went in, turned on the heat, and then got back in the cab. He dropped us off at Old King Koles, a supermarket my parents shopped at when I was a child, and we lived on 15th Street. The room I got was a kitchenette with one full-sized bed. I bought some lunch meat and crackers, milk, juice, cookies, Vienna sausages, bacon, eggs, bread, margarine, chicken, rice, cooking oil, hot dogs, polish sausages, pork and beans, paper plates, and plastic silverware, plus one pot and one cheap pan to cook my kids a hot meal. I got a jitney to give us a ride back to the room.

Upon entering, the roaches were running everywhere. I hurriedly closed the door and ran with my kids to the office to tell the manager what I saw. "The whole kitchen area was moving. These were full-grown roaches that had been there for a while."

He didn't seem shocked at all. "I will not stay in there with my kids," I declared.

"I don't blame you," he responded. "I can give you another room in the newer building next door. It has a kitchen."

"Yes," I said, relieved. The new room was a little cleaner and offered no roaches. I inspected it thoroughly, turned on the heat, and everything seemed okay for the moment. I cooked dinner, gave the kids a warm bath, and by 7:43 PM, they were asleep.

Finally, after being up for more than 24 hours, I fell into a light sleep across the bed, still in my clothes. Gunshots and loud arguing woke me up. Peeking out the cracked window, I saw two men and a cab driver fighting over the cab fare right in front of my door. "God, please make them go away." They did, and I heard no more gunfire that night.

Monday morning, before checkout, I called Buffalo Projects and explained my situation; they added my name to the long waiting list. I paid twenty-three dollars for one more night at the motel. Then, it was off to Cots, another shelter for just one night.

They put everybody out at 7:00 a.m. It was cold, so I got on the bus and rode from one end to the other. I returned to the Cots, and they were full.

I got the Joy Road bus and rode to Diane Smith's house on the lower east side of the city. My plan was not to tell her that I was homeless; she was my girl and had been since I was nine years old. But I was highly embarrassed, and I didn't want anyone to know what happened. Diane Smith was too happy to see me. She made us feel welcome, and she invited us to stay with her for a few days. "Hell, she said if you're going to stay in Detroit, you can move in with me. We'll split the bills. Diane always had financial support from her father.

Not knowing my situation, as bad as it was, I needed somewhere to stay. I knew that her lifestyle and mine were totally different. Diane was out there. Her house stayed full of all types of men. She would fuck anything and everything; she didn't care what her kids thought. She had four children. Three boys and a girl.

Her house was clean, and she was a good cook. She made the best homemade spaghetti from scratch you ever ate. We had crackers, spaghetti, and Kool-Aid for dinner. Then, I put the kids to sleep on her couch so I could watch them. Diane and I sat in her kitchen at the table and drank a pint of Canadian Club, no chaser. We talked about Burnella's funeral and who was there. She told me that Ollie called her and asked if he could come over and that he needed someone to talk to. She agreed, and they ended up in bed together. "Damn, Diane. You shouldn't have done that," I said. "It's not personal. I just can't pass it up," she replied. "Well, you need to learn how to," I said.

We played the Blues that night—Johnny Taylor, Tyrone Davis, Bobby Blue Bland, Lattimore, and Buddy Guy. We reminisced, and we cried. I told her what Nina did to me. And she said that I could stay there as long as I needed to. The next day, I used her phone and called my mother. She was glad to hear from me. I told her where I was and gave her Diane's phone number and address. "Mama," I said, "you can call Diane, because she'll always know where I am. Don't worry. I just got us a nice apartment on the west side. I'll be moving in on Monday." I told her that lie because I didn't want her to worry; her health was deteriorating. I called Buffalo Projects, and I was still on the list. The manager said that because of my emergency situation, I could move in on the next available date. I thanked her. Buffalo Projects was as close to the alley as I could get without living outside. But if she gave it to me, I'd take it.

Late that night, as I was sleeping in bed with my kids, I heard this scratching, gnawing, chewing sound. It woke me up. I felt something moving in the bed with us. I pulled back the covers, and there was a big rat in the bed with us. I jumped up and turned on the lights, grabbing my kids in the same breath. I ran out of the room into Diane's bedroom, which she was sharing with God knows who. I put the kids on the couch and grabbed the broom. Diane and I went back into the room and grabbed their clothes and jackets. I dressed them, and we left.

"Don't go," she said.

"Girl, I've got to go. I can't stay here with these rats running over me and my kids. I'll call you and let you know where I'm at."

"It's late," she said.

"I know. I'll be alright. I called the few shelters they had in Detroit, knowing the numbers by heart. They were all full. We rode the Gratiot bus that night, all night. Diane lived on Van Dyke off Gratiot Avenue. The buses ran fast. As soon as we got to the bus stop, the bus was pulling up. I was tired, but I knew that I had to stay up all night and watch over my kids. I was running out of money; if it weren't for Diane giving me twenty dollars, I would have had only five.

Two days later, I was back at Cass Corridor. The manager remembered me and gave us someone else's room. Outside my room, I used the pay phone to call Diane, letting her know that I was alright. She informed me that the lady from Buffalo Projects had called and left her number for me.

It was Friday after 8:00 p.m.; they were closed.

That morning, they had cleared out the shelter. All I had were twenty-five dollars in food stamps and three dollars in my pocket. We had nowhere to go. It was cold, cloudy, dark, and dreary, much like our future seemed to be. We crossed the street to the vacant lot that housed everything from abandoned cars and old sofas to scrap metal. It was a deserted, depressing graveyard of a lot.

Seeking shelter for my kids, we got inside an abandoned car. That's where we stayed until lunchtime. I took my kids inside, and we stood in the soup line in the kitchen. They gave us soup and crackers. I didn't eat anything; I tried to keep to myself, avoiding mixing and mingling. After lunch, we were thrown back onto the streets. The shelter doors wouldn't open again until dinner time.

I walked back over to the car I had claimed as my own. A man was getting ready to climb inside. I yelled at him, "Don't do that. That's my car for my kids. If you get in, there's going to be a fight." He was half-drunk. He called me a bitch and my sons bastards.

I took all my frustrations out on him. I approached him with my fists balled up and hit him with all my might, knocking him to the ground and demanded, "You better apologize to my children right now, or I'm gonna tear you a brand-new asshole."

He apologized and tried to touch their hands. I warned him, "Don't touch my children." He got up and walked away. I hurt my hand. I was the shelter hero. I surprised myself; everyone saw what I did. I was mad as hell. "Don't anybody call my kids out by their names again. I will kick your ass," I declared.

I put the kids back in the car, and we waited. At 5:00 PM, it was time to go back in, but my name wasn't on the list; they had no room for us. They were full. I practically begged a woman to give us a room. She was callous and cold. "No," she said. "We need our rooms." The manager, who had helped me before, had gone home for the weekend.

My eyes filled with water, but I didn't cry.

The real deal was that she was using the room for tricks, and she wanted to make sure that she got her cut. I was hip to it.

As I turned to walk away, a prostitute with blond hair approached me. I pulled her aside and offered to sell my food stamps for half price. She agreed, tearing a ten out of the book and handing me fifteen in return, along with a twenty-dollar bill.

"Take care of your business," she said, winking. "Thank you," I whispered." God bless you."

"No need to thank me; this is what I do for a living. They don't call me Goldie for nothing. I earned that name from the sweat on my brow. I'd rather give it to you and those babies than to my pimp. I just gotta turn an extra trick to make it up. That's all; it ain't nothing. You remind me of my little sister. Be cool, little sister, and take care of those babies."

Now I had twenty-three dollars and fifteen in stamps.

We walked up to the liquor store on Woodward to get change for the phone. I fed the kids at White Castle, then we returned and made the abandoned car our home for the night. We huddled together to stay warm; the kids didn't want to fall asleep right away—they were cold, and we were damn near on top of each other.

Goldie brought us two clean blankets and two clean pillows.

"This is what I do; I work the streets. I pick up my tricks right here. So, I'll watch over you until 5:30 in the morning," she told me as I hugged her and thanked her.

"I'd give you my room," she said, "but I'm working. I gotta make so much money or take a chance at getting my teeth knocked out. I'll take care of you like my little sister."

I could tell she had once been a nice-looking woman, but life had taken its toll on her. I stayed up all night, praying and rocking my babies in my arms. "God, please have mercy on us. Help me so I can take care of my kids. Look after us, and don't let any harm come to us this night. I pray this prayer in Jesus' name, Amen."

White Castle had become my friend—a safe haven. I was washing my children up, brushing their teeth, and feeding them right there.

Sunday morning, I took the kids to the shelter and signed us up. The house manager could see in my face—she knew to come correct, or I'd be beating her ass soon. She gave me a room immediately.

"If we stay hidden, you can stay inside your room for the whole day," she said. "I guess so," I replied, "you made your money last night at our expense." She never said anything.

I received my key, and we were nearly frozen. We walked back to the liquor store for milk and small food items. On our way back to the shelter, a church on the street corner was selling barbecue and chicken dinners. I bought two—one of each. The meals came laced with baked beans, coleslaw, string beans, fresh bread, and a Faygo Pop—a local Detroit brand from Gratiot Avenue. The church mothers looked clean, as did the food. It was the best I could do under the circumstances.

After giving the kids, a much-needed stand-up bath, I put them down for a nap. I washed and dried their clothes on the radiator, then took my own stand-up bath and did the same with my clothes. I could feel my body and hands thawing out.

We woke, blessed our food, ate dinner, and went back to sleep, warm at last.

Monday morning, I got up early to use the house iron. At 7:10 AM, I left Cass Corridor for good, determined never to return. I was going to do everything in my power to avoid going back. As we walked out, Detroit's finest were outside, questioning everyone about the previous night. My eyes scanned the crowd for Goldie, to thank her and say goodbye.

A partially nude female body had been found, her throat cut from ear to ear. The police questioned everyone but me. I was trying to get out of the way when a lady mentioned they had found Goldie's body in an alley on Second Avenue near Cass. She had been murdered by one of her clients.

You could have knocked me over with a feather.

In disbelief, I stammered, "Are you sure it was her?" Just then, an officer flashed Goldie's picture. I felt sick to my stomach and started walking fast to get away from there. I felt bad for her and her family, but what could I do? So, I prayed and asked God to forgive her sins and welcome her into heaven. I couldn't even cry for her. My heart was numb with pain.

"Any tears that I had left. I needed for me."

We boarded the Woodward bus and transferred to the Conant bus line. I was walking into the Buffalo administration office just as they were opening. I met Mrs. Ford and told her about our living conditions and what had happened to Goldie.

Mrs. Ford said she had heard about it on the radio that morning on her way to work. "Well, this will be a better day for you," she said, offering me a two-bedroom apartment on Gable Court. "It's not cleaned, and it needs to be painted."

"I'll clean it up and paint it if you just give me a place to stay with my kids," I offered. "You got a deal," she replied. "Fill this application out, and I'll take care of the rest."

I hugged her and thanked her. Right there, I called the social worker and gave her my new address. Mrs. Ford handed me the keys and pointed the way. When we walked in, I couldn't believe my eyes at how filthy it was, but I thanked God anyway. Someone had left an old couch, and the telephone, lights, and gas were on. "Thank you, Lord," I said out loud.

I called Diane and asked her to come over to sit with the kids while I cleaned up and ran a few errands. "This place is so filthy; I don't want the kids to get down off the couch."

"I'm on my way," she said, "because Daddy got my kids."

I found an old broom and mop in the apartment, so I cleaned until she arrived. I called Laura, forgetting the time difference, and we talked. She said she had been leaving messages for me at Nina's house. I told Laura what had happened and where I was now. Laura mentioned that Mr. Martinez had mailed my last check and food stamps to my post office box in San Jose.

"Oh my God," I exclaimed, "open it." "And by the Grace of God."

She did. It was a check for six hundred fifty-four dollars and fifty cents and three hundred dollars in food stamps.

I had a check from the daycare center where I worked for one hundred twenty-seven dollars. I couldn't believe it, and I started to cry.

"Don't cry, baby," she said. "I'm gonna help you." Thank you, God."

Laura told me she would deposit my check into her account and would give Western Union the money that day. She also promised to pick up my food stamps and mail them to me right away.

Relief washed over me immediately. I hugged my kids and reassured them that everything was going to be alright now. I called the utility companies and Michigan Bell to transfer everything into my name. An hour and a half later, Diane knocked at the door. I shared the good news, took some sheets and blankets from the shelter, and cleaned off the couch for the kids to sit on. "Take care of my kids," I told her. "You know I will," she replied.

Diane had only ever been harsh to her kids. "You all be good," I said as I hugged and kissed them. "Mama will be back soon, and I'll bring you something good."

"Yeah, and bring me a pint of C.C.," Diane called out. "You got it," I replied, then left.

Walking to the bus line, I headed downtown to Western Union, where Laura had sent me nine hundred and eighty-one dollars—two hundred of which were out of her own pocket. I was in good shape now. "Praise God"

I took the Gratiot Bus and alighted at Coulter Brothers' goodwill store on the corner of Gratiot and Chene, a mile and a half from Aunt Janie's. The owner let me redeem my voucher for a couch, two big fluffy chairs, two lamps, a sturdy kitchen table with four chairs, a big rug, and a used bed for me. However, he couldn't deliver it until the next day, after 4:00 PM. I thanked him and caught the bus back downtown.

At a furniture store downtown, I bought a new set of bunk beds for the kids, scheduling the delivery for the next afternoon. Then, I went over to K-Mart, where I stocked up on new linen, towels, Batman sheets, blankets, plenty of towels, toothbrushes, clothes, coats, boots, underwear, tee shirts, hats, gloves, mittens, diapers, new baby bottles, socks, thermal and flannel shirts, books, a few toys, and candy. I also grabbed cleaning supplies like a mop, broom, oven cleaner, Lysol, curtains and rods, pillows, vitamins, and Father John.

I even bought myself some size 12 blue jeans, down from 14. I'd lost weight.

Satisfied, I got a Jitney to give me a ride home. We stopped at the Americana Hotel near Hamtramck, where I paid $69.00 for a room with two double beds for one night. He helped me carry some pages inside. I kept the bag with the clothes in it close.

Me and Diane loaded the kids in the car, and he took us to get Chinese food before dropping us off at the hotel. I asked him to come back in three days to take me to Amtrak to get the rest of my stuff. Meanwhile, Diane had the Jitney take her to the liquor store. She returned with a fifth of C.C., a pack of Kools, and his phone number 40 minutes later.

After giving the kids, a bath and feeding them, I propped them up in bed to watch some TV. They were happy and tired, and so was I. I threw away everything they'd been wearing in the garbage can. Diane knew I was going back to the apartment to clean up. She told me to be careful and promised to take care of my kids and not to drink until I returned.

I hailed a cab, and by 6:38 AM, I was walking through the hotel door. I'd cleaned that nasty apartment until it made me throw up. My hands were raw sore and bleeding, but I didn't give a damn.

I had a clean place to take them to. The whole apartment was stark, made of cement, with cinder block walls and concrete floors, warmed by radiator heat.

But I got the job done. They were still sleeping. Slipping into a hot bath, I allowed the heat to soothe away the exhaustion. Afterwards, I descended to the hotel lobby and ordered a hearty breakfast of French toast, bacon, eggs, sausages, orange juice, milk, toast, oatmeal, and fresh fruit.

I returned to our room, waking the kids with kisses; they were ecstatic to see me. Diane was still fast asleep on the floor.

After breakfast, we dressed and hailed a cab to Farmer Jack's, where I spent one hundred and forty dollars on groceries. Highland Appliance was right next door. There, I bought the kids a brand new 20-inch color television. With our shopping done, I arranged for a Jitney to take us home.

Virley Coulter and his brother Willie were already waiting outside our apartment. They were early, which turned out to be a blessing given that my right hand was jammed at the wrist and aching and swelling—something I had ignored until then. The Coulter brothers didn't just deliver my furniture; they lingered, helping to assemble the beds for the kids and me. They even brought in the groceries and hauled away the old sofa to resell.

"God is good!" I exclaimed, thankful. I hugged and kissed Mr. Coulter, offering him twenty dollars for his help. He declined, suggesting I spend it on the boys instead. "Buy them some socks, or something," he advised. There was a gentle wisdom about him that I admired, a quality I found in those who, like him, had lived rich, challenging lives.

Mr. Coulter was a principled man who believed in helping out, particularly when it came to black folks during hard times. Though a few white families lived in our depressed area, he helped them regardless. His empathy stemmed from a painful past; white folks had lynched his oldest brother when he was just fifteen, a year before they moved here from Macon, Georgia, in 1927—he rode the same train as my mother in 1926.

He was the only literate one among his six brothers. They worked tirelessly, saving enough to rent—and eventually buy—a building from a Jewish man, where they started a moving company and a used furniture store.

As his parents aged, Mr. Coulter cared for them in his home until they passed, just a month apart. I learned that Mr. Coulter, like my mother, walked to school barefoot. That's why he suggested buying socks.

"Did you know my mother?" I asked.

He chuckled as he took a pinch of snuff from his butternut can, wiping his mouth with the back of his hand. "We could all be cousins down south," he mused, his eyes twinkling with mirth.

As the afternoon waned, Diane left with the Coulter brothers. She had taken a liking to Willie. Meanwhile, with help from my boys, I managed to put away the groceries and make the beds despite my throbbing hand.

In the oven, I baked pork chops with sides of gravy, baked potatoes, biscuits, spinach, and hot apple pie. After dinner, I gave the kids a warm Mr. Bubble bath. Then, on our knees together, we said our prayers, a family united in gratitude and hope.

Finally, as the harsh winter yielded to the promise of spring, I began my search for a new place to live. The Buffalo projects were never meant to be more than a steppingstone, a temporary refuge from the storms of life. Each day, I'd walk through the dangerous streets with my children, buying newspapers as we maneuvered past the lurking shadows of addiction, violence, and despair.

Once the kids were napping and dinner simmered on the stove, I'd hunker down with the classifieds. My eyes would cross as I circled phone numbers diligently, calling each one in hopes of finding a better home. But each call ended in disappointment—either the rent was unaffordable, welfare wasn't accepted, or the waiting lists were interminably long. The nice, clean neighborhoods to the west, with their inviting houses, remained just out of reach, demanding more than I could afford.

The reality of the Buffalo projects was grim—addicts, users, murderers, rapists, and break-ins were part of the daily tableau. Yet, what I had in my favor was street smarts. My demeanor, distant and uninviting, kept many would-be troublemakers at bay, especially men. I became a master at invisibility, blending into the background to protect my family.

For added security, I wedged a large butcher knife in the back door and cut shade stick rods to fit snugly into every downstairs window, a precaution left by a previous tenant. It was a meager existence at the bottom of society's barrel, surrounded by my own kind but not of them.

Yet, outside these confines, the world opened up. We spent countless days at Detroit's grand institutions—the Main Library's vast collections, the Detroit Institute of Art's inspiring exhibits, the Historical and Science

Museums, and occasionally a movie or church service. We even explored diverse cuisines, enriching our lives beyond the projects' grip.

On some days, I would simply teach my children about life. Yes, they were young, but I believed in starting their education from the cradle. We'd ride the bus through Detroit's tougher neighborhoods, down Woodward into Highland Park, where the streets were alive with the vivid and sometimes shocking realities of urban life—streetwalkers, pimps, brawls, and the ever- present liquor stores.

"It's by the grace of God that it wasn't me," I'd tell them, pointing out the destitute figures on the sidewalks. "And if you're not careful, that could be you. Education is your exit from this life."

I was adamant that they should not mingle with the other kids we passed on our walks. "You have to pick and choose your friends carefully," I would instruct them. "If you lay down with dogs, you'll get up with fleas." Learn to discriminate. Pick and choose your friends.

It wasn't that I believed we were better than anyone; it was that we were on a different path—I wanted more for them. This was the ethos I instilled, the same one my mother passed down to me: "You're always better than your circumstances."

We seldom played outside. When we did step out, it was to leave the neighborhood for the day. The rundown playgrounds were littered with discarded syringes, a constant reminder of the peril just outside our door. Every day, my prayers were the same: for God to grant me the strength and time to raise my children away from this.

To give me strength and to help me find another place to live, I'd stay up at night listening out, watching over my kids, checking the stove and walls for fire, and praying.

This particular day, I received a telephone call. It was an old man returning my call. He said that he had a property to rent—a two-bedroom upper flat that was clean and safe. "I will rent it to you if you like it," he offered.

I asked if I could come and see it right away. He agreed and gave me his address. Immediately, I dressed the kids and myself, and we caught the 7-mile bus. We got off and walked to his house. He was friendly and welcomed us in. His wife made us tea while we talked. His wife introduced herself as Mrs. Ruth Gronowski; he asked to just be called Walter.

I filled out the application. Walter mentioned he would waive the security deposit if I took care of the property. It was newly painted, and he wanted $250.00 a month for rent. "If you like it, you could move in right away," he said.

His wife took a special liking to my children, continuously remarking how well-behaved they were. Unfortunately, Mr. Walter was unable to show the flat, so he gave me the keys and pointed the way.

The building sat right around the corner from his house. It wasn't what I was hoping for, but it was better than where we were—3833 Wexford on the corner of East Seven Mile Road.

A deserted office building where Mr. Walter ran his real estate company and had retired. Two side-by-side upper flats are divided equally by cement and drywall. Facing the front, it offered a clear view of Pershing, a predominantly black high school where the Detroit Dramatics had gone to school. It was clean, with plenty of windows and hardwood floors. The bonus was that it was free of rats and roaches. A second-story building on a rooftop, with no safety features whatsoever to prevent one from falling. I'd never seen so many steps in my life. It was like a long walk to heaven.

I told him that I didn't have any money, and if I gave him a deposit of fifty dollars, would he hold it until the first of the month? He didn't want to leave it vacant that long, so he said, "Take the keys, and pay me when you get it."

"Oh my God, thank you," I thanked him. "Bless your heart," he said to me. "I've never seen anyone as young as you take care of their kids like you do. You can't be a bad person. And you're clean, I can tell. You're a good mother, and that's all I need to know."

He handed me the keys, and his wife gave me a hug.

"Call us after you move in," they said, standing on the porch and waving goodbye. I couldn't believe what just happened. God heard my prayers. I felt good inside, and it showed. We boarded the bus, and I gave the kids the individual lunches I'd made for them. We had a long ride home, so I was able to think and plan my next move.

I didn't know how I was going to get the money to move. Only that, I was. I was ready to move now; I didn't have time to wait. It was getting hot outside, and I know from living around black folks that's when the brothers come out.

I stopped by the party store near home and got some boxes. "Thank you, Lord," I said out loud. I was tickled inside at God's merciful work.

On the way home, a car pulled up to me and offered me a ride.

I never looked around. "No, thank you," I said. "I know that walk anywhere," he said. "Don't you remember me? It's me, Bob. I lived up under you on Elmhurst and 12th Street. Don't tell me that you don't remember me."

I turned around and looked into a familiar face from the past. "You used to take care of your mama over there. Your mother's blind. isn't she?" he asked.

"Yes," I said with a full smile on my face. "I remember you." His face was the friendliest face I'd seen in a while over there anyway. He offered us a ride in his yellow and gold two-tone car. He asked if I was moving and offered to take me to Farmer Jacks to get some more boxes. I accepted.

He helped me in the house with the kids, and André fell asleep in the car. Bob stayed for dinner, and he waited for me to give the kids a bath and read "Jack and the Beanstalk."

"You got your hands full, don't you?" he observed, watching me juggle the demands of the moment.

"Yes, I do, but I'm hanging in and taking care of my business," I replied with a half-smile, masking the exhaustion beneath.

"Do you have kids?" I asked, shifting the focus back to him. His head dropped slightly as he answered, "Yeah, a girl and a boy."

"Are you still at home with your kids?" I probed further.

"No," he said curtly, his expression clouding over. Sensing the tension, I quickly asked, "So, you're still married?"

"I'm getting a divorce. We've been separated since I last saw you," he confessed. The weight of his words seemed to fill the room, prompting me to start packing some nearby items. As I worked, I muttered to myself about the tasks awaiting me: "I just got one baby potty trained; now I have to work on the other."

Andre and Terrance, eleven months apart, were still in bottles and in diapers, but I was managing.

"Don't you worry about my boys; I'm taking care of them. You just take care of yours," I said sharply, not looking up from the box I was filling.

"I'm not worried, and I didn't mean to offend you," he quickly clarified. "Actually, I'm impressed at how well you take care of your sons. And I'd like to come back and visit you, if you don't mind."

"Visit me for what?" I asked, skeptical.

"Just because," he said with a slight shrug. "You know that I've always liked you. I've been trying to get you to be my girlfriend for a long time. And now that I found you, I'm not going to lose track of you again."

I blushed, despite myself. "Well, you have a wife, and you should be focused on your relationship with your family."

I walked him to the door. "Good night, and thank you," I said formally.

He leaned in and kissed me on the cheek. "Good night to you. See you tomorrow," he replied, his confidence unshaken.

"I don't know what for," I muttered under my breath.

He laughed. "You'll see," he teased, adding as he stepped out, "Oh, and I like your haircut."

Before turning in, I got down on my knees and thanked the Lord for the good day He had given me. The telephone rang—it was Laura. She called to tell me that the man, Mr. Hall, a neighbor who had stolen my car from in front of her door, was involved in a bad accident that closed the roads in San Jose. The accident was so severe that Mr. Hall had to be cut from his truck, both of his legs amputated while he was in the hospital, and then he died two weeks later.

"See, it doesn't pay to mistreat God's people. You're blessed and loved by the Creator Himself. If you just hold on, God will work it all out," she said.

"God has His unchanging hands on you and your children. God loves you," she added before hanging up.

Later that morning, I lay awake in bed, pondering Laura's words about Mr. Hall. Despite everything, I couldn't help but feel sorry for him. Her words about God's love lingered in my mind, and with that comforting thought, I turned over, scooted up under my baby Terrance, and fell asleep.

Early the next morning, I woke up and called my mother. I told her I was moving and suggested that maybe Nina could bring her and Tina down to stay with me for a while.

Then I called Mr. Coulter. "How much will you charge me?" I inquired.

"Not much," he answered. "You don't have that much to move. As a matter of fact, if you fry me some chicken and make me some turnip greens and cornbread, I'll do it for nothing."

"You got a deal. I'll be ready this Saturday," I agreed. "Okay, just call me," he replied.

Around 10:05 that morning, a knock came at the door. It was Bob with his mother, and he had a surprise for the boys. I couldn't believe it. I let them in, and he introduced her as Lettie Matthews, his mother. They came there to help me pack and do my running around. She was instantly nice and eager to help.

"I can't let your mother pack and move boxes," I protested. "Oh no," she chuckled. "I'll babysit while y'all do everything." I hesitated but finally agreed.

Bob went to the car and came back with something moving under his nicely pressed red pinstriped shirt.

It was a puppy—his surprise for the boys. They loved it. Under my breath, I muttered, "What the hell am I going to do with a puppy? I already have two babies in diapers."

I asked him what kind of dog it was, was it vicious, and would it bite my kids. "He's a 'sooner,'" he said.

"A sooner? What's a sooner?" I asked, puzzled. "Soon to be anything," he joked. We all laughed.

"Mama, can we keep him?" the kids pleaded, their eyes alight with excitement. "We love him, and we'll take care of him."

"Yes, but let me give him a bath first," I replied, trying to mask my weariness with a smile.

After Bob took me to get boxes, we returned to find the kids, Ms. Matthews, and the puppy all asleep together in the same bed upstairs. I didn't want to take her kindness for granted. Before we left again, I left her a note explaining that we were heading over to the apartment to clean up. "I'll call you later," I wrote.

In the car, Bob tried to hold my hand. I gently pulled away. At the apartment, I cleaned the cupboards and bathroom, swept the floors, and wiped down the walls. Bob mopped the entire house, including the long flight of stairs, and checked the locks on the doors. We stopped by the

Dairy Queen on our way back; I bought ice cream and banana splits for everyone—it was the least I could do.

When we returned, I hugged Ms. Matthews and thanked her warmly. Bob took his mother home and then came back, his presence increasingly persistent.

Saturday morning, bright and early, Mr. Coulter and his brother Willie knocked at the door. Bob and his mother were close on their heels; they nearly walked in together. Ms. Matthews drove her car with the kids inside, while Bob helped Mr. Coulter and Willie move me in. After everything was set, I hugged and thanked them, promising Bob and his mother a dinner invitation soon.

I was exhausted, mentally and physically; my hand was hurting. Nevertheless, I managed to serve the kids hot chicken noodle soup, sandwiches, milk, and applesauce for dinner. Meanwhile, Bob busied himself assembling the beds. He noticed my discomfort and offered to rub my back, then suggested, "Let me give you a bath."

"No, thank you," I said firmly. "I can bathe myself."

Every day, Bob came to my house after rehearsals. He was in a singing group called the Quixotis, performing lead tenor alongside two girls and another guy. Time passed, and my relationship with Nina had cooled considerably by the time she dropped off Mama and Tina. Sometimes I'd keep them for weeks because of Mama's legs. I didn't mind; it gave me plenty of time with them. I took them to movies or Bell Isle just to enjoy the scenery. Mama was doing fine now, and I was even considering moving back to San Jose.

It was a hot summer, and the kids lacked a proper place to play. Bob would often take us to the drive-in or to visit my old friends from the neighborhood, to picnics, barbecues, or just for a ride—anything to get out of the house. Sometimes, he brought us to his rehearsals. He had developed a lasting relationship with the boys, teaching them things that only a man knows. They loved him, and he loved them back.

I watched carefully as their relationship developed. Anyone I chose to love would have to love and respect my children too. I thanked God for our flat on Wexford, but it was only a steppingstone to something better. When my children napped, I spent that time daydreaming about the past and the loved ones gone. I dreamt of the day I could move into a better home and lifestyle with my children. I had big plans for them—they were going to college. They weren't just going to hang out on the streets and become gang members, bums, drug dealers, pimps, or addicts. My road might be long and heavy, but I was more determined than ever. I must stay focused. I was nineteen and a half.

No man was ever going to come before my kids. I was going to be the biggest influence in their lives. Nobody could love them more than me. They were mine, and that's all that mattered.

As "Rock Your Baby" by George McCrae played on the radio, my eyes filled with tears. I thought of Burnella, her smile, and her beautiful, sweet spirit that surrounded her. I wondered who was raising her children now and how much they must miss her.

I remember the last time we spent together—smoking cigarettes, learning new dance steps, putting on lipstick, and trying on clothes and shoes. "Burnella, London," I whispered, the name echoing softly in the emptiness. "I missed you so much. You'll always be a part of my life." My heart was heavy, laden with baggage from the past. I sent this up to you, Miss London. One of our favorite jams. Remember the night we bopped to it? Together, we shut the basement party down.

Just Me and You: The Four Top 1964 "Baby, I Need You Lovin"

June 7, 1974, Before Mama returned home to Nina, I planned a grand dinner party. It was also my son's birthday. He'll be turning 2 years old. I invited Mr. Coulter and his brother Willie, Diane, Ms. Matthews, and Bob. The menu was a feast: fried fish, fried chicken, barbeque ribs, turnip greens with the bulbs, potato salad, coleslaw, baked beans, macaroni and cheese, hot water bread, pepper salad, corn on the cob, and my first attempt at peach cobbler. And you know I nailed it. I took great pride in cooking for my children. And my house was clean.

And just as I put the cornbread in the oven to stay warm, I heard an interruption on the radio. And the announcer said I hate to interrupt this program. A man was killed last night on Grandy Street. Lawrence Blackwell was gunned down. As soon as he said it, I screamed, "Who?" And he repeated it to me as if he heard what I said. Again, he said Lawrence Blackwell was killed last night in an altercation on Detroit's East Side. Oh my God, I screamed. Please don't let it be him, I begged. I tried to calm myself while I looked for Margies phone number. When she answered, I called her Margie; that's all I said, and she said yes, baby, it's true. I dropped the phone and fell to my knees, covering my mouth with both hands from the loud scream. She told me what happened to Lawrence; she said that Tyson and Lawrence were playing around, or so he thought. Tyson showed Lawrence his gun, and he pulled it on him. And Lawrence said, laughing, "Shoot me; I ain't never been dead before. Tyson, his best friend from kindergarten, shot Lawrence in the chest. Looking up at Tyson with disbelief, Lawrence dropped to his knees. Then she said that Lawrence begged for his life. And Tyson stepped around the back of Lawrence, still on his knees, and shot him in the backside of his head, killing him.

The tragic news and disbelief of Lawrence's death upset me so much that I had to go to the bathroom throughout the party, cover my mouth, and cry. I was in shock, holding it all in and remembering that that's the same son of a bitch that I didn't want to meet that morning. And I recall the cold wind that passed through my face that day when Lawrence hugged me. Oh, my God. I couldn't wait for everyone to leave. I couldn't wait to be alone. So, I could open my windows and turn the speakers outwards and play his song, our song by William Bell, 1971 Jam

"Till My Back Aint' Got No Bones." A dedication to his memory. Lawrence Blackwell was twenty-one years old.

Everyone ate until they were full, then sat around reminiscing about the past. Ms. Matthews engaged Mama in a deep discussion about the Bible. It was a perfect evening. Everyone complimented my cooking and my haircut—a bold shaved style not commonly seen here in Detroit. "It takes a lot of nerve to cut your hair off," they said. Bob, ever the gentleman, offered to take me and the kids to the movies the next day. I wanted to see Claudine with James Earl Jones, Diahann Carroll, and Lawrence Hilton-Jacobs. We had just seen Three the Hard Way and Enter the Dragon. It was sweltering inside, so whenever I could afford a movie with air conditioning, I took it. Claudine made me cry and think, resonating deeply with my own life.

Exhausted, I wanted nothing more than to go to bed. Bob lingered, sniffing around me like a dog in heat, but I wasn't interested.

I called Laura, updating her on Mama's improved condition and expressing my desire to return. "Come on, you don't have to stay in the shelter. You can stay here with me," she insisted. She had moved from her apartment in San Juan Bautista to a townhouse on Senter Road. Knowing I had a safety net was a relief.

I shared my plans with Mama. "I don't blame you for wanting to leave Michigan," she said, supportive as ever. "You have to do all you can to provide for your kids. Don't worry about me; I'll be just fine." I asked if she had heard from my brother, Rickey. I hadn't spoken to him since I'd been home. "Yes," she replied, "I'm not sure where he's living. I think he's on Rangoon and Tireman, in a four-family flat, driving a City Cab."

"City cab?" I exclaimed, alarmed. "He'll get killed! These brothers are robbing and killing Black people. I don't want him driving a cab."

Determined, I asked Bob to help me find my brother. Rickey was lucid. It hurts me to know of him like this. As the youngest of the two, we had always been close; I didn't judge him—I prayed for him. Rickey was a devoted father to three children, treating his stepdaughter as his own. Despite his struggles, he loved his family more than life itself.

I hugged him tightly, kissed him, and urged him to call me and to find a safer job. As I left, the weight of our shared struggles and hopes filled me with a determined sadness, pushing me to keep moving forward, no matter the cost.

My sister Charlie pulled up in a cab just as I was about to leave Rickey's place. We embraced warmly; she complimented my new haircut, as did Rickey. Deciding to stay a little longer, we gathered on the front porch, reveling in each other's company, sharing gossip, and confessing our love for each other. They sipped on beer while I stuck to Faygo Pop, finding it too hot for anything stronger. Bob excused himself, promising to return at 6:00 p.m. to pick us up. It was only the second time Charlie had met Bob and, I thought, the first for Rickey.

Later that night, after Bob had driven me and the sleeping kids home, he asked if he could come up to talk. He seemed to have something pressing on his mind that he felt I needed to know. After tucking the kids into bed, I listened as Bob shared his tumultuous past. And thinking about Lawrence's funeral that day at James H. Cole's Funeral Home, right on the corner from Motown. I caught the bus and went. It was overflowing with well-wishers and friends. His poor mama and sister sat and cried quietly as I bent down to kiss him. I couldn't stay long because I had to get back to my kids'. I saw Yogi, and he tried to hug me, and I pulled away, lighting a cigarette and looking through the crowd for Big Dot, Margie, and Little Dot.

When I returned home, I was sad. I was seeking some fresh air to clear the heavy atmosphere, so I suggested to Bob, "Let's sit on the rooftop. I'm having a glass of wine. Would you like some?"

"No thanks; I'll grab a beer from the store. I'll be right back," he said, pausing before adding, "I just don't want to go home tonight."

We talked into the early morning, seated under the stars. My feelings for him were evolving; I wanted to be sure I wasn't making any mistakes. He broached the subject of my sons, expressing a desire to be a father to them. I told him that I'm their father, and I'm not looking for any man to be a father to my children. I'll take care of my own kids.

"I've grown to love your sons.," he confessed earnestly.

The kids do love you; I'll consider a relationship." I paused, my thoughts drifting to my future plans. "But I won't be here long. I'm planning to go back to California soon, though we can hang out until then. He looked at me with a mix of hope and desperation in his eyes. "I don't want to go home. Can I stay here tonight?"

I agreed, but with conditions. "You can stay, but you'll have to sleep on the couch." My children have to see you sleeping on the couch. He understood.

Every attempt to pay rent to Walter or his wife had been met with procrastination. As I strolled with the kids to make payments, they'd always say, "Oh, just give it to me later," echoing each other's sentiments. I had seven hundred and fifty dollars of his money saved up in blank money orders, but Walter and Ruth wouldn't accept it. "Just hold onto it," they would say. "Maybe I'll collect next month." I had mentioned to them that I might be moving back to California, promising to keep them updated on my departure.

Occasionally, Bob would arrange for his mother to babysit the kids so we could enjoy some time together, either at the movies or hearing him sing at a club. He was keen on integrating me into his life, ensuring I met all his family, and proudly introducing me as his girlfriend. Resolved, I decided to move back to San Jose, and Bob expressed his desire to join me.

I shared the news with Laura, who encouraged, "Bring him with you. He could start a new life here and maybe get some help with his career. You know I'll help anyone trying to help themselves.

I've got people here from Chicago and Alabama. Give him a chance, especially if he loves you and the boys."

Taking her advice to heart, I began making plans to leave soon. When I informed Walter and Ruth of my definite plans to leave, their response was unexpected. "Please keep the rent money you owe us and use it to help yourself," they insisted warmly. "We just really wanted to help you along with your kids. You're not the only young person we've let live here or that we've tried to help. But you're the only one who showed us any backbone. You're the only one who took care of the place and offered to pay your rent on time. We have enough money to live on for the rest of our lives. We need our health back; we don't need money."

"God bless you, child," they said, their voices laden with genuine affection. "Let us hear from you before you leave."

I was stunned. "Oh my God," I murmured to the boys, shaking my head in disbelief. "Did you see what just happened?"

My thoughts then turned to the puppy. I worried about how to handle the situation without upsetting the kids. There was a little girl living next door, so I tentatively suggested to the kids, "What if we give the puppy to her? You could still play with him before we leave."

They were attached to Bosco, and I couldn't bear the thought of hurting them, so I added, "He can't ride the train because he doesn't have a license, and I can't get one for him." They seemed to accept this reasoning.

Internally, I laughed darkly at my own frustration. I really wanted to throw that little stinking, whining, crying mutt, along with Bob, off the rooftop, I thought, but dismissed it as a fleeting, morbid joke.

Training the dog had taken up time I could have spent with my son, who still needed help with potty training. Sometimes, I'd catch a cab to the laundromat, lugging clothes, sheets, and blankets down the long flight of stairs, but other times, I washed clothes and diapers by hand in the bathtub. It was hard, but I persevered.

Bob giving the kids a dog should have been a red flag, among many. but at the time, it didn't see it. When I accepted the dog, it was out of a desire to make my children happy. I loved Bosco, but I was exhausted.

With that realization, we caught the bus to the Salvation Army Goodwill on Woodward and Clairmont, where I bought the kids some pants, shirts, and lightweight jackets. Then we took the Woodward bus downtown to Hudson's. We could have taken the elevator, operated by a real person, but I wanted my sons to experience riding the moving stairs.

Chapter 18

"God Answers Prayers"

There was always a sale in the basement of Hudson's, a place we frequented when I was a child with Mama and Rickey. You could find decent clothes at a reasonable price, and it felt like I was reliving pieces of my childhood as I watched my own children explore the same space.

I managed to buy them new underwear, socks, six pairs of pants each, jackets, and shoes. Though finances were tight, I seized every opportunity to clothe my children well. Pride swelled in my heart at how they presented themselves—they were good boys, and I made sure they knew how proud I was of them at every possible moment. I couldn't always give them much, but I was determined to give them the best of me.

That day, I also picked up some dusters and house shoes for Mama and popcorn from Otto's before treating the boys to dinner at Big Boy's. As we caught the bus home, my mind was at peace, filled with the simple joys of the day.

Arriving home, Bob was there, waiting on our doorstep. "You could have called me," he said, a hint of disappointment in his voice. "I would have taken you shopping."

"Thank you," I replied, "but I just wanted some time alone with my sons today." I paused before asking, "What are you doing here?"

"I just stopped by to see how you are. How's your mother?" he countered.

"That's why I'm here," he continued, his tone shifting. "We had another fight. Can I stay here tonight?"

"Yeah," I agreed, albeit with reservations. "You can sleep on the couch." My empathy for him was tinged with caution; I liked him, but there were clear boundaries I would not cross, especially not with my sons in the picture.

As he helped with the bags and took the baby from my arms, he broached another subject. "So, what did your friend say? Can I go to California too? I'll pay my own way and take care of myself. I'll even pay her rent if she wants. I'm afraid that if I don't get away from here, I might start using again." Yeah, and you don't want that. "I won't be bothered with a drug addict.

I hesitated, then responded, "Yes, Laura said you can come too. She said, I should give you a chance."

Before leaving, I hosted another dinner party, this time inviting only those who didn't mind seeing me in my current state. My old friends looked up to me, and I maintained that image carefully, heeding my mother's teaching to "never let your right hand know what your left hand's doing." I wasn't proud of living in a deserted, dilapidated real estate building or of being on welfare. To collect my food stamps, I'd drive to Redford, Michigan, far from anyone I knew, to avoid bumping into familiar faces.

When friends inquired over the phone about my means of support, I lied, claiming Eric was sending us allotment checks and savings bonds each month. My dinner party was a success, filled with nostalgia and blues music. I'd invited some of Mama's old friends, and she wept with joy at their reunion. It was these little gestures that counted.

I cooked a massive meal and played blues from my extensive record collection, spanning from the 1950s to the 1970s—artists like Howlin' Wolf, Robert Johnson, Muddy Waters, and Detroit's own Little Sonny. People filled the room. The evening was lively with drinks, dancing, and loud conversations, while Mama sat quietly, soaking in the stories of the good old days.

I'd made her favorite sweet potato pie.

Yet as we headed to California, tears streamed down my face. I was torn. The pull to stay and spend whatever time my mother had left wrestled with my desire for a fresh start. Over and over, I asked myself, *"Was I making the right choice?"*

As we arrived in California, the smog blanketed the sky, a stark contrast to Bob's look of enthusiasm and eagerness. He was eager for a fresh start, his eyes scanning the horizon for opportunities. I had loaned him the money to buy his ticket, and he assured me he would repay it once his group manager wired him the funds.

I had managed to save $1,000—a down payment for an apartment and some money to put towards a car. Laura, ever the friend, took me around on her days off, and on other occasions, I would drop her off at work. I had applied at several places but was particularly hopeful about Santee Apartments off McLaughlin Road. It was nice, clean, and, importantly, low-income. I didn't waste time applying for state aid and was soon on it, grateful that the funds and food stamps were retroactive.

Every day, I would drop Bob off at the employment office, as he claimed to be looking for work. In the cool evenings, he would engage the boys in various activities—throwing the football, shooting hoops, wrestling, or playing baseball. They seemed to connect with him, and I appreciated the time he spent with them. But I made sure to spend just as much time with my sons, mirroring Bob's activities. I didn't want them to grow overly attached to him, not after the way they'd become attached to the dog.

Eventually, Bob and I took our relationship to the next level. We had just moved into a two- bedroom unit on the second floor of Santee Apartments. I was thankful for the relief and for Laura's indefatigable support, especially in helping Bob try to find his footing.

I enrolled Shawn in school and kept the boys at home since I couldn't afford daycare after their previous program closed. As days turned into weeks, I found myself questioning my decision to bring Bob along. He had already borrowed money from Laura and two of her friends, and he still owed me for the ticket.

Two months passed, and Bob was still without a job. My patience thinned, morphing into resentment. I was beginning to lose all respect for him, feeling he was leeching off what little we had. The food stamps were meant for my children, and it pained me to see him consuming what should have been theirs. Yet, a part of me wrestled with the notion of charity—wouldn't God want me to help him?

Each day brought its own set of challenges, and as I lay awake at night, I pondered the balance between helping a struggling man and protecting the well-being of my children. My faith told me to give, but my motherly instinct screamed to prioritize my sons. It was a dilemma that weighed heavily on my soul.

After securing the funds to buy a car, furniture, food, and pay the bills for the kids and myself, I asked him to leave and go back. I couldn't stand him—the sight of him made me sick. I didn't want him to touch me. First, I kicked him out of my bed, then to the couch, and finally out of my apartment.

He went over and stayed with Laura, but that arrangement was short-lived because Winston didn't like him at all. He said that Winston made him feel uncomfortable when he called him "Farmer Jack," even though Winston claimed he was just playing. Maybe Bob felt intimidated because Winston was much taller than him.

I scheduled appointments for me and the children to have our annual physicals. Shawn and Terrance were healthy. Andre was diagnosed with asthma, eczema, and a heart murmur that could be treated with medication. He had to use a breathing machine. They wanted to put him on medication that would make him sleepy. He needed to wear all cotton clothes, and I had to wash any dye out of them before he could wear them. His diet had to change—no dairy—and I had to monitor his behavior, restricting his activities. Amidst all this, I discovered I was pregnant— almost three months. I nearly fainted; I had used protection.

"Oh my God, what am I going to do?" I'm worried about André, but I was determined not to hinder his growth. My boys were rough and tough; I had taught them how to fight and climb trees. That night, I worried myself to sleep, and a little voice deep inside woke me up, saying, "This is your last child. Have your baby and raise it with the others. I'll be with you through it all." I didn't know if that voice came from God or if I just needed reassurance, but one thing I knew for sure was that God would not forsake me. I'm keeping my baby—that goes without saying. I didn't even entertain the thought. All things come through God, and he breathed life into this child that I was carrying. I quickly glanced into the future.

It didn't matter to me whether Bob would be around to help raise his child or not. Relationships are not etched in stone. I knew that I would always be here because I'm their mama, and they're mine. I was dedicated and committed.

I didn't tell Bob at first. But I did tell Laura, and she told Bob in so many words.

"Girl, you're gaining weight; your hips are getting rounder and bigger. Look at your nose; your skin is so bright. You're glowing. Are you pregnant?" she asked me right in front of him.

"Yeah, I am."

Bob was so excited that he grabbed me and hugged me, kissing my face and hands tenderly. For a moment, I could tolerate him. "I'm going to get a job and help you. I'm going to be a good father and take care of business."

"Well, seeing is believing," I said to myself. *"It doesn't matter what you say or do; I'm going to make the way for this child."* The Bible says, 'Put your trust in no man; all things come from God.' I wasn't waiting on Bob for anything.

Time passed, and Bobby sang with a local band—there wasn't much else he could do. His gigs were infrequent. He dreamed of being discovered, harboring the delusion that the world awaited his emergence as the finest tenor alive. I often reminded him that Eddie

Kendricks and Terry Huff of Special Delivery singing "I Destroyed Your Love" were the greatest tenors to ever live, without comparison. Eagerly, he awaited an opportunity to appear on Soul Train. Despite his persistent attempts to contact Don Cornelius through letters and tapes, Bobby received no response from Don or his staff.

Bobby was his own hero—a legend in his mind. I never received such good care as I did at Alexian Brother Hospital. Bob drove me to all of my appointments. I remained independent; that was his way of using the car. I was still cooking, cleaning, washing, ironing, and taking care of my children. I carried my baby through the entire summer, and Tina was there to visit.

Bobby was some help, but not enough. It was hot, and I was tired. My weight had almost doubled. My feet were swollen, and I weighed in at 178 pounds. I had special cravings: pork n' beans with watermelon, fish sandwiches, and pickle juice. Occasionally, I'd ask Bob to go to the store for me, and he was Johnny-on-the-spot. I prayed and asked God for a healthy baby, for it not to hurt, and for a girl.

Bob was getting around pretty well in San Jose. He had made friends in the neighborhood, unlike me—I didn't care to be bothered. I took care of my kids, kept my apartment clean, and found another love: growing plants. I kept myself busy with reading, cooking, or just learning something new. I was active in school with Shawn, and on the weekends, we spent time at the water fountain.

A huge water fountain sat in the heart of the valley. The city turned the water on, and families came from everywhere—Blacks, Hispanics, Whites. I'd pack picnic lunches, blankets, and dry clothes. We'd stay all day. One day, the city held a treasure hunt. There was a lot of money buried in Fountain Park. We never found the treasure, but we had fun looking.

Twice, I went to hear Bob sing. I didn't drink, but I had picked up the habit of smoking again. On this particular day, I went to the food stamp office. The line was wrapped around the building. The clerk, left alone, became frustrated and overwhelmed. She opened both doors and started throwing boxes and boxes of food stamps into the air. It was raining food stamps. Everyone scrambled, diving to the ground. People of all colors were picking up free food stamps, including me, on my hands and knees. I was eight months pregnant. People were careful not to knock me down.

I left there with six hundred twenty-five dollars in food stamps. What a good day! I thanked God, shopped for my house, and bought food for a lady I met while walking Shawn to the bus stop. Occasionally, I'd send her a hot meal throughout the week.

That day, she knocked on my door. I was surprised she made it up the long flight of stairs. Her cane trembled in her hand. She pointed downward; she had to show me something. I walked downstairs, where there were nine boxes for me. I didn't know what was inside. I couldn't accept this; she was old and frail, someone's mother. She said, "You're the only one who thinks about me. My grown children left me and never turned back. Take the boxes upstairs."

"I can't accept this," I said.

"Yes, you can," she insisted, "and you will. You prayed for help, didn't you?"

She walked into her doorway. "You need help with those kids. God answers prayers." She closed the door behind her. Bob carried the boxes upstairs. I opened them and, to my surprise, found baby clothes, tee shirts, diapers, rubber pants, rattles, several pacifiers, blankets, sheets, bottles, ointments, powder, lotion, a bassinet, and gift certificates for Similac formula—you name it, it was inside the boxes. She also bought the boys short sets. She gave me so much that I didn't need a thing for the baby. I went back downstairs to thank her again.

I was having a good day. God really shined down on me today. I'd prepared a place for my baby in the bedroom with me. I still had the boys' baby bed; it was in good shape, but how did she know I needed sheets? I was going to wait until the end of my eighth month to go shopping, but now I don't have to. Mrs. Meyers made it possible; she ordered everything from the Sears catalog.

I thought about what God had said to me that morning when I found out I was pregnant. Several months passed, and I noticed that Shawn didn't want to go to school. He was always eager to learn, but now he didn't want to go. I asked him why, if something happened to him that he needed to tell me about. I taught the boys about their body parts and not to let anyone touch them in certain places. To always tell me if anyone touched them—I didn't care who. Just tell me. I held my breath and asked if Bob had put his hand on him in any way. Quickly, he said no.

"Well, you go to school today, and I'll be home here waiting for you. Do you want me to go to school with you?" I asked him.

His reply to me was no. "I'll be alright." His head was dropped as he talked to me.

I put my hand under his chin and raised his head. "There's no need for you to look down. You can tell me anything. Is someone bothering you at school?" I saw how fast he was running yesterday after he got off the bus. He never answered.

"Well, I'll be waiting for you today, just like every other day. And when you come home today, I want you to tell me what's wrong," I said.

He replied, "OK. I love you, mama. I was just getting ready to tell you the same thing," as I tucked his shirt inside his pants. I checked his little body for bruises and marks of some kind to tell me what was wrong. I walked him to the bus stop and put him on the bus. An hour later, I drove to the school and watched him play, still trying to see something.

So, I went home and waited for his bus. I was uneasy the whole day. If my kids are unhappy, then it's my job to do something about it. Bob's friend Chuck came over, and they rehearsed an LTD song, "Back in Love Again." Hell, Chuck was a better tenor than Bob.

I was distracted by thoughts of my son. At 2:45 pm, I went downstairs to watch for my child. I stood still behind the big tree in front of my apartment. When the bus pulled up, I stepped out into view. My son was running as fast as he could, just like the Gingerbread Man. He was running so fast that he ran past me.

I asked him, "What are you running from?" Just then, he turned around and looked into the eyes of what he thought was terror. There stood a bigger boy in every way, balling up his fist to hit my son.

"I promise you, if you hit my son, I'm gonna beat your mama's ass. Now, you hit him if you want to," I said. He quickly unballed his fist.

I turned to Shawn and said, "Is that what you're running from? Shit, he better not hit you. Where do you live? Take me to your house right now. Is your mother at home?"

I knocked on the apartment below mine, and a Spanish woman answered. "Listen, I live right upstairs. If your son's having a problem with mine, you knock on my door, and we can resolve this before it gets out of hand," I said.

"Patrick does what he wants," she said.

"Well, he better find someone else to pick on. He's making my son's life miserable."

"My son's not going to be running from Patrick, and I'm telling you in front of Patrick. If he hits my son again for any reason, I'm coming back down these stairs, and I'm going to hit you. Do you understand me?" I turned to Patrick and warned him again.

"Keep your hands off my son, you bully!" I exclaimed, anger boiling within me. This boy, nine years old, was much bigger, fatter, and taller than my son. I took Shawn upstairs, gave him a snack to hold him until dinner, and changed his clothes. Then, I sent him back outside to play with his little friend, Raleigh. and Adrian I was looking out the upstairs window, and I kept a vigilant eye on him.

Soon enough, Shawn came running upstairs, on the verge of tears. "Don't you cry," I commanded sharply. Cutting my dinner preparations short, I grabbed a knife from the drain board, hiding it by rolling it under my maternity shirt. Clutching his hand, I led him back downstairs.

Initially, I knocked gently on her door, but as she didn't answer, my knocks grew into a furious pounding. Even Patrick joined in beating on the door. The longer his mother ignored us, the angrier I became. Through the window, I could see a man sitting in a chair, motionless.

Finally, she cracked the door open and muttered, "I do not speak English," before slamming the door shut. In a flash of rage, I stepped back and kicked the door in with all my might. Grabbing her by the collar and the back of her shirt and neck, I dragged her outside. Holding her with one hand, I slapped her face. "I told you to make your son leave mine alone. You claimed you don't understand English; well, maybe you'll understand this!" I yelled, throwing her to the ground. Turning to Shawn, I said, "Go over there and get yourself an equalizer. We're gonna make this fight fair. You better whip his ass, or I'm gonna beat yours."

To Patrick's mother, I hissed, "If you move, bitch, I'll cut your throat." Shawn didn't need a stick; he started wailing on Patrick. Bawling up his fist, he struck him right between the eyes. As Patrick's body folded forward, Shawn dropped him, beating him down with all the strength and moves that I and Bob had taught him. That day, Shawn made sure Patrick would never bother him again.

That night, after his bath and prayers, I tucked him in. "Shawn, remember, it's not the size of the dog in the fight. It's the fight inside the dog. Always remember that. Do you understand?" "Yes," he whispered.

Patrick never bothered him again. I was eight months pregnant.

Bob had taken my car and stayed away all day and into the night, knowing I wanted to go to the laundromat as my time was near. My bags were packed, and there was plenty of food I had cooked up for the kids in the refrigerator. I hoped my stay wouldn't be too long away from home.

This pregnancy felt different from when I carried my boys. My oversized stomach sat higher; I was carrying this baby in my hips, butt, and breasts. My breasts were full of milk, swelling to a size 40 double D.

Early the next morning, Bob slipped in quietly, grabbed his covers, and settled on the couch. Not feeling up for an argument, I kept quiet. I just wanted him to move on.

The next morning, I got the kids dressed for a full day: a morning at the laundromat, an afternoon at the museum where the car President John F. Kennedy was assassinated in was on display, along with the ambush car of Bonnie and Clyde, and a night at the drive-in. After mailing Mama's homemade buttered pound cake for her birthday, I was taking the boys to see the movies of their choice. They had picked "Saturday Night Fever," starring John Travolta, and "Three the Hard Way," with Jim Kelly.

Today, the sky was the limit. They had been such good boys, and I had saved a little money for outings with them.

I packed their lunches and left Bob at home; he was tired from God knows what. On my way out, I stopped at the mailbox. Inside, I found a letter from the Section 8 Housing Program inviting me to come in and fill out an application—they had openings.

"Oh my God!" I screamed, overcome with joy. "Thank you, Lord! Praise Your Holy Name." This was my ticket out—the answer to my prayers. But who submitted my name? I wondered, curiosity mingling with gratitude.

Grooving to the Eddie Kendricks "Shoe Shine Boy" This' stirred up deep emotions. I didn't want Bob in my life. I was all emotional, reminiscing about Robert Howard and my friends back home. What were they doing for the holidays? In the same breath, I prayed they were all still alive.

Have you ever heard a song so beautifully crafted, with music and lyrics woven together like an ice-cold glass of buttermilk with hot buttered cornbread? It makes you stop and think— remember when? It makes you want to cry inside. The Staple Singers were jamming with 'Let's Do It Again,' and Detroit's own Special Delivery with 'I Destroyed Your Love' parts 1 and 2 played next. I was grooving. It didn't feel like it was three weeks before Christmas.

It was a bright, beautiful, sunny Saturday morning—my favorite day of the week. People were washing their cars and hoopdies; the smell of barbecue filled the air. As quietly as the butterflies flew, children played on the playground in their shorts, sleeveless shirts, and sandals.

California is truly a beautiful place to live, and I appreciated God for granting me this chance at happiness. For a brief moment, I felt a sigh of relief. Every time I stepped outside, I felt as though I was being hugged by the mountains. The clear, serene blue sky engulfed my spirit with certainty. The grass, so green and crisp, gave a whole new meaning to being alive.

They were playing all the oldies. Chaka Khan's 'Smokin' Room' was thumping loud. For a minute, I thought I heard Chuck singing Rose Royce's 'I Wanna Get Next To You.' I was feeling good and positive about my life and my future with my kids. After this baby, I can go back to school and get off welfare. Stand up on my own two feet. Set an example for my children.

I left the clothes in the brown push-button station wagon for Bob to bring upstairs. That whole afternoon, Bob seemed really upset with me. He complained that I didn't want to have a sexual relationship with him, that I didn't want to spend any time with him, and that I didn't want him sleeping in bed with me.

"Bob," I said to him, "why don't you just go home?"

"No," he said. "I'm staying here with you and the boys; this is my family. I love you all. Don't you love me?"

"Yes," I replied, "I love you. But I don't think I'm in love with you. I appreciate the time you spend with the boys, and I love you for that." But that's it.

Well, what did I say that for? He started another argument with me.

Bob wanted me to give him something I just wasn't feeling. Plus, let the truth be known, he had a circumcision status and size that left much to be desired.

He played me, Dirty.

Bob brought the last of the clothes upstairs, and I went down to the store for banana popsicles for me and Superman popsicles for the boys. After opening the box of popsicles to eat on the way home, I dropped the keys down on the car floor. Unable to bend forward, I had to get out of the car to retrieve the keys. They had fallen between the seats and landed under the seat.

I pulled and pulled until they popped back in my face. The keys were attached to a pair of big, bloomer-flowered panties. Everyone knows what their own underwear looks like, and these weren't mine. I spun the car around and drove as fast as I could back to the apartment. I ran up the stairs two at a time. Bob heard me coming. As I grabbed the doorknob and stormed inside, he saw the look on my face and the panties in my hand. He took off, running down the hall toward the bedroom.

"So that's why you're trying to start an argument with me?" I shouted and hauled off, punching him in the back of his head as he tried to dodge away sideways.

"This is your fault," he said, panting. "I did it because you won't."

I attacked him even harder, punching him in the face and neck. We were fighting between the kids' bunk beds. Bob didn't fight back; he just blocked my punches and pushed me down onto the bunk bed. Mid-air, I grabbed onto Bob and pulled him down on top of me. I held him tight and bit him on top of his shoulder, feeling my teeth meet together. He hollered like the scalded dog he was.

He blamed me for everything. Thank God the boys were outside playing, and Terrance was down for his daily nap.

After the fight, I rolled off the bed and grabbed my son and my keys. I was leaving—going over to Laura's, anywhere away from him. I wobbled down the stairs, gathered my kids, and got into the car. At this point, no one knew we had been fighting; everything was still quiet. I put the car in drive, and Bob jumped onto the hood, straddling himself across it. Holding on, he placed his hands inside the window to stop me from rolling it up.

Guess what? I rolled them up anyway, trapping his hands. I asked him again to get off the hood. "No, you're not going anywhere," he said. I grew angrier by the second, as he refused to let go. "I want to tell you what happened," he pleaded.

"I don't want to hear it!" I snapped. "Get off my car!" I demanded it for the last time. He wouldn't let go, so I hit the accelerator, throwing him forward off the car. He fell, but then threw himself onto the back of the station wagon, clinging on like an ape climbing a tree.

I hit the brakes; he fell off and skinned his entire body. He jumped back onto the hood, and I hit the brakes again, throwing him off. This time, he landed under the car. By this time, people were starting to come outside their apartments. Bob was bleeding from head to toe, covered in abrasions.

His friend La Rue, who comes over whenever I bake pies, helped him up. I put the car in drive and drove off, leaving him to lick his wounds.

Bob loves an audience; he always played the victim. But I had seen through his act. I didn't dare tell Laura—I was too embarrassed. She thought I was just over for a visit.

I returned the next day and asked him to leave again. Can we talk about this?" he said. "OK, let's talk," I responded.

"Bob said that the day he kept my car for so long was the day it happened. He said her name was Beatrice, and he picked her up at the bus stop. And it happened in my car. He said that he was sorry, and he asked me to forgive him. It just happened so quickly. "I believe that," I said. I looked at him and said, "How do you think this makes me feel? You're a grown man, and you contribute almost nothing to the household. I share everything with you. I loaned you money intended for my children. I've tried to help you every way I can. And this is the best you can do for me?" I said.

"Nothing in your life is going to matter because your heart is dirty and selfish. This is your baby that I'm carrying in my stomach, and you haven't bought one damn thing for it."

"You have the nerve to borrow my car, burn up my gas by picking up some trick—Bitch—and fuck her in my car. That's pretty low down." My voice was cold and measured. "For as long as it took you, you could have screwed a whore like that in an alley. No, I don't forgive you."

My accusation hung heavy in the air. "You didn't have enough respect for me, or yourself, to take your business elsewhere. What kind of dog are you?" I glared at Bob across the table. "You sit here, eat my food, look me in the face, and cut my throat with my back turned. You have no sense of loyalty. I don't want to hear any more excuses from you. I want you out now, today. Get your stuff and get out."

My fury didn't stop there. "I'm not upset because you screwed her, because I know what she's getting. I'm upset that you totally disrespect me, and you take my kindness for granted."

He tried to touch my arm, his expression softening. "Look, don't ever put your hands on me again," I said, pulling away sharply. "I'm giving you one week to get out."

I went to bingo for the first time that night, and for someone who didn't know how to play bingo, I did exceptionally well. I hit the last jackpot and walked out alone with $600.00 in my pocket. I was thrilled; now I could get that big wheel for Shawn and a tricycle for Andre. I planned to save the rest for our upcoming move.

The next day, Mama called to let me know she had received the cake I'd baked and sent it via overnight mail. It was still warm. I told her about the money I intended to send her and Tina for Christmas. She protested, as expected, but I sent one hundred dollars anyway.

Chapter 19

"God Will Open a Door"

The children had a wonderful Christmas. I did the best I could, cooking everything for them and whoever else stopped by. Holidays always brought people to my door, eager to enjoy my home- style cooking. I didn't mind feeding anyone—God fed me. The menu was extensive: turkey, dressing, giblet gravy, potato salad, turnip greens, macaroni and cheese, string beans with white potatoes, Waldorf salad, chitlins, crackling' bread, peach cobbler, Jello, apple pie, lemon meringue pies, sweet potato pies, gingerbread cookies, a gingerbread house that I let the kids decorate, and homemade ice cream.

The house was a festive explosion of Christmas candy, fresh fruit, nuts, plenty of candy canes, and Christmas cookies. It was a joyous time for the kids, and I was happy just seeing them so delighted. "Thank you, God, for making the way." And plenty of toys.

On December 27, 1975, at around 1:47 a.m., there was a knock on my door. Startled, I got up to answer it and was surprised to find Winston and T.C. on the doorstep, both unmistakably drunk, Winston more so than T.C. Two shades to the wind, Winston was. They had been out partying at Ojay's Jam, "Living for the Weekend."

I was happy to see them. We exchanged hugs and kisses, and I welcomed them inside. They didn't refuse my offer of something to eat. Seeing Bob asleep on the couch, they teased him a bit before he woke up. After I cooked bacon, a mushroom omelet with sautéed potatoes, and toast with jelly, I was ready to lay down on the couch myself. As I squeezed past Winston, he rubbed my stomach with one hand and placed the other in the small of my back. His touch conveyed a tenderness that surprised me.

"Don't get mad at me, Bob," Winston said, a serious tone cutting through his drunken haze, "but I love this woman. I always have. This should be my baby."

I pressed past him to sit on the couch. "And if you're not careful, she'll be my girl," Winston continued. "She would have been mine if I hadn't let her go back to Detroit. Man, I wasn't thinking—that's when I lost her. She's a good, strong young woman who takes care of her kids. I have all the respect in the world for her. She's an amazing woman; she's going to do great things. She deserves better… better than you, I don't know," he said, turning to Bob, who remained silent.

I could see then that Bob was weaker than I needed. He had no heart. What did I really need him for?

Winston's confession lingered in the air. "I fell in love with her the first time I met her. The connection is still there. I'm just being a man, telling you how I feel about your woman to your face."

"I don't mean disrespect. I love her, man, and I always will. If you ever screw up, she knows where to find me."

I showed no expression and kept my feelings hidden as I went to bed, leaving them to their discussion. Winston ended up staying the night, sleeping on the couch, while Bob took the big brown round chair.

T.C. was long gone. Bob had driven Winston home that morning; I never saw him leave. That afternoon, drained from being woken so early, I lay on the couch, attempting to nap during the kids' quiet time. Heavy and miserable with my pregnancy, all I could think about was the impending labor.

"God, please don't let it hurt," I whispered before drifting off.

Just before the New Year, I received my certificate from Section 8. I was entitled to a three- or four-bedroom house or apartment. The program I was enrolled in would cover 75% of my rent, and I would only need to pay 25% of my income for shelter. "God's Blessings"

New Year's Day, 1976, found me dragging. My feet were swollen, and I couldn't tie my shoes. Bob had gone to the store and bought me a pair of slip-ons, but I refused to wear them. I couldn't stop moving; I drove the kids around different areas, searching for a new place to live without telling Bob. He knew better than to question my kids about it.

On my last day of pregnancy, I deep cleaned the entire apartment from top to bottom. I moved the refrigerator and stove and cleaned behind them. I swept the carpet and mopped the floors. I had Superman energy. I made lasagna and baked a German chocolate cake for the boys. Bob waited until we had all finished eating before he had his dinner. He avoided me at all costs.

The boys sensed the tension; they knew he was in the doghouse. He should have felt shame—I would have. It's not in my nature to be mean or mistreat anyone, but I felt sorry for him because he was so lost and foolish. Yet Bob thought he was cunning. I knew my time was near; I was rapidly approaching my due date.

At midnight, my water broke for the first time in my life. With my boys, they had to break my water. I was watching *The Honeymooners*. I got up to take a shower, and as I dried off, water ran down my legs like a faucet had been turned on. I had to call for Bob's help; the floor was wet, and I didn't want to risk falling. He rushed in, helped dry me off, and dressed me.

He grabbed my suitcase, which had been sitting by the door for a month, ran out of the house, and left me behind. He ran down the stairs, screaming, "She's going to have the baby!" over and over, as loud as he could.

I called him a stupid motherfucker under my breath.

I'd made arrangements with Laura to keep the kids, but she had to go back to work. I didn't have anyone to leave the boys with, so I planned to take them to the hospital. Bob could drop me off; I really didn't want him there, and I had told him so. After he dropped me off, I wanted him to take my boys home and put them back in bed. "I don't need you to deliver this baby," I had said. "I can deliver my baby by myself, just like my other children. All I need is God with me."

It must have dawned on Bob that he left me behind, because on his way back, he ran into LaRue, his friend, who was wandering around. Bob told him I was in labor. LaRue looked up to see me standing, waiting for Bob to help me down. Bob explained that the boys were asleep and asked if he could sit with them while he took me to the hospital. Without hesitation, LaRue agreed. "No, thank you. They're awake now; we'll take them with us," I said.

Now LaRue was a drummer, and he and Bobby were putting together a band along with his wife Cheryl that had a gravely soul-searching singing voice to be reckoned with. Together, they had three children. And it wasn't until we became close that she confided in me about the physical abuse she suffered at his hands. Towards my delivery date, Cheryl and I would take daily walks, and we would talk about our personal lives. In our talks, I asked her to help me come up with a name in case I had a girl. And she did. I named her after her little girl. Cheryl cried about LaRue on most days, and although I advised her to leave him, she was also afraid. Cheryl and I became close, and after meeting her entire family—her mother, Mrs. Blackmon, her sisters, Carolyn Brenda and Kim—I couldn't help but love them all. This friendship remains today.

I don't have any respect for a degenerate man who fights a woman. Still, I tolerated them rehearsing at my apartment. It gave Cheryl time to help herself heal. Additionally, she expressed a desire for a father figure to raise her children. That ain't a good reason. I didn't feel that way; I stepped up and assumed the role of both parents. I will not have any man beating me up in front of my kids. For the sake of having a so-called father.

"Okay, well, good luck," LaRue said. "Thank you," I responded.

When Bob put me in the car, I made him promise to take care of the boys, as we had discussed. "Don't let any harm come to them. And don't leave them with anybody," I pleaded. He assured me he would take care of them.

I kissed the kids goodbye and cried at the same time. The labor pain was almost unbearable; it was severe and consistent. I prayed for it to stop, but it seemed the more I prayed, the harder it got. I had my hands straddled across the headboard, and I rode it all night. At 7:00, my baby was coming, and the doctor instructed me to transfer from one bed to another. They had me sit on the gurney, my legs dangling on each side.

"They could have placed me on my side in a cradle position to administer the spinal I requested." That position pinned me against nature, and my baby was pushed back up inside and turned around. I felt it turn." I told them my baby was coming—they could see the crown. I cried out, but they paid no attention to what I was saying. They were busy preparing me. My baby was in distress.

My regular doctor was unavailable, so his partner, Dr. Majors, was scheduled to deliver my baby. Dr. Majors had one arm shorter than the other, a remnant of an accident years ago. I overheard the nurses whispering that he hadn't delivered a baby in a long time.

He didn't know me at all. But in that critical moment, it seemed God himself guided Dr. Majors' hands. With his injured arm, Dr. Majors cradled my baby's head, gently turning it so it could breathe. I could see the strain on his face and the concentration. My baby was turning blue, struggling for oxygen, and I was helpless, lying there with my spinal cord numbing my senses.

I prayed with a desperate fervor. "Please save my baby; it's not breathing." I cried silently. The nurses held my head down, trying to keep me calm, but panic was setting in. Then, amidst my screams for divine intervention, I heard the sweetest sound—my baby crying.

Dr. Majors, with diligent care and perhaps a touch of divine grace, had saved my baby. At 7:36 AM, I gave birth to a healthy, beautiful, bald-headed baby. The first cry pierced through all the tension, and tears of relief and joy streamed down my face. Gratitude, love, and a profound sense of connection overwhelmed me. For nine months, this baby and I had been close companions. I remembered feeling its first kicks, and even the night I'd rocked it to sleep from within my belly, craving watermelon, pork, and beans.

Emotions washed over me as I cried through it all, falling in love for the fourth time in my life. "What is it?" I asked eagerly. "What is it?"

The nurses gently laid the baby on top of my stomach. "See for yourself," one said softly, "but try not to lift your head."

I couldn't resist. I lifted my head just a bit and used my thumb and first finger to gently part its legs. I could feel what it was, and when I saw it, I cried even more. My baby, weighing in at 5 pounds, 8 ounces, and seventeen and a half inches long, she was as cute as a button.

Inwardly, I prayed and thanked God for being there with me and for blessing me with this beautiful bundle of joy. Later that day, Bob and Laura brought the boys down to meet their new little sister. Their faces lit up with wonder and curiosity as they peered at the tiny addition to our family.

I named her Kyham Nichole. Exhaustion mingled with elation as I cradled her, my hunger momentarily forgotten. Laura was more than willing to take the boys home with her, leaving us some quiet time. Bob announced he was going out to celebrate; he never said where, and I didn't ask—I didn't care. His journey now was on foot unless he found another ride; he wasn't using my car unless it was to bring the kids down or in an emergency. I had long ago warned Laura against loaning her car to Bob— he'd surely wreck it without means to replace it. Just before he left, Bob leaned in for a kiss, but I whispered to him, "You can go back to Detroit now; the baby's here."

Time passed, and I continued my search for a better place to live. Kyham was almost two months old when the weather turned wet and chilly. Concerned she might catch a cold; I asked Bob to babysit while the boys and I "went to the store." I wasn't really headed for the store; I was going to look at a house. Bob, ever jealous, disliked me going anywhere without his knowing. He'd driven away almost all his friends. The Commodores' new song "Brick House" was popular, and baby, that's what I was; only my measurements were 36-24-46. Bob was trying to straighten up, but I didn't want him anymore. The kids and I found the perfect house. It was breathtakingly beautiful, perched on the edge of the foothills overlooking San Jose, complete with three bedrooms, a living room, dining room, fireplace, dishwasher, all new appliances, and wall-to-wall carpet. There are two large bathrooms, a manicured front lawn, and a large backyard with a dollhouse that is perfect for Kyham and the boys.

"Oh God, please let me have this house for the kids." I prayed and laid my hands on it. Before returning home, I treated the boys to tacos and chocolate shakes at Jack in the Box. When we got back, I washed my hands and went straight to my baby. I asked Bob how long she'd been asleep.

He said it some time now. I'd been gone just over an hour. Picking Kyham up to kiss and play with her, I found her unresponsive. Panicked, I tried to wake her—no reaction. I screamed at Bob, "What did you do to my baby? She's not responding!"

He said nothing. I grabbed her blanket and ran out, the kids and Bob following. I raced to the emergency room, her lifeless body in my arms, and cried to the staff that she wasn't moving. They quickly took Kyham from my arms, checking her over and sniffing for odors. "Only milk," I cried when they asked what she had ingested. Just then, Dr. Shelly, her pediatrician, who was on call, arrived. She checked Kyham, drew some blood from her foot, and rushed it to the lab.

"My guess is she's drunk," Dr. Shelly told me. "Someone gave this baby something to drink."

I confronted Bob in the waiting room. "Before I make a scene," I demanded once more. Bob confessed to giving her 8 oz. of beer in her bottle. I relayed this to Dr. Shelly, who scolded me about the beer. "I totally agree," I said, "but I didn't give it to her. She's my responsibility, though, and I bet it'll never happen again."

We stayed with Kyham until she woke up and was discharged. I didn't speak to Bob afterward; he knew I was furious. I would pick my time to deal with him.

On February 22, 1976, forty-six days after Kyham arrived, I was giving her a bath when I saw on the news that Florence Ballard, lead singer and founder of The Supremes, had died. "Oh my God," I cried out, "please don't let it be true." They flashed her picture and footage of her house body, from a rundown neighborhood in Detroit. She was said to have died penniless and on welfare.

I called home to confirm the devastating news. Florence Ballard, my favorite of the Supremes, had passed away at only 32 years old. She was not just a celebrity to me; she felt like family. I was sick inside, my thoughts racing to her three children. Who would raise them now? I knew the Detroiters, known for their solidarity, would give her a solid farewell. Even from afar, the weight of her untimely death was palpable, and all I could do was pray for her and her grieving family.

Amidst this turmoil, I was grappling with the financial pressures of moving. An idea struck me— to send sixty dollars to Mrs. Brazil in Detroit. She could play the street numbers for me if I dreamt of a lucky number. Although I had nearly four hundred dollars saved, it wasn't enough to move out of Santee. I relayed my plan to Mrs. Brazil over the phone, a seasoned number player, telling her to take thirty for her troubles.

No more bingo for me, not until Kyham was older. I was determined to leave Bob behind when I moved. I also placed an ad in the Detroit News for a live-in babysitter, offering room and board. It was a step toward assembling my future, with my ducks methodically lining up in a row.

During the days Bob was out, I packed in secret. Occasionally, Winston, T.C., and Jackie would drop by, but running the streets was out of the question—I made them feel at home with me instead.

Chapter 20

"God Made the Way"

One cool evening, exhausted, I put the kids to bed early and settled down myself. A nightmare jolted me awake. I was fighting off spiders in my sleep. Shaking, I threw back the covers—it was just a dream. The next morning, I called Mrs. Brazil, who assured me that dreaming of spiders was lucky. So, I played the numbers 519–915 in Detroit and 195–591 in Pontiac. That evening, Mrs. Brazil's excited voice came through the phone—I had won! Each ticket paid $500.00, totaling $2000.00. I was ecstatic, silently rejoicing to keep Bob in the dark. I played the number again, and 519 hit straight in Pontiac—an additional $500.00.

In two days, I'd won $2500.00, enough to move and furnish a new home. When I received the call about the house at 3341 Inspiration Ct., rentable for just $169.00 a month, I was overwhelmed. God truly answered my prayers. My children now have a house to live in.

I tried to offer Mrs. Brazil three hundred dollars for her help, but she refused, insisting I needed it more for my children. She even sent me five money orders totaling $500.00 each. By March 1976, the move was seamless. I gave away almost everything we owned, explaining to the kids that this was for the best. "Santee is decent," I told them, "But you have to want more from life. Don't get stuck here." This is a stepping stone.

In our new neighborhood, the only black family in the court, we settled quickly. The community was close-knit, even boasting a family that housed horses in their backyard. Shawn would have a school bus pick him up right at our door when school started.

I bought new furniture—a green and white tweed sofa with matching chairs, a floor-model color TV, and new household items. A cockatoo puppy and a Chinese golden pheasant added to our new beginnings. The kids quickly adjusted, playing with other children on the court. In the evenings, we sat outside, enjoying the tranquil city views, savoring the stability and the promise of better days ahead in our elite working-class neighborhood.

My station wagon was gasping its last breaths, and I needed another car. I had just enough money to make it happen. Laura couldn't take me to the dealership, so she sent Bob instead. He'd been crashing with her until his record deal came through, after which he planned to head back to Detroit. The kids chatted with him freely, but I barely spoke.

At the car lot, my budget limited me to a stick-shift Toyota Corona. I didn't know how to drive a stick, but I bought it anyway—it was all I could afford. Bob promised to teach me. Predictably, he didn't. He'd sit around, dragging out each visit under the guise of instruction, but on the road, he always took the wheel. It didn't take long for me to see through his tactics—his way of keeping me dependent and housebound.

Three weeks later, he failed to show up. I seized the moment. With the kids napping, I faced my fear and headed outside. I'd never driven a car with three pedals. Around the court I went, stopping, jerking, and stalling—a chaotic dance of gears and gas. But two days later, I was driving smoothly, a silent victory over my fears.

One sunny afternoon, I drove to Laura's house. She was retrieving her mail as I pulled up. Bob came out, kissed the kids, and pointedly ignored my role as the driver.

That summer was a blissful chapter of zoos, museums, beaches, drive-ins, and trips to Sleepy Hollow Park. But one visit to the park was cut short when a pit bull attacked a little girl. I hustled the kids away, bewildered and angry that such a dangerous animal was allowed in a family space.

Eventually, someone responded to my ad for a live-in babysitter. After countless hours on the phone vetting Gloria, I sent her a bus ticket. I watched her closely with the kids, easing only when I felt confident in her care.

Bob's visits grew more frequent, filled with grand plans for his future that no longer concerned me. My own future was bright.

One evening, discomfort led me to the emergency room to treat a urinary issue. Overnight hospitalization meant leaving the kids longer than expected. Panicked, I called Gloria, who mentioned Bob's visit. I reluctantly asked him to ensure the kids were okay until I returned. He agreed, noting he'd be leaving town in two days.

I returned home early the next morning to my children's sleepy embraces, ensuring their safety first. Then I noticed my bedroom—a mess, which was unlike me. I wondered if the kids had sought comfort there, but dismissed the thought without much concern.

Bob returned later that day for a lengthy farewell. After all the turmoil, he was finally leaving. The children were melancholic, so I planned a grand birthday party to lift their spirits. We invited everyone and drove around to spread the word.

Six days later, the party was a vibrant success. Guests arrived with gifts, money, and warm smiles. I baked cupcakes, churned homemade ice cream on the patio, and grilled barbecue. Amid the laughter and chatter, I watched the children's spirits soar—happy once more in our new beginning.

The summer unfolded with visits to zoos, museums, and beaches. One day at Sleepy Hollow Park, chaos erupted when a pit bull mauled a little girl. I herded my children away, my mind reeling at the irresponsibility. Never to visit again.

As autumn approached and school resumed, I placed Andre and Terrance in daycare while I attended classes. Mornings were a flurry of activity as I prepared crockpot dinners before heading out, ensuring Gloria didn't need to cook.\One late evening, Gloria requested a serious talk, her tone suggesting urgency. We sat at the dining room table; the air thick with unspoken words. She confessed her desire to return to Detroit, her discomfort rooted in something she hesitated to disclose. Pressed for clarity, she admitted to an unthinkable betrayal—she and Bob had been intimate in my bed during my hospital stay. It wasn't their first encounter.

I felt the room spin as she pleaded for two days before her departure. Rage and disbelief gripped me; I demanded she leave immediately. In the dead of night, I drove her to the bus station, a silent ride filled with the weight of betrayal.

After her departure, I confided in Lettie, knowing she would spread the word. Bob's facade of decency needed shattering. He had used my home, my sanctuary, to carry out his deceit. I recounted his earlier indiscretion in my car, emphasizing his habitual disrespect.

Resolved to find a more trustworthy babysitter, I eventually hired Bridgette, a streetwise fifteen- year-old from Oakland. Despite her rough exterior and troubled past, she showed potential. I took it upon myself to mentor her, hoping to steer her clear of the harsh realities that awaited on the streets.

Trouble found us again one day when Shawn ran into the house, crying from a blow to the eye by a neighborhood girl. Fueled by maternal instinct, I confronted the girl's mother, a towering figure dismissive of my concerns. Her threat to sic her Hugh son on me ignited a fury within me, setting the stage for a confrontation that would not be easily forgotten. He was even bigger than her. I stood my ground, making it clear where I lived and that I was not to be fucked with.

In those turbulent days, each challenge was met with a fierce determination to protect my family and uphold my dignity, lessons I hoped to imprint on my children as we navigated the complexities of life at 3341 Inspiration Ct., which is where I live, I said right across the street.

As I left the confrontation, I was brimming with anger. I pointed assertively across the street and drove back home with my son. Inside, I instructed the kids firmly. "Whatever you hear, don't come out of this room," I said as I closed the door behind me. In my bedroom, I retrieved Bob's shotgun, loaded it with a calm resolve, and stationed myself on the couch, the weapon stretched across my lap.

Muttering to myself about the injustice and the threats, I prepared for the worst. "I came over there to talk, to resolve this peacefully, and you threaten me with your son? Send him, and I'll leave his ass dead on the front porch."

Minutes later, a timid knock came at my door. It was her, standing off to the side, her voice shaky. "Ms. Lady, I'm here to apologize," she called out.

"I don't want to hear it," I snapped. "Where's your son?"

"I'm sorry," she pleaded, sensing the gravity of the shotgun across my lap. "That's all I wanted; it was an apology." One by one, the kids left their room, sensing the tension easing.

She continued, "Please, Ms. Lady, I'm sorry." I had taken Shawn to the emergency room earlier, and his eye was badly bruised—the white now streaked with red—a sight that fueled my simmering anger. Despite my outrage, I knew better than to retaliate physically; I needed another way to settle scores.

A few nights later, I hatched a plan and enlisted Bridgette's help, giving her forty dollars for her trouble. I pointed out the girl during recess, and Bridgette executed the plan perfectly, ensuring the girl learned her lesson the hard way. Satisfied with the outcome, I even tipped Bridgette for her effective, albeit brutal, intervention.

As days turned into weeks, a homesickness for my mother grew within me. I was still having recurring thoughts and dreams about my past being raped, held against my will, and beaten up. Although Welton Smith was dead to me, it still wasn't enough for what they did. And I wanted my revenge on the man.

I thought to myself, *"How could they do that to me? I was only a child. How helpless and powerless I felt."* Over and over, I played it in my mind to silence the pain. Having to face the facts and relive what happened was unbearable. In my prayers at night, sometimes I'd ask God for the answer. Why? But we're not supposed to question God, so that means that I have to live with it. I tried hard to hide my feelings and thoughts. I never want my children or anyone else to know what happened to me on that August night. "In Times Like These" was an old spiritual hymn that the elders used to sing in my mother's church when I was a child. This song invaded my thoughts and soul throughout the night. When I woke up, it was there. Throughout the day, I could feel it inside.

It was Sunday, and I was taking the kids to the State Fair for the day. After they rode all the rides and ate all they could, on the way back to the car, we walked past a little church. I could hear them singing what appeared to be the song God had put in my heart that morning. The closer I got, the louder they sang. As I walked towards the church, I could hear the hymn. I couldn't believe it. Was this a coincidence or what? I turned around to walk back to the car with the kids, and a lady stepped out onto the doorstep and said to me, "Come in. Gods got a message for you," she said, beckoning with her hands towards me.

I quickly looked down at my clothes; we were dressed in jeans and sandals. "I can't," I said to her. "I'm not dressed to come into the house of the Lord." She beckoned again and said, "You're always welcome in the house of the Lord. Come inside and get your blessing." She opened the front door even wider. I could really hear the song they were singing; it got louder. Everyone was standing up. They turned around, faced me, and welcomed us in. It was only a handful of people, all dressed in white.

The minister said to me, "Come here, child, and get your blessing. God has a message for you. Sit right down front." He told me, "Your load is heavy now, but God has wonderful things in store for you. We don't always know or understand why bad things happen in our lives. But just remember God and the persecution he felt when he carried the very cross that he was crucified on, up Calvary Hill." The minister pointed to me. "You just hold your head up and remember God first. God told me to tell you that he'd fight your battles for you. He knows about everyone who has ever hurt you."

Tears streamed down my face. I cried that day like I never cried before; it was as if everything that ever hurt me in life had been washed away. "God wants you to go down in the water once again," he said. "I know you were probably baptized as a child. But God wants you to be baptized again. This very night," he said. I agreed, got undressed, and the old mothers placed me in a cap and gown. The minister placed his hands on the front and back of my body, and down I went. When he brought me up, I had the Holy Ghost. I started to shout right there in the water.

I remember them getting me out of the small pool and turning me loose. I shouted through the whole church, through the entire service, until I got tired. That's the second time in my life that I received the Holy Ghost. I left there feeling free, empowered, and renewed!

I called Mama and told her of my new experience; she was glad and encouraged me to continue on. "You're a special child," she said. "I knew that when God gave you to me after Joyce died."

I slept like a baby that night.

On July 12, 1977, I'd planned a birthday party for Andre at White Hill Park. He was six, Terrance had just turned five, Shawn was eight, Kyham was eighteen months old, and I was twenty-one. I didn't invite anyone, just his brothers and sister. To my surprise, the whole gang was out there. It was a beautiful day. When the kids saw their old friends, they forgot all about me and took off running.

Winston, T.C., Bitsy, Lonnie Brown, Jackie, and their children were there. Jackie was pregnant with T.C.'s baby. They rushed over to help me get the birthday food out of the car. Winston spent most of his time flirting with me and talking about Farmer Jack Bob. I made the picnic table pretty; I decorated it with all the birthday trimmings. I set things up on the table for the kids to eat whenever. I had plenty of food; I always cook a lot. Winston and T.C. put the volleyball set together, the badminton set, and the plastic horseshoe setup together. And then Jackie and I sat down, whipped their asses in dominoes, and bid whist.

We drank, smoked, danced, and partied with Earth, Wind, and Fire, The Tramps, and all the Motown jams one's heart could hold. On the radio, of course. We stayed until late in the evening. It turned out to be a glorious day.

Kyham spent most of her time peeing in her panties, making mud pies, eating worms, or stuffing them in her pockets. Her head was still bald; she had just a few strands, just enough for one barrette. Shawn spent most of his time sabotaging my towel, making capes for himself as Batman, Terrance as Robin, and Andre as the Joker. They played nicely together. I never allowed them to fight or argue with each other. "I wouldn't allow them to go to bed at night upset at each other. That creates animosity," I said. "All you have is each other; you must love your brother like you love yourself. It's four of you; you all have one sibling apiece." Every day, I taught them something new.

I love my children more than life itself!

We had a nice summer together; school was getting ready to start again. Andre was getting ready to start first grade and Terrance was going to kindergarten. I couldn't afford daycare for Kyham; I had to buy school clothes for them all. Times were tight, but with prayer, we were going to make it through. Asshole Bob hadn't sent a penny to help his child. When he called, I would hang up on him before he could say hello. I didn't want anything from him. "I'll take care of my baby myself, with God's help."

I wasn't able to work or go to school right now, so I turned my kitchen into a moneymaker.

I started taking orders ahead of time. I used my cooking talent to move forward. I baked sometimes two days straight, making homemade pies of any kind: peach and blueberry cream cheese cobbles, apple strudels, homemade cakes, lasagna, corned beef and cabbage—you name it, I cooked it. Just place your order.

Everything sold for $17.00 apiece. Laura's friends, married and single, had become my best customers. Most times, they'd give me a three-dollar tip. They'd swing by the house to pick up, or I delivered to her job. Some days, I could make as much as one hundred and two dollars. If I had a good week, I would have made over six hundred. I use this money to stay afloat. The reason I had repeat business is that I was clean, and I cooked from scratch using all-natural ingredients. In between the cooking, I was cleaning, cooking, washing, ironing, mopping, and taking care of my kids. I didn't have a life of my own. My day began at 5:00 a.m. After I got the kids off to school, I turned on the radio. Kyham would play quietly with her toys; I'd stand in the kitchen and cook. Johnny Nash's song "I Can See Clearly Now" had become my bridge of strength. I shed a lot of tears, but I knew that one day things would get better for me.

This day, I was making two million-dollar pies for a lady on Laura's job when I heard the announcer over the radio say that Elvis Presley had died. "What?" I screamed at the radio. "Oh, God, it can't be true." They announced it again. I ran and turned on the television, and there it was, plastered all over. I sat down and cried. I called my mother, and she said she knew. Mama was upset and crying, too. Mama was so upset that I had to call Rickey to go out there and check on her. I was in shock.

He was one of my favorite people in the world. And the world would never be the same without Elvis. I grew up watching all of his movies. It was a sad, sad day for people all over the world. In my opinion, Elvis loved God and Elvis grieved his mother; he was never the same after her death. I understood because I loved my mother dearly too.

Chapter 21

"Mama"

That was in August. In September, Rickey called and told me that Mama was sick and having headaches. She always said she was doing fine whenever I called her. He said, "I think you should come home. Mama's real sick." Immediately, I started to pack up the things we weren't using. I called Mama and told her that I was coming home. I could hear in her voice that she was sick. "God, I prayed; please don't let my mother die." I never told the children about my plans. I had to move out of the house because I didn't know how long I'd have to stay. I was going to have my car shipped to Michigan, so I wouldn't be on foot. The price was twelve hundred dollars—hell, that was more than I paid for it. But I knew I could only afford a piece of junk in Detroit. I had some money saved; I would sell everything in my house to raise more money. I called Lettie and told her about my mother. I asked her if I could stay there until I found a place to live. She said yes; she was only too happy to help out. I knew she had more than enough room for us in her four-bedroom home. "I'll start to get things prepared for you," she said. Plus, it would be her first time meeting her grandchild. I knew, and she said that Bobby was living somewhere else on the west side. She said they'd fallen all the way out.

She wasn't speaking to him. I called my mother several times a day just to hear her voice. It was reassurance for me that she was alright. And alive, I was able to sell my furniture for the extra money that I knew I'd be needing. I packed all the kids' clothes that I could carry on the train, and I spent three days driving twenty-six boxes of household items back and forth to the San Jose terminal to ship with Amtrak. The night before we left, I drove my car over to Oscar's to be shipped to Michigan within three weeks. I left a six-hundred-dollar deposit and some other new and old items in the trunk. "It's guaranteed," they said.

I remember the morning we left. I stood outside, looking up into the beautiful, bright, sunny sky. The rolling hills took my breath away. Nobody but God could have created something so beautiful and serene. I couldn't help but cry. I thought about the lyrics to a song written by Frankie Beverly and Maze, 'Look at California.'

Somehow, I knew that would be my last time standing on the soil in the land that had so much promise and so much to offer. I was torn between the two, but I knew that I was doing the right thing. Nothing in this life, not even myself, was more important to me than my mother and my children. This was a sacrifice that I had to endure.

I said my goodbyes once again, and I headed back to the city filled with strife and disappointment.

We arrived in Detroit one week before Thanksgiving in 1977. And I must tell you, nothing has changed. It was dark, dry, cold, and wet. The winter months could break you down if you let them. Lettie barely made it to the station. The roads were slippery, closed, and wet from the relentless falling snow. In the days to follow, we were snowed in. All the schools were closed. I couldn't go anywhere. I wasn't able to see my mother until Thanksgiving Day. Lettie dropped us off, and my brother Rickey promised to take us back.

Nina welcomed us into her home, and most of my small family members were there, including Poppi and Aunt Janie. For a while, we were cordial to each other.

My mother looked sickly and sad. It broke my heart to see her. I went into the bathroom and cried. I begged God to give me strength. Mama's health was in rapid decline. She could barely walk with arthritis in both knees. To me, it looked like her head increased in size from the brain tumor growing. I sat down on the floor next to her, laid my head on her lap, and she stroked the side of my face with her hands. I cried tenderly at my mother's touch. The tears streamed down her leg. "I love you, mama," and she said, "Don't you cry. I'm not afraid. You shouldn't be either. God loves me, and we all have our cross to bear. I'm going home to be with the Lord, and that satisfies my soul. You are strong for me and your kids. When God gets ready for me, I'll be ready to go."

We formed a circle and held hands in prayer before dinner. Everyone except for Geri, she pretended not to see. Everyone was glad that I was back at home. They loved Kyham, as I knew they would. Poppi and Aunt Janie were glad to see Mama. They hadn't seen Mama in years since Nina moved her so far away; nobody had transportation. I told them that I would pick them up and drive them out when I got my car. My father really loved my mother; to keep from crying, he stayed away. I was trying hard, for the sake of my mother, to forgive Aunt Janie for what she did to me. I could hardly look her in her black face. We won't even talk about Geri and Nina.

Rickey drove us back to Lettie's that evening, and he came inside and met her family. Rene, her youngest daughter, and her two little girls live with her too. I stayed there as long as I could. A little over a week. I had to move because of the roaches. It looked as if every roach in the city of Detroit was living there with us. I left her house running in the daytime; at night, I stuffed the kids' ears with cotton balls. I cleaned an area for us to live in, but it wasn't going to work.

I stayed up all night watching over them. I wouldn't cook or feed my children there. The house was constantly nasty. I won't subject my children to living in filth. I caught the bus with my children, bags, and luggage to the Monterey Motel, and that's where we stayed. My money was running low, so I went over to social services and waited in the long, long line to apply for assistance. We stayed so long that I packed lunch. I called Mr. Brazil to take me around to look for housing. I filled out a multitude of applications with my four children. I was weary and tired. I had to figure out what to do. And I was embarrassed. Mr. Brazil offered us to come and stay with him, and I thanked him. I knew that his plate was already full having to take care of his three grown children, their spouses, their children, three of his daughters' children, and his wife.

His daughter Evelyn had three boys; she left them there to live with her parents for so long that they adopted them. One day Evelyn said that she was going to the store, and she never looked back. That was five years ago. She was heavily on drugs. I told Daddy that I wanted to see if I could make my own way.

In December, I found out that my oldest sister Charlie was living on 14th Street near Dexter. So, I decided to surprise her. But I was the one surprised! We spent the entire day laughing, eating, and talking about the past. It got so late that she invited us to stay the night. This was the type of area that you didn't want to get caught in after dark. So yes, I agreed to stay. She had two bedrooms, and I slept on the couch.

Around 3:30 AM, I heard someone stick a key in the door and turn the knob. I was sleeping with my back to the door. I lifted my head to see who was coming into the dark room that was lit up with the stove light. Charlie never mentioned she had a boyfriend. So, I sat up to get up and focus, and guess who walked in—Bob. I maintained my facial expression, but you should have seen his. Nervously, he spoke, and I didn't. A few hours later, I left before Charlie woke up. I later found out through Mama that they'd been living together since he came back to Detroit. Mama said she couldn't remember him, and nobody in the family knew what was going on. Everybody was so spaced out.

I also found out that I visited my brother Rickey at his house a couple of years ago. When I was living in Wexford, they'd already been together. That's why Bob left us there and picked us up later. Well, you could have knocked me over with a feather. Charlie and I never spoke about it. Maybe she did know about me, and I sure didn't know about her. He was just that sneaky.

It was getting close to the new year, and I wasn't content with having to stay in the Monteray with my children on New Year's Eve. I figured that we'd get down on the floor and stay there until after midnight. The Monterey was located on Woodward; the motel itself wasn't too bad, but the area was polluted with drugs and prostitution. I knew this was only a steppingstone.

I swallowed my pride and called Geri to ask her if we could stay at her apartment for two weeks until I could find a place to live.

Three days later, I received a message from the front desk that my sister had called and to call her right away. From the message I received, I prayed there was nothing wrong. I wasn't able to call my mother as much because all calls were toll calls. I called her to find out what she wanted. And she said, "I was calling you back; there's nothing wrong. What do you want?"

I told her that I needed a place to stay with my children and that I could stay at her apartment for two weeks. I heard the hesitation in her voice. "Yeah," she said, "but I don't want you there any longer than two weeks." My first thought was to tell her to never mind and to kiss my ass. But for the sake of my children, I took a deep breath and said, "Thank you."

Geri was never at her apartment because she worked two jobs. I knew that she'd been at the American Red Cross for almost ten years; she said that she key-punched at night. The only reason she ever came home was to change clothes, and that wasn't often. She started to write down her rules and regulations, her dos and don'ts. I was made to feel uncomfortable by the jump street. She lived in Bellville, Michigan, even further away than Nina. The suburbs of Michigan are in Lemon Tree apartments.

She said that I'd have to wait until after the New Year because she was having some friends over. I thought to myself that she's nicer to her friends than she is to me. Two days later, she called in a huff. She asked me if I was ready to meet her there because she had to go to work that evening. "I have to let you in," she said. "I'm not going to give you a key to my apartment." With such short notice, I told her that I'd have to get someone to bring us up there. Mind you, Geri only worked about six miles from the Monterey Motel. She never offered to pick us up, and I didn't ask. "I'll be there for a couple of hours." I had to scramble to get a ride, get the kids ready, and pack.

Mr. Brazil's journey began on the east side of town, navigating through the thickening snow from Hurlbut Street and Gratiot, almost downtown, to reach us in Belleville. But upon our arrival, she was absent, and the night offered no shelter but her doorstep. The children and I huddled together, sharing bologna and crackers, as I fought the weariness that clawed at my eyes.

Dawn brought no reprieve. At 8:30 AM, I approached the front desk, the cold still biting at our bones, to call her at the Red Cross. Her response was a torrent of anger, berating me for not being present upon her return. "I can't leave my job to let you in. You should have been there when I told you to," she raged before the line went dead. Tears blurred my vision as I stood in the snow, my children's shivering forms clinging to me. Mr. Brazil was beyond reach, his duties taking him elsewhere. It was then that the lady from the front office noticed our plight. With a kindness that seemed foreign in that frigid morning, she ushered us inside and offered a cup of hot chocolate, her words a soothing balm. "Calm down," she assured. "I'll handle it from here."

Her suggestion to call Ms. Lee back was met with my reluctance, but her insistence prevailed. With a heavy heart, I dialed the number and passed the phone to her. "Ms. Lee," she began, "this is Shelly from the front office. I have your sister and her four kids here. If it's alright with you, we'll give her a key to let herself in." Though Ms. Lee forbade the key, she permitted entry. Gratitude filled me as I thanked Shelly; her act of compassion was a beacon in the storm. The shrill ring of the telephone pierced the silence as I stood at the threshold of her apartment. It was Geri's voice that greeted me, her words laced with venom. "I don't want you or your kids sitting on my furniture; don't touch my TV; and don't eat my food. You all can sleep in the back right bedroom on the floor. I mean it, Pat," she spat out, "don't touch anything in my apartment." The line went dead with a slam, leaving me feeling less than a stray.

Despite the sting of her words, I tried to make the best of our grim refuge. I bathed the children, clothed them in clean garments, and prepared a humble meal of soup. As they settled on a makeshift pallet for a nap, the urgency to find a new home gnawed at me—school was looming on the horizon. Defiant, I used Geri's phone to tend to my affairs. "To hell with Geri," I muttered under my breath. A call to Lettie revealed a troubling visit from Child Protective Services. "What is Child Protective Service?" I asked, a knot forming in my stomach. "I don't know," she replied, "but you better call them." The call to Social Services only deepened my anxiety. The worker was tight-lipped, offering nothing more than vague warnings of neglect and the threat of custody. "Take my children from me? That's not true," I protested. "I take care of my kids." But the bureaucracy was unmoved. "You can't get anything from us until they clear you of all charges," she said. My address was questioned, and my existence at my own home was denied by an unnamed accuser. I decided to stay put to weather the storm from within these hostile walls. A call to my mother shed light on the situation. "Someone reported you," she said, her voice heavy with concern. "They're going to try to put your children in a home. They will separate them. Be careful." Her warning was clear, and her tone bespoke the knowledge of Geri's treachery. In my heart, I knew—it must have been Geri who called. Or Aunt Janie.

Almost two weeks had passed, and Geri was coming back and forth to the apartment to make sure we weren't sitting on her precious furniture. In between those times, Mr. Brazil was traveling back and forth to take me to the store to buy food for the kids. The market was across the busy freeway; I needed a car just to go to the store. I was trapped. He would also drive me to the city to look for a place to live. I spent days and days homeschooling my children and reading books to them. At night, I stayed up worrying and praying about how I was going to get us out of this situation. I called about my car; they said it still hadn't arrived. My money was funky, and time was of the essence.

I could tell that Andre wasn't feeling well; he had a cold and was having some trouble breathing. He had a slight fever on and off. I gave him soup, orange juice, and aspirin. He didn't seem to be feeling any better. On this day, it was freezing rain on top of the seven inches of snow we received. I never got too comfortable in her apartment; we were living out of bags and living out of one room.

Geri stormed inside her apartment and said, "You got to go. Now, today! I don't give a damn where you go, but you get the hell outta here." We had some words, and then my son Andre started to vomit. He was choking. I rushed him to the bathroom. I'd never seen anything like it in my life. He threw up blood clots. It must have been a million of them. I told her to call an ambulance; he was strangling. She didn't budge. I patted him on the back and tried to help clear his nose. He threw up like a faucet. They were everywhere. Finally, I got him where he could catch his breath and breathe. I cleaned him up and removed all the mucus. Geri stood there and watched it all. She stood in the bathroom doorway, and she said, "You got to go." I gathered my children and my belongings and went downstairs to the office building. I called Mr. Brazil and waited for him to come.

That was Friday. Mr. Brazil took me down to the Children's Hospital on Beaubien Street near Mack Avenue, across the street from the American Red Cross, where Geri worked. When we left the emergency room, we drove down Mack Street. I looked over, and I could see Geri's car in the lot. Andre was treated and released; he'd had nosebleeds and was swallowing blood in his sleep. Mr. Brazil took us to his house for the weekend. Although I was catching pure hell, it sure was good to see the whole gang from the neighborhood.

Everybody was glad to see us; it was like old times again. Although the house was severely crowded, they made us feel welcome anyway. Mr. and Mrs. Brazil officially adopted me as one of their own. That really meant a lot to me because I felt so alone and thrown away. The Brazils always treated me like their own. I remember one time, Me and Emory were having a bad fight over something silly, I'm sure. Daddy told us both to shut up, and, of course, we didn't, and Dad put both me and Emory out of the house. We all laughed about it later. Mr. Brazil was no angel by a long shot. You could almost call them the most literal parents I know. A hippie in their own day. They had many friends on the block. Dad was the president of Hurlbut Street Block Club, and he would see that things got done.

The Brazil House was home to many. Old friends always came by to visit. If you ever wanted to reconnect with an old friend you hadn't seen in years, the Brazil home was the place to go. They welcomed everyone with open arms, offering a hot meal and plenty of love

That night, we played cards, drank beer and liquor, and listened to the blues. I needed a break.

I cooked while they caught me up on all the local gossip. The kids even joined the party with potato chips, Twinkies, and soda. Mrs. Brazil babysat so Emory and I could roam the streets, searching for old friends. I looked everywhere for one of my dearest friends, Gramps, but couldn't find him. I even stopped by to see Robert and his parents. Everyone told me how good I looked. Daddy kept my secret about Geri and what she had done; he simply told everyone that I was moving back home. I stayed at the Brazil house long enough to take care of my business and to pray. I found a private spot in the bathroom where I kneeled down to pray for strength and guidance.

Three days before I moved out, I dreamed about Michael Martin. In the dream, he was a baby in diapers, crying. I played his name in the streets in Detroit and Pontiac, and the numbers 628–849 came up straight in Detroit. I won a thousand dollars. Michael brought me some money.

I was happy, but I still felt uneasy from the dream. I couldn't shake the feeling that something was wrong with Michael. So, I started to look for him. I called some of the old gang, but no one had seen Michael. Then, I called Information, but his number was unlisted. I placed an emergency phone call through the telephone company, asking them to get in touch with Michael and have him call me back.

An hour later, I received a call from Granny, Michael's grandmother. She told me Michael had been in a bad car accident and was at the University of Michigan Hospital in Ann Arbor. Michael was visiting friends in Belleville when one of them asked him to go to the store. Michael had a bad feeling but went anyway. The driver was speeding down a back dirt road when their car became airborne over a hill and was blindsided by a stalled tractor, hitting it head-on.

The driver of their car died instantly; the engine came through the dashboard and cut him in half. Michael was thrown 50 feet into the air and landed in a cornfield on top of his head. Granny relayed that Michael had broken his neck crack and was unable to move.

The paramedics only realized there was another passenger because Michael had been knocked out of his shoes. Horrified, I immediately called to confirm he was at that hospital, then I took a train to Ann Arbor with the kids. When I arrived, Michael was lying in a baby bed, in a diaper, with monitors connected to his body. His neck was broken in several places paralyzed from the neck down and would never be able to walk again. Michael was a Quadriplegic.

Michael was twenty-two.

All I could do was cry for him. Michael tried to comfort me before breaking down himself. He lamented, "What makes this so bad is that I can't skate anymore." I leaned over, hugged him, and said, "My legs still work; I'll take you to the skating rink, and I'll skate for you."

Michael was in pretty good spirits, doing all he could to comfort me.

This accident happened at the end of 1977. The kids and I spent the whole day with Michael. While he continued to recover in the hospital, I continued my journey on the streets. I called to see if my car had arrived. They said no. I paid Mr. Brazil to take me over to check on my car. When

I got there, they pretended like they couldn't find the paperwork. Then the owner of the company said that the clutch had gone out and they couldn't drive it here. It was left stranded on the road. Heartbroken, I realized not only did I have no transportation, but I was also out six hundred dollars. I pitched a fit with the owner.

I accused them of lying, stealing my money, and my car. I threatened to sue them. Afterward, Mr. Brazil dropped us off at the Monterey Motel where we stayed until my money ran out. We've been homeless now for eleven months.

Chapter 22

"Survival of the Fittest"

1980

I struggled to survive on the streets, living everywhere from shelters, parks, libraries, and friends' places to sleeping in abandoned cars, riding buses, and even outdoors on the ground and under bridges. We washed up and changed clothes at White Castle and any other restaurant that I could. I couldn't get any help from social services because they were collaborating with child protective services to take my children from me. Whenever I was fortunate enough to get a room at the shelter, I used an alias. As fate would have it, I got lucky; I found an abandoned house.

For me and the kids to live in. We were riding the Grand River bus early one evening; I'm not even sure where I was headed. My mental state was fragile; I was in a deep funk, feeling discouraged and tired. Life had become damn near impossible to live. It hurts for me to breathe. I thought to myself, maybe I should end it all. Feelings of hopelessness weighed heavily; my children were starving. I couldn't remember the last time they had a hot meal. With no money left, I rode the bus line from one end to the other for two days. I almost didn't recognize the familiar blocks. It was the middle of September; the moisture in the air helped the fall leaves change color.

The bus was getting ready to pass an old street we used to live on. Something in my gut told me to get off and walk down the long block to the house I once lived in when Nina owned it. The sky was cloudy, and it was getting dark out; we had to try and find shelter somewhere, somehow.

As we walked, my eyes searched both sides of the street for a house to sleep in. Most of the homes had been vandalized, either by the homeowner, Detroit Stress, or the Big Four. The clannish group was assembled by a White Supremacy Commander-in-Chief, and they had the full right to kill. It didn't matter to them if you were old, young, or a child; as long as you were black, you fit the criteria.

A group of all-white police officers is on a mission to kill black people. Hiding behind the Detroit Police Department, they roamed without their hoods and ropes. The special unit known as Stress was infamous for kicking in doors, drawing guns, and pistol-whipping people. Sometimes, they even killed people in their homes. It was revealed by *The Michigan Chronicle* that Stress had beaten a sixteen-year-old to death. His face was profiled on the front page, causing widespread fear among the black community about becoming the next victim.

Now, the Big Four consisted of three white cops riding shotgun and one black driver. They were a backup for Stress. They rode in unmarked black cars and dressed in plain clothes. Black people marched down Woodward Avenue to City Hall to have Stress abolished. Detroit's newly elected Mayor Young, aware that blacks were in imminent danger, immediately ended Stress. It has been reported that at least 60 blacks were killed by Stress. No whites were ever killed during what was referred to as open season on NIGGERS!

The empty houses on Freeland Street looked dangerous and cold. We continued to walk; my children were tired, lifeless, hungry, irritable, and cold. I carried Kyham and our few bags of clothing in my arms. Shawn and Andre each held hands, with Terrance in the middle. They walked ahead of me. With every step toward the house, I prayed, "God, please help me; please, I feel like I can't go on." The warm tears streaming down my face reminded me of a summer day and butterflies. For a moment, I remembered when I was a little girl. When I looked up, I knew that we had found refuge on Freeland Street. The house, all too familiar, was standing vacant. It was Nina's old house before she moved to Canton Township. All of a sudden, I felt great strength growing from within. I was determined to make this house work for us, regardless of the obstacles. I was afraid, yes, but also determined. I thought about my mother, and I thought about Curtis Mayfield's song, 'Keep on Pushing.' 'You can't stop now!'

I secured my children inside the backyard fence, raised the window, and climbed inside. The back door had been barricaded with a large 2x4. My children and I moved in with no hesitation on my part. The electricity was still on, and the phone was on, but the furnace had been stolen, and the water was off. With very little daylight left, I scrambled to clean up and make a place to live out of nothing. I found some old blankets, an old broom, and a few towels. It was so cold inside the house that I used the funny pages of an old newspaper to cover the windows so no one could see in. And I folded the paper down to stuff in the cracks. We moved into this house with nothing but what we had on our backs. I found a small space heater in the basement and used it for heat. 'God is good!'

I don't know what time it was, but there was a knock at the door. I tried to peek through the funny paper to see who it was. It was my brother, Rickey. He said that God led him to me. He had been looking for me, and nobody knew where I was. He didn't know why he thought to come to the house on Freeland. That night he didn't have much money, but he went to the store and bought the kids bologna, cheese, bread, milk, and four cups. Rickey was also on foot and catching hell. He was riding with his new white girlfriend, Judy.

He promised to come back and check on me, and I made him promise not to tell anyone where I was. He gave me twenty dollars.

I thanked him and hugged him.

We were all living in one room. In the months that followed, I found myself walking to the nearest church, holding my head down in shame, looking for food to feed my children. St. Vincent de Paul distributed food on Tuesdays only. They gave me canned goods and boxed food. We ate out of those cans for over six months.

We didn't even have a fork. I found an old butcher knife in the house. Using it to stab the can along the side, I cut up, up, up until it opened. I sat the kids down on the newspaper, then placed the food into my hand and then into their mouths; we were eating out of cans. I'd walk three or four blocks to the gas station and carry water back in a big plastic bucket for them to drink and wash their faces in. I kept in touch with Mama and Mrs. Brazil as much as I could. I told my mother where I was living, but not how I was living. I told her not to tell Nina, for fear she would come over and put us out. I didn't know if she still owned the house or not. Thanksgiving, Christmas, and New Year's passed us by without even a thought!

I remember seeing two good old friends of mine. I told them about my situation. I was embarrassed, but I told them anyway. I told them that I was homeless and without food for my kids. It was cold as hell out, and my feet were wet. This happened three days before Christmas.

They were living life high on the hog! Margie and Little Dot—you couldn't hit them in the ass with a red apple! They said, "Come on, get in the car." They pulled their mink coats back so I could get in. They could look at me and see how I was living. I was clean, but I was living from hand to mouth. I got in the car, and we drove over to their laid-back home that they shared together on Cheyenne.

When I walked inside, the aroma of the food greeted you at the door. Bowls and bowls of fresh fruit, nuts, and candy overflowed onto the tables. The Christmas tree lights only enhanced the beautiful wrapping paper on the many gifts stacked up to the ceiling, cascading onto the floor. The house was warm, and the atmosphere was friendly. We walked upstairs into their bedroom, where I waited for them to get dressed.

They were going out to play cards. They didn't pay much attention to me; they were busy in their own worlds, snorting cocaine and drinking champagne. The sound of water running from the shower put me to sleep. When I woke up, they were gone. I remember thinking to myself, "My, my, how we've changed." I remember us walking to get free commodities together. What hurt my feelings was that they didn't even offer me an orange or a candy cane for my children. I left there, walking back to Freeland.

I left Rickey to babysit the kids while I combed the area, scrounging for food. I felt guilty. I felt like I had done something wrong. I went to their house, got warm, and fell asleep. I left them in the abandoned house, but that was not my intention.

I thought that Margie and Dot would feel some empathy and show us some love. We were like sisters, I thought; we'd weathered some storms together. I thought they were better than that.

I loved them so much that I wanted to believe they would show some compassion and want to help me out without me having to lower myself by asking. You find out who your real friends are in times of need! I learned a lesson that day: All that shines ain't gold.

We survived an entire winter living like that. I never stopped praying and asking God for strength, guidance, and money. "Please, Lord," I prayed day after day, "I need a miracle." One day, a knock came at the door. I peeked out and told the kids to remain quiet. I could see two white ladies; I knew it was Child Protective Services. They left a card on the door for me to contact them. "That'll never happen in this life," I thought to myself.

On January 13, 1980, I took the kids to Cappuccin Soup Kitchen on Kercheval and Mt. Elliott on Detroit's lower east side. While standing in the long soup line, I noticed a small color television set on the same counter where they were serving food. Channel 7 Action News with Bill Bonds reported that Donny Hathaway marking the one-year anniversary of his death. Recapped the story now under investigation. He was found dead outside his apartment window. My heart sank. I didn't know that Donny Hathway had died a year ago. Donny sang his songs with so much raw funk and class—it was unbelievable. "The Ghetto" came to mind; his words had hit home for me. I've been a faithful fan of his since the beginning. As bad as I was feeling watching my children grow and adjust from one situation to another, like jumping through hoops in such little time, the death of Donny Hathaway truly crushed me. It was like saying goodbye to an old friend. He was tremendously talented.

After getting off the bus before dark and walking back to the abandoned house, I prayed silently in my heart. "Lord," I said, "I don't know what to do; I don't know where to go; my babies are cold and hungry; they need to eat. Please, Lord, provide for us, as you said you would." Amidst these prayers, I was battling negative thoughts about my situation. "You said that you'd never forsake me, Lord. Help me get through this; stay with me. Lord, please protect us. Don't let any harm come to us as we walk these streets. Help my babies, Lord, your children that you gave to me. It's my job to take care of them; you're their Father in Heaven. I'm asking you to make a way. It's by your grace that they're mine. Please don't allow them to suffer for my mistakes."

It took all the energy I had to pray this prayer to the Lord, and He knew it. I was at an all-time low! That night, after checking the house for safety, I laid down on the floor in the other room. It was cold; I balled up like a fist. I was sleeping hard, but at the same time, I could feel someone standing and watching over me. I was so tired I could hardly move. I struggled to turn over, and when I did, I could see Lawrence Blackwell standing in the corner of the room with his arms crossed, smiling down at me. He was wearing the white suit he was buried in.

I was too afraid to move. I shut my eyes, and before I could cry out to him that he was scaring me, he was gone. I hurried up and got out of there. I laid down next to my children. I couldn't help but think about my dear friend Lawrence. He came to me because he knew I was in distress. He was there to watch over me. With him in mind, I felt safe, so I fell back to sleep. I dreamed there was a tarantula spider climbing up my leg. I knocked it off and stepped on it, and when I rolled my foot back, there was a big ruby jewel in its back.

I woke up screaming, "031 bit me!" Hot damn, I knew I had the number, but I didn't have any money. My right hand was itching; I had to get this number in before 12:00 noon. I had five hours; this was my only chance. I scrounged through the house looking for any money to help me. I searched high and low.

"God is good!" In the basement, I found a rack of old coats. They belonged to Nina; she loved coats. In the dark basement, I began searching the pockets. In the third coat pocket I searched, I felt two balled-up pieces of paper. I pulled them out but couldn't see. I started to leave the paper in the coat, but my mind said to take it upstairs and look at it. I stood by the kitchen sink with daylight barely peeping through and unballed my hand. It was a twenty-dollar bill and a ten- dollar bill—$30.00. I screamed, "Thank you, Jesus."

I couldn't believe it. I got the kids cleaned up, and we left there running with everything we owned to the bus stop. I knew two things for sure: I had the number, and I would never go back to Freeland again. We caught the Grand River bus downtown, I fed the kids a hot breakfast, and we caught the Cadillac bus to Mrs. Brazil's house. Whenever I visited Brazil's, it was an all-day thing, so I planned it just that way. When I opened the door, Mrs. Brazil and I had a love-mate call, something we did between each other. So, I sang out to my love mate, and she sang out in tears. I hurried in to see what was wrong. Just then, Daddy was entering the room, and with his full hand open, he crunched his eyeglasses on his face, pushing them up. He took a stance and fixed his suspenders. They hugged the kids and asked us how we had been doing. He went to the kitchen to put on the percolator for coffee. I made our cups of coffee and proceeded to tell them about my dream.

I played Lawrence's name, and Spider- 519, and 031 in Detroit and Pontiac. And I spent the entire day with them, cooking, listening to them argue, laughing, and gossiping. Mrs. Wynn came over, and Marlene, the oldest girl, came over, and we walked to Jack's store and got three dollars' worth of mild hog head cheese, crackers, and a beer. We walked back and sat down on the front porch. As soon as I noticed that it was getting dark outside, Mrs. Brazil screamed, "You hit the number! 031 fell straight into Detroit. I'd won five hundred dollars." "You might as well stay here," she said. "It's getting dark; I don't want to have to worry about you. Plus, Mr. Charles is not going to pay you until tomorrow anyway." So I stayed, and we had dinner, watched TV, and played cards—3, 5, 9. All was quiet at the Brazil home.

That morning, I had Daddy drive me over to the projects on Warren and Connor. They immediately accepted my application. They showed me the unit available; when we walked inside, I started to throw up from the smell and filth there. I told her, "No, thank you; I didn't want to live in this. It was squalor." There was smeared blood on the walls; it was infested with rats, roaches, gangs, drugs, guns, and break-ins. "Shit," I thought to myself, "I'll take my chances on the streets."

While I waited for Mr. Charles to come, I called and talked to Mama. I reassured her that I was doing just fine. She told me that Laura called and wanted me to call her back, but Mama couldn't see to write the number down; Laura had changed her number. I also called Amtrak to find out that I had lost all of the boxes I shipped from California. They made one attempt to contact me at Lettie's but were unsuccessful. After I got my money, just like before, I had Dad drop us off at Monterey. The reason I stayed at Monterey was because they had a kitchenette and refrigerator. I gave the kids a warm bath, fed them dinner, and we got down on our knees and said the Lord's prayers. I thanked God for his many blessings.

I paid our motel bill for six weeks at $65.00 a week, which gave us some time. With less than one hundred dollars left to spend on food, my babies and I walked to the nearest corner store, where I bought them as much food as I could afford. I could see that Andre wasn't feeling well; he was coughing and looked tired.

I knew that if I had to rush him to the closest emergency room, we were in close proximity to doing so. "If you ever get sick, get sick on Woodward Avenue," I would say. Detroit's most outstanding hospitals are located on the strip or within walking distance. I worried about him, about them, about everything. But I was determined and continued to pray.

We walked through the hallway to check on any messages left from before. The motel clerk was cool like that; we'd become friends. He watched my back, always ensuring we had the safest room available, and kept a pot and pan in the back for me. Jean was as sweet as pie, and he loved my children. I hurried to the room to feed and bathe my kids and put them down for the night. Through the night, Andre's temperature elevated; I couldn't get it down. He started to wheeze, and his eyes rolled back. I grabbed the phone and told Jean to call an ambulance because André was having trouble breathing. I sat him up and splashed some cold water on his face, which seemed to help him catch his breath. I woke the kids up in a hurry, yelling, "Get dressed!"

I hurried to put on my clothes. As I was running out to the front, the paramedics were running in. I briefed them on his history; they strapped oxygen on him and drove us to Children's Hospital. They rushed him back, and I had to leave the kids in the lobby to accompany Andre. I could still see them, but nonetheless, they were left alone. After being there for almost four hours waiting on test results, the kids became tired and restless, squabbling a bit. I told them I was leaving Shawn in charge and to behave. Andre had another asthma attack compounded by a cold. They administered breathing treatments and gave us prescriptions as we were preparing to leave. I planned to hail a cab to the pharmacy and then the motel.

As we were leaving, I noticed two women walking towards me. Their approach was as if we were old friends, smiling at me. I never smiled back. They both wore long beige polyester lightweight coats. My antennas went up. I stopped my kids for a moment and started to fix their coats. I huddled them close and whispered, "These women are coming here to take you away. I want you to be very quiet and let me talk; don't say anything." When I stood up, they were standing over me. I stretched my arms out to push my kids back and take a step back. They flashed their IDs and introduced themselves as Ms. Loran and Mrs. Smitz, one black and one white. They asked me to come with them to their office as they had several complaints that needed to be investigated. I told them it was late and asked if I could make an appointment to come in. "No," they said, "Ms. Lee, I'm afraid not," addressing me by my name.

"Well, I'm not going anywhere with you until I get my son's prescription filled," I insisted. We got in the car, and not only did they get the prescription filled, but they also bought the kids something to eat. In my heart of hearts, I knew not to trust the enemy. On our way down to their office, I asked them what they were going to do to us now that they had found me. I told them my children were well taken care of and that I loved them very much. Instead of trying to separate us, why don't you help me stay with my kids? "That's why we're here, Ms. Lee, to help you," Mrs. Smitz said. "The judge will decide what to do." The judge' I thought to myself. They asked me how I had been living; I avoided the question, steering the conversation in another direction.

I already knew what I was going to do; I was just waiting for the opportunity. My mind was made up—nobody's taking my kids from me. When we drove into their parking lot, Mrs. Smitz walked to her car and said goodbye to her coworker. She drove off. I saw with my eyes the building exits as we walked up the long flight of stairs. Ms. Loran led the way. I turned around and put my finger to my mouth, signaling silence. Quietly, we walked into the office. The building itself was dark, but the office light provided enough illumination for me to see that it was 4:20 in the morning. As soon as we sat down, she started to question my children. They never answered. I stood up and told her that if she wanted to know anything about me or them, she better talk to me directly. "Do not question my kids," I insisted.

Ms. Loran sarcastically replied, "You're right, leave that up to the judge. But tonight, I'll be placing your children in temporary custody. I'll try to place them together, but that's going to be hard." Just then, Ms. Loran's telephone started to ring; it was her daughter. From the conversation, I understood her daughter had a fight with another girl at the skating rink over a boy. I heard Ms. Loran tell her daughter, "You're only fifteen; there'll be other boys." She hung up and turned to me, and before she could speak, Terrance said, "I have to go to the bathroom," and the telephone rang at the same time. Then they all said they had to go to the bathroom. That was my cue.

I pretended that I didn't know where the bathroom was, so I asked. Hell, I'd scoped it out when we first walked up. It was right by the stairs. Ms. Loran, distracted by her child, pointed the way and continued to talk on the phone. I grabbed my babies and walked back through the dark hallway. Quickly my eyes adjusted to the darkness. I opened the bathroom door and walked inside so she could hear the door open.

I never closed it. For a second, I stood there listening to her conversation; the police were there to take her child to juvenile. I whispered to the kids to quietly walk down the first flight of stairs and when they hit the second flight, to run like hell. I picked up Andre and Kyham and hauled ass out of the building. We ran down the back alley up to West Grand Blvd and cut over to Second Avenue. I hailed a cab, threw the kids in, and we drove off. I told the driver what was happening, so he took some shortcuts to make sure no one was following us. He dropped us off at Mrs. Brazil's.

I ran up and started to beat on the door. Dad came down. I cried with relief as I told the story. "Well, you're safe here. I ain't gonna let nobody take your kids from you. You're a good mother; I wish Evelyn was like you," he said. I put my kids to bed on the couch and called Jean at Monterey. He said they had been there looking for me around 10:00 pm, the time I left to take Andre to the hospital. They must have come after I left. Jean said to wait a few days until it cooled down, that he'd change my name in the register and move me and my belongings to another room in the back. Jean was the house manager; he lived on the premises. I thanked him.

The couch was right by the door, so every time I heard a car drive down the street, I woke up. We stayed at the Brazil's a little over a week; they wouldn't let me leave. Dad drove me to the Monterey, to pick up clothes; I was in and out in a flash. Jean and I had a signal; if it ever happened again, he showed me a hiding place.

All this happened because I didn't have an address. I needed a place to stay before I could get an address. Housing was crap in Detroit. We'd been living on the streets for a total of sixteen months.

Someone told me about the organization named Westside Mothers; they were known for helping mothers with children. With the kids, I caught the Oakman bus down to see them early in the morning. I was on my last leg. I had only three dollars in my pocket and no way to feed my babies. We had been living on whatever little food I could carry from the Catholic Churches. Last night we spent riding the bus and eating White Castles.

Westside Mothers is a group of mothers that fights for the rights of welfare recipients. They have access to resources to help get you on your feet. They were located between Hostess Bakery and Focus Hope in a small little building in the basement. I walked down the concrete stairwell, engulfed by cinder block walls that looked like they hadn't been painted in years. The honey beige walls were starting to blend with hunter green trim. I was welcomed in and made to feel at home. These Black women were here to restore hope.

I explained the situation to them. I told them that I believed Lettie was the one who reported me to Child Protective Services, and now they were on my case because she felt that I thought I was better than her. I didn't want to live in the filth they created. I don't want my children to live under those circumstances. Additionally, I observed that she attempted to distinguish between my children based on their skin tone. Andre is browner, like my mother, than his brothers and sister. I noticed Lettie when she slighted Terrance for Andre. She gave Andre more cookies than Terrance, then whispered something in his ear and laughed at Terrance. But what she didn't know is that I taught my children to share and love one another, and that's exactly what André did. Shared.

Westside mother, Mrs. Larry, called and talked to the worker. She explained that the allegations made against me were not true. Mrs. Larry said that she met with me last week and that my children were clean, fed, and safe. "Where are they living?" the social worker asked Mrs. Larry. After some quick thinking on her part, she said that I came into their office for help and left no address. The social worker also stated to Mrs. Larry that she had me down as living and receiving a check and food stamps at 2265

Mack Avenue. Mrs. Larry wrote the information down right in front of me. I was sitting across from her at her desk; I could see. Mrs. Larry took the information and told the worker that she'd call her back after lunch. As soon as she hung up the phone, I told her that was Aunt Janie's address, and I hadn't lived there in years. In the same breath, I pulled out my California Driver's License to prove to her that I was telling the truth.

The mothers bought me and my children a hot fish and chicken dinner with all the trimmings for lunch. We had been there that long. Mrs. Larry was doing all she could to help me untangle everything. Mrs. Larry called the worker back; she was a Black woman like her. The worker told Mrs. Larry that she had been sending my checks and food stamp card there for over nine years. Mrs. Larry told her that she had my driver's license in her hand and that she could prove that Aunt Janie had been receiving my checks in my name. She'd also been the one receiving and filling out my renewal papers. She also told the worker that she spoke with Mr. Martinez to confirm that I was living and receiving aid in San Jose, California. The worker said that she would cut my checks off to Aunt Janie immediately and open a case for me as soon as I got an address. She said that she'd mail a copy of her letter explaining the situation and recommending that Child Protective Services close my case with their agency.

She also authorized Westside Mothers to give me a shelter voucher, rent authorization, used furniture and second-hand clothing voucher, bus tickets, and one-time emergency food stamps for the past two months. "Oh my God," I cried. "Thank you," I said, hugging her with what little strength I had left. Mrs. Larry said, "I'm not through yet." Mrs. Larry called a cab and paid them to take us to Labelle Shelter off 14th Street near Davison. I left there with two hundred and twelve dollars in stamps, bus tickets for two weeks, plenty of snacks like Hostess cupcakes, Twinkies, Better Made potato chips, Focus Hope food sundry items, and all of my vouchers. I thanked God for hearing my prayers. Mrs. Larry also wrote a note to the administrator at the shelter asking them not to put me and the kids out in the morning because of Andre's asthma. When I arrived at the secluded shelter, I was treated with dignity and respect. They gave me a large bedroom with three beds and one baby bed. It was clean and warm.

After feeding the kids and giving them a bath, I put them down for bed and walked outside the room to smoke a cigarette and clear my head.

In the lounge were several Black women, like me, struggling to stay afloat. We united, exchanged ideas, and made plans for the future. Labelle wasn't the best shelter—I'd become an expert! But it was clean, secluded, and warm, and the staff was very kind to the kids. And it was a steppingstone.

As I walked through the doorway, I instantly struck up a conversation with a small-framed, brown-skinned, likable woman. She said she'd been living there for a year. It was nearly impossible for her to find decent housing. She placed her hand on her side, swayed her back, and sat down.

"I'm the mother of eleven children, and I'm pregnant with my twelfth," she said.

I couldn't believe it at first, but then they all started to gather in the room, climbing and stepping on top of everybody—I knew it was true. I remember at least two other large families like hers: but I was still surprised. Her name was Shirley Pringle, just like the potato chips, and Charlene was a friend of hers. Before long, our friendship developed. Charlene was out there, but I liked her. I'd watch her children for her so she could fill out applications, or she could get us a ride during the day with some of her old male friends to look for a place. We made our phone calls from the shelter the night before to look for a place to live the following day. I'd been there for two weeks.

On this particular Saturday, I got a call from the front saying that I had a visitor. I walked through the hallway and saw Nina's face—my heart was in my throat and beating fast. "Is there something wrong with Mama?"

"No," she said. "Mama told me where you were here, and I just came by to see where you were."

Flaunting her diamonds and fur coat, she looked sharp from head to toe. Looking down at her hands, she straightened her diamonds. "Geri and I are on our way to Carl's Chop House for dinner; we're meeting some friends for drinks," she added. Again, she said, "I just wanted to know where you were. Mama's doing much better; she's gaining weight."

"Well, that's good," I said. As we walked back towards the door, I could see her brand-new Delta 98 silver-gray car—it was sharp. Nina went inside her pocket and handed me a folded twenty dollars.

I instantly refused it; she forced it into my hand again, and I backed up and told her, "That's alright, I don't need anything; thank you anyway.

We'll be fine." "Are you sure?" she said. "Take it for the kids." "No, thank you; we'll be fine," I said. "See you later," she said.

It was the weekend, and I was feeling blue. Charlene had just come back from turning a trick in the car; she had some money and was ready to party. I overheard a conversation on the phone with a man she called Hoot. Hoot and Hazel owned an After Hour Joint on the north end of town. Shortly after, he came over and invited us all to his joint on Clay near Oakman Blvd. "What the hell?" I said, "Yeah."

He seemed nice enough. I dressed the kids, and we went over. Secretly, Charlene turned tricks all night long with various men, making enough money to move out of the shelter. 'Thank God I still had my vouchers.' She didn't think I noticed her working the upper third floor, but I did. 'Charlene only held her head up long enough to take a drink. ' Hoot and his wife Hazel were so nice and warm; they were good to the kids. She cooked us a fabulous dinner, and we were safe. Charlene and Pringle's kids were at the shelter; the girl on duty was cool. Hazel put the kids down in her big room, right next to where I was sitting. And baby, we partied—we drank liquor, played the blues, and everybody cried about their lives but me. I wasn't in the mood to cry.

On our way back to the shelter, Hoot propositioned me. I told him briefly that I appreciated his offer, but I was only interested in finding a place to live. "I can tell you love your kids," he said. "You're a nice, clean woman." Hoot was a nice-looking older man who handled a lot of money. Plus, I said, "I like your wife, Hazel; I couldn't do that." So, he had to settle for Charlene. Monday morning, I called Lettie's looking for Bob.

He answered the phone, and I told him that I needed a ride to find me a place to live. He said that he'd been looking for me and that he had moved back to his mother's since I saw him at Charlie's. I didn't care; I just needed a ride. I left when Bob came; Charlene left with Hoot; Pringle had her own transportation. Charlene gave me the address of an apartment building on Ohio and Grand River. They had plenty of openings. Sure enough, I went there and waited until early evening for the owner to return. He accepted my vouchers and showed me an apartment on the 8th floor that was clean. I could move in tomorrow. It was far from the best, but it got us out of the shelter and off the streets.

Charlene had already started a relationship with the owner, so she secured a downstairs apartment, no better than mine. The three red brick apartment buildings housed over two hundred poor black families. We moved into the apartment without even a sheet. It had one bedroom, a bath, a small hallway, a living room with a Murphy bed stuck in the wall, and a kitchen so narrow I had to turn my body sideways to move through it. Once in the kitchen, I could do a complete turnaround by the counter. The refrigerator was so filthy and had such a foul smell that it hadn't been cleaned out in years; it made me gag. The peeling moss green paint matched the splintering and lifting hardwood floors perfectly. The units were so close to each other, I knew there were roaches; I just hadn't seen any yet. I had to leave Bob with the kids to go down to Charlene's in search of some sheets to lay my babies on.

I was ashamed, but I had to do it. As I was approaching her door, I walked into Hoot. He spoke first, saying that Charlene was gone; she left the kids, and no one was answering the door. I said okay and turned to walk away. Hoot grabbed my hand, and pressed something into it, and held it tight. "I know there's nothing between us, and you made it clear that there never will be. And I appreciate that; I respect you for it," he said. "I told Hazel that I wanted to make you my next girlfriend."

"What?" I exclaimed.

"Actually, I wasn't looking for Charlene; I was looking for you," he continued. "Hazel knows that I'm through with Charlene; our relationship ended over a year ago, but we remained friends. Hazel and I have an arrangement. I take care of all the bills, buy the food, and give her money. She does what she wants, and I do what I want. Hazel has been friends with many of my girlfriends, but she likes you. That's the way it is between us. Look, I want to help you with your kids. Hazel would want it that way."

I pulled my hand back from his and opened it—four fifty-dollar bills unraveled in my hand. "Hoot, I can't take this," I said, pushing it back.

"You better take this," he insisted. "Hazel sent a hundred, and I'm giving you a hundred. You can help your kids with this money. Hazel and I never had kids, and we were talking about what a good mother you are. Your kids are intelligent and well-behaved. They're going to be somebody someday. God has a special calling for you through those kids, so take the money. Please, from one friend to another."

"Okay," I said, hugging him. "Thank you. Give Hazel a kiss for me."

He said he would stop by sometime and pick me and Charlene up to go party at his joint. It was getting dark, so I took the stairs, happy I had some money to help my kids. I thanked God for Hoot and Hazel.

The apartment was so nasty that I had Bob drop us off at the motel in Redford. I told him to come back the next morning bright and early; I needed to use his car. I washed and dried all of our clothes right in the room. At 7:30 AM, Bob knocked at the door, and I was ready. I fed the kids a hot breakfast at Albert's Restaurant, then ran over to K-Mart to buy cleaning supplies, sheets, blankets, coloring books, and crayons. We drove over to Virley Coulter's furniture store. After we hugged, I filtered through the stuff he had, but it wasn't the same quality as before. He said he was having financial problems. He let me pick out a couch, a chair, and a small dinette table with mismatched chairs.

I gave him the address and a hug. He was only too pleased to help. We got back to the apartment, and Bob took off, mentioning he had an early rehearsal. I told him I needed him to come back so I could go to the market and get the kids some food. Before I could start cleaning, I had to situate my children on something clean. I told the kids to stand back. I put two socks on my hands and reached up to grab the worn-out rope of the Murphy bed. I was afraid to pull, fearing what might fall out when I let it down.

I closed my eyes, turned my head, and pulled down the Murphy bed. The two front legs collapsed to the floor with a loud "boom," and the filthy mattress slid forward—it was dirty enough to belong in the alley right behind us. Someone had been sleeping and bleeding on it, not to mention other things. The kids stepped way back as I opened the window, folded the flimsy mattress, and pushed it out. I took the broom I had bought, brushed the frame off, and swept away all the dust and cobwebs. I sprayed it down with Lysol and washed the entire bed off with bleach water. I threw the new blanket over the frame, sat my children down, gave them their coloring books, and said, "Don't get off the bed; it's nasty and filthy in here."

I cleaned the whole apartment, washing the walls from top to bottom. Yet, I still couldn't bring myself to clean out the refrigerator. There was evidence of roaches; I could see droppings and smell the spray. Charlene came by just in time. I asked her to fetch Gary, the owner. An hour later, he came to my door. I showed him the refrigerator and the mattress that had taken a dive of its own, landing in the lower trees. Not only did he provide a decent mattress, but he also had the caretaker bring me a clean refrigerator from the lower level.

Pringle came by; she drove me to the market, the goodwill, and to buy Chinese food. Then we waited for Mr. Coulter. He arrived around four o'clock with another fellow. He overheard me say at the furniture store that I needed a stove, so he brought me one. The elevator had been working off and on, but Mr. Coulter, with his friend's help, managed to drag the couch up eight flights of stairs with a dolly and the stove up four flights. I was glad Pringle was there; she kept me company and helped me keep my mind off the rats and roaches for a while. Her daughter played with the kids, but all good things come to an end.

She had to go home and check on her kids. Pringle found a four-bedroom house on the west side of Lesure and Fenkell. Before she left, she talked about her husband—a serviceman who left her for the woman around the corner with six fewer children than her. Pringle said her husband and her doctor told her to stop having so many children, but she was going to wait for him to come back home to her and their children. We hugged goodbye. I barricaded the door with a knife and lay across the Murphy bed with the kids. Finally, I dozed off and woke up to a scratching sound in the kitchen. I knew what it sounded like but was too afraid to put my feet on the floor or to look.

Bob knocked at the door; I ran to open it, hopping back onto the bed. I told him to be quiet and listen; I didn't want to scare the kids. He heard the sound too. "Give me some money," he said. "I'll be right back." I gave him ten dollars, and I threatened him; he returned with a bag full of rat and mouse traps. Too afraid to move, I stayed on the bed. He set the traps and caught 32 mice nesting in the bottom of the stove. I remember counting how many times I heard the traps snap. Bob used the traps over and over again until he caught them all. The next morning, I took his car and went to the goodwill to buy a hot plate; I wasn't cooking on that stove. My nerves were shot; I could hardly walk on the floors. I didn't let the kids play on the floors at all. On my way, I prayed to God to help me find a decent place to live with my kids. I'm scared and alone.

I enrolled Shawn and the boys in school and soon started to receive my checks and stamps. I walked my sons to Sheryl Elementary every day and was there to pick them up when school let out. I went to Sheryl when I was a kid; it was nice and clean then. But times had changed. Sheryl Elementary was now infested with poor, malnourished, underachieving children who lacked love, supervision, and proper home training. My heart went out to any child without a parent to love, teach, hug, feed, and take care of them.

One day, Kyham and I had been out on foot looking for a new place to live. I filled out applications and took numbers out of the phone book. It had been a while since I called my mother, or Mrs. Brazil. I hadn't planned to stay long enough to need a telephone, but having one would have made things easier.

I was cooking dinner for the kids—frying pork chops, cabbage, rice with gravy, and hot water bread on the hot plate. The kids were watching Batman when, out of the corner of my eye, I saw a huge rat run from behind the counter I was cooking on. It startled me so badly that my hands flew up, and when they came down, I accidentally hit the handle of the skillet, flipping it over onto my forearm. At the same time, Bob was knocking at the door. He rushed us to the Henry Ford emergency room, where I was treated and released with a third-degree burn. My mind was made up; I wasn't going back there. I had Bob drive me over to Rickey's house on Burgess and Outer Drive. Rickey was upset about my arm, and he was even more upset when he saw Bob. He said they'd been looking for me because Judy's brother-in-law had a three-bedroom house he wanted to rent.

"Oh my God!" I almost dropped to my knees. "Thank you, Lord," I screamed. "Where is it?" Judy said it was on Greydale, two blocks from Fenkell. "Is it vacant now?" I asked. "Yes," she said, "stay here with us tonight, and I'll call him and let you talk to him right now. Tomorrow morning, I'll drive you over there."

"Thank you, God!" I screamed and hugged my kids. Judy called him, and I talked to Scott Miller, the owner. He said I could move in tomorrow. It was clean and freshly painted, with a front and back yard. The carpet had some stains, but overall, he said I could have it. "My God, my God." I couldn't believe it. "Thank you, Lord," I cried, "for hearing my prayers." Just that quickly, the Lord had made a way out of no way!

I let Bob go, and Rickey and I walked to the store. We got a beer and a half man and embraced the evening outside on the front porch, enjoying the cool air and having a long, overdue heart-to- heart talk. The next day came and went, and before I knew it, I was setting up shop at 15737 Greydale, a predominantly all-white "trash" area, but I was grateful to God because I knew this was only a steppingstone! The little white house, trimmed in black, was just what the doctor ordered.

The house had a living room adjoined by a dining room, a large kitchen, one bath, two bedrooms, and a full basement. He let me move in on my word that I would pay him when I got my check—two hundred and fifty dollars a month, one hundred and twenty-five every two weeks, more than half of my check—but I was determined to make it work. I had some money when we moved in, but I explained my situation with the rats and roaches and that I needed to buy beds and furniture for my kids. He said he trusted me and that he could wait.

The second thing, because the kids had been so unhappy, was to have my jitney friend Frank take us down to the dog pound, and they picked out Randy. He was as big as his name—a three- month-old St. Bernard puppy with a beautiful, rich, deep brown coat with honey blonde and white highlights. His paws were as large as their hands. They were so happy, and I was happy— it felt good to see a smile on their faces.

I made a clean home for them the best I could, and they made many friends. I was back to cooking, cleaning, and being a mama. I went and found my cousin, whom we called Bird. She was out of school for the summer, and I asked her to come and babysit the kids, just to be there with me if I needed someone to watch them. She was all too happy about it because she loved to cook and experiment with recipes, especially making new desserts. She was a nice kid who needed some love. I knew I could trust her; she was like an old mother hen. Although it may have been too late, I didn't want her to become a product of her environment—she had more potential than that. Her mother was my first cousin, and Bird was a twin; she and her sister fell in the middle of five children. She got packed, and we left. She stayed with us, and I barely had to cook. The kids preferred her cooking because she cooked junk, and I made them eat healthy. I didn't mind because they were eating.

I became acquainted with the girl to the left of me, Chris, and the Black woman, Cardonal Murphy, who lived across the street. She was a nurse; I found out later that she and Nina worked together. My children played with her son, Thomas. He was a nice kid, but she always left him home alone. So, I asked her to let him spend the day with us when she was gone. I made sure he ate, and I treated him like one of my own.

I had Mama and Tina come and stay as long as they wanted. The summer was fine with me. The kids had birthday parties and plenty of fun time to play. I continued to look for a place to live. This area was only good for a year; the Black Brothers were starting to move in quickly. The whites were leaving the area, running. I wanted to run too, but I couldn't, not yet.

On Saturdays, we had a pancake eating contest. Whoever ate all the pancakes they ordered from me would have the entire day free of chores. I had plans to go out for the evening; I hadn't been anywhere in such a long time without the kids. I was invited to a wedding, but I split the day with my kids—I was only going to the reception.

I could hear the ice cream truck coming down the street; my bedroom faced the front porch and street. Kyham was screaming at the top of her lungs with excitement, "Mama, the ice cream truck is coming!" All of a sudden, I heard her screaming and gagging. I ran outside to help her and screamed too, "Bird, call an ambulance!" I tried not to panic; her bright yellow shirt was covered in blood. They rushed her back and started working on her immediately. They took her vitals and looked at her mouth. Kyham was spinning around with excitement about the ice cream truck; she had a stick in her hand. She put the stick in her mouth, got dizzy from all the twirling around, and fell into the house wall. Kyham ran the stick down her throat, and it broke off in the back of her throat, almost coming through the back of her neck. I was hysterical inside; she had a mouth full of blood. I had to think fast. I could see the stick breaking off in the back of her throat. I prayed to God right then and there: "Please God," I cried, "don't let the stick go down her throat and choke her." The ambulance was there before I could finish praying. The sirens were on, and we rushed to the Mt. Carmel emergency room. Thank God they were able to remove it without surgery. God answers prayers.

She got sixteen stitches, a tetanus shot, plenty of popsicles, and a lot of love from me, her brothers, and Bird. As school was getting ready to start,

I took Bird home and enrolled the boys in Houghton Elementary, across from Bert Road—a fast-moving intersection. Every morning, I walked the kids to school after feeding them a hot breakfast and ensuring they were clean. My afternoons were spent with Pringle looking for housing, picking up food from the Catholic churches, reading a book, or homeschooling Kyham. In the early evening, I'd Walk back and pick up my children after school, letting them out at 3:00 PM. I never let them walk home alone. I gave them a snack, taught them to get their clothes ready for the next day, helped them with homework, and fed them a hot, complete meal for dinner. I did this every day; I never sent my children to school without a hot breakfast.

Finally, I was able to find Laura's phone number, so I put the kids to bed and waited to call so I could talk without any interruption. I knew we'd be on the phone for a while, catching up on old times. After their baths, I put them down for the evening and called Laura—she wasn't home.

I talked to Winston, who told me that he had a kid on the way with Denise. He asked about the boys and my mother. Winston said that he would have QT—that was his nickname for Laura— call me back when she got in.

At 11:00 p.m., the phone started to ring. It was Laura, and we didn't do any small talk at all. "Where have you been?" she asked.

"I've been trying to get in touch with you; I called and left two messages for you to call me." I explained what happened and my situation.

Laura said, "The first time I called, I just wanted to know how you and the kids were doing. But the second message I left you was more serious."

She said she saw my biological father's daughter Tracy last week, and she said that your sister Jenny killed herself. I all but fell to the floor. I couldn't believe it; I started to cry. She said that Jenny was found dead in the bathroom. She put a.357 Magnum in her mouth and pulled the trigger, blowing the back of her head off. I screamed at the very thought!

Laura said she was found dead by her boyfriend. I was in total shock, in disbelief, and speechless. Jenny killed herself six days before her twenty-first birthday. After the news about Jenny, I looked at life differently, taking each day in stride. I tried to get in touch with Tracy and offer my deepest sympathy. Although we weren't raised together, I felt a sincere loss.

I made the holidays as happy for the kids as I could. For Thanksgiving, we had a dinner party, and I cooked a lot. I wanted to make sure my kids had enough of every kind of food and pie they wanted to eat, and then some. I invited all of my family members over, including Charlie. I wasn't really mad at Charlie, or even disappointed. In shock, maybe. Christmas was fabulous; Santa Claus tried to make up for the lost holidays and suffering on the streets. The kids got pretty much what they asked for through their many letters to Santa. On New Year's Eve, Nina and Roy, her male friend, Mama, Tina, me, and the kids—we all brought the New Year in together. We fried chicken, made mashed potatoes with gravy, fresh spinach, rolls with butter, and made homemade apple pie. We made our toast to the good year ahead of us. Roy spent the entire evening playing "Zoom" by the Commodores. We didn't care; all that mattered was that we were all together at last.

We made it through the winter, and I was still looking for suitable housing. I really wanted to stay in Detroit; I love my hometown, but the school system was subpar. The areas where poor people were forced to live were pure slums. I had no intention of raising my children in the projects where the only view we'd have would be one of an alley or subjecting them to live on the lower eastside, in places where not even a tree or grass would grow.

'To each his own.' That's not for me. I want more for my kids. Some children survive the projects, accepting defeat, and it becomes a lifestyle for them.

I call those families "lifers"—families that live in the projects year after year, their misery passed down from one generation to the next. Some feel they have no other choice. Others feel that life has beaten them down, so they give up trying.

My attitude is simple: if I'm still breathing, I'm getting up. If God wakes me up in the morning, that means I have another chance to get things right in my life. I'm strong enough, and my mind was made up about their future. They were going to graduate from high school and college; they were not going to prison, selling drugs, using drugs, becoming prostitutes, pimps, or thieves; and they were not going to bring me a house full of babies by different mothers or fathers. I knew I had my work cut out for me, but I welcomed the challenge. If I ever wanted them to amount to anything, I had to try.

I was smart enough to know that if I were to demand this type of discipline from my children, I'd have to teach them to set their standards and goals high. I encouraged them to aim high and live by example. That required me to live a certain way in front of them. I was never going to marry; I didn't want any man over them telling them what to do or how much of something to eat they could have. I was going to be the biggest influence in their lives.

When I first felt my baby's heartbeat alongside mine, I knew there were certain things I wouldn't tolerate, certain matters they would have no say in—no questions asked. I was determined to give my children a chance at life and to make sure they got the best education possible. Times were hard in Michigan and not even fair. Black single mothers had to step up and be counted, take a chance on life, take a chance on their children's future, and not accept the ill-fated fate that may lie ahead. I always encouraged my girlfriends to try and do better, to change their situation, and to do something about it. My wings were open and spread wide, ready to take on new challenges for the sake of my kids.

When it came to raising my kids, there would be no obstacle too large and no mountain too high to climb. In between my busy schedule, I was baking pies, cobblers, and cakes, selling them for $17.00 a pop. I had to add to my income and stay home with my children. Someone has always had to stay home to raise the kids. I was constantly going to and from the school, checking on Andre's behavior.

Sometimes I'd Walk to school to check on him four times a week; they always called me. I didn't even have to stop by the office anymore—we were on a first-name basis.

He was constantly in trouble at school for fighting, disrupting the class, or bullying another child. He was hard-headed and didn't want to listen, but I warned him that if his behavior didn't change, he would be headed to jail. Before I let him go to prison, I'd discipline him myself. School let out early, and we hurried home; an ice storm was coming. I'd seen ice storms before, but never in April. It started to hail ice balls the size of golf balls. Rain and slush mixed as I opened the door to look out; everything was frozen in time—trees, bushes, telephone poles, streets, and porches. It was absolutely beautiful; it looked like something in three-D. The kids and Randy were slipping and sliding all around outside.

The last week of May 1980, my father Poppi came over to visit us. He stayed for three weeks, and during that time, he and the boys were inseparable. They stayed up all hours of the night cooking, eating popcorn, and watching old black-and-white movies. I'd find them all asleep with their grandfather on the floor. It meant a lot to me, the time he spent with them. They couldn't wait to get home to see him. Pretty soon, I could see that it was time for him to move on. I couldn't help but feel the same sadness in my heart and the sick feeling in my stomach that I felt when I was a little child when he'd leave. Sometimes we never knew when we'd see him again, and that would make my heart ache. I didn't want him to go, but he said he had to get himself together and that he'd be back to see us real soon. I wasn't sure where he was headed; Nina dropped him off in Highland Park.

The house was quiet, and we were sad, so I popped popcorn and we watched "The Wizard of Oz." Two weeks later, Nina called; she wanted to go to the Eastern Market for their notorious Wrigley's Corn Beef. She asked if Mama and Tina could stay at the house with Bird and the kids; she was there for the weekend.

After shopping at the market, we stopped by a rooming house off Woodward. We walked in and asked for our father, Poppi. He came downstairs and introduced us as his children, as he always did. "This is my baby," he said, pointing to me.

Everyone in the house seemed nice, and they liked him. They called him Poncho. We talked, hugged, and kissed. He said, "Come and pick me up on Tuesday, three days from now. I'm coming back out there to stay for a while." He walked us to the car, and as he always did when playing, he said, "Come on and give me my kiss, thang." His face was sweating profusely, and his short, stubbled beard scratched me as I kissed him anyway. He kissed me on the left cheek, a feeling I could still sense after we drove away.

When I got home, I told the kids that their grandfather was coming back on Tuesday to stay. They were elated. I thought that if he arrived early enough, he could attend Shawn's graduation with me. Shawn had been double promoted into his right grade, and, against my better judgment, he was also a safety boy. We had a big celebration planned.

However, early Monday morning around 1:32 AM, someone was beating on the door—it sounded like the police. It was Nina; she stepped inside, having been crying. "Oh God, I knew something was wrong," I thought, fearing it was my mother. I held my breath as I screamed and asked, "What's wrong?" Nina revealed that someone from the rooming house had called her to say that my father was dead, having died from a heart attack. I screamed and doubled over in pain, my stomach knotting up.

"Oh God, no," I cried. "Please don't let it be true." Barely holding myself together, Nina asked me to ride with her. Bird was still there, so I could leave to find out if it was really him.

We drove downtown to the morgue, crying all the way. After identifying ourselves, we were asked to identify his body. The examiner removed the sheet from his face, and it was indeed him. Our life together flashed before my eyes—the only father I ever knew, the only father who ever loved me, was gone.

I saw the warm blood trickling out the side of his nose; he lay there so peacefully that I couldn't believe it was him. I got sick to my stomach and started to vomit. We left the morgue; Nina had to go to work, and I had to get the kids ready for school. She dropped me off at home.

When I was walking in, Bob pulled up. Seeing my distress, he asked what was wrong, and I told him. I couldn't tell the kids right then; I didn't want them to have to carry that bad news all day at school. We attended Shawn's graduation, which was lovely. He earned two medals and two certificates for being a good student and moved forward to the fifth grade.

Later that day, I told them that their grandfather had passed away in his sleep. They couldn't believe it; they cried and cried. It hurt me to see them in such pain. I told them to remember the good times they shared with him, and it seemed to comfort them when I told them he was resting in heaven now.

I had Bobby drive me over to Rickey's house before he and Shawn left for the Sugar Ray Leonard and Roberto Duran fight—Bob's gift to him. When I knocked on the door and Rickey answered, I fell to my knees, unable to get up. Rickey helped me up, and sensing something was terribly wrong, I stood still. "Is it Mama?" he asked. "No," I cried. "Is it Poppi?" "Yes," I cried again. I bent over with grief. Rickey walked into the other room of the house, and I could hear him crying, his body folding in pain, and his arms stretching across his side. I walked over, and we comforted each other.

He asked how it happened. I explained that he had walked to the store and come back. They said he stayed downstairs for a while, then went upstairs to his bedroom. Two hours later, when he didn't answer a call for dinner, someone checked on him and found him dead, lying across the bed with his hand over his heart. The paramedics tried to resuscitate him, but it was too late.

The word of his death spread quickly, and soon people were gathering at my house from all corners—east, west, north, and south. They brought food, cards, and their deepest sympathies. My old friends from the hood came to pay their respects. He had been a father to many and a good friend to all. In the days that followed, I did all I could to cope with my loss. I dreaded the thought of his funeral and seeing him that way. "My God," I cried, "how will we deal with the pain?" Then I remembered my mother. Had Nina told Mama? I was sure she had.

I was up early, sitting on the side of my bed, praying for deliverance and strength. I got up, walked into the kids' bedroom, and gave them a warm kiss. I snuggled them in and started breakfast. Standing at the sink, looking out the kitchen window, I sliced golden apples for their breakfast. The cold water running down on my hands reminded me of the cool water hose showers my father used to give us on hot summer days. For a moment, I could still feel his kiss. I could still feel him nearby; tears streamed down my face as I barely managed to slice the apples.

Suddenly, I snapped back to reality when I realized Randy had run away. The stake that was driven into the ground to hold him was gone too. I ran outside to look for him, but he was nowhere to be found. I called Bird to get up and help me find Randy. Soon, everybody was up looking for him. "Oh my God," I prayed, "please don't let him get hit by a car. Please send him home." Time was near, and I had to get dressed. Without a ride of my own, I had to go with Bob.

I took the kids with me to pick up his floral cross arrangement so they would feel a part of what was going on. On the way back, as we dropped the kids off and "Color Him Father "by The Winstons played on the radio, I cried some more. There was no way I would take my children to his funeral; they weren't ready for that. I kissed them goodbye and instructed Bird to keep them inside the house until I returned. It was a cloudy, partly sunny, light rainy day. I wanted the kids to stay inside and do something they wanted to do.

On the way to Stinson Funeral Home on West Grand Blvd. and Warren Avenue, I prayed for Randy's safe return. My eyes combed the streets and alleys as we drove away. We drove to Telegraph Road, a distance out of the way from the house due to construction. Out of the corner of my eye, I saw a brown and white fluffy dog with a wagging tail. I couldn't believe it—Randy was on the other side of Telegraph Road, a street that acts like a highway with traffic moving at least 55 miles an hour. Randy was standing there with a little boy smaller than him.

"God, don't let them get hit before I get to them," I prayed. Bob had to fight through traffic to get over, but he did. We pulled out, and Bob grabbed Randy and put him inside the car. I told the little boy to cross the street at the light. "God answers prayers," I thought as we drove Randy home. The kids were overjoyed. I told them to lock Randy up in the basement until I returned home.

I wanted to hand-carry the beautiful blue and white carnation ensemble in myself. When I entered the large room at the funeral home, I couldn't help but see the many friends and well- wishers waiting for the family to enter. We gathered in the hallway and formed one line to walk down. Bob tried to walk with me, but I walked ahead of him. The closer I got, the more I said to myself, "That's not him." The man in the casket was almost a deep chocolate brown, but the hair looked like his—all black and wavy with a silver streak in the front. I could feel my knees buckle. I reached and grabbed my brother's arm; he was in no better shape than me. First him, then me. I walked closely to the casket and looked down into his face, still as the night. I leaned over and kissed him on the forehead. A tear, my tear, rolled down his cheek. I stood tall and threw my shoulders back because I knew that's what he would have wanted, and I walked away. I looked for my mother to sit with, but she wasn't there. I couldn't believe that Nina didn't bring Mama.

There must have been a hundred and fifty people there, even his 87-year-old father, who I later found out had bought the beautiful, enormous headstone with an eagle spreading its wings. All of his children were there except for Geri, who was on assignment in Malaysia for the Red Cross. The people who spoke had something nice or funny to say, and I appreciated that, but it was a sad day for us as a family—no one had died in twenty years.

I remember standing at his gravesite, feeling the light rain and sun peeping through the cloudy sky that shone down on my face. I thought to myself, "I thank God for bringing him into my life at a time when my mother really needed someone. Thank you for the time we had together."

Two weeks after the funeral, I heard that Geri had returned home; she came back a week after the funeral. She was on vacation and looking for some investment property when she spotted two children who looked like my sister's children, stolen from Charlie in 1967. Mama relayed the story: Geri approached the kids, realizing it was them. She told them to get in the car, saying that she was their Aunt Geri and they had been stolen from their mother thirteen years ago. Cathy remembered her when Geri started to call out names, recalling her grandmother.

They got into the car, and Geri took them to their mother, Charlie, who was living on Davison in Detroit. "My God, I couldn't believe it! God is truly amazing," I said to Mama. I called everyone and shared the good news. Two days later, everyone came to my house for a welcome home party. The kids had grown tall and were teenagers now. Cathy remembered us, but Man didn't; he sat quietly. Charlie asked if I could take Cathy until she found a bigger place to live. "Yes," I said without hesitation. Nina took him to live with her mama and Tina in Canton.

Time moved forward, and I enrolled Cathy at Redford High School. It wasn't long before I discovered she was skipping school, leaving to smoke weed and cigarettes and hang out. I asked her why, knowing we could talk because we quickly developed a relationship. I was only five years older than her, but I demanded respect and gave it. Her mother talked to her, trying to get her to straighten up and finish school, but I could tell she was headstrong and ready to do her own thing. Now, I wasn't only going to school for Andre; I was going for Cathy as well.

One evening, I was looking in the paper and saw a house for rent in Fort Lauderdale, Florida. The ad stated that this three-bedroom house would become available in mid-fall. I called and spoke with the lady who owned the house, and she said she would send me pictures. I had nine hundred dollars saved to move. Because all the time that I lived on Greydale Scott Miller, would not accept rent from me. I would give it to him, and before he left, he would lay it on the coffee table and walk out. He'd say he didn't need it because the house was paid for. Use it for the kids, he said. Every rent day, Scott would come over, and I'd give him the rent money for that month, and he would refuse it. All he wanted was some cornbread of any kind and for me to play his favorite song, My Jam by Hank Williams. (1949), "I'm So Lonesome I Could Cry." He would sit there and drink out the neck of his favorite liquor bottle.

The following day, Geri came by my house with Rickey. She asked me to ride with her to the Eastern Market for corned beef. I wasn't doing anything, so I went along. They shopped for corned beef, and I bought the biggest watermelon I'd ever seen for $7.00. I knew the kids would be surprised by its size. I spent my last because I knew I had a ride home, or so I thought. Geri started an argument with me, and I was forced to defend myself. She pulled her car over and told me to get out. "I will get out of your car!" I screamed back at her. Rickey tried to quiet us down, but it wasn't working. Geri screamed at me, "I hate you; you're not my sister. I wish you would die. I should spit in your face," and I said, "If you do, I'll whip your ass for you."

She screamed again, "I hate you; you're not my sister." Rickey got ready to get out of the car, and she grabbed his arm and told him, "Forget her; come on and go with me." Rickey snatched his arm away from her, got out, and carried my watermelon on the bus and then home for me. Geri and Nina always tried to separate me and Rickey, but they couldn't because we were close.

That night, I could smell Welton's hand across my face and Donald Malone rapping me. It was a mixture of dreams; the man was beating me up.

I was in the kitchen, cooking dinner, when I heard a knock at the door. I opened it to find Balma, Little Dot's boyfriend. I was surprised to see him without Dot. Balma said he was there for two reasons: he wanted to buy one peach cobbler and one butter pound cake from me. "I'll sell you the cobblers," I said.

Balma was a good catch for Dot—working full-time for General Motors, tall, good-looking, owning his own home, driving a new car, and having plenty of money stored in a safe—he made side money by selling drugs, which I couldn't condone. He paid me sixty dollars for the pies and tried to give me a hundred-dollar bill as a tip. I refused the money at first, but he insisted, suggesting I use it for the kids. Reluctantly, I thanked him and gave him a kiss on the cheek as he departed. Just then, Bob burst into the house, gasping for breath. I paid little attention as I walked Balma to his car and said goodnight. Returning inside, I found Bob just catching his breath; he had siphoned gas from one car to his, and it had backed up into his mouth, cutting off his breath. Once composed, he admitted he was stealing gas because he needed to get to an audition and didn't have the money for fuel. Aware that I had just pocketed $160, Bob knew better than to ask me for anything.

Five days later, Pringle came over to visit and eat, and the pictures of the Florida house arrived in the mail. I shared my plans to move, and although she tried to talk me out of it, I remained firm. "Girl," I said, "I can't continue to live here under these conditions." She understood but expressed sadness about my potential departure. Together, we opened the envelope; the house was beautiful and rented for six hundred dollars a month—a sum I knew I couldn't afford without a job.

As we were examining the pictures, Bobby pulled up and got out of his car. I quickly hid the pictures on the sofa. He was brimming with excitement, having made the audition; they would live, record, and perform in a club in Fort Lauderdale, Florida. "What?" I exclaimed. Bob revealed that his new group, Flight Control, would be relocating in late August and were set to perform on Soul Train in mid-December. Pringle and I exchanged glances in silence, overwhelmed by the coincidence.

After Pringle and Bob left, I washed my hands and went into the kitchen to prepare dinner for the kids: tripe, coleslaw, rice, okra, and hot water bread. The kids weren't fond of okra but enjoyed everything else. Suddenly, I heard a choking sound. Turning around, it was Kyham choking on the tripe. Frantically, I tried to dislodge it, but it slipped further down her throat, blocking her airway. She was turning blue. In desperation, I ran onto the porch, crying out for divine intervention. The children sought help from Cardinal, a nurse across the street, but she wasn't home.

On my knees, with Kyham in my arms, her eyes rolled back. I was at my wit's end. I sat her up hit her on the back and screamed, "Jesus, help me!" Miraculously, the tripe ejected from her mouth, allowing her to breathe again. Her color returned, and her throat cleared. Shaking and crying with relief, I thanked God for answering my prayers once again. Back inside, I threw out all the tripe and vowed never to cook it again.

That evening, after bath time and reading a Bible story to the kids, I climbed into bed, unable to sleep. I tossed and turned, thinking about all the day's events, along with my past and future. I lay awake, contemplating whether to move to Florida or strive even harder to find a decent place to live here. Exhausted from trying to make things fit in my life, I was unhappy with it all.

Cathy had been missing for three weeks. Despite filing a missing person report with the Redford Police Department, it seemed they hadn't found her, or perhaps hadn't even looked. I had a gut feeling that something was terribly wrong, which left me doubled over in pain. I prayed fervently for her safe return. Amidst this turmoil, I was wrestling with the decision to move to Florida. Feeling like I had nothing to lose, I knew what I wanted out of life, but my goals were lofty and fraught with struggle. I was tired of struggling.

On August 17, 1980, after discussing it with my mother, she encouraged me to try, saying, "Nothing beats a failure but a try!" That was all the encouragement I needed; I started to pack without hesitation. I arranged everything, making reservations and planning for my brother to take care of Randy for the kids. Let me just go and try.

I mailed nine hundred dollars to Mrs. Dorothy in Florida—six hundred for the first month's rent and three hundred for the deposit—along with a letter to secure the house, giving her our arrival date. Bob had already left, but he gave me his address and phone number in case I needed him. I threw a going-away party for me and the kids, cooking up a feast that everyone attended, including Cathy. When she walked into the backyard, I couldn't help but cry. We hugged, and she explained that she didn't know I was moving. She had just stopped by to let me know she was alright and that she was pregnant, introducing us to her boyfriend. Cathy said she was living with his family on the east side and was alright. "God answers prayers," I thought to myself.

I'd found a family to buy my furniture, asking them to wait until the day before we were leaving. It was our last Saturday in this house; the kids were sad and excited, dealing with the mix of emotions. On Sunday morning, we had our last pancake eating contest in this house, and I wanted it to be memorable, so I made homemade blueberry pancakes. Andre said he could eat six, Shawn eight, Kyham three, and Terrance five. As they placed their orders, Shawn went to the bathroom to run his bath, and Kyham followed him into the kitchen. Suddenly, I heard Kyham scream. I ran toward her and found her bleeding; her finger was caught inside the linen closet, and Shawn had slammed the door shut without knowing she was there, cutting off her fingertip. Shawn called the ambulance, and when I opened the door, her fingertip fell out. I screamed, picked it up, and tried to stop the bleeding by tying off her hand. Amid the confusion, Andre grabbed the fingertip and ran outside to show it off, but he dropped it in the grass. I couldn't find it, and the ambulance rushed us to the emergency room. They asked me for the fingertip, and I explained what happened. The plastic surgeon filed her fingertip down and sewed it back together. Shawn felt terrible about his baby sister and did all he could to make it up to her. Andre apologized to Kyham for losing her fingertip in the grass.

Two days later, we went outside to feed Randy, but he was gone. We looked everywhere, called the Dog Pound and the Humane Society, and posted pictures, but we never saw Randy again. I believed that someone had stolen him and was hiding him in their house. "Oh God," I prayed, "I feel so bad for my children and their loss of Randy." The last few days, the kids were quiet and sad, until the night Pringle came over in her station wagon, and we drove to White Castle. She was pregnant with her thirteenth child. When I placed my order—eight cheeseburgers, three fries, and five orange drinks—the kids burst out laughing when Pringle ordered seventy-six cheeseburgers, eighty-two hamburgers, sixty orders of fries, and fifteen pops. I never laughed so hard in my life; I almost fell out of the car.

When we got back to my house, the telephone was ringing. It was Mrs. Dorothy wanting to confirm that I was still coming before she cashed my money orders. I assured her to go ahead because I was on my way. Two days later, we arrived at the train station. I waited for Pringle, as she had promised to say our goodbyes, but she didn't show up. Pretty soon, we boarded the train and slowly moved down the tracks. I took one last look at the dreary city I was leaving behind and saw Pringle and her children running alongside the track, waving goodbye. My heart was filled with sadness. I cried and blew kisses.

We arrived in Fort Lauderdale three days later, around 7:00 p.m. To my surprise, Bob was there to pick us up. I was startled to see his face among the crowd. My plan had been to get a cab to a motel room near the station until tomorrow, then take a cab to Dorothy's to pick up the key. I asked Bob how he knew what time and day my train would be arriving. He chuckled, "I know everything about you," and laughed to himself. We were tired, and the kids were restless from the scenic cross-country trip. Bob drove us around in a car he had borrowed from his manager, proudly displaying his connection to the area. He mentioned meeting a lady across the street from where he lived with the group, calling her 'Dorothy.' I was stunned to learn that his manager, Tom, was renting a house from her for them to live in and that Tom had introduced Dorothy to his group, Flight Control, who were renting the house right across the street from where she lived.

Bob revealed that during a conversation about Detroit, Dorothy mentioned she had just rented a three-bedroom house to a lady moving here with four kids from Detroit. Bob realized then that it was me. "The Black people here stick together," he said, noting that Tom and Dorothy were good friends. Bob offered to let us stay with him for the night, but I refused. Instead, he took us to check into the motel and put our luggage in the room. I figured I might meet Dorothy and get the keys.

When we got to the cramped house he shared with nine other members, I asked him to show me where Dorothy lived. Quickly, he looked across the street and said she wasn't home because she was at church. "Show me anyway," I insisted, and he pointed to her house. I walked across the street and knocked on the door. She wasn't expecting us until tomorrow; no one answered, so I left her a note stuck in her door with the name of the motel and phone number. After letting the kids visit for an hour, I had him drop us off at the motel. Bob asked if he could stay the night with us, but I declined, saying, "I'll see you tomorrow."

The next morning, I called Dorothy again, and no one answered. I called again, and a girl answered, saying she was her granddaughter and would give her the message. As checkout time approached, I started to panic; these rooms were going for sixty-five dollars a night. I called Bob and left a message for him to call me back. Three days later, he called. I told him I needed a ride to Dorothy's since she hadn't returned my calls. He didn't drive us there right away; he had to make a few stops along the way. When we pulled up, I looked to see if Dorothy was there; someone was standing on the porch. I walked over and introduced myself to her. It was her granddaughter; she said that Dorothy wasn't in; she was volunteering at the church and would be back later. So I waited, walking the kids around the block, ending up at the corner store located in the ghetto.

Two young girls approached us as we left the store. Introducing themselves as Jackie and Cheryl, they mentioned they knew us through Bob and lived down the street from the band. Excitement filled their voices as they spoke about the neighborhood's enthusiasm for having a group of musicians nearby. Cheryl mentioned that her mother knew Tom and had been cooking and sending food to the destitute group of men since they arrived. They even invited us to meet their mother, who lived just a few doors down from where Bob was staying. Curious and wanting to stay nearby in case Dorothy appeared, the kids and I accepted their invitation and spent the afternoon on their porch, the sound of the band rehearsing floating over from nearby.

Hours later, with no sign of Dorothy, we returned to our temporary motel home. At 9:00 PM, after another unanswered call and message left for Dorothy, frustration began to set in. Two weeks and a thousand dollars later, Dorothy finally called, but her words brought more confusion than relief. She accused me of backing out of the house rental because Bob had told her I'd found another place in Florida and that we were reconciling as a couple. Shocked, I tried to correct her misunderstanding, insisting that Bob was lying and certainly not my husband, but she talked over me, eventually hanging up after revealing she had returned my nine hundred dollars to him.

Attempts to reconnect with Dorothy failed, as she kept hanging up. Desperate, I called Bob's place but only got a promise of a message being relayed. I even asked Jackie and Cheryl to check his house, but no one answered the door.

Distraught, I couldn't stay still. Later, Jackie and Cheryl drove to the motel. They explained that their mother felt terrible about what had happened and wanted to speak with me personally. As we drove to their home, the girls shared more unsettling news: they had seen members of Flight Control with drugs. This revelation had led their mother to ban them from visiting the band again, recognizing the group wasn't the positive influence she had once thought.

When we arrived, I tried to confront Bob, but he didn't answer his door, though I saw a curtain twitch. Defeated, we returned to Jackie's. While we sat on the porch, venting about Bob and his group, Pearl, Jackie's mother, made an unexpected offer. She had a fixer-upper house around the corner that she was willing to let me use until she could get it repaired. "It's not the best," she admitted, "but it will get you out of that motel for now."

Grateful for any semblance of stability, we walked over to see the house. It was far from ideal— one-bedroom, old furniture, and appliances were left behind, and crucially, two walls were missing, one in the living room and one in the kitchen. Yet, with Jackie, Cheryl, and their mother's help, I saw potential for a makeshift home. They also helped me secure a job at The Red Cross in Broward County as an intake worker, providing food and shelter for transients— ironically, a service I was almost in need of myself.

Jackie and Cheryl became like family, dropping me off at work and watching the kids during my shifts. The children quickly grew fond of them, finding solace and care in their company. Two weeks after starting my job, I received my first paycheck, and on that same day, I learned that Flight Control had moved out. Despite my daily attempts to confront Bob, he was nowhere to be found. I was relieved yet vigilant; I had plans for him should our paths cross again, my resolve as firm as ever.

Flight Control seemed to relish my misfortune, snickering and laughing behind my back while pretending to be my friend to my face. One day, I saw Dorothy in her garden, and she could see the rage burning in my eyes. She asked if we could talk, but I snapped back, "If you don't have my money, there's nothing to talk about." From across the street, she shouted that she was sorry about what had happened and wanted to make it up to me and the kids. I kept walking, my mind heavy with thoughts of my children. Jackie walked beside me, murmuring, "It ain't worth it; they'll get theirs—just wait and see."

I clung to that hope. Despite my efforts to pay them for babysitting and some rent, Jackie and her mother wouldn't accept the money. Instead, they simply asked for pizza. They had practically moved in with us, and Pearl didn't mind. Jackie, nineteen, and Cheryl, seventeen, could stay out of trouble this way, she reasoned. As I continued to work and save whatever I could, we were just getting by. I enrolled the kids in school while Kyham stayed home during the day. The lack of money and absence of a car made finding a decent place to live incredibly difficult. I prayed constantly for strength and to keep out of trouble.

My world seemed to be crumbling when, with only one week left at work due to layoffs, Pearl's ex-husband was awarded the house we lived in as part of their divorce settlement. He wanted it back since he had nowhere else to go. Forced to move, I found refuge on the street for one night and shelter, which unexpectedly became a turning point for the better. Within two weeks, the shelter's social worker secured for us a three-bedroom apartment through my Section 8 voucher, along with new beds and food stamps. She drove us to Crystal Lake Apartments in Hollywood, Florida—a big, beautiful, and clean complex surrounded by water, palm trees, and canals. Overwhelmed with gratitude, I kneeled and thanked God for not forgetting us. Our new neighbors were a diverse mix of Haitians, Blacks, Mexicans, and Whites. The grass was lush, and the flowers still bloomed beautifully.

That evening, Jackie and Cheryl unexpectedly knocked on our door. I asked how they found me, and they explained that they had gone to the shelter, where they saw Bob trying to get information on my whereabouts. When he left, they inquired inside, benefiting from their mother's former connections there as a housekeeper before she fell ill. We embraced warmly, and this time, they brought the pizza.

That night, we all slept on the floor. The next day, I enrolled the kids in school, transferred utilities, ordered a phone line, and awaited the delivery of our new beds. Jackie asked if she could move in with us to babysit while Cheryl went away to school. Gratefully, I accepted her offer. Finally, things were looking up. I landed a job driving a school bus for the Broward County Board of Education.

I worked diligently, saving enough to buy my children new bunk beds and essentials for the kids. They were thriving, making friends in a school that was clean and free of graffiti and drugs. Determined to make the most of our new life, I enrolled the kids in Bible study, winter camp, and various activities available to them. Our apartment, filled with sunlight streaming through open windows and equipped with new appliances, felt like a true home—despite the occasional palmetto bugs, lizards, and red ants. Making $8.00 an hour and receiving $377 in food stamps each month, I had finally saved enough for a down payment on furniture. Jackie took us to the store, where we picked out a nice blue and white sofa, a loveseat, and a matching chair, marking the beginning of our new life in this sunny enclave.

I left a two-hundred-dollar deposit. As we were leaving, the salesman walked us to the door. It was getting dark out. He mentioned I might need a co-signer and promised to call if that was the case. He opened the door to let us out, and guess who walked in? Dorothy. She was there to pay her bill and overheard some of our conversation. Looking past her, I saw Bob getting something out of her car, but he didn't see me.

I told Jackie to take the kids to the car, and before he knew it, I rushed at Bob. When he looked up, I balled up my fist and hit him square in the face, starting to whip his ass. Dorothy came out and tried to stop the fight, asking Bob if he was alright.

Dorothy—an older, ugly woman that resembled a mud puppy in every way—was smitten by Bob's good looks and the attention he showed her. She had to believe everything he said. I beat him with my fists and scratched his entire face.

"You took my money, and I'm out here with my kids! I'll kill you!" I screamed. "Bitch, I'll kill you!"

I was on top of his back, scratching and clawing my way to the top. Bob screamed like the little bitch he was.

"I'm sorry! I'm sorry!"

Dorothy screamed, "Stop, you're hurting him!"

"Bitch," I said, "you better get the fuck out of the way before I kick your ass. You dumb bitch, you gave him my money without even knowing him."

Jackie came to Bob's rescue. The kids could see me fighting; they were crying for me to stop. When we left the furniture store, we went and got Chinese food and laughed all the way home.

Two days later, the furniture store called; they said that Dorothy co-signed for it.

At first, I said no. I didn't want anything from her. But then I thought about it and all the changes she and Bob put us through.

"Yes," I said, "deliver my furniture right on time for the holidays."

December 8, 1980. I was getting off work early. I stopped inside to pick up my paycheck. While waiting in line, I overheard some people talking among themselves about John Lennon. At first, I didn't pay much attention to what they were saying until they mentioned he had been shot and killed in front of his apartment building.

"What?" I said, and they turned to me and repeated it.

I almost dropped to my knees. "Oh God, no, who would do such a thing?"

I cried. Not John Lennon; he was my favorite of the Beatles. I've been a fan since the 1960s. I remember when they first came to America—the first time they appeared on the Ed Sullivan show. My mother took me to see their movies, and I had all of their music.

It was a sad day for many. The world would never be the same without John Lennon. I felt the loss; it was like losing an old friend. I scrambled to buy his last album, *Double Fantasy*. My favorite track on the album is Beautiful Boy. I couldn't help thinking about his son, whom he left behind. I know he wanted to live to see him grow up. I prayed for him.

When I returned home, the kids said that Bob had come by and wanted to talk to me. Shawn said that he tried to talk to him about what happened, but he didn't want to hear it.

Shawn said that he left Bob standing outside my door, and he went back to play. The only reason I allowed Bob to come around was because the kids loved him, but that was no more. My children had lost all respect for him, and he was no longer their hero. They saw him for who he really was.

We talked about him over dinner that night, and I told the kids that I didn't want Bob to come around them anymore, and when I see him, I'm going to tell him. They agreed; they didn't want him to come around anymore either.

Having a relationship with Bob wasn't healthy, and I didn't want to get into any trouble.

On Christmas day, Bob came to my door empty-handed; he wanted to see the kids. I refused him, and I told him that I didn't want him to ever come to my door again.

He stood there, crying like a little bitch. He said that he didn't have anywhere else to go.

"I guess so," I said. "You probably burned all your bridges. Go back to Dorothy's, or maybe you should call Charlie, or you should call Soul Train. I don't know what to tell you, but if you ever come to my house again, I'll kill you."

Chapter 23

"Merry Christmas, My Ass"

I slammed the door in his face. I called to wish Mama a Merry Christmas and to see if she had received the two dusters and house slippers I sent her. We talked, and she was doing fine; she said that she missed us and told me to give the kids a kiss and hug for her. I brought the New Year in with my kids, Jackie, Cheryl, pizza, and two bottles of Harvey's Bristol Cream. They didn't want me to cook; everyone wanted me to relax and not worry, so I did just that. We danced, played Monopoly, and Uno. We had a lovely evening until Bob came knocking at the door. I pulled the blinds back, looked him in the face, and then I went back and sat down. I didn't even open the door. I ignored Bob just like he did us. He left a note at my door; it read, "I'm sorry, please let's talk." I balled it up and threw it in the trash.

By the first week of January 1981, there was a knock at my door, and there stood two men from the furniture company; they were there to repossess my furniture. I hadn't been late with any payment, and they knew so, but they said that Dorothy wanted my furniture picked up. I called the furniture store, and they said that Dorothy and her friend Bob were there, and she had signed the order to have it picked up. It was broad daylight for everyone to see. I was mad as hell and embarrassed. I let them take it. Now my children and I had to sit on the floor; the children ran inside to see what was happening along with all their friends.

Three months later, I lost my job because I had to leave work early; André was expelled from school for fighting. I had to go and get him from the office right then. I didn't have much money saved—just enough to pay my rent, lights, and gas bill and a little over. To make matters worse, Pearl, Jackie's mother, slipped and fell down a flight of stairs, hitting her head, fracturing her skull, and breaking an arm. She had to be hospitalized. I was worried about her and my situation; I was unable to sleep and feeling depressed. I made one last telephone call before they shut my phone off, and that was to Laura. I explained what was going on and that I needed some money desperately. She sent me five hundred dollars via Western Union.

I had a friend of mine take me to pick it up. I filled up her tank, and then I had her take me to the State Department to apply for state aid. My application was denied; they wouldn't give me money, only food stamps, and no medical care for the kids.

I knew that all I had was less than five hundred dollars to live on, no transportation, no babysitter, and that next month I was going to be behind on all my bills. I lay awake thinking about how I could get my hands on some money. I was desperate. I paid my bills for the month, and I went down to the bus station and bought tickets to Detroit.

Two days later, we went home for a short visit. I applied for state aid using my sister's address; I was eligible for assistance. I spent one day with my mother and two days with Diane. The night before I left Detroit, I went down to the east side and bought a handgun from Emory, then went back to Florida.

When I returned home, my apartment had been broken into. Some of the windows were open, and the blinds were pulled closed, all but one that was stuck in the frame from the wind blowing. I told the kids to stay outside in the open yard so I could check inside.

I didn't know what to expect. I went to put the key in the door, but it was already unlocked. I went inside, my purse in hand, and put my hand on the. 38 I brought back from Detroit. I pushed the door open and walked inside, and I couldn't believe my eyes. My apartment was destroyed. I walked in, and I could hear the glass crunching underneath my shoes.

Empty beer bottles, broken, leftover alcohol bottles thrown against the walls, food splattered on the walls.

I passed the kitchen; all my food was gone, and broken glass was all over the floor. The refrigerator doors were open, and the stove was left on. All of my dishes and glasses that weren't smashed were left dirty in the sink.

I continued through the apartment with my gun drawn down by my side. My children's rooms had been destroyed. Used condoms, with semen still in the rubber, were in their beds. I found stained panties in their beds, blankets sprawled over the room, broken glass, and their clothes were pulled out of the drawers. Something red poured all over the beds and walls. Ants were everywhere.

I walked back into my bedroom and found stains on my sheets, bras, and panties left in my bed, and all of my clothes were destroyed with this red dye liquid. I slipped on a wet condom left on the floor. Empty wine bottles, marijuana, empty plastic bags, pills, and traces of cocaine were left on a mirror on the floor. My waterbed had been stabbed, cut with a butcher knife; the mattress was split in half, the knife still in it. Feathers from my pillows filled the air, and a picture of my mother had been stomped on and broken. The bathroom mirror was smeared with feces and broken, barely hanging on the frame. Someone had used the toilet and left it there for me to see. The shower curtain and rod were ripped from the wall, and the bathtub was stuffed with towels and filled with water trickling down the side.

Kyham's room had used condoms all over the floor and in her bed, stains of semen on her sheets, traces of cocaine in the bed, marijuana papers, wrappers, and stems. Her room was destroyed; her toys were wet with water and broken. Her doll heads were cut off. The kids' big wheels had been broken as well. I was at my end with troubles and problems, one behind the other.

My first instinct was to call the police, but I said no, I'd handle it myself. I knew that Bob was responsible for this destruction of my apartment and the repossession of the furniture. He was mad because I wouldn't let him move in with me. It seems that everything I tried to do, everything I tried to accomplish, he would go out of his way to sabotage.

Well, this time, he got lucky. I'm finally going to give him what he wants—what he's been waiting for. On the inside, I was enraged, but I didn't want the kids to see; I didn't want them hurt anymore. I'm gonna handle it from here, I thought to myself. I remained quiet; my mind was made up.

I put the gun away for now and walked outside to where the kids were playing in the dirt and climbing trees. My neighbor emerged from her apartment and approached me with concern. She mentioned that she saw a man climbing through my window one night; she described Bob in full detail. He had told her that he had lost his key. Initially, she thought to call the police, but after his explanation, she changed her mind. The kids wanted to come inside to look at the damage, but I refused them access. I didn't want my children to see the nasty, filthy mess that was left inside on their beds; they'd never been exposed to anything like that.

Instead, we walked to the store where I bought them hot sandwiches, pickled eggs, potato chips, candy, pop, and popsicles. They stayed outside to eat and play while I cleaned up the mess inside. I opened the living room blind to watch the kids. It took me four hours to clean the apartment and air it out. I threw away the sheets, blankets, and everything else that was destroyed inside.

Later, I walked over to my girlfriend's house. Kate was her name, and she seemed to know all about it. I listened to her talk. I had Kate take me to look for Bob, but he was nowhere to be found.

That evening, I gave the kids a bath and put them down for the evening. I was on my last fifty dollars and had no way to feed my children. I was worried as hell. Living in Hollywood, Florida, demanded transportation—if you didn't have a car, you were stuck trying to get around.

Jackie came to my apartment that night to borrow twenty dollars from me for gas to see her mother. I had to give it to her. We walked to her car, and she mentioned that she'd been wanting to tell me something for a long time now, but she didn't know how. I told her to just tell me, and she did.

Jackie lit a cigarette, and we leaned on her car. She said that Bob had been talking about me like a dog to anyone who would listen. He had spilled all of my business to everyone and claimed that my sons didn't belong to him—only Kyham was his.

"And who is he to talk about me, and who is he to belong to? Bob ain't shit; he never will be, and his future looks dim. Bob is and always will be an opportunist—anyway the wind blows, that's the way he's headed. He damn sure ain't nobody to belong to; he always got his hand out or a trick up his sleeve. That's who he is."

I told Jackie about the children he had in Detroit and that he walked off and left. He tried to screw me the night his wife went into labor with his son when we lived in Detroit. I got a letter from his wife in my apartment, asking him to take care of his children or just send them a card. I never told that lie—that Bob was my children's father—hell, you can look at them and tell they're mine.

Jackie's telling me what he said only added fuel to the fire. The next morning, she came back to watch the kids for me so I could go downtown to PG&E and make arrangements on my gas and electric bill before they cut it off.

On my way there, I looked out the bus window for Bob, hoping I could see him. When I walked into the building, I stood in line, waiting for my turn. I walked up to the window, and the man behind the counter introduced himself to me. His name was Jim Gibbs—he was friendly, funny, and flirtatious with me. He made arrangements for my light and gas bill to stay on for one month without worry.

"If you don't have the money when this arrangement expires, you call me, and I'll pay your bills for you," he said.

I laughed, and he added, "You're too pretty to be worrying. Let me take you out tonight."

"I can't let you take me out; I don't even know you, and I have four kids at home, and they're not used to me leaving them at night. I don't even have a babysitter," I replied.

"If you get a sitter, I'll pay the bill. I just want your company. You seem like a nice lady, and you will get to know me if you just give me your number."

I was so embarrassed, but I had to tell him that I didn't have a telephone.

"Take my number," he said. "If you ever need to talk to me anytime, please call me."

He grabbed my hand and slipped his card into it, then walked me out. Jim Gibbs stood about 6'1", was dressed nicely, his nails were clean, and he spoke in a kind and intelligent manner. He seemed sincere. I must say he made me blush with his kindness and compliments. I smiled and laughed with him; it felt good for a change to have someone to talk to. It took my mind off killing Bob for a brief minute.

When I returned home, Shawn told me that Bob came over to the house. He was dressed in a navy-blue three-piece suit with matching leather-blue shoes and a navy-blue Stetson hat, driving a new car, and showboating with a pocket full of money. He looked down at Shawn's shoes and pointed out that he needed a new pair. Shawn said that Bob pulled out a pocket full of money, showed it to him, and then put it back in his pocket. Shawn said that Jackie let him in; he stood by the door.

I lost my mind in anger. I exploded on the inside. That night, I borrowed Jackie's car and took my gun. The pressure was mounting; I felt like I was losing my mind. I drove to Pompano Beach and waited outside his so-called manager's house in the dark for over three hours.

I combed the streets of Fort Lauderdale, looking and looking for Bob. I went to the club he performed at and sat in the parking lot behind the parked cars, waiting. I made up my mind that I was going to kill him on sight. I can't explain what I was feeling, but I'm thankful to God that I couldn't find him. In my state of mind, it would be premeditated murder, and I'd be facing life in prison. The sun came up and shone down on my face like never before. As I drove the quiet freeway, I unloaded the gun, wiped it off, and threw the bullets out the window. I drove over to the beach, got out, took my shoes off, and walked in the sand over to the pier. I dropped the gun in the water. I cried out to God, thanking him for bringing me back to my good senses.

In the days to come, I was in a deep funk. It seems like everything I tried to do failed. I was stuck and unable to help my children or myself. I quit eating, and the weight was falling off. Sixty days later, Charlie mailed my first check to me from Michigan. In exchange for the favor, I gave her all of the food stamps. Not that she wanted them; she actually refused them. But I really appreciated her helping me out. I only needed the help from the state temporarily until I could figure out what to do next.

On July 27, 1981, Kyham Terrance and I walked a half-mile to the bus stop. It was hot as hell outside. We rode the bus to Sears in Hollywood, Florida. Shawn and Andre were at summer camp. Kyham needed shoes, and Terrance needed pants. I made up my mind that I wasn't going to buy them anything else out of goodwill. I was tired of my children wearing other people's clothes. I wasn't going to worry about it because I knew that God would make a way.

Terrance was growing tall like a weed, his legs and arms long, wiry, and thin. Not only was I going to buy them some new clothes, but I was also going to cook crab legs for dinner as well. We looked for pants and shopped for shoes. The kids wanted to play in the toy department right next to where I was shopping, but I wasn't having it. I said firmly, "You wait here with me."

We'd been in the store for around an hour or so, and there were many children running around freely from one department to another. Kids up and down the aisles, and I remember saying to myself, "Where are their parents?" It seemed like the parents just brought the kids to the store and let them run free. I knew better. I didn't trust anyone. I guarded my children with my life. I knew from my past experience to be careful and watch your kids.

Over the loudspeaker, I heard an announcement that a little boy was missing, and then they went into a full description and detail of what he was wearing, the color of his hair, and the clothing he was wearing. They said that his mother was waiting for him. If you see this little boy, bring him up to the front office.

I looked at my two children, and they were standing right in front of me. I took my clothes and my children's hands and walked toward the register to pay. They continued to announce that this child was missing. I proceeded to the front counter, looking for this child between the aisles.

They announced his name as Adam, and they said that he was six years old. Security locked all the doors, and no one was permitted inside or out. I was worried about this child that no one could find, but I did remember seeing a child with dark, thick hair, missing teeth, and a funny smile in the store. As I thought to myself, I remembered the bold striped tee shirt he had on, and if I wasn't mistaken, he wore a baseball hat. And then I remembered his sweet face and bright, full smile, with his teeth missing in the front.

I took my children's hands and held on tight, walking at first and then running through the store, looking underneath the clothing racks, bathrooms, and stairways. I got sick to my stomach; the child was gone. I couldn't believe it. I cried and prayed for them to find him.

The store was locked down; no one could get in or out. I cried uncontrollably for his return. The more time that passed, the more afraid I became of him. The police ushered us out of the store in a single line, one by one, and I remember looking around one more time for little Adam Walsh. I couldn't get home fast enough to hug my kids. I told them what happened that day in the store. By that time, everyone was looking, and his picture was all over the news. Still,

I couldn't believe that he was gone. In the days to come, me and my children walked the streets in the hot sun, looking and searching for this child that was nowhere to be found. We walked and searched the empty fields and canals that surrounded our apartment. Days and days went by, and I couldn't eat or sleep. I wouldn't allow my children to play outside at all, not without my supervision. I prayed for Adam, and I watched his parents beg and plead for his safe return. And then they found him. Bless his heart!

Depression had consumed me. It took all the strength I had to get up in the morning and go about my day. While the kids were still involved in their daily activities, I sat motionless on the floor day in and day out. I played Teddy Pendergrass over and over, "You're My Greatest Inspiration." It's funny how certain songs come to mind and locate feelings and thoughts about life. I had almost died on the inside. I mean, I kept my appearance up and all, but I wasn't motivated to do anything for myself. My children knew that there was something desperately wrong with me, but they didn't have an idea how serious it really was. I had two gentleman friends calling on me, but I wasn't interested beyond friendship. My kids encouraged me to go out and enjoy myself. I did go out with Jim Gibbs three times, and he asked me to marry him in front of my children. He said he would provide for us. In spite of him being a nice guy, I just wasn't feeling it, and I didn't want a relationship with him like that.

I never led him to think otherwise. I believed he was decent the day he came to my apartment without my knowledge. Me, Shawn, and Kyham were at home. Jim asked me why Shawn was home. I told him that I couldn't send him to school because he didn't have any shoes to wear. He's already missed three weeks of school. Jim Gibbs reached into his pocket and handed me a hundred-dollar bill. I refused to accept it but thanked him anyway. Without argument, he gave the money to Shawn to buy the shoes he wanted. Shawn was taught not to accept any money from anyone; he thanked him but also refused the money. Jim then insisted that I take the money and buy his shoes so he could go back to school.

"Don't let pride stand in your way," he said. "Let me help you," and that's what he did until I left Florida. God will send help.

Jim monitored my gas and electric accounts and paid the bills to keep them on. Somehow, he understood hardship and strife. He said that he came from a family of ten and that his mother, who lived in Pennsylvania, raised them all after his father left them for another woman.

"I'd be less than a man," he said, "not to help someone that I care about."

The shoes that I mention are the same shoes that Bob came over and teased Shawn about; he wore them as long as he could.

In December of 1981, I decided to go back to Detroit to live. It was too hard to live in Florida without money. I got a part-time job working at the daycare center four days a week. My rent was only $79.00 a month, and I could barely pay on time. I scrimped and saved all I could to make ends meet. Thank God for Jim Gibbs; he kept my lights and gas on. Occasionally, he'd let me use his car to go grocery shopping or run errands.

Kyham and I went to the market, and I saw Bob and Kaye loading groceries into her car. They never saw me; I followed them home. I waited and watched; my first thought was to run him down with Jim's car, but I said no, I'll wait and see. He dropped her off and left. I waited outside until the coast was clear, and then I knocked on her door. She came running to the door, her eyes stretched wide.

She offered us to come inside, and I didn't. She tried to play it off by smiling.

"I said to her, 'It all makes sense now about my apartment being broken into and trashed.' She said that she had nothing to do with it and that she and Bob had just started living together for the past few months. She knew about it because he told her that he had a party at my apartment, but not what he did to my apartment."

She was surprised that I wasn't angry with her.

"I have no reason to be angry with you," I said, "because Bob is nothing to me, but I truly thought you were my friend, and that hurts more than anything he ever did to me. I'm disappointed in you. Bob will use you just like everyone he comes in contact with, and pretty soon you too will be disposable. Bob preys on women with low self-esteem, women that are far less attractive than others, women that are fat, older, and feel they have nothing else to offer. He lays waiting in the wings, scoping out his next prey, and then he moves in for the kill. When you can no longer provide for Bob, when he can no longer drive your car, eat your food, and steal your money, when he can no longer use you, then he'll move on to his next victim."

I turned around and walked away.

This was truly my day of excitement. When I got home, I put the groceries away and started to cook dinner. I waited for the kids to come home from school. Later that afternoon, Shawn was riding his bike, and Andre was riding his big wheel. Shawn lost control of his bike as it came around the curb of the complex. He fell off and rolled down the hill through the wire fence that had been pried open by fishermen. He rolled into the murky water that surrounded our apartment, almost into the jaws of an alligator. Praise God!

An hour later, Terrance came inside the house. I looked at him, and he appeared to be in shock and was unable to speak. I asked him what was wrong, and before he could get it out, I saw a complete handprint on his face. He burst out crying and said that he was playing in the sandbox when this little girl slapped him, and he hit her back. She started to cry, and when he looked up, her mother had slapped his face and left the handprint. "What the hell?" I said.

I went crazy; I mean, I really lost it. I went into my room, digging deep down in the box to arm myself with something. Flash Back from the day the man slapped my baby Andre.

I ran over to her house. I was crazy mad and out of control.

"I begged her to come out, and she wouldn't. I cursed and screamed, you hit my son. Please come out!' I begged her." It's like I couldn't believe it, like I was losing my mind. All of the neighbors came out, including the guy who liked me; he lived across the way from me. He walked me back to my apartment. Soon, I was able to calm myself down. And I called the police. They came, and I explained to them that she slapped my son. I never mentioned that I went to her apartment like a crazy woman to kill her.

An hour later, the lady who slapped my son came to my apartment crying, and she apologized to me and my son. I was still very upset with her. I accepted her apology alright, and I offered her a cup of tea, but I said to her, "If you ever put your hands on any of my kids again, I will kill you, with my bare hand without hesitation, and I mean it. You're a grown woman, and if my children do anything to yours, I'll chastise them. You don't know how close you came to getting yourself hurt over some kid shit. You're wrong for putting your hand on anyone's children. Let them settle their differences themselves."

She offered me a hug; at first, I hesitated but then hugged her back. I thank God that Mr. Lucky took the gun away from me. A lesson learned!

I realized that I didn't have enough discipline to own a gun, especially when it came to anyone threatening my children's safety. The next day, I took that shotgun to the pawn shop and sold it for seventy-five dollars. And I never touched a gun again.

On my way back to my apartment complex, I stopped by the mailbox, and then I walked through—and you will never believe who was standing in the doorway: my brother Rickey and Judy! I couldn't believe it. I ran to them and hugged them, asking how and why they were here. Not that I wasn't happy to see them—I just thought something was wrong.

"There's nothing wrong," he said. "I just miss you and wanted to see how you and the kids are doing. I needed to put my eyes on you," he explained.

I was so happy to see them. The kids were totally surprised when they came home from school to see their uncle Rickey and aunt Judy. We caught up on all the latest gossip and spent our time sitting outside in the evenings, sipping beer, and just being together. It was good enough for me.

My brother was clean and free from the drugs that had consumed his life since he was fourteen. He told me how he did it. Rickey said that what started the ball rolling was that he and Judy had a bad argument. He told her that he didn't want a drunk woman and that he was tired of worrying about her, seeing her drunk, and throwing up blood when she came to visit him on the weekends. He told her that she was going to die if she didn't quit drinking.

Judy screamed back that she didn't want a junkie for a boyfriend and that he was going to die or overdose if he didn't stop shooting up. He told her to go home that day and not to try to contact him again.

Rickey said he thought about her words—they pierced his soul. That was on a Monday. He said that he locked himself in his apartment on Grand River and decided to quit right then and there. Rickey said that at first, he tried to relax and watch TV, but he couldn't be still. That night, the symptoms got worse; he tossed and turned and was sweating profusely, and his stomach cramped with pain. His joints and legs began to ache. He got up and tried to eat something, and he started to vomit. Barely crawling back to bed, he laid down and tried to sleep but couldn't.

On the second day, he was in a lot of pain. His neighbor came to his door, knocking because she hadn't seen him. He talked to her through the closed door—he couldn't open it; he'd used the bathroom all over himself and was too weak to clean it up. Judy called, and he was too weak to answer the phone. Sweating and cramping, all he could do was lay there. He rolled his lifeless body out of bed and fell on the floor face down, crying out to God to help him. "Just give me the strength to get through this; stay with me, Lord," he prayed.

On the third day, he was in agony, really weak, and in constant pain, weak to the point that he could hardly stand up. He called Judy and asked her to come over and fix him something to eat. On his knees in pain, he stripped the bed down and managed to clean himself up. Judy came over in a hurry and fried him some chicken, mashed potatoes, and green beans. He didn't eat much; in fact, he threw it up. Judy lay there in bed with Rickey, doing all she could to comfort him.

On the fourth day, he said that he started to feel better; he could feel the drugs were out of his system. He's been clean ever since then. Judy is also alcohol-free. Back in 1978, this was the first time he tried to kick it, and he failed. But this time, he said, was different. He was determined, and he did it by the grace of God.

They stayed one week with me. I told them that I would be right behind them. I was on my way back. On the last day of February, I spoke with Nina. I told her what a hard time I was having here, and she told me to come home and try again. She said that everyone missed me. I told her that I was homesick. I really missed my friends and, most importantly, my mother.

On March 8, 1982, we took our last train ride, headed back to Michigan. Believe it or not, this time I was actually excited about going home. The kids were looking forward to seeing their old friends, and we made plans for the future. I thought about the few friends I was leaving behind. I smiled to myself: my old fishing buddy, Mr. Lucky; Jackie; Cheryl; Jim Gibbs. We exchanged phone numbers to keep in touch. I had enough money saved to find something decent to live in, I hoped.

Nina picked us up from the train station, and we hugged and kissed like never before. She couldn't believe how much the kids had grown and how the Florida sun had baked our skin. We drove up to Canton, and I rushed inside to hug and kiss my mother and niece. We made our home temporarily in her basement. In nine days, thanks to Pringle, I'd found a nice three- bedroom brick house to live in on the west side of the city.

Pringle was so excited that we were home. She came to pick us up and drove me to Detroit. She introduced me to a friend of hers who was helping low-income mothers with children find a clean, decent place to live. I thank God for Mr. J.D. Patrick!

J.D. Patrick was a real estate broker, and Elaine was his real estate agent. Together, they made magic happen for those families who were less fortunate. Being poor doesn't mean people don't have the ambition to want to live better. J.D. Patrick made it happen! We walked in; the office was crowded, so we waited our turn. They introduced themselves and were impressed at how well-behaved and mannerly my children were.

They were professional and understood the struggle; with one hundred dollars down, I was able to move in that day. 17637 Trinity. I had all the utilities turned on and enrolled my children in Holcomb Elementary and Shawn in Emerson Middle; both schools were behind in teaching. An all-black school assigned by the district. We slept on the carpeted floor until I was able to buy some used furniture. The area was nice and clean; I could tell that most of the families in the area were homeowners. Black people were moving in fast, and whites were once again on the run. I didn't blame them!

Pringle was at my house every day after I walked my children nine blocks to school. We spent the days trying to put our lives in order, and I looked for work. Pringle was pregnant again; this made her number 15. I couldn't believe that she was still having babies after all that was going on. But she said that she believed that if God didn't want her to have these children, she wouldn't get pregnant. Pringle had thirteen children with her husband and the rest with her new boyfriend, Emmette. He only came around when her check was due, and when the money ran out, he was gone home back to his mother's house in Ecorse, Michigan. I told Pringle that he was only using her to get high, but when I spoke of him, it would result in an argument between us. So, I tried to keep my mouth shut. But it was hard!

I managed to scrape up enough money to buy a car—a brown 1976 Catalina. I paid one hundred and twenty-five dollars for it. I bought it from my neighbor across the street. At first, it ran well, but pretty soon, it started to give me problems. "You get what you pay for!" I needed transportation to take the kids to school—Shawn's school was not within walking distance. I wanted to take them to church and recreation, not far, just around. We spent the summer at the museums, library, movies, parks, zoo, picnics, cooking, dancing, or visiting Mrs. Brazil. Anything to keep my children's minds occupied, plus it was hot and we didn't have any air. I even got my babysitter Bird to go out to the bar and dance my ass off. After being there for a while, I was able to locate all of my old friends—Michael, Sam, and Dickey Bird—everybody except for Gramps. Cathy came by with her son and new husband-to-be.

I really liked this one; he was a sweet young man with ambition and was nice-looking, mannerly, and a master mechanic. "Sometimes God will put people in your life ahead of time because he knows that you're going to need them down the road. God is good!" All I had to do was cook for Tee-Tee, and he'd keep my car running. Sometimes it would stop at every other block, but God would make the way for us to get home somehow. I was twenty-seven; Shawn was twelve; André was ten; Terrance was nine; and Kyham was five. I must say that I'm very proud of my kids and proud that God chose me to be their mother. Andre was still doing dumb things, but overall, they didn't give me much trouble. I told them that I loved them each and every day.

One Saturday, I went over to Brazil's for a family cookout; they were fabulous with excitement and fun. You never knew who you were gonna see. The excitement was real and very much alive. I took my records, and, baby, we'd party. This time, after the party, I went back the next day to help clean up. Later that evening, I was standing on their porch and a car rolled up, and someone hollered, "Damn baby, you're still fine, and you still got those big hips." I started to laugh; they called out to me, "You don't know me, do you?" I couldn't see who was inside the car. They pulled over, and this small man in stature could only be Gramps. As he came into view, I recognized him right away. It was him. We hugged and talked about how long it had been since we'd seen each other. It had been fifteen years since I'd seen my dear friend Gramps. He couldn't stay long, so we made a date to meet next week on Tuesday and catch up on old times. He was married now and had a son named after him. Man, my heart skipped a beat when I saw Gramps. I ran in the house and told Mrs. Brazil about seeing Gramps; she wasn't as excited as me because she sees him all the time—he lives right behind her house across the alley.

Well, it warmed my heart to see my old friend Gramps, one of my favorite friends in the world. We drove home, and I told the kids stories about how much fun we used to have when we were kids. It was just good to see everybody again. I spent a lot of time with Michael Martin after his car accident; he was left completely paralyzed from the neck down, but Michael was optimistic about his recovery and future. I went to most of his doctor appointments with him at Henry Ford Hospital, as well as his rehabilitation appointments. Most days we spent singing old Motown songs, sipping and reminiscing about the good old days, or just being together. He said I was his inspiration for wanting to get better. He had a motorized wheelchair that he'd let the kids ride on the back with, along with his baby brother Ike.

After leaving Michael's house, I headed home. I could hear the phone ringing from the driveway. We ran inside; I answered the phone. It was Mrs. Brazil calling me to tell me that Gramps was in an altercation with a much bigger man on Bewick Street. In fact, the incident happened right in front of Robert Howard's parents' house. She went on to say that Gramps was strolling his young son down Bewick when he got into an argument with John C. He was the kind of person that everybody knew but nobody wanted to be around. Mrs. Brazil said that John followed Gramps down the street and pulled a knife on him, starting to stab Gramps repeatedly all over his body, to the point where he couldn't defend himself against this much larger man. She said that after he stabbed Gramps, he took the large hunting knife and stabbed him in the groin, splitting him open. My God, I cried.

She said that everybody saw this, but no one helped Gramps. I got the number and called Ms. Coleman, Gramps' mother. She said that the hospital just called and told her to come back down there right away—that he'd taken a turn for the worse. She told me that she couldn't talk to me right then. I hung up and called Henry Ford. I told them that I was his sister, and they told me that they'd called the family in. Right away, I jumped in my car and drove to Henry Ford Hospital. They let me in. His mother stood there crying over her eldest son; he lay motionless, with blood bags and tubes, IVs, and God knows what else connected to him. I took his hand in mine and prayed for his life and that of his family. I asked God to please have mercy on him. I could see the many, many stab wounds on his body—so many I can't count. He was in the ICU on the critical list. I left his mother and family there to go home to my kids and cook dinner. I was grateful that Cathy lived around the corner; she'd come and babysit for me sometimes when I needed her to. I lay in bed tossing and turning, thinking and praying, worrying about Gramps. The thought of what he did to him made me sick to my stomach.

The next morning, after breakfast, I drove to Mrs. Brazil's house and talked about what happened to Gramps. "He is a nice guy that never hurt nobody," we all said. "Gramps is a cool little motherfucker that got your back; he's down." There were so many people gathered at the Brazil's that we were standing and sitting on both porches, front and back.

Me and Emory looked up to see Gramps' sister walking towards us. I felt a knot in my stomach. I grabbed a hold of Emory's arm. Before she made it to the porch, she burst out crying, "He's dead, he's dead!" she fell to her knees. "He killed my brother." My God, I cried, "Please no, God," I screamed, "please don't let it be true." But it was. Kirk (Gramps) Coleman died of 47 stab wounds. His sister said that the doctor thought they treated all the stab wounds; it was so many that he bled to death from his kidneys. He was in surgery for four hours. He weighed about 110 pounds and was less than 5 feet tall.

We all went to his funeral at Cantrell on Mack Avenue, two blocks from Bewick. John was arrested and sentenced to seven years; he was released in three and a half months for good behavior. No one ever knew why he killed Gramps. I say he killed him because he knew he was bigger than him, and he knew he could. Gramps was twenty-seven years old. As time moved forward, I thought about him; nothing could fill the void he left. I prayed for understanding and forgiveness so I would not hate the man who killed my special friend. "God help me."

Summer was ending, and the leaves were starting to change, and pretty soon it was Halloween time—time to go trick-or-treating. I dressed the kids in homemade costumes, and off we went. Door to door, until they filled their brown paper bags to the top. I also gave them a small Halloween party, inviting Mama and Tina. They had cupcakes, candy, caramel apples, hot dogs, punch, popcorn, and potato chips. I combed through their bags. I was happy because I got to eat all the candy I wanted too. I love candy! I kept Mama and Tina as much as I could because the weather was changing fast, and I wasn't sure if I could get to Canton in that car this winter; that worried me.

Chapter 24

"God Knows Best and He Has the Final Say"

On Thanksgiving Day, everyone came to my house. I cooked a feast. Two days later, I called my mother, and I could hear her voice and words sound slurred. I asked her if she was alright, and she sounded like she was fading away. My God, I screamed. Mama had a stroke. I prayed to God, "Please let me get to her; don't let her die, God, please." I hung up and called Nina at her job; she was closer to Mama than me. I left the house running. I drove to Canton with no problems. When I got there, Tina told me that the ambulance had taken Mama to Mercy Hospital down the street from where I live. When I got there, my mother was barely talking; she'd had a stroke on her left side. We waited and waited in the emergency room for hours while they ran tests. Afterwards, my mother was placed in a private room and made comfortable; she slipped into a coma and remained that way for a period of time. I moved into the hospital and cared for my mother around the clock with the help of Bird, who kept the kids. I'd go home every other day to check in on them, but mostly I was at the hospital.

I prayed to God for a miracle. I never left her side. I bathed her and changed her linen; the nurses didn't have to do anything for my mother—I took care of her myself. I spent days and days reading the Bible and crying, begging for my mother's life. I lay in bed with my mother as much as I could.

Nina had to work, but she came every day after work to care for her sick mother. I called Elder Travis, a dear old friend of hers, to pray and anoint my mother with holy oil. I opened the Bible and laid it by her bed. Her doctor came in and wanted to talk to the family; I wouldn't go—I didn't want to hear. As the door opened, I could see the doctor shaking her head. I refused to accept the inevitable; I kept praying to God. I prayed to let her live to see her birthday, December 5, and He did. I prayed to let her live to see Christmas. Her doctor sent her home by ambulance. We spent Christmas with her in Canton Township. We didn't celebrate; we were just happy to be there. On Christmas night, Nina had to rush Mama back to the hospital. She had taken a turn for the worse. I couldn't give her up; she couldn't die. I prayed. "She'll get better," I said to myself, playing tricks with my own mind. Everyone gathered at Mama's bedside and cried, including Aunt Janie. That was her baby sister—her only sister. I went to the large picture window and said, the verse 121 Psalms "I look to the hills from whence cometh my help. My help cometh from the Lord, Jesus Christ, who created the heavens and the earth." Lord, give her the strength to fight this battle. I could hear my mother's death rattle breathing; it sounded like every breath she took was her last. She opened her eyes and said, "My son, my son, my son." Her hands reached out. She closed her eyes, and the light in her room that hung directly over her bed started flashing out of control, and then it went out. I stood looking out the window, and I continued to pray. I told God not to let her suffer anymore, that she was tired, and to take her home. I said, "Lord, let your will be done."

"Please, Heavenly Father, give me the strength to accept it." We moved Mama to another room. After we settled her in, Nina and Roy went for dinner—it was his birthday. December 29,1982

I stayed with Mama. I pulled my chair close to the edge of the bed and held her hand in mine. I prayed the 23rd Psalm; Mama lay still in a coma. She sat halfway up, opened her eyes, and focused on the corner of the wall. She pointed. I could tell that Mama could see. "There's my

Jesus right there; don't you see him?" I told Nina what happened when they came back.

I drove home to check on the kids and change clothes. I had to deprive myself of her and all the hugs and kissing because I caught a cold. Almost when I stepped in the door, the phone was ringing—it was Roy telling me to come back down to the hospital. I asked if she was alright, and he said for me to hurry up and come. I scrambled, tripping over my pants leg. When I got there, I couldn't remember where she was. I searched the floors, and the information was closed. I ran up the stairs and opened the door. Roy was sitting there; the look on his face told it all.

I opened her door, and there she lay—her body was still and warm; all the tubes were gone. I looked at her with disbelief and sadness; my best friend was gone. I crawled over and got in bed with her. I scooped her in my arms, held her hands, and kissed her face—my mother was gone from this world at 10:46 p.m. I think I was hysterical; I cried and laughed at the same time. I believe I was in shock; my heart was numb with unbearable pain. How was I going to live and breathe without my mother?

On the way home, I could see the sky open up, and one bright star twinkled more than any other in the sky, then the clouds covered it up. I knew then that Mama had made it in; she was safe with the Lord. 'The Question Is' by the Winans played on the radio.

Mama passed away on December 30, 1982; she was 63 years old.

That night, Nina and I drank a half gallon of Vodka straight, and it didn't faze us. I was cold- sober, and so was she.

Standing at her gravesite, I remembered that before she died, Mama said that she knew that Poppi had passed away. Nina didn't have to tell her because his spirit came to her after he died. I prayed that he would be there waiting for her to welcome her in so she wouldn't be alone. Mama was buried next to her husband, the man who went to his grave loving her.

"Floyd Crammer's 1960 "Last Date" 'forever reminds me of the love they shared; that was their song.

After Mama died, Nina moved into my basement until she closed the deal on her own house around the corner from mine.

I can't explain in words how bad I felt. I lay on the couch for nine months, depressed over my mother. How was I going to live without my mother? Every day was a new day for me. I did the best I could and did the bare minimum to keep myself alive. I tried to reassemble my life. One morning before breakfast, I looked at my children; they were going on full force with life. They were getting good grades, staying out of trouble, and living the examples I set before them. I was encouraged by their behavior. I said to myself, "Stay focused." With that in mind, I got a second wind. I said to myself, "I can look further back than I can head; I got to keep on pushing." I drove over to Virginia Farrell Cosmetology School on West Seven Mile Road and enrolled myself in classes. I now sport an asymmetric haircut with a W-drop cut line in the back.

My hair was whipped to perfection.

I felt the pressures of life mounting; the nightmare from my past continued. Most days, I just didn't feel good. I couldn't wait to get home alone so I could cry in peace. Some days, it was so bad that I could feel my insides swelling up and bursting open. Sometimes, in the middle of a meal with the kids, I calmly walked into the bathroom, turned the water on, flushed the toilet, and cried my eyes out. But my nose would sometimes give me away; whenever I cry, my nose always turns red. Then I'd assume my position as a strong woman and their mother. I'd throw my shoulders back and hold my head up, walk back out, and finish having dinner with the kids.

December 1, 1983, almost a year ago—Mama's birthday and the last Christmas we spent together—played in my mind as though it happened yesterday. It was so clear and vivid that I relived every moment, every emotion, and every tear. The first anniversary of her death was approaching, which was devastating. I felt sad and blue, but I had to remind myself that I had asked God to let His will be done. So, I prayed for the strength to accept it. I thanked God for giving her to me as my mother, and I remembered that she belonged to Him first. I was grateful for the time I had with her and all the fond memories that will forever live on inside of me.

December 1983

On December 17, 1983, I was visiting with my mother's first husband, Matthew, at his house on Snowden Street. He had always loved me since I was a little girl. I loved him too, but I knew he made my mother's life harder by not providing for them. My mother loved him—they were still good friends, and she forgave him. Who was I not too? I was sitting there talking with him, waiting for Aunt Janie to come home. She was coming to visit me for the holidays. We had talked about it last week. Believe it or not, I was looking forward to her coming. She was my only aunt. I wanted to forgive her, but I still hadn't reached that point. I was nice and respectful the way my mama raised me, even though she didn't deserve it. We were sitting there, and he was drinking a beer. He invited us over for Christmas; there was always a party at his house when we got together. I kept calling Aunt Janie's house but couldn't get an answer.

I called Gene, the owner of the record store she frequented. He said that she had just left to go home several hours ago. Well, the roads were getting bad, so I wanted to hurry up and pick her up. I called back, and my cousin Billy answered. I asked for Aunt Janie, and he said that she was dead. Just like that, with no emotion. I couldn't believe it, nor did I cry. Billy was so calm, it was frightening. "What happened?" I asked. Billy said that when he came home from work, he found her dead behind her bed. "James Brown, Song "Payback" came to mind.

He thinks she had a series of seizures. Apparently, she'd been there for a while. I was in shock. I told Matthew and everyone else I could. No one seemed to be sad about her death. Aunt Janie was dead so long that the undertaker asked Billy and me if we wanted her arms broken to straighten her out in the casket, and together we said yes.

Mrs. Maggie said she heard Aunt Janie fall and that Billy was at home when it happened. He had to pass her bay window to go upstairs, and she saw him. Aunt Janie died eleven months and twelve days after my mother. She was 67. She wasn't buried with her sister, or even in the same area near her sister. Aunt Janie was buried with the church and choir members she loathed, despised, and envied. She hated them so much that she slept with all their men, smiled in their faces, and ate Sunday dinner with them in the basement cafeteria at Friendship Baptist Church on Beaubien Street.

Mama used to say, "If you want to find a whore, go to church!" Maybe Billy did kill Aunt Janie, but no one cared enough to find out. In my opinion, Aunt Janie was a dirty, low-down bitch! Straight up. I'll stand by this.

I'd been having trouble with my old car; it was barely running, and some days I'd be stranded at school. I couldn't take the kids to school, or I'd have to get a cab for us.

I went to Matthew, whom I called Daddy, and asked him to help me get a car so I could continue going to school. He said he would think about it. I offered to repay him once I graduated. I hadn't heard anything from him since.

One day, he called me over. He wanted to drink some beer and play records. Every time I went to his house, I'd play "Victim" by Candi Staton over and over. "Hell, I wasn't doing anything else," I thought, so we went over. I'm sitting there, sipping Tequila straight, and he says to me, "I thought about helping you get a car and you paying me back. But you can't afford to pay me back. You got those kids."

My heart stopped because I knew that I couldn't make it without his help. "No, I'm not going to help you get a car," he continued. I didn't say anything. "Well, that's alright," I said. "I'll make it somehow."

"Please take my keys and go outside and get my cigarettes," he said. I grabbed his keys and tried to open his car door. Daddy and the kids were standing on the porch. "They don't fit," I said to him.

"Try that car right there," he pointed. I tried the door, and it opened. "Start it up," he said, and I did. "That's your car," he announced. Raring back and being proud of himself. I see you trying to help yourself and your kids, he said. So why not help you?

I couldn't believe it. He had bought me a black 1979 Cordoba with T-tops, all leather bucket seats, and a stick column on the floor. I cried out, "Thank you, Lord!" I hugged him. He laughed.

This was an iconic year for triumph and tragedy in Motown. The beloved legend Jackie Wilson passed away; I went to his funeral on Northend Oakman Blvd. Michael Jackson burned his scalp while filming a Pepsi commercial. And if that wasn't enough.

On April 1, 1984, I was in school when I received a page to call my sister, Charlie. I prayed that nothing was wrong. And it was April Fool's Day. She told me that Marvin Gaye was dead, killed by his father. I got sick to my stomach, signed out of school, and stayed home. The grief was too much to bear; I lay down on the couch and cried every time I heard his name mentioned on the news.

Marvin Gaye was my main man; he got me through a lot of hard times in my life. I saved his music for special occasions. It hurt me to see them remove his body from the house. Then the circumstances that surrounded his death—I couldn't comprehend. In my opinion, Mr. Gay lay in wait, contemplating the day and the opportunity to kill his son. Because Marvin reminded him of all the things he wished he was.

I played Marvin Gaye's music for two weeks straight. My life will never be the same without my main mellow. The kids and I went to the Motown Museum, and I touched the piano keys he had played on. I also attended a tribute to his life at the Music Hall.

His death was not in vain. Marvin Gaye was simply trying to show us how to live.

So much was going on about Marvin Gaye's death that very little was mentioned about Detroit's own Philippe Wynn. His death was barely reported. I was having such a hard time dealing with the death and the shock of it all that I had to stop myself in my tracks and regroup. I read a small article in the Detroit News. It was so small that I could hardly see it. I was offended and saddened to hear about the death of the lead singer for The Spinners. Although he wasn't singing with them at that time, he was dedicated. I remember going back to the first time I ever heard the Spinners, which was in 1963. We were living on Epworth. I was going to the penny candy store on the corner of Linsdale. As I poked around, I heard a car pass by, stop, and park. He ran into the store before I could get there. I heard his record player playing from his candy apple drop-top car. 'Truly Yours'. I stood there and listened to it all. I've been in love with the Spinners ever since.

Phillippe Wynn and Marvin Gaye were tremendously talented. They inspired me to want to live. They provided me with a profound outlook on life through their vision, through their love, and through their music. Peace!

Looking out the window one day, Pee Wee came over to my house on Trinity Street. She was driving a red and white car and playing her music loudly. I ran outside to hug her and welcome her in. For the first time, she got to meet my children. She hadn't seen Shawn since he was Choo-Choo. She encouraged me to take him to meet Eric. I refused at first, but I gave in. The next day I took Shawn out of school, and we all drove over to Promenade Street to one of the many homes owned by his dominating mother, Ms. Florence, and for the first time in his life, Shawn was face-to-face with his biological father. Eric was glad to see me. We hugged, and he showed me his tattoo with my name spelled out on his arm. I still loved Eric, but I was resentful of him because he could have helped me with his son in so many ways. Their visit was warm and memorable, with Eric telling Shawn how much he still loved me and how proud he was of both of us. I want to marry your mother, he said". That afternoon, I introduced my children to Pee Wee's children, and they became cousins and inseparable. Friendship that still endures today.

Every other Friday, I would drop them off to visit while Pee Wee and I would go dancing at a local bar up th street. Just to get away.

Today I met Father Marcan; he was the head of the poverty fund at Dun Scotus Catholic Church in Southfield on Nine Mile Road. I was there to sign my children up for summer camp. In my interview with him, I told him about my children, what I expected from them, and what I wanted for their future. I told him that I feared for my son's life with the gangs, drugs, and violence coming in by the boatloads. I wanted to transfer him to another school; I needed to move out of the area. I lay awake at night trying to figure out what to do next. I thought I'd place the kids in the Oak Park School District.

I had to try!

I knew I could be prosecuted for this, but I was willing to take the chance. I called JD, and he let me use an address in Oak Park, a house he owned. I enrolled the kids and explained to them to keep their mouths shut about the address or they could be thrown out. All was well until the day Andre told the kids in his classroom that they didn't live in the area; his teacher overheard the conversation and reported it to the administration. They called me in. I explained the best I could, but with prejudice, as they were, my children were expelled. I was threatened by the principal that he would call the police and have me prosecuted for falsifying information. I wasn't afraid because, if asked, I'd tell the judge the truth. I'm afraid to send my children to Detroit public schools in my area. That's why I did it. I left there worried about where to put my kids next. I had to send them back to the same old school, with Black people swarming the area like locusts.

I got a part-time job working during the day for the Mina Suka distributing company. My job was to stand in the stores I was assigned to which were Black areas and give out coupons for a carton of Kool cigarettes, and pass out Trident gum. I was only assigned to give these cigarette coupons out in the black communities and neighborhoods. In my house, I had boxes and boxes and boxes of Trident gum in all flavors, and I had boxes and boxes and boxes of coupons for Kool cigarettes.

I called Sam, and he came with his brother-in-law, Nottie. I told him my fears that I had to place Shawn in Benedictine on Outer Drive. Shawn had the grades, but I didn't have the money. Long story short! We spent the next three weeks going from store to store, busting coupons, and accumulating cartons of cigarettes. Pretty soon, with their help and 'God's grace,' I turned those cigarettes into enough money to pay Shawn's tuition for two months, buy his books, and buy his clothes from the goodwill. I sold the cigarettes to my friend Martin; he was from the West Indies and owned a store on the lower east side of the city. He gave me $600.00, and I put him in the same school that Tina went to, Benedictine High. And I started looking for a place to live. J. D. left a message, and I called him. He told me to start looking for a place to live because he was in bad financial trouble. and he didn't have anything else available right then.

I went to work and school, cooked, cleaned, did homework, and looked for a place to live every day. I also became a member of Acorn. I found a nice house on the corner, 16801 Gilchrist. I'd left my number in the door several times; when I'd go back, the number was still stuck in the door from before. I placed my hand on the house and claimed it in Jesus' name.

And to add to my problems, someone stole my T-Tops off my car, sitting right in my driveway. I went outside to my car to dry the inside out with a towel. I couldn't get it to start; my car was soaked and wet. Shawn had to get to school; he had perfect attendance and a test. While we wiped the car dry, I happened to look up into Nina's face; she was driving by. She looked at me and kept going. Nina had to drive past my house to take Tina to school; there was no other way. She saw my hood up, and she drove right past me and my son without even stopping to give him a ride to the same school that he went to with Tina. "God bless the child that has its own!"

I called a cab and took all my kids to school. Shawn had track practice.

For the next few days, I had to take a cab. One day I picked Shawn up in a cab; he and Tina were standing side by side, talking to each other. Nina called Tina to the car and drove off; she never spoke or offered to give us a ride.

Time was moving on. Satan is a liar. "By the Grace of God," I'm going to make it with my kids. We'll see who's gonna have the last laugh.

My oldest brother Matthew came home for a visit; he spent his time at Nina's house. He called me on the phone, and I asked him if he would use part of his VA benefit to buy a house here in Michigan and rent it to me. I humbled myself and cried to him to help me find a decent place to live with my kids. He told me that he had to talk to Nina and Geri to see what they had to say about it. Well, you know what they said: "NO."

I say this: if I want to truly help a person, I don't need anyone's approval or input on what to do for that person! There's no way I would see my baby sister in the streets, homeless with four children, and not help her! Especially if she's trying to help herself. Nina, Matthew, and Geri could have gotten together and bought a house to help me, but they didn't. They never contributed anything positive to my life; they were sitting back, waiting for me to fail. Yeah, Nina bought them a new jacket, but what the hell is a new jacket if you can't take it off? God hears my prayers; I kept moving forward.

Chapter 25

"Keep Your Eyes on God"

Pamela Gorman called and invited me to Mr. Gorman's retirement party. I was in a bad mood and pressed to move out of this area. If it wasn't for being able to see all my old friends from the hood, I would have said no. I called Bird over, and I got dressed. I was sharp. We had a fantastic time, and I danced my ass off. I'm glad I went to see all my old friends; on my way out the door, Mr. Gorman asked me if I was married yet. I said no; he said that for a fine-looking woman like you, I'm gonna introduce you to two of my buddies that work for Ford's Tractor Plant. I smiled and replied, "Don't do me any favors," he said, "these guys are nice; you need somebody to be good to you for a change.

One guy's name is Funky Worm, and the other guy, his name is Ronnie Harris." Well, don't give my number to anybody named Funky Worm; my luck is bad enough. We laughed; two weeks later, on a Thursday night, I had just come home from winning the $300.00 jackpot at bingo at the corner Catholic Church. and getting ready to watch Knots Landing on TV, my telephone was ringing. This soft-spoken voice asked for me and then introduced himself as Ronnie Harris. We talked and laughed until after midnight. He wanted to come by and take me out next week. I didn't want him to because we were sleeping on the floor. Anyway, I told him my situation, and he wasn't pressed. I just want to meet you and your kids. He said.

I agreed; he showed up at my door right after work in his work clothes. He met my children, and the love between them evolved. He was nice-looking with curly light brown hair; he stood 5'11, and he was tender spoken. I fixed him dinner, and we watched television; he loved my cooking. He asked me if I believed in love at first sight, and I said maybe. He said, "Well, I'm in love for the first time in my life; I'm gonna make you, my wife." I laughed; I had one more day left of school before graduation next week, and I had to be at school at 7:30 to take my finals. I told the kids to walk together in a group to school, and I'll call to make sure they made it. My constant prayer was for their safety.

I was sitting in class when I got a page to call home immediately. When I called, Roy answered my phone. "What the hell are you doing at my house?" I wondered aloud.

"Come home right away," he urged. My hands began to tremble. "What's wrong?" I asked. "Nothing," he replied curtly.

I drove like a bat out of hell. Upon arrival, a trail of blood on the porch, leading to the sidewalk, greeted me. Panicked, I ran inside and found Kyham lying on the couch, her face and wrist covered with a bloody towel.

"What happened?" I cried out.

They didn't have time to explain. I grabbed Kyham, placed her in the car, and we sped off, passing an ambulance on the way to MT. Carmel Hospital. At the hospital, as they removed the blood-soaked towel, my heart sank. My child's face had been cut in half, from the bridge of her nose straight down, and her wrist slashed. She had pushed a glass window door with her hand, causing the glass pane to fall out and slice her.

Kyham was in surgery for two hours. During her recovery, Child Protective Services was called. They asked me to step out of the room, but then I could hear them questioning her. "What happened? You can tell the truth; did your mother do this to you?"

I heard Kyham say no, and then I pushed open the door and raised hell with them. Child Protective Services came in to question both Kyham and me. "You're gonna have to kill me before I let you take my kids," I declared, blood in my eyes from tears and rage. "Now go, leave me alone." And they did.

When we got home, Ronnie called. I told him what happened, and he came straight from work to sit with us. He ordered pizza, pasta, salads, and rented videos. He spent the entire evening with us. On graduation day, Ronnie had two dozen red roses delivered to the school with a personal note inside.

My two new friends, Erma Hunt and Mollie Seawart, read it. We'd become inseparable, doing all of our dirty work together. Sometimes we'd sneak out to go to the bar and drink our lunch responsibly. They were like the big sisters I never had, always teasing me about having a boyfriend and wanting to meet him. "He's not my boyfriend," I told them, "But I'll introduce you."

JD called; he was in financial trouble. The court had ordered him to relinquish his properties and holdings. I had to move immediately. The next morning, I went down to Acorn, an organization developed for squatters. The house on Gilchrist was on their list—abandoned for over six months. I could move in immediately, and they would protect me if anyone tried to evict me.

Sam, Nottie, and I pulled all the plywood off the windows and doors. I called a locksmith and changed the locks, cleaned, painted, and got the house ready to move in. The four-bedroom house, just six blocks from Shawn's school, was a blessing.

After a long day of cleaning, as I started cooking dinner, a white man came to my door with a court order. "You have 24 hours to move; this property has been seized by the bank," he informed me.

"It's raining," I noted, and I invited him in. I explained that I only rented the house and knew nothing of it being seized. "I've been paying rent." I showed him my receipts and introduced him to my four children. I asked for a week to move.

He understood, having been a single parent who lost his wife the previous year. "If you promise you'll be out in seven days, and if you'll give me a piece of that fried chicken in your kitchen, I'll let you stay," he proposed.

"God is good," I murmured as I put three pieces of chicken on two pieces of bread and made him a sandwich to go. I was out in five days. The house was absolutely decent, larger than Trinity, with a nice fenced-in backyard.

I made it my own. Ronnie and I spent a lot of time together, although he was still living with his sister, taking care of her and her two kids along with her seldom-home boyfriend. He told me that he wanted a family of his own. Ronnie showered me and the kids with expensive gifts and money.

He bought me a car and gave me money. I was deeply in love with him, and he was deeply in love with us. He took the kids kite flying, to the drag races, to the rodeo, to see the monster cars—he was absolutely wonderful. I knew that God had sent him to me.

One evening, his sister Bonnie called me. She wanted to invite me to a lingerie party at her house. I hesitated at first because I knew some trouble was brewing, but I agreed. I called my old friend Pee Wee, and she said she would go with me. Ronnie told me that he would see me after work at his house. We arrived at the same time, and I thought I was seeing double when two little ladies approached him. They stood there waiting for me; he pointed. When I walked up, he introduced them as his mother's—one was his aunt, and the other woman was his mother. They were identical twins. In all the time we had spent together, he had never told me.

They pretended to be nice and friendly, but I could see them looking me up and down out of the corner of my eye. I was sharp from head to toe and smelled sweet. I shook their hands and kissed him, then he escorted me inside the house he shared with his sister Bonnie. I'm glad I brought Pee Wee, or else I wouldn't have had anyone to talk to. The party was filled with close friends and family. All they did was introduce themselves and wanted to know if I was the woman Ronnie ranted and raved about. Soon, Ronnie's old girlfriend came through the door. Bonnie introduced us; she flaunted herself all she could, but I knew the real reason she was there, and I could deal with it. Ronnie came downstairs after his shower. He asked me what I ordered; I told him, and he paid for my entire order in front of everyone, including his ex. He grabbed my hand, and we left. I thanked God for Ronnie—he was so good to me. He made the difference.

Saturday morning, Father Marcan called and told me that he had a sponsor for Shawn starting next year. Dr. Turner wanted to contribute to his education at Benedictine as long as he kept his grades up. Shawn was a straight-A student. God is good! Ronnie called and invited us to lunch and a movie. We picked him up and had a glorious time. I loved him so much. Our time spent together reminded me of Al Hudson's song 'Now

That I Found You,' Lionel Ritchie's 'Penny Lover,' and 'Sail Away' by the Temptations. On Sunday, we went to Matthew's house for the day. While we were talking, I told him what Nina, Geri, and Matthew Jr. did to me. I told him that I asked Matthew Jr. to help buy me a house, and what he said.

"Hallelujah"

He said, "I'll buy you a house for those kids to live in. You're a good mother." I thought it was the alcohol talking, but sure enough, Monday morning, he went down to the VA and applied for the loan. He said it's just sitting there; I might as well put it to good use. He called me and told me he was approved. He told me to find the house that I wanted for no more than $40,000 and call him back. I couldn't believe it. Thank you, God! I screamed. God touched his heart to help me. I had been on the streets for over five years with my children.

Ronnie came to my house one Friday evening after work. I was cooking in the kitchen. He kissed me and stole a pork chop. He walked into the dining room and asked me if I thought we could live together under one roof with one name. We turned to face each other at the same time. He asked, "Will you marry me?" Without hesitation, I said yes.

Ronnie proved to me that he was in my corner and that he loved us as a whole. He stepped in and took care of business. I no longer lay awake at night trying to figure things out; he lay awake with me and worked it out. He respected me and my kids and what I was trying to accomplish, and he supported me in every way. We were his family, he said.

I was thirty years old and had never wanted to marry. I prayed and asked God for guidance. I really did love him—not for the financial stability he offered, but because Ronnie was a sweet, kind, compassionate man that you couldn't help but love.

I discussed it with my kids; they knew that nothing would change. I'm still their mother, and no one disciplines my children but me (within reason). They loved him; they knew Ronnie was good for me and gave me their blessings. Ronnie took care of business. He gave me three thousand dollars to plan our wedding. He also paid for the limousines, tuxedos, and my dress, and the wedding was catered. I wore a beautiful white full-length embroidered puff-sleeve dress with a white pearl-beaded half veil. I carried a yellow and white cascade bouquet. My handsome son, who is now 16 and stands 6'0", walked me down the aisle.

Ronnie and I married on Saturday, June 29, 1985, at 3:00 PM at Solomon Temple on East 7 Mile Road—a large, beautiful church that was first built in the shape of an ark, later torn down and rebuilt into a temple.

The problem came when I asked Charlie to be a bridesmaid, and I chose the color yellow. Over the phone, she said, "Change your colors; I don't like yellow." We got into an argument, and not only did she not participate in my wedding, she didn't come at all. I thought to myself, it's not about the color—my sisters must really be jealous of my happiness. They all knew that Ronnie made the difference; he was picking up all the slack in my life. I thank God for him.

His family was unhappy about his decision to marry me. First of all, I have four children, and he didn't have any. The fact that he told me out of his own mouth that he was the breadwinner and that I was taking money out of their hands didn't help. They would spend his money and save theirs. They didn't care if he was happy or not. He said that when he got paid on Fridays, his family, including his mothers, would meet him at the door with their hands stuck out, like he was only a meal ticket. They were judgmental and unhappy about their own failed marriages. I knew they were sneaky when I first met them. They hovered like vultures. I wasn't trying to get in or even try to fit in—I didn't give a damn. It was all about living. Me and Ronnie. We spent a fabulous weekend in Ontario, Canada. He fed me breakfast in a rose-petal-covered bed. After we counted the money we received as a gift, we went shopping for the kids.

About three months after we married, I got a call from the principal's office concerning Kyham. They said that someone came there to take Kyham out of school. I panicked and drove to the school. She was safe in the office. I asked them who it was, and they didn't know. I said they should have called the police on them. The principal said that it was a young man. He came to the office and told them that he was her father but couldn't prove it. I told them that his name is not on her contact list, and she's not to go with anyone but me. I signed her out and took her home. Bob called my phone—how he got the number, I don't know. He said that he wanted to take Kyham to live with him, and if I didn't let him have her, he would find a way to steal her from me. I got instantly mad. I told him, "If you take my child, I'll find your mother and kill her."

I had to find someone of equal value. I figured he was living somewhere in the area watching me and the kids, but I meant what I said, and he knew it; he never called back and threatened me again. As added reassurance, I went back to the school and told them again not to let my child go with anyone but me—to call me if they had to. I gave them Bob's full name. "If he comes up here again, please call the police." I went to the police department and notified them as well. I wasn't really going to kill his mother any more than he was going to raise Kyham.

In Bob's heart, he didn't really want the responsibility of providing for her. She'd be a hindrance unless he figured out a way to hustle her with a sad story. He was trying to hurt me and upset me, but it didn't work.

Three days before Christmas 1985, Ronnie said he wanted to buy me a new winter coat from J.L. Hudson's. I told him the coat I had was fine, but he insisted, saying, "Yes, it's OK, but I want to buy you something better." So, we drove to Hudson's. Ronnie took a seat while I looked for a coat. I really didn't see anything I wanted until he pointed over to another area—all that was on the racks were mink coats. Just then, a sales lady came out and said, "Mr. Harris, I got the coats you picked out earlier still on hold," and she started bringing out mink coats from the back. I looked at him in disbelief. He sat back down and urged, "Try them on." I protested the expense, but he simply said, "I want to."

He bought me a beautiful Mahogany full-length mink coat with a hat and muff and had it monogramed with my first and his last name. On Christmas Day, the Christmas tree was full from top to bottom with gifts. He bought me a microwave oven big enough to cook a turkey, two leather suits complete with silk blouses and matching suede boots from Saks Fifth Avenue, perfumes, and gifts from Lord& Taylor and Macy's. Also in my stocking were a three-carat champagne diamond to wear opposite the four-carat wedding rings and one thousand dollars stuffed in the bottom of my stocking. The kids got everything they asked for and then some! I got him a full-length maxi leather coat with matching gloves, hat, and knee-length leather boots, cologne, silk pajamas with matching robes, sweaters, slacks, shirts, and socks. I had every charge card there was to all the department stores, and I also had credit cards in my name only with a $25,000 credit limit to be used in case of an emergency. I had two bank accounts with at least five to ten thousand in them.

Nina, Geri, and Charlie could see that we were a happy family, and we had plenty of everything—new furniture and all new appliances. Nina and Roy spent every Friday at our house, and they didn't want for anything. Ronnie knew how they treated me, and he showboated for them. They pretended not to see, but they were looking. We had happy times on Gilchrist when he got paid on Fridays—he handed me his check in front of them. I would give it back and say, No, Ronnie, you can't do that. Yes, I can, he said. Spend it on the house and the kids. Every Friday, without fail, Ronnie handed me his check. We partied, I cooked, we sang songs, soul trained, played karaoke, and played the blues—Brook Benton, Dinah Washington, Jackie Wilson, and Nina's favorite song, "Part-Time Lover" by Stevie Wonder. And the kids had fun with some new friends.

My sister Charlie called me and asked for a favor. She'd been sick, and she needed someone to clean her house. I took Shawn over to her apartment and cleaned it from top to bottom. I was suffering from a strained back. She tried to pay me, and I told her that she didn't owe me anything. That's what families are for. I could tell that my sister was sick—her eyes were yellow like she had jaundice, her coordination was off, and she seemed to be confused.

Charlie said that she had a doctor's appointment next week and asked me to take her. Of course, I said yes. I drove her to Henry Ford's hospital and listened to what the doctor told her. He told her that years of drinking were taking a toll on her liver and that she needed to stop drinking so that the liver could heal itself. She was headed for a triple bypass if she didn't stop. She said that she would.

We filled her prescriptions, and she had me drop her off at the bar on Davidson. I said to her, "Charlie, you got to stop drinking. You heard what the doctor said." Charlie said to me, "This is my life, and when I die, this world won't owe me anything!" She thanked me, and we said our goodbyes. She knew that I would worry, so she said, "Go home and take care of your family. You know, I think you're a good mother. You take good care of your kids; I'm proud of you."

I said, "Charlie, you're scaring me, girl."

"Don't be scared; I'm gonna do what the doctor says." I'll be alright. I'm not going to be drinking much. I can't stop today, but I will stop. I'm just visiting some friends up here, catching up on the gossip, that's all."

Charlie was well-loved by many friends. She had a magnetic personality. She was bright, beautiful, and bubbly—truly a sweet sister. I have a lot of respect for her. I love her very much. I was going to trust her decision and respect her wishes, and more than anything, I'm going to pray for her.

I felt better just hearing her say that.

That night, I got a call from Cathy that Charlie was in the hospital; she'd been rushed there by ambulance. I drove down there; she was fine. She said she fell and hurt her leg. At 3:00 in the morning, I drove her home. She told me that Nina was mad at her. I don't remember why, but I know it was something petty—it didn't take much to set Nina off. It seemed as though she was looking for anything to get mad at. The wrong look, making your own decisions, or not agreeing with her—she'd hold onto a grudge for years. Then, if you asked her for help, that's when she'd really let you have it.

"Anyway, Nina is coming to take her to an appointment in the morning. She asked me to go with her."

"Yes," I said.

The next morning, they picked me up, and I noticed that Nina had made Charlie ride in the back while I was in the front. I offered to switch places with Charlie to make it easier for her, but Nina wouldn't hear of it. "That's alright; you can ride up here," Nina said tersely. Nina had very little to say to Charlie, and what little she did say was insulting, snappy, and nasty.

When we pulled into the parking lot, Nina could have dropped us off in front of the building. Instead, she pulled down to the end of the large parking lot, forcing Charlie to walk a considerable distance. I got out with my sister, grabbed her under her arm, and walked with her. I held onto her tightly—it was cold, wet, and slippery, and Charlie's legs were hurting so badly she could hardly stand. All Nina had to do was drop her off in front of the building, but that would have been too much like, right. She did it out of pure meanness. I just looked at Nina and shook my head in disbelief.

I had Nina drop us off at my house. I wanted to take my sister inside, fix her something to eat, and give her time to visit with the kids whom she hadn't seen in a long time. I'd cooked turkey and dressing with all the trimmings; I didn't need a special occasion to cook turkey and dressing. As a matter of fact, it was Charlie's recipe that I used. Charlie asked me to fix her a small plate— she was never a big eater.

I went into the bedroom for a minute and then heard her throwing up in the bathroom. I rushed in to help her; she was on her knees, her eyes filled with water. I helped her off the floor and cleaned her up. "I wasn't able to keep anything down," she confessed.

"Well, I'm gonna take you back to the doctor and let him know. You'll be alright," I reassured her. "Oh yeah, girl," she replied, "don't worry about me."

I asked her to stay the night so I could look after her, but she had to get home to William, her live-in boyfriend. I could tell that he loved her very much; he took good care of her. The kids and I drove her home.

The next day, I took her over to Henry Ford Hospital's emergency room, and they kept her. I was glad because I knew they would find out what was wrong. I stayed there and got her settled in. I paid for her TV and telephone and went to the gift shop for books, puzzles, and candy. I sat there until William came, then left to go home and cook dinner.

Charlie stayed in the hospital for one week. The doctor said that she had a hole in her stomach the size of a fist. She was bleeding on the inside; they were giving her blood by the bag fulls. They couldn't stop the bleeding without surgery. She was scheduled for immediate surgery at the University of Michigan in Ann Arbor. I was worried because she had lost so much blood, and she didn't weigh much. I called on the Lord to go with her into the operating room, to guide the surgeons' hands, and to take care of her. I spent the entire day at U of M, praying and waiting for her safe return. William, Charlie's boyfriend, was worried; he paced the hospital floors. I told him, "God is real, and He's almighty. He will fix whatever is wrong in your life. Just trust and believe. I know He's gonna give her back to us whole, and she won't be sick anymore."

God is good! Not only did she come out of surgery alive, but the doctors said she would recover and live if she quit drinking. He asked me if Charlie had a reason why she did so much damage to herself by drinking. I told him the story about her children being stolen from her by her ex- husband and years of depression. He told me that it was a good thing that I took her to the emergency room—that's what saved her life. I hugged him and thanked him for his kind words, then said, "God saved her life through you."

Charlie had a triple bypass.

I got home around 7:30 p.m. Pringle was sitting outside my house; she said she just drove up to tell me that the Feds got JD. They seized everything he owned—properties, bank accounts, everything—and he's been sentenced to ten years in federal prison. I didn't want to believe it. Pringle said that Elaine, his assistant, was also found guilty and sentenced to five years in the federal penitentiary.

"For what?" I asked. Pringle said she didn't know all the particulars, only that it was true.

"Wow, I feel bad for them both; they were nice and really helped me, and everyone they could," I said.

Pringle said she meant to tell me the last time I was at her house, but we got into it. "I will pray for them," I said.

Pringle and I hugged, kissed, and said our goodbyes.

Three months before we moved into our new house, Ronnie surprised me with a Yellow Lincoln Continental, fully loaded. I couldn't believe my eyes when he drove up with it. I cried and hugged him tightly. That same evening, Matthew called and said my house was ready and that he had the keys in his pocket. He'd closed the loan on 20106 Heyden Street, two blocks from 8 Mile Road—a four-bedroom brick house in a predominantly white neighborhood on Detroit's west side. He didn't ask me for a penny; he paid all the closing costs even though he knew I had the money.

Ronnie knew that I had asked Matthew, before we married, to help me buy a house. As much as I loved Ronnie, I wasn't going to put the future of myself or my children solely in his hands. I'm responsible for my kids— that's just the way it is. If Ronnie ever leaves me, I still have somewhere to stay with my kids, and no one can ever put us out on the streets again.

I maintained my independence. Ronnie wanted me to stay home so he could provide for me and the kids, but I worked anyway, doing hair out of my home, and still took care of my children. I didn't depend on Ronnie for anything, but it was nice to know that I could. I learned a long time ago, 'God bless the child that's got his own!' Ronnie paid all the bills. He insisted that I keep my money to do whatever I wanted, so I had money saved for a rainy day.

Charlie was released from the hospital, and she was back to her old self. She wasn't drinking. She and William were happy and doing fine. On February 7, 1986, Charlie called me early, which was unusual for her because she usually slept late. We talked on the phone for six hours, going back and forth about everything and everyone, reminiscing about it all. She told me stories about things that happened before I was born. I managed to take my bath, clean the house, and cook dinner without laying the phone down, thanks to a long phone cord. I really enjoyed our conversation; we laughed a lot that day. I told Ronnie about it.

That night, I received a telephone call from Cathy. She said that she and her husband Tee-Tee had rushed Charlie back to the emergency room in Chicago and Wyoming. I jumped up and got dressed, and when I got there, the room was full of everyone. Charlie was comatose, with plenty of IVs all over her hands and arms; she even had one in her neck. Seeing her like that, my God! I asked Cathy what happened. Cathy said that she was talking to her mother on the phone for about two hours, and Charlie said she would call her back. When she didn't hear from her, Cathy called, and Charlie didn't answer her phone. Cathy got up, went over there, knocked at the door, and no one answered, so she called the police, and she got the landlord to open the door.

She found her mother unconscious on the floor by the bed. William was still at work. The ambulance rushed her to the hospital. Charlie never regained consciousness. She was found lying in a puddle of blood. "Where is she bleeding from?" I asked. Cathy said they had to stabilize her first and then run some tests to find out. I cried on my way to find the chapel in the tiny hospital. I got down on my knees and prayed. I begged God to help my sister, to give her the will to want to live. I pleaded with Him to give her the strength to live, to touch her body from the top of her head to the bottom of her feet, and to heal her, Lord, inside and out.

When I went back into the room, I sat down near her bed, rubbed her feet, and talked to her. She lay still and asleep. It was almost daylight, so I left to get the kids ready for school, with every intention of going back. I wanted to talk to the doctor. I stayed home for about an hour, getting the kids breakfast and ready for school. When I got back down to the hospital, I stayed and waited for the doctor. I was worried and afraid; she was still asleep. I got into the bed with her and held her hand softly, whispering in her ear, "Fight, Charlie, fight to live. If you can hear me, squeeze my hand." She didn't squeeze my hand, but she held on to it. I knew it was a sign from God that my sister was going to live. She was weak and frail, but she could heal and get better. I whispered in her ear, "Charlie, don't you go anywhere and leave me here with those two bitches." She smiled, and a single tear rolled down the side of her face. I lay in bed with her until the doctor came in. He examined her and asked me to call the family in.

"Call the family in for what?" I asked, scared.

"He said, 'She's not responding to the medication, and there's nothing else we can do but make her comfortable.'"

"What are you saying?" I asked.

"I'm sorry. I wish we could do more," he replied.

It felt like all my insides had dropped to the bottom of my stomach. I doubled over in pain, dropped to my knees, and then onto the floor. I had to just sit there for a minute to get myself together. I couldn't believe what was happening; there had been so much pain in my life that my heart felt numb. In disbelief, I started to laugh out loud, then I started to cry, and then I started to pray for God to save my sister, but she had the same death rattle breathing like my mother.

I called everyone to come back down. We gathered in her room and waited to talk to the doctor again. He called us into another room and told us that it was just a matter of time—that nothing had changed. We all couldn't believe it; we cried. I prayed silently, 'God, please have mercy; please don't let her suffer.'

February 9, 1986, 3:42 a.m.

My oldest sister passed away. She was 42 years old. I've never felt so sad in my life. It was different with Charlie because she was so young and beautiful, and the fact that she had just gotten her kids back made it even sadder. We have to understand that God makes no mistakes, and I had to accept that it was His will. I thank God for giving her to me as my sister; no one could ever fill her shoes in my life. I will always remember her laughter, her jokes, her cooking, her wisdom, and her love.

Her wake was held at Swanson's on West Six Mile Road, and it was standing room only. Her friends and buddies came out of the woodwork—people I'd forgotten about and some I hadn't seen in years, her old boyfriends, people she went to school with, and those she worked with at the Post Office. Even the man who killed her was there—the one who started it all. He sat with his son, Man, and his latest victim, his wife of twelve years; they had a six-year-old child together. They talked quietly among themselves, but Ronnie's sisters and his mother interrupted their comments with laughter and giggles, making fun of my sister in her casket.

They don't know to this day that I overheard their comments and jokes about my sister. I even heard Charlie's son, Man, say, 'Let the bitch die the same day she did.' He stood by the casket and talked to his father. Ronnie's sisters laughed and pointed at the many needle marks left on Charlie's arms, evidence of the pain she endured and suffered.

'Vengeance is mine,' says the Lord, and I had to remember that to keep myself out of trouble.

On Valentine's Day at 11:00 AM, we held her funeral service at Greater Grace Temple on Schafer and West Seven Mile Road, the home of Detroit's own Bishop Ellis. Charlie wasn't a member there or anywhere and hadn't been a member of any church for years—maybe that's why they charged us. I didn't mind paying, but it would have sounded better if they'd asked for a donation.

I felt Charlie's constant spirit of protection around me after she passed away. I could feel her in my house, especially in the kitchen when I was cooking. Before they closed the casket, I took one last look at my sister, and her entire facial expression had changed; she didn't look peaceful anymore. I prayed the 23rd Psalm for protection, asking God to let her in, knowing that Mama would be waiting for her. I will miss and love my sister forever. I prayed for our strength in the Lord. I forgave Charlie years ago for everything she'd ever done to me. I pray she forgave herself, and God will give her peace. Charlie was buried next to my mother and father. Nina didn't attend Charlie's funeral; she said she had to work.

Old friends showed up from the Majestic Bar and Grill, the Lincoln, Muriel's Bar, Bachelor 2 Lounge, Tanqueray, and all of her pinochle buddies. There wasn't a dry eye in the house. I later found out from William that Charlie never stopped drinking; she hid it well from us all. Charlie told us what we wanted to hear. William said that Charlie would stand in her walk-in closet and pour wine into a tablespoon and drink it. Charlie was in denial. I will always believe that my sister died from a broken heart.

I was so depressed by her death that I stayed in bed and around the house for three weeks. Ronnie was very supportive in my time of grief; the kids were hurting too—everyone close to me had died. We finally got moved and settled in; the house was really nice, but I knew the neighborhood was only good for about four years before we'd have to move again. There were Black people in the neighborhood, just a better class. I'll cross that bridge when I come to it; for now, I was going to enjoy my new house. It was only a stepping stone!

1986

The children were thriving in school. Shawn worked as a caddy at Plum Hollow Gulf Course in Southfield and was learning how to drive—that is, when I wasn't interfering too much. Andre, ever the challenge, was placed in a private school because he had been kicked out of almost everyone within the district. I paid his tuition of $3,500 with the clear understanding that there was to be no fighting. If he was caught, he would be expelled. Sure enough, after three weeks, he was expelled, and I lost all the money I'd planned to use for Shawn's tuition.

For the time being, the kids went to Taft. I applied to Luddington Elementary/Junior High for Terrance and Kyham, but there was a waiting list for the next semester. Luddington was the best thing going, next to a private school with only room for seven hundred students. I prayed and asked God to make a way for my kids to get into Luddington. It was safe, clean, and the teachers and principal were dedicated.

That summer, I hired a tutor to come to the house three days a week to tutor the boys. I also had them all enrolled in track and field, basketball, and recreation at the YMCA. We spent time going to church and taking trips to Canada. There were gangs in the neighborhood, and I worried about them being pressured to join. I had enough faith in my children to know that they would do everything possible not to become members. But sometimes, that shit doesn't work!

I had a sick feeling in my stomach for two weeks that wouldn't go away. Although Shawn was graduating, he wasn't grown yet, and I had to make him understand that when I said 'No,' that's what it meant. Shawn was invited to a party by his friend Melody. He wanted to go badly; all his friends were going to be there. But I said no. The night of the party, Shawn was still upset with me, so he stayed in his room.

At 11:00, I turned on the news, and there she was. Melody Rucker, 16, was shot to death by some boys she refused to let into her sweet sixteen birthday party. I was shocked and saddened. Shawn said he had walked with her that day, coming from football practice. All I could do was pray for the Rucker family. I promised myself that I would never forget her.

1987

I had to remain focused on my children's future. I can testify when I say that prayer changes things! Shawn was graduating from Benedictine High School on May 17, 1987, at 6:00 p.m. He was accepted to Eastern Michigan University in Ypsilanti, Michigan.

I prayed for this day. I knew now that all my suffering was not in vain. The seniors were getting ready for graduation rehearsals, prom night, and plenty of parties.

On the day of his prom, Nina, Geri, Matthew Sr., and his wife Alma gathered at the house, offering words of encouragement. I thought to myself about Nina and Geri: You're a little late for that conversation. Ronnie and I showered him with gifts, money, and photographers, both video and still. Shawn and his date were picked up in a black-and-white stretch limousine with all the trimmings. They had dinner at the Bonny Brooke Country Club, and I let him stay out until 3:00 in the morning. I couldn't sleep until he got home. I relished every moment the evening my son walked across the stage to receive his diploma. I could do nothing but cry and praise God. I wished my mother were here to see this, but in my heart, I knew she could. Shawn was nominated for having the best walk, and when he accepted his diploma, he did the James Brown splits across the stage; paying homage to Fast Eddie the man that made sure that we ate. Everyone stood up and applauded.

Then they had a moment of prayer and silence for Melody Rucker, with Isiah Thomas as the guest speaker. My family did not attend Shawn's ceremony, and I wasn't invited to Tina's the year before.

In August 1987, I received a call to come up to Luddington and fill out an application to enroll my children in school. She gave me two serial numbers to show when I got there. I was excited and trusted God. "Does this mean they'll be enrolled?" I asked. She said, "I'm not sure if we'll have room for them, but we have to take all applications anyway."

When I got there, there was a line wrapped around the corner waiting to get in for applications. I got in at the end of the line and waited. It's one thing about people from Detroit—if you get the right crowd, you can have a ball with a bunch of strangers. And that's just what we did. We laughed and talked; the time passed quickly. When we got inside, I filled out the applications, and I put the serial number on the top right-hand side of the paper: 111 and 112. We sat back down, and I noticed that no one but me had a serial number. We were the only ones.

The principal walked out and shook my hand, introducing herself as Mrs. Shelton. She walked us back, pulled out the kids' folders, and talked to them directly. I was so proud of them; they knew how to conduct themselves and hold an intelligent conversation with her.

After the interview, Mrs. Shelton stood up and walked towards the door, her reading glasses hanging around her neck and resting on her ample bosom. I could tell she was old-school. She looked at me and said, "I like your children. They're intelligent, and they will go far if they just apply themselves. I can tell you spend a lot of time with your kids; you've raised them well." She paused, then asked, "Let me ask you a question."

"Yes?" I replied.

"Why did you stand in that line when the receptionist gave you a serial number linking you to an application?" Mrs. Shelton inquired.

I looked at her, puzzled. "I don't understand," I said.

"Your children have been accepted into Luddington. That's why she gave you the numbers, so you could come right in," Mrs. Shelton explained. I didn't know I said.

I couldn't believe it. "Thank you," I said, my voice trembling with gratitude. "I prayed and asked God to help them get in, and He did."

"God answers prayers, but I don't have to tell you that," she smiled, adding, "Plus, your children have the grades they need to qualify. Most parents who apply here find their children can't keep up."

We were there for an open house, and we met their teachers. It was a moment of relief and pride.

November 1987

I was inside the house cleaning up and getting ready for the holidays, making plans to go to Bingo that night, when my telephone rang. It was a Big Dot on the line. I hadn't talked to her in a while, so I was glad to hear from her.

"Girl, you need to sit down. I've got to tell you something," she said. "Is it bad news?" I asked. She replied, "Little Dot killed Balma." "What?" I exclaimed, and she repeated it.

I had to sit down on the couch to catch my breath. "How? When?" I managed to say.

Through tears, she explained that Balma had rented a van for Dot to drive while he had hers repaired. They were driving a rental, and Dot wanted to use the car to go to Chuck E. Cheese's, while Balma needed it for work. They were living apart in separate houses, but Balma paid the rent on both. It had been snowing out.

The argument happened over the phone. Balma hung up and walked to Dot's house to take the car, and the argument escalated. Balma was standing outside on the steps; Dot was inside the house in the doorway. "You wait here, bitch, you're gonna make me kill you and play crazy," Dot had warned. Big Dot said that Dot walked back into the house, pulled a gun from underneath the couch cushion—a gun Balma had given her for protection—and shot Balma through the screen door. He was hit in the throat, dead center, and fell off the porch into a pile of snow, gurgling through the blood and begging for help.

"The only thing that kept him alive was the snow," I murmured.

Big Dot continued, saying that Dot then let Balma lay there while she instructed her oldest son and daughter to rob him of all his jewelry and money. These were the same kids that Balma had provided for and cared for. "From my understanding, they didn't want to, but they did," Big Dot added. Then, Dot concocted a story and coached them on what to tell the police. They agreed on the story, and then she called the police. Forty-five minutes after she shot him, Balma had been laying in the snow, fighting for his life. When the police arrived, they called the ambulance, and as they lifted Balma to put him inside, he drew his last breath.

"I knew that Dot was going to kill Balma. I could feel it in my soul," I confessed, recalling how she always used to tell Balma, "You're gonna make me kill you and play crazy." The reason she always told him that was because she received disability for seizers and that was the leverage she and her lawyer used.

I asked Big Dot where Margie was when this happened. "She left town the same night, headed for Chattanooga, Tennessee," she replied.

I couldn't believe it. I remembered the last time I saw Dot; we were talking, and she was bragging about using Balma for his money and the fact that she was screwing his best friend, Darrell, when Balma was asleep in the house. I knew she was getting high because she kept going into the bathroom. When she came back into the living room, she sat down to talk to me, and blood was dripping from her nose—she didn't even know it. Her face was numb from the cocaine. I got up and left; that's the last time I saw Dot. Before we hung up, we both agreed to go to the trial together.

It was raining really bad that night. I had a lot to think about at Bingo. Ronnie had insisted on driving me despite the downpour. He walked me to the door with an umbrella, shielding me from the rain. That was the last I saw of him—until 1:53 AM. He claimed he'd fallen asleep at a friend's house and apologized for not picking me up. I didn't say a word; I just listened. He knew I didn't believe him.

A week later, he did it again: he left me at Bingo. But this time, when I got home, he was there, waiting. He said he had to see about his mother. I never asked her anything. The next day, she called to confirm that he was with her. I didn't believe it, and we got into a light argument. The tension in the house was mounting. Ronnie stayed home after that and didn't go anywhere. I told him, "It's not the fact that you go out—it's that I can't trust you anymore. You leave me standing outside in the dark, depending on you."

Ronnie responded, "I wouldn't ask you to get a ride home." "It's no different than you leaving me stranded," I countered. He dropped his head.

"Is there someone else? Is there somewhere else you'd rather be?" I asked.

"No, I love you. I'll prove you can trust me again. I'll never leave you like that again," he swore. I found out later that he lied. There was something going on.

During the holidays, we spent a lot of time together. He was off on changeover and showered me with gifts, money, attention, affection, and love, as he always did.

Occasionally, my friend Sue and her husband James would stop over. They knew they'd have a good time at my place because I cook and I have all the old music they love. That evening, as Sue and I talked, I played some blues from the fifties—Ruth Brown's "5-10-15 Hours of Your Love," Ray Charles' "Nighttime," Lowell Fulson's "Reconsider Me," and Charles Brown's "C.C. Rider."

Ronnie and James went to the store. "I'll be right back," he said. "I said, 'Take your time.'" Two hours later, he was coming through the door.

I loved my husband dearly, but I wasn't taking nonsense from him or any other man. Well, that was short-lived. The following weekend, Ronnie didn't come home at all. I called the morgue, the police, and his family to see if he was alright. His mothers were evasive about his whereabouts; they answered the phone together—one on each end—and claimed they hadn't seen him. They didn't seem concerned. In fact, they seemed a bit relieved that he wasn't home with me.

The following day, I was dragging, tired from a lack of sleep and worry. Then the telephone rang. It was Ronnie. He apologized and wanted to take me away for the weekend.

"No," I said, but he had already made reservations—special arrangements for me.

"It's a surprise, and we need to talk. Pack our suitcase, and I'll be home right after work," he said. I called a babysitter.

The surprise was the newly built Embassy Suites in Southfield, with a glass elevator. The room was filled with red roses that covered the bed, and champagne, chocolate, and strawberries awaited us. We got dressed, and he took me down to dinner, where he paid the trio to serenade me at the dinner table. All this was fine and well, but I still wondered, *Where the hell were you last night?*

"Baby, let's not talk about it now, okay?" he pleaded. "I swear to you, I wasn't with any other woman. I swear to you on a stack of Bibles. Let's just enjoy each other and set our differences aside for now."

I looked into his eyes and said, "Alright."

On Monday morning, I cooked breakfast for Ronnie like I do every morning. Before he left for work, he said, "When I get home, we'll talk. I promise." He kissed me and left.

My day started early, so I cleaned the house, mopped floors, stripped the bed down, and washed clothes. I sorted through Ronnie's work clothes, and as I picked up his socks to turn them inside out, I felt something. I rolled the sock right side in, and something hit my foot. I bent down to pick it up, held it in my hand, and realized it was a small screen that looked like it belonged on a small pipe.

When Ronnie came home, I showed it to him, and he said, "It's time we talk."

I fixed his dinner, but he didn't want to eat. That was unusual. We went into the bedroom and sat down. He told me that's what he wanted to talk about. The nights he stayed gone—that's where he was: smoking crack and getting high.

"I'm sorry to put you through this," he said. "How did this happen?" I asked.

Ronnie explained that he grew up in a world that lacked communication. He stuttered badly and had astigmatism, turning to drugs as a way of communicating. Then one day, he was watching the 700 Club, and the pastor was praying. Ronnie said he placed his hand on the TV set and was healed from stuttering and astigmatism.

"I thank God for his blessing. He opened the doors for me to be able to talk," he said.

He admitted that he'd been experimenting with heavy drugs since he was a teenager. He named them all: crack cocaine, mescaline, LSD, cocaine, heroin, marijuana, pills, and acid. There isn't a drug out there that I haven't tried. I couldn't believe it. He cried out to me, "Please don't leave me. I'll get some help." I wouldn't dare leave him in this desperate hour.

As shocked as I was, I supported my husband, and the fact that he wanted help made it even better. Ronnie hung his head in shame. He knew that I was a private person and wouldn't tell anyone, especially the kids.

The next day, he did everything necessary to enroll himself in the Shar House Drug and Rehabilitation Program on West Grand Blvd. He got his bonus check and had some other money transferred into his savings account. He took Shawn down to the bank and opened a new account, placing Shawn's name on it first. Ronnie deposited $25,000 in the bank in case we needed something. Shawn could go to the bank and get it.

He also made arrangements for his work check to be mailed directly to me to maintain the household bills. I was sad and didn't want to see him go, but I knew the only way we could survive this marriage was if he got help—and meant it. I suffered too hard for this. I sacrificed my life to raise my children, and I wasn't going to subject them to this kind of behavior, especially in my own house. Children live by example; nothing from nothing leaves nothing every time.

I fought my whole life to keep my kids away from drugs and drug addicts. All the preaching, praying, and crying I did, asking God to protect us, I remember asking Emory to talk to my children about the harsh realities of addiction—showing them the track marks on his arms and legs. They listened intently to him and asked him questions.

As for Ronnie, I couldn't control or condone what he did. He was his own man. At least he had the decency to take his habits away from home, a gesture I respected, albeit grudgingly. We decided to tell the kids that Ronnie had to go away for work at Ford's Tractor in Romeo. I was too embarrassed to reveal the truth.

In the following months, I supported Ronnie in every way I knew. I spent hours in counseling sessions with him, bought him new clothes, shoes, and pajamas, and the kids and I wrote him letters. I made sure he had money and never missed a visit. He'd be there, standing with his arms stretched out, waiting for me. Ronnie stayed six months in rehab, and when he left, he was clean. We were happy and a family again.

Chapter 26

"Time Brings About a Change"

1988 was a pivotal year. Terrance was finishing his last year at Ludington, and Andre was at Taft Junior High. I worried incessantly about where to enroll them next; Henry Ford High School was just three blocks from home on Evergreen Road, but it was notorious for its violence—killings, shootings, robberies, gangs. It was like a trap with no escape; every school I considered was either subpar or charged exorbitant tuition fees.

Eventually, Ronnie suggested we ask Nina if we could use her address so the kids could attend Southfield High School, offering to pay her a thousand dollars. She agreed, and he paid her.

I bought the boys' clothes—Terrance was wearing size eleven shoes and André was ten and a half. They were all taller than me, towering at 6', 6'1", and Terrance at 6'3". I always made sure they looked presentable: hair combed, clean, teeth brushed and flossed, shoes tied.

I drove the kids to school every morning and was there to pick them up in the afternoon. I didn't want Ronnie to pay Nina, but we were out of options. I didn't want any favors from her that she could later hold over our heads. I prefer to pay my way in life, but she saw a window of opportunity to exploit. A deal's a deal, right?

But what kind of person—what kind of aunt—accepts a thousand dollars to help her nephews? Ronnie wasn't even their father, yet he tried to help my children. Meanwhile, I was paying tuition for Shawn at Oakland Community College, helping him dip his toes into academia before university.

Then came the call from Big Dot about Little Dot going to court for Balma's murder. Personally, it was not my decision it seemed clear that they were going to get her on premeditated murder. Everyone that spoke about it agreed. Dot had waited for the opportunity to kill Balma; because she talked about it. Was it a dark intent harbored in her heart? I asked myself? I don't know.

Big Dot and I went through the metal detectors at the 36th District Court on Madison, near downtown Detroit, across from Stroh's Factory. For two weeks, we sat and listened to her children cry, defending their mother in vain. They were torn because, although Balma had been like a father to them for over ten years, Dot was their mother, and they knew all too well her flaws.

I felt a profound sorrow for Balma. His siblings had come all the way from Alabama, took him home for his funeral, and returned for the trial to show solidarity. Despite their support, Attorney dissected the story into so many pieces during the trial that I lost track. They concocted a narrative of self-defense that the jury accepted, sentencing Little Dot to just eighteen months for possession of the gun.

Not a day more for the killing of Balma. No weapon was found on him; they never found the gun, and she had shot him through the door using his own gun. The money for her attorney came from Balma's savings hidden in a floor safe. She killed him with his gun in a house he paid rent for, just so she and her children could have a place to live.

It's all so sad for Balma.

Well, Balma's sister let out a cry that I've never heard before, and they had to be helped to their feet. Little Dot was led away to the county jail to be transported to prison. It was a tragic situation—Balma's family had opened their doors and hearts to Little Dot and her kids. Balma used to take Dot and her children down south for the entire summer, and they were welcomed with open arms. They talked over the phone and exchanged personal thoughts and feelings; Balma's mother even included

Dot and her children in her prayers. I felt so bad for all of them, including Dot. What had driven her to kill the one man who had been good to her?

This situation reminded me of a night I want to forget—the night I thought about killing Bob. I don't believe I had enough nerve to do it, but I thank God I had enough discipline not to. On the flip side, Little Dot and I are different people. I knew that when she left me alone at her house that Christmas holiday when I was homeless. Little Dot lost most of, if not all, her friends.

In April of 1988, my oldest brother, Matthew Jr., invited me, Ronnie, Nina, and Roy to attend his retirement ceremony in Fort Belvoir, Virginia. As happy as I was for him, I didn't want to go. I knew that Nina had tarnished our relationship; she would talk negatively about all of us to Matthew, which influenced his opinion towards his two younger siblings. Matthew, Nina, and Geri always sat high and looked low at me and Rickey. She had nearly severed our relationship with Matthew, pushing hard until she pushed him out of our lives. I bypassed the drama, knowing I may never get this opportunity again to see my brother, who worked so many years to accomplish this—retire thirty-three years and out. I didn't want to miss that.

I got a babysitter, my cousin Bird, and her sister, and I instructed them to only allow my kids to sit on the porch, no roaming the streets, and I went for the weekend. Before we left, Big Dot called and said that Balma's mother dropped dead at the kitchen table the morning she got the news that Little Dot only had eighteen months, and nothing for her son. I packed, and we drove down together, staying at the Marriott Hotel in downtown Alexandria, Virginia.

While there, we visited Arlington Cemetery, John F. Kennedy's gravesite, and the site of the Unknown Soldier. The soldiers looked like toy soldiers; they were so still, professional, graceful, and precise. They performed honors. We went out for a seafood lunch on the pier, and I called and checked on the kids at every payphone. The ceremony was nice, and the seven-course meal was lovely. We sat at the dinner table with Matthew in a show of support. The general talked about all of Matthew's accomplishments in his thirty-three years in the Army—to name a few, he was a demolition specialist, served with the 7th and 2nd Divisions in Korea, and was a 1st Sergeant in the Special Forces. To make a long story short, there must have been a hundred and sixty accomplishments; I counted over thirty-six schools and places he was assigned to, including Vietnam three times. He'd traveled all over the world. He stayed focused. Matthew is a great inspiration in my life. I have a lot of respect for him and am proud to call him my brother, even if he hasn't always acted like one. He doesn't even know what my favorite ice cream is or what kind of cookies I like best. He retired as a command sergeant major. I cried because I knew in my heart that if anyone deserved it, he did. He earned it. I cried because I wished my mother was there to see it.

We celebrated a bit that night at the NCO Club. Everyone was dancing out but me, especially when the DJ played one of my favorites, I first heard in Detroit on WJLB Jay Butler's Blues station. Tony Trottman's "Your Man Is Home Tonight"—he played it back-to-back for me. I couldn't get enough of this song, so he gave me the cassette before we left.

"He said here, take this Detroit."

I hugged him, and I thanked him because I couldn't find it in Detroit; it hadn't hit the shelves yet. The night before I came home, I dreamed of Mrs. Blackmon, but in my dream, she looked like Pringle—in all honesty, Mrs. Blackmon and Pringle favored each other; they had the same facial structure and skin color. In my dream, Ms. Blackmon was waving goodbye to me. I tried to shake the dream and the bad feeling associated with it, but I couldn't. The closer I got to home, the more the feeling overpowered me. I have a knot in my stomach. I said a prayer. I began to worry about Mrs. Blackmon, knowing that she was an older woman who had been through a lot.

"Lord, please protect my children and cover them in your blood," I prayed.

Then the knot in my stomach vanished just as quickly as it had appeared. We drove up, and I jumped out to run inside the house. I looked for my children—they weren't in the bedrooms. Then I heard laughter. Peering outside my back bedroom window, I saw them safely in the backyard, cleaning up. I thanked God, hugged, and kissed my children tightly. They asked me about the trip, and as we talked, I could hear my telephone ringing from outside my bedroom window. I walked inside, using the bedroom side door to answer it.

"Hello?" I picked up the receiver. "It's me, Lollie," a voice replied.

I was surprised. "Where are you? How's your mother? Where is she? I've been looking for her." "You know Mama died. We had her funeral yesterday," Lollie said, her voice heavy.

I screamed, "No, no, God, please!" I had a dream about her, but it wasn't her I was worried about. I felt sick to my stomach, crying, and I fell across the bed.

Lollie explained that Shirley Pringle died last week. The state had taken her children from her and placed them in a home. She fought long and hard to get them back and finally did. Pringle then lost her house because she couldn't pay the rent, so she went back into a LaBelle Shelter—that's where she was staying when she died.

"Pringle had a bad headache, was vomiting all day, and laid down early in the in the evening," Lollie continued. "At dinner time, she didn't want to eat and kept complaining about her head hurting." She was rushed to a private suburban hospital, which refused to treat her because she didn't have insurance—and we won't even mention the fact that she was black and poor. They sent her back to the shelter, untreated, in a cab.

Lollie said that Pringle threw up in the cab, and the driver, despite pleas to help their mother, cursed them out and put them out of the cab three blocks from the shelter. Her children all but picked her up and carried her back to the shelter. When they got back, Pringle passed out from the pain in her head. They called an ambulance again, but it didn't show up until later that evening. She was rushed back to the hospital, this time to Detroit Receiving—a county hospital for the poor, a distance away from the shelter. When she got there, she threw up again and was on her knees in pain with this headache. Lollie said she died before they could place her on a bed against the hallway wall. They'd run out of rooms.

"Her doctor told Pringle not to have any more children, or it might kill her," Lollie added. "She had one more child, her seventeenth baby." Pringle died three months after her last child. Lollie said that Emmette never showed up for Pringle's funeral on April 18, 1988, and didn't contribute a dollar towards her expenses, not even a flower. The funeral was held two blocks from where Emmette lived with his mother. Pringle was 42 years old.

The doctors said that Pringle died from a brain aneurysm. If they'd treated her at the first hospital, they might have been able to save her life.

I was devastated by the news of her death; I felt like I was coming apart. I would have liked to have had the chance to say goodbye to my friend. In good times and bad, we were sisters in life, sisters in the struggle. One thing was for sure—my words had hit home. I remember telling Pringle that all she had in this world was her kids; they were there for her through it all, even in death.

Peace.

Later that evening, before I went to bed, I knew what to expect. Despite everything going on around me, I needed to have my own private nervous breakdown somewhere I could be alone with myself. It was getting harder to suppress my feelings of sadness. I was still having nightmares about my past. I was experiencing bouts of depression; sometimes I felt like I was choking on different ranges of emotions. I could still smell his hands.

I held it all inside myself—I still hadn't told anyone what happened to me, not even Ronnie. I lay awake, all crying out, wondering, what are her kids going to do without her?

I prayed for them and let them know that if they needed me, I was here. Her children were dispersed among her older children and family members. I picked Kyham up from school, and she told me she wanted to visit her friend Stormy, a classmate of hers.

I told her that Stormy could visit here, but I didn't want her over there. She said that she had walked home with Stormy today at lunchtime. When she walked in the door, her grandmother Lettie's picture was sitting on the end table, facing her. Bob then walked downstairs. She recognized him at once. He pretended as if he didn't know who she was.

"What's your name?" he asked. "Kyham," she replied. "Where were you born?" "California," she said.

"And what's your mother's name?" he continued.

When she told him, he said, "I know a lady with that same name," and walked back upstairs.

Kyham told me he pretended not to know who she was because he's Stormy's mother's live-in boyfriend, and he's afraid that we'll tell her about him.

"You're a smart young lady, and we're gonna leave it just like that," I said. "Let her find out on her own. And don't you go to Stormy's house again, or you're gonna get yourself grounded. You know better."

That dirty mother——I said to myself. Well, good. Don't you say anything to him at all.

I really didn't feel like company when Sue and James dropped by. They wanted to talk to me and Ronnie because they were having some personal issues. I muttered to myself, Hell, nobody has more problems than me right now. Sue revealed that James was using drugs, and she was at her wit's end—she wanted to know if we could talk to him because she was on the verge of throwing him out if he didn't clean himself up. They knew nothing about Ronnie's issues.

Ronnie stepped up and said, "Yes, James, come and go with me to the store. We'll have a man- to-man talk." They stayed gone for four hours, which left me wondering what took so long. When I asked Ronnie, he simply said they were talking.

That same day, I picked up Kyham from school. "Guess who came to the office today?" she asked excitedly.

"Santa Claus?" I joked.

She laughed. "No, Mom. It was Bob." She explained how Bob walked into the school office with a McDonald's lunch for Stormy. Kyham, who worked as an office aide, escorted him through the hallways to Stormy's homeroom. They walked side by side, and he said nothing but a casual hello to her. Kyham dropped her head, visibly upset. "Don't hold your head down; he is nothing to you. "If anything, you should be ashamed and embarrassed for him." I said.

I offered her words of encouragement. "Kyham, look at it this way. You haven't lost anything. Bob doesn't care any more about Stormy than he does about you or even his own mother. He doesn't love Stormy; he's just pretending because that's the face he has to show to slither through life. Do you understand what I'm saying?"

"Yes, I do," she replied quietly.

"See, my dear, you don't have to hang your head about anything. I'm your mother, and I'm the one who loves you. If the Lord lets me live to see you all grown up, that's all that matters. You're better off without him in your life. When you see a pile of shit in the street, what do you do?"

Kyham answered, "Step over it."

"Exactly, and that's what you do about Bob—step over him; he's nothing."

I hugged and kissed my baby, then took her over to Hudson's at Northland, where we did some shopping.

Friday came, and Terrance and Andre needed a ride to practice. Ronnie was late coming home from work; we waited. He finally called, saying he was on his way and was helping a friend start his car. Ronnie came home at midnight, offering only a terse apology. I said nothing, but I knew trouble was brewing.

Saturday morning, he lay sleeping in bed. I got the kids together, Shawn included, and went to Pamela's house. We got her kids, and all of us went skating at Northland Roller Rink in Southfield. Pam and I, old school as we were, had learned to skate in the hood. We had an enjoyable day together. When I got home, Ronnie was gone again. He came back that evening, using James as an alibi. This behavior continued for months; each time Ronnie had a different excuse. It had gotten so bad that I never knew when, or if, he was coming home.

Then one Friday, Ronnie didn't come home at all. He didn't call, and I sure as hell didn't call around looking for him. Monday morning, Ronnie's foreman called to say he hadn't reported to work. I became worried because he always went to work—sometimes he drove, most times he had a rider. I did the usual: I called the morgue, the police department, and I dreaded calling his mother, but I did. No one had seen him.

Then Sue called and said that Ronnie and James had left together. She came to my house and told me that James had stolen three hundred and eighty dollars from her after she cashed her check from Cadillacs. She had her pistol in the car. It didn't take much to talk her out of killing him, but she declared that James couldn't come back to live with her. I told her I understood.

Ronnie came home that Monday night, and I asked him to sleep on the couch because I didn't know where he'd been, and I couldn't believe anything he said. While he was home, I told him I was out of money. He signed a bank withdrawal slip, laid it on the TV, and told me to use what I had whenever I needed it. He was good that week, and then Friday came and went—no Ronnie. This time, he left for four months. No calls, no nothing.

Monday morning, his foreman called again; he hadn't reported for work. They threatened his job if he didn't show up or take a medical leave. I called his mother and relayed the message.

Thursday brought more excuses from his mother. I got a letter out of the mailbox for Ronnie to sign; he was on suspension. I called his mother and told her Ronnie's job was in jeopardy if he didn't contact Ford's. They took the threat lightly, seemingly because Ronnie was in contact with them, telling a different story. That afternoon, UPS delivered a box to the house. I opened it to find a full-length $5,500 beaver coat charged to our account at Hudson's. I called them, and they mentioned it was charged by Ronnie but sent to the wrong address, then they inadvertently mentioned another woman's name. I personally delivered the coat back to Hudson's and had it removed from our charge.

The next afternoon, a delivery from Highland Appliance in Highland Park arrived. When I called, they told me Ronnie was in the store, charging all kinds of things to a new account he just opened. I asked the staff not to alert him to my arrival. I drove there, and Ronnie spotted me as I walked through the door. He ran out, got into another car, and drove away like a bat out of hell. I slowed and let him pass. Another week went by, and I drove to Bingo. When I got out, my car was gone. I didn't report it to the police because I knew Ronnie had stolen it, leaving me no way to get the kids back and forth to school. I rented a car.

This continued until a dope dealer called, wanting the beaver coat he bought for his woman. He claimed he paid Ronnie a thousand dollars in cash and drugs. I told him I knew nothing of their transaction and that Ronnie didn't live here anymore; he should take it up with him. Before we hung up, he revealed that Ronnie was taking orders from people—drug dealers and associates— buying things on credit for cash.

Time moved forward. Ronnie lost his job after seventeen years. All I could do was pray for him. I had a good cry for him and my kids because they loved him so much, and then I changed my attitude about things. I was looking forward to the future with my kids; there was nothing else to think about. It's like pouring water on a drowning man—Ronnie didn't want any help. As much as he said he loved me and the kids, I knew he loved drugs more, and I accepted that. Ronnie used all the money we had in the bank and on the charge accounts. Cash advances were disappearing fast. I had all the locks changed on the doors. I couldn't trust him; he was no longer my husband; he was a drug addict, and I was going to treat him accordingly. I didn't hesitate; I filed for divorce on December 31, 1988—New Year's Eve.

The kids were older, and I spent New Year's Eve in New Haven, a small rural town with no streetlights. Ms. Blackmon invited me to her party, and I didn't want to sit home and be sad. I needed to hear some music, laughter, and dance. I had Bird come to the house and babysit the kids, even though they were teenagers; I still wanted an adult with them. I got dressed and drove to New Haven, arriving around 9:00 p.m. The party was on. I was watching the clock because I wanted to wish the kids a happy new year and to get down on the floor because of the shooting. At 11:15, I received a phone call from the kids; my heart was racing. Terrance said that Ronnie was there, and they opened the door for him; he wanted to talk to me. He came to the phone and said he came for his stuff; he couldn't get himself together and wanted his clothes and shoes to sell to get high.

I was at peace with that; I was in no position to argue. "Just don't take anything that belongs to me," I said.

"Alright," he replied.

Ronnie took everything that belonged to him and left. I stayed on the phone until he was gone, then I told Shawn to put his hand in my mink coat pockets hanging behind the bedroom door to feel in each pocket that my money was still there. He did. I had five thousand dollars in each pocket. Ronnie's leather coat, which he took, was hanging right in front of my mink coat. God is good, I thought; Ronnie never knew the money was there.

Early Sunday morning, I lay drifting in and out of sleep, worried and praying for protection. Around 3:46 AM, I heard God say to me, "Go get that money out of the bank." I looked up, and the withdrawal slip was still laying on the TV. I couldn't fall back asleep. At 7:00 AM, I got up and told Shawn to get dressed because he was going to be late for school at OCC. I took the kids to school and drove to the bank on Schafer. I waited an hour for them to open, and we walked in with them.

I told Shawn to sign the withdrawal slip above Ronnie's signature, and I withdraw all of it but five dollars. I was nervous and waiting. God is good, indeed—the money was still there. The teller counted out twenty-five thousand dollars, and we walked out. I dropped him off at school, went to another bank, bought a cashier's check, and locked it down. Then I drove to New Haven and looked around the town for a house to buy.

When I came home that evening, there was a message on my phone from Ronnie and the bank manager. She said Ronnie walked into the bank to withdraw the money fifteen minutes after I left.

Terrance and André were doing fine in school. Terrance was on the track team, and Andre was involved in an art class after school. I was still worried; the neighborhood was getting bad. We had our schedules mixed up, and Terrance and Andre took the school bus to Nina's house to call me to pick them up. When they knocked at the door, Nina pretended not to hear them. I felt something in my stomach; my nerves were on end.

Terrance and Andre walked to the pay phone and called me. They said they were at Nina's house, but she pretended that she wasn't home. They saw her car and the curtain move. I told them to wait for me at the pancake house. I'm on my way. I was afraid to leave them anywhere because kids were getting killed right and left over nothing. They just killed a child over a pair of shoes. I drove fast and picked them up. When I got home, I called Nina to ask her why she wouldn't let my sons in her house so they would be safe. She pretended like she didn't hear them knock, then she told me they couldn't use her address anymore. "That's fine and well," I said, "but you could have let them in." I quit speaking to Nina for a long time after that.

February 8, 1989—almost three years to the day after Charlie died, her ex-husband Teddy's nine-year-old daughter died. I'm sorry she passed away. When I heard, I sent flowers and went to the funeral to look Teddy in his face. I never approached the casket. Teddy was distraught. Maybe he can feel the pain that he's inflicted on so many others in his life. From what I understand, Darlene was running through the school hallway, and she fell dead. On the flip side, "God only knows how much abuse this child suffered at his hands. Maybe that's why God took her so soon." I prayed for her, but not for him.

There was too much sadness surrounding my life. I was going through it. So much was going on, and I wanted out. But I had to keep on going. I prayed, "Help me, God, to stay focused."

I like the looks of New Haven—a small town with plenty of kids, dairy farms, dirt gravel roads, horses and buggies, plenty of underdeveloped land, and everything within walking distance. From what I had heard, the last person killed in New Haven was over thirty years ago. That was good news to hear.

There just weren't any houses available to buy or rent, but that wasn't going to stop me from praying and searching. I looked through the surrounding areas, unable to find what I wanted. For the first time in my life, I was able to pick and choose. I made up my mind that this was something I had to give to God; He was going to have to make the way. I knew He would because He's never let me down. God Almighty is the only one I can depend on, the only one that has always been there for me in good and bad times. He stood and watched over me day and night when I was living in abandoned cars with my children—the one who blew the match out the night the man tried to set me and my babies on fire, the one who provided shelter for me and my children in my hours of darkness, the one who fed my children when I couldn't. God's list is endless with me.

Yes, I'm going to put all my faith and trust in God. That's the position I took. I stood strong in faith because I knew in my heart that I believed in miracles. I was a faithful believer in what I could not see. I believe that Jesus raised the dead, that He arose in three days, that He fed a multitude of people with a single loaf of bread, that He died for our sins, that He restored sight to the blind, and that if God is watching over the butterflies, then He certainly has his eyes on me. I knew that I had a direct line, and I knew how to call on God; He could solve it all. Everything in the world belongs to Him.

With that being said, I found myself having a good conversation with Him, one-on-one. I said to myself out loud, "I can look further back than I can ahead." God has brought me a mighty long way, and I can attest to that. I was praising and thanking him. I felt good, and I encouraged myself to feel better. I was still talking to myself out loud when a carload of people looked over at me to see who I was talking to. I continued to praise the Lord. "God has done a great many things for me in my lifetime, and I'll praise Him wherever I want to."

I was rejoicing and testifying at the same time. One after another, heavy drops of tears streamed down my face and dropped into my lap. The feeling of relief from life's repetitive, tiresome pressures, restrictions, holds, boundaries, shackles, and roadblocks that had consumed me was no more—like peeling layers and layers of life's disappointment and fears from my soul. Remembering the past, where I used to be, and where I am now was only possible by God's grace and the sweat of my brow. I paid the price and some.

I reminded myself of the way things used to be, and I didn't ever want to forget where I came from; it's too painful and a lesson well learned. I drove myself home, praying, crying, and testifying to the goodness of the Lord. I stepped outside the car after a long day of searching and looked up into the bright, sunny sky. I could do nothing but call His name, Jesus. I knew in my heart that everything was going to be alright.

I cooked us dinner and hugged and kissed my children like I've done since they were babies before they went to bed. I wouldn't let the sun go down without telling my children that I love them. Before I went to bed, I got down on my knees and prayed to God to guide my steps, open the doors and windows, and pour out a blessing for us. I prayed for protection, the 23rd Psalm, and I asked for a house in a neighborhood—someplace clean and safe that wouldn't deteriorate before my eyes.

I asked God to cover us in His blood. I asked for a house in New Haven. The families that lived in the Village of New Haven were those whose homes had been passed down from one generation to the next, like old money—they weren't selling. I wish I could have found a place like that to live in when my children were little and I was struggling so hard. Why has life been so hard for us? Everyone has their own cross to bear. I answered my own question.

I left my phone number with William, a man I met in New Haven at Ms. Blackmon's house. He said he knew everyone there; he'd lived in the village all his life. I asked him to be on the lookout for a house for us to move into. Andre and Terrance were still out of school. I wasn't going to send them to Henry Ford if I didn't have to; I was scared for their lives. Especially after hearing about his death last year. Maserati Rick was killed at Mt. Carmel Hospital. Drugs and gangs were taking over the streets of Detroit. Senseless killing of kids over jewelry, shoes, and coats. I made sure they had study time and read plenty of books until I could figure out what to do. I was in a pickle!

Unable to sleep from the excitement, I laid across the bed in the same spot where Ronnie used to lay. He crossed my mind briefly, but I knew I had to stay focused, not emotional. I had a mission to accomplish, and that was to move my children to New Haven.

Later that evening, Lollie called to see how we were doing and to tell me that Emmette had died—Pringle's boyfriend. He was found dead in the bathtub by his mother, having died from a drug overdose. "Well," I said, "God has a way of making things even." No sooner had I hung up from Lollie, Diane, my old girlfriend, called, and we talked for hours. Before we hung up, I asked her if she had ever heard anything from Ollie, Burnella's husband—the man who killed my girlfriend 15 years ago.

Diane said, "Girl, I don't know where you've been, but Ollie is dead. He dropped dead running to catch the Grand River bus several years ago. He had a massive heart attack."

"Heart attack my ass," I said. "His conscience killed him. Ollie knew he should have gone to prison for killing her. It doesn't pay to mistreat God's children," I said. Burnella had everything to live for; she'd only been on this earth for 19 years, and she was three months pregnant with his child. Ollie took it upon himself to end her life; he shot her down like a dog. I call it payback. 'Vengeance is mine,' said the Lord. 'You shall reap what you sow. If you put it out there, it's coming back.'

Ollie was a weak, spineless, undercover coward who finally got what he deserved. What kind of punk-ass brother is that? Those kids will never forget what they witnessed that night; they will never get to know what a nice person their mother was and how much she loved them," I said. Plus, they were left without a mother to raise them, and now his dumb ass is dead. I feel sorry for the kids; I feel sorry for the situation as a whole." Ollie was 32 years old when he died. "Yeah," I said, "he still outlived her by thirteen years."

Well, I heard all of everybody's problems, more then I cared too. I was bombarded with my own. I really just wanted to concentrate on moving my children to New Haven—that's all I cared to think about this evening. I needed to relax myself, so I played Detroit's Clark Sisters' "You Are the Sunshine" and Mavis Staples' "God Bless the Children." I went to the kitchen, and she made me a drink. I got a glass of ice, and I poured one pre-measured or pre-mixed can of Jack Daniel and Coca-Cola into the glass, and I lined the rim of the glass with lemon. I sipped on that and then poured another. I gave myself a pedicure and changed the polish on my toes from tasty orange to bright light red.

Saturday morning, I got a phone call from Margie. She said that she was back from Chattanooga and wanted to see me and talk. I was so excited to hear from her. I loved her like a big sister I always had, in spite of the way she treated me and my children. Plus, I wanted to know what led Little Dot to kill Balma. I called a babysitter and drove to her house, arriving at 6:00 p.m. that same evening. Margie was no longer profiling and fronting—life and drugs had broken her down. She was so low; she could sit on the curb and swing her legs! Margie had lost it all; her reputation and her status in the good life were no more. I could look at her and tell she was catching pure hell. Her life of drugs and the good times had hit like a cinder block; it was more than she could bear. She tried to hide, but I could see. I didn't relish in her misfortune; I felt genuine sorrow for all that she'd put herself through. All the diamonds, mink coats, and fake friends were gone.

Margie met me at the door when I drove up, as if she were sitting and looking out the bay window, waiting for me. We hugged, and she screamed out my name, "Pat! Where have you been, girl? I've been looking for you. I've asked everybody about you," she said. I would have recognized her anywhere; she still looked the same, and she still had that floor-model television big ass. Margie lived off Joy Road and Evergreen in a house with her old boyfriend—the one she dogged in his time of need, the man who worked hard every day and gave her all of his money on Friday, the one that she put out of her house on many occasions; she treated him like shit when life was good to her. Margie was now living in his house; the tables had turned. I'd lived life long enough in this world to know that the people you see going up are the same people you see coming down. She had hit rock bottom, and God let me live to see it. I had to buy her a pack of cigarettes; we smoked the same brand, Benson and Hedges Menthol. That evening, we sat out in her well-maintained backyard and killed mosquitoes. Margie faithfully cooked dinner for a boyfriend who didn't care if he ate with her or not. She barbecued and had all the sides.

She told me she had a surprise for me, and just then a car pulled up in front of her house. She urged me to walk with her to the car. I hesitated at first because I wasn't sure about the kind of crowd she ran with anymore. I stood on the sidewalk and watched as an old lady emerged from the parked car. The street light provided enough light for me to see that this woman was old and frail. Then she called me by name and said, "You don't know me anymore." I studied her face; I didn't recognize her, but I recognized the voice with a southern drawl—it was a voice from my past. Then she reached out for my hand to help her come closer to me, and it was Little Dot. "Well, shut my mouth and call me Hushie," I exclaimed. I wouldn't have ever believed what I was seeing except with my own eyes. My God, she looked so worn; the stress lines on her face had finally met. Her hair was snow white; those eighteen months had kicked her ass, I thought to myself. The Little Dot I knew was as fine as all outdoors, built like a brick house, with olive- colored skin, hazel eyes, blonde hair, and a southern accent. She was as pretty as she was treacherous. Dot had it going on at one time.

We hugged, walked to the backyard, and sat down. She lit a cigarette, the same brand we both smoked. She confessed to me then. Dot told me that she was sorry she had killed Balma and that she wished she could take it back. Dot said that she had served time in prison with Balma's spirit haunting her cell every night. She said that Balma would come and sit on her bed, and sometimes he stood up. Dot said that she had conversations with him every time he appeared; Balma continuously asked her why she had killed him. He told her that he still loved her and that he would wait for her no matter how long it took, and that he forgave her. He cried and told her that he wanted to live. I listened to her confess her sins.

Dot had lost it all—her home, her children, the majority of her friends, and her mind. No one wanted to be around her. Little Dot didn't stay long, and she kept looking around her like she was expecting someone the entire time she spent with us. She talked about Balma, then she left. I felt sorry for her; she wasn't the same woman I once knew. I prayed for her.

In the days to come, Margie called on me a lot to take her places or give her money, and I did. I didn't treat her as she had treated me. As for Dot, God had taken care of her; she didn't have to play crazy anymore.

Reluctantly, I enrolled Andre and Terrance in Henry Ford High, and they attended for the remainder of the semester. I was afraid to send them. I had to really trust God. I prayed and checked with the school every day for their safety.

Six nights later, William called and said he had found me a house. He couldn't tell me any particulars because he hadn't seen the inside, but I didn't care. It was in the right location, and I was claiming it. I was going to make it work. I thanked God. I was unable to sleep, thinking about it all

The next morning, I kept the kids home from school and drove up. William had found a nice three-bedroom house that was for sale on a court with eight other houses. The owner, an 88-year- old man living in a rest home, Mr. Bradford, said he wanted five thousand cash dollars for the house; then he would sign the deed over to me. I had to pay two years' back taxes associated with the property. I couldn't believe it. First, I paid Mr. Bradford in cash, and then he signed the deed over to me. Let me show you how good God is! I cashed the $25,000 cashier's check, took the tax bill down to the county building, and bought the house that day for $11,700.92, including taxes. I owned the house outright; he'd paid the mortgage off years ago when his wife died.

Hot damn, I hit the jackpot! I was happy and screaming with joy on the inside. I had bought my babies a house in an area I didn't have to worry about anymore. "God is good!" He showed up today. I could feel the tension that I had lived with for so many years leaving. No words could describe how I felt. It was as if I'd touched the hem of God's garment and I'd been made whole. It was a miraculous feeling—for once in my life, I didn't feel afraid.

For once in my life, I didn't have to struggle; it just came to me. By the grace of God, I was able to buy a house for myself. I no longer had to lay awake at night listening to suspicious sounds of someone breaking into my house or stealing my car out of the driveway. God gave me and my children another chance at life. He blessed us as a family with a safe place to live and a school for my children to go to without being gunned down. I didn't have to worry about having to move in two years again and again. All the things I prayed about; God worked out in a matter of hours. Just that quick, God worked another miracle in my life, right before my eyes. God lightened the heavy load that I was so accustomed to carrying. God solved all my problems in the blink of an eye.

I cried and praised the Lord all the way home. I thanked Him all my life for the good and bad times; He had been there through it all, and I thanked Him for it. I cried out to my mother and thanked her for being the only true person that I knew loved me. She didn't have to love me because she gave birth to me; she loved me because she was my mother. She could have abandoned me like my so-called biological father, but that wasn't even an option with my mama; she chose to love me instead.

I quickly threw his no-good ass out of my mind; I didn't want to ruin the moment. It was her love and suffering that I had watched her endure that made me strong and strive to do better. I thanked God for Ronnie—he told me to use the money for the kids, and I knew that he would have wanted me to do just what I did: help my children. Versus him smoking it up in a crack house, on the flip side, $25,000 worth of crack… I laughed to myself; I'm sure I saved his life.

I couldn't wait to get home and tell the other kids. I had the keys in my hand. When I got home, they greeted me at the door like they always have, making me comfortable in our own home. I told the kids about the three-bedroom house on a court with eight other houses. I described the laid-back atmosphere it had. Children were able to ride their bikes on the sidewalk or walk to the store without getting robbed; the speed limit is 25 miles per hour; and they had their choice of safe, clean high schools they could graduate from.

I screamed, "Thank you, Lord, for hearing my prayers! Thank you, Lord, because all my suffering was not in vain." I could see their future in full scope. They were excited. I sure didn't feel like cooking tonight, and the sky was the limit, so we ordered takeout from Red Lobster, and for the first time in a long time, I was truly hungry. While we sat at the dining room table and had dinner, I told the kids that we were going up there in two weeks to look around. The house needs a little work, but most of it is cosmetics, and I have enough money for that, and I have enough money to give you all some.

I gave the kids three hundred fifty dollars apiece to buy what they wanted. I said after dinner I wanted to do some dancing. By now, all of my children had mastered the latest and the old- school ways of dancing—they knew their mama wasn't no slouch. Of course, I pulled out all my records from the past and present, and baby, we got down. We ballroom danced, and I did the mashed potatoes for them and the bop with all the steps from the sixties. We laughed, and they hugged me and said that they were proud of me. I had an enjoyable, memorable evening with my children.

The next day, I started packing and throwing away things I didn't want to take. I wanted a fresh start in life. Immediately, I became familiar with the area. I shopped for new furniture at Art Van's furniture store. My children were older now, so I knew I could buy white if I wanted to.

As happy as I was, I still felt sadness tugging at my heart day after day because I knew that the day I had waited for so long was quickly approaching. I wondered how I was going to turn my son loose—the clock was ticking. Shawn was offered and accepted into Eastern Michigan University in Ypsilanti, Michigan, about thirty minutes from Detroit and an hour's drive from New Haven. I didn't let him see me cry, but every time I thought about it, the less I pushed forward by purchasing all the things he needed to start college. I paid for his tuition and books.

Soon thereafter, we drove up, and the kids couldn't believe it. I could see the signs of relief leaving their faces. They jumped out of the car and ran inside to look around while they patrolled the area. We spent the entire day in New Haven, familiarizing ourselves with the small village. We checked out the schools, and the boys checked out the basketball and football teams.

In the weeks to come, I hired a company to put new floors in the house. I ordered white custom- made blinds with gold pin stripes for the living room and a gold mirror for the dining room. I put fuchsia carpet in both rooms and new carpet in the kids' bedrooms. I had the entire house painted inside and out, and I had the walls mirrored. I had the front stair repaired, put in new plumbing, and bought brand new appliances. Every time we drove up to New Haven, I'd take something from the old house to lighten my load before we moved completely in. We drove up each time in a different car that I'd rented. I couldn't afford to stretch out and buy a car yet, so I continued to use my credit card to rent a car. The first weekend we stayed all night in New Haven, we were invited to a barn fire birthday party by William on the back road. The women seemed somewhat relieved to see me walk in with him.

He introduced us to everybody there and was very protective of us. When we returned to Detroit two days later, my side door was standing open. Someone had broken into our house and stolen my stereo, speakers, video camera, and whatever else they could grab. I never thought for a minute that Ronnie did it, but later that day, the word on the streets was that some of my children's acquaintances had graduated from chasing the ice cream truck to breaking into homes. I thanked God; we weren't there when it happened. They were looking for money to buy drugs. I reminded my children that these were the same young men who had sat at my table on many occasions and had dinner with us. I could see then that they were going astray, and I stopped my children from hanging out with them. I reminded my kids that they had to learn to discriminate when picking and choosing friends. "Don't spend your life loafing," I said. "Let this be a lesson for you."

That same day, I rented a U-Haul truck, paid some guys to load it, and drove the truck to New Haven myself. We never slept in that house again. I went back and had it boarded up. I could hardly get the kids to help me around the new house; they were too busy running the streets, having the time of their lives playing basketball, going to barn fires, birthday parties, skating, watching movies, and making new acquaintances. My children were tremendously happy, and it showed. I was happy decorating my home and planting flowers, and it showed. Everyone wanted to know that I moved to New Haven couldn't wait to come and see. We spent the entire summer with ease. William showed me around, riding the dirt roads and shortcuts. I can't remember when we'd all been so happy.

When I returned this day, I walked into the house, and the telephone was ringing. The voice on the other end caught me off guard—it was Ronnie. "Oh my God," I said, "how are you?"

He was glad to hear my voice. We did a lot of small talk. He said he got my phone number from Mrs. Brazil, who told him that we moved. Before I could get the words out, again Ronnie said, "You beat me to the bank that day, and I'm glad you did.". "I was out of my mind. Yes, I did take the money out of the bank. What did you do with the money?" he asked.

I said, "I bought the kids a house, paid the taxes on this house, and I'm in the process of buying new furniture. I paid Shawn's tuition; you know he's going to college in the fall."

"Well, I'm glad you used the money for yourself and the kids. I've caused you all enough pain," he said. "Thank you," I replied. "I knew you wouldn't be mad at me."

He said, "I'm never mad at you. I'm sorry that I messed up so badly, and I can't straighten it out."

I asked him if he was clean, and he said, "No, I'm still out here getting high; I'm still chasing Jason." He chuckled, "and look at what it cost me— everything, my job, and I lost it all."

I could hear his voice cracking. I listened to him talk. "I understand how you feel, and I'm sorry for you, but I cried my last tear when you made your choice." I asked if he received the divorce papers, and he said no; he never stayed in one place long enough to receive anything; that's how he lost his job, he said.

Ronnie paused in complete silence; his voice cracked. He asked, "Is it too late for us?"

With no hesitation, I said, "Yes, but I wish you well, and I'll always love you, but I can't live with the drug problem you have. I want my children to have a fair chance at life and not be directly influenced by drugs. There's more to life than getting high. I don't want my kids to be exposed to living with someone they love and respect and then finding out you have a drug problem. What then?" I said. "It's my job as their parent to protect them and teach them right from wrong. As much as I love you, I love my children more."

Ronnie said that he understood. "If you need a place to stay, you can live in the house on Heyden. I'm still paying the note until you get on your feet," I said.

"No," he said, "I'm still chasing drugs and getting high, and I'm not ready to stop. I don't want to cause you any more sleepless nights."

"Well, if I can ever do anything to help you, please call me. Let us hear from you, and please take care of yourself," I said.

"Ronnie, I'm not going to worry about you anymore. I have already grieved for you. I'm going to pray for you."

"Thank you," he said. "I'll love you always."

We hung up the phone. That was the last time I heard from Ronnie.

In August of 1989, it was time for Shawn to go, and I spent the whole time crying and preaching the dos and don'ts of living away from home. I followed him in my car on I-94 to Ypsilanti. William and I helped him move into his dorm. I felt somewhat relieved that he was going away to college with some old close friends, Anthony and Crumbly, that he'd grown up with.

I couldn't help but feel worried about his girlfriend, who was also enrolled in the same school, being by his side. My constant worry was that she was going to get pregnant, and that would be the end of his dreams and career. Shawn always listened to me. For years, I preached to him that this girl was like her mother, looking for a way out. She knows that you're going to be successful someday, and she's needy. "Make no mistake with her; don't trust her. She'll put you in a trick bag, and it may cost you everything. She's not the one, and by all means, protect yourself at all times." I spent the next two months crying, unable to sleep or eat.

I talked to Shawn every day, and he was taking heed to my words. I raised Shawn to be responsible and trustworthy, so I had to believe God would watch over and protect him. Shawn had a job working at Briarwood Mall at Bass Shoe Store. This was one of many jobs he'd hold down.

In November of 1989, we spent our first Thanksgiving in New Haven, and I invited all my family over for dinner. Even Matthew Jr. came home; he drove all the way from Virginia with his new family. I cooked a feast and laid it out on the beautiful dining table that I spent two days decorating and coordinating colors. I pulled out all my old music, and after we blessed the food, thanked God, and had dinner, everybody was too full to dance but me. Matthew Sr. went to his Chrysler Aero Van and presented me with two gifts. He made a toast to me, telling me how very proud of me he was. "I was a hell of a woman to raise my children single-handedly like I did," he said. "I did a great job." He gave me the deed to Heyden and the 'Candi Staton' album that I played so much at his house, autographed from him to me, 'Candi Staton 'Victim.' He knew that song alone was my personal testimony to life. Of course, Nina, Geri, and Matthew Jr. dropped their heads and pretended not to hear his toast to me. I said to myself, they should all be ashamed of the way they treated me, but deep down inside I knew they weren't. They were envious of my successes.

This was a man who knew the blood that flowed through my body was different from his, yet he reached out and helped me at a time in my life when I really needed someone. I thank God for Matthew Sr., and I told him so. After all the sentiments and tears, we partied. We soul-trained and reminisced about Mama Charlie and my father. I dedicated Matthew Sr.'s favorite song to him, "I Love You Just the Way You Are" by Billy Joel. He stood up, placed his hand on his stomach, held the other in the air, and wiggled his hips from side to side, doing his own dance. We had a ball that night.

The children had a terrific Christmas, and there was peace in the house. I invited Margie up for New Year's, and I showed her a good time.

In fact, she stayed with me for a week before I took her back to Detroit. She talked about old times and told me she remembered where I came from. She told me how proud of me she was. Margie admitted that she hadn't always made the right decisions and choices in her life. She said she was going back to Chattanooga to live because Bobby, her boyfriend, had moved her out of his house and put her things on the porch while she was at the doctor's office. He moved his new girlfriend the same night. I said to myself, "That explains why she had me pick her up at her daughter's house. All that time, I thought she was visiting her daughter because of the holidays."

I invited her to go back to the house and stay with me, but she said she'd be alright. Then she turned to me and asked, "You would do that for me?" I said yes. "I remember when I didn't have anywhere to go, when Aunt Janie was mistreating me and stealing my baby's money, you and your mother took me in."

I started to cry. "I was just fifteen years old with my baby, and I was outdoors. My mother had been taken away from me. I had no one to help me; no one loved me, and you and your mother took me in. I lived there with you all, and every time she ate, I ate. She taught me about things I didn't know as a young girl. Ma' Dear never treated me any differently than she did anybody else. She treated me like I was her child, and when she chastised one, she chastised us all. I'll never forget that, and I thank God for Ma' Dear."

Wiping the tears from my eyes with one hand and driving with the other, shaking my head, I said, "Yes, you're welcome to come and live with me for as long as you want."

Margie said, "Thank you, but I'll come back another time when I get myself together." I offered, but she refused. I think she was embarrassed and felt ashamed of the level she had allowed herself to stoop to. The fact that her grown children knew what was going on. Not only did she use drugs, but she also encouraged her daughter to get high with her.

In 1990, in New Haven, I came out swinging full force; my back was strong. I sold the house on Heyden and bought another in New Haven—a five-bedroom brick house. I was able to get a bank loan. I was happy with the purchase, and they gave me a courtesy credit card with a $5,000 credit limit."

I'll keep it for emergencies and for the kids."

Immediately, I applied for a state adult foster care license. While I waited for approval from the state, I hired a company to modify the home so I'd be in compliance. One day before my birthday, I received my license. Let me show you how good God is: there was another larger licensed home in the area, and it caught fire that same night. My licensing worker called me at home and placed five clients in my home. Four of them were paid privately. God blessed me to be able to own my own business doing something that I loved—helping people. This was the beginning of me making money hand over fist. Still, this was only a steppingstone.

Chapter 27

"God Give Me Strength"

Saturday, early morning, 1991

My favorite day of the week. We'd been living in New Haven for almost two years, and life was good. Standing at my open bedroom window, I could hear the church bells ringing from several blocks away. Looking out, I saw old farmers plowing their gardens, the smell of barbecue filling the air. Butterflies fluttered around my front yard flower garden. I thanked God for His goodness and mercy.

My business was doing great; I had a decent staff that I worked with. Besides being on call twenty-four hours a day, every day, spending time on the riverbank and looking for new fishing holes made it possible. Andre and Terrance were on their way out—graduation from high school. Andre was accepted into Michigan University with a two-year scholarship. Terrance was going to be with his brother at Eastern University. "One more to go," I'd tell myself.

My friend Michael and the others always came to visit. They boasted about how proud of me and the kids they were. Most of my friends were still using some kind of drug, but never around my kids—they wouldn't dare. They all had big respect for me and my accomplishments; they knew our love was real. They encouraged all we had achieved together, as a whole, as a family. I appreciated that.

Andre and Terrance's ceremony was scheduled for June 26. I was ecstatic and felt very blessed that God would bring me this far with my kids. I was ahead of schedule, getting things ready for their prom, graduation, and plenty of parties. They were also scheduled to take their pictures in their cap and gown.

I'd reserved a limousine for Andre. I rented a car for Terrance and reserved a suite for both of them to have an after-party. I thought it over and agreed—it was safer than them driving on the road at night. I gave them more freedom than I had given Shawn. The locations were different, and they proved to me that they were responsible. I raised them to be young men. I had to turn them loose, somewhat, and let them learn to fly on their own. I raised them old-school style; they were ahead of the game. I taught them all their lives about girls and the games they played. "Always protect yourself," I tell them. "It doesn't matter what she says; you should be responsible and take care of your own business." I gave them money to handle their business.

My children and I are very close, and I didn't pull any punches. My life had been an open book; I was straight up—they knew at all times where I was coming from. I raised them to be trustworthy. When the time came, I knew my sons wouldn't have a problem supplying me with the names and addresses of their friends they planned to spend the evening with. I'll have them call me when they make it to the hotel. Those would be my conditions, and I knew they would comply.

On June 1, before I sat down at the kitchen table to address the invitations to everyone, inviting them up for a dinner celebration for Andre and Terrance, I sipped on a cup of hot lemonade. I stood at the back door, looking out at the kids' dog, Moc ca Do Do, as Kyham named her. Any day now, she was getting ready to give birth to her first litter of puppies.

I walked back in from the laundry room and turned on the television set in the kitchen. I wasn't really in the mood for the news, so I flipped through the channels. Suddenly, I saw a picture of

David Ruffin. I hurriedly turned the volume up, dreading to hear what I didn't want to believe when I saw his face on TV. They said that David Ruffin was dead and, in the morgue,

I attended his viewing scheduled for Sunday, June 9, 1991, at 1:00 PM.

I merged into the long line outside Swanson Funeral Home on West McNichols Road. As I stood in the long, hot line, I could hear David Ruffin's mighty voice singing 'I Wish It Would Rain' over the noisy crowd of onlookers.

The bellows of outdoor speakers filled the street with plenty of Temptations songs from the past. I was crying so hard I couldn't see. I remembered back to the first time I ever laid eyes on David Ruffin—it was at the Motown Revue at the Fox Theatre on Woodward Avenue. I was mesmerized by his voice; it sounds like he's crying as he delivers the message in the song. My heart was heavy as I thought about the members of the Motown family that had gone on before him and the ones destined to leave. 'Motown is like family!'

I was still in denial about his death, playing games with my own mind. Eventually, they let us inside, and my eyes searched the room for David. They had us merge upstairs, above where his body lay. I thought I was going to collapse from fear of what I might see. "Move forward," they said. "No pictures," they instructed. I asked if I could go down and see him up close and personal. "No one is permitted downstairs," they said. "Follow the rope." Just then, I unleashed the latch on the rope that separated me from him and proceeded to David's casket. I moved in fast and looked at his face. I was close enough to touch him. I put my hand on his shoulder and rubbed his face. My tears dropped on his white lapel. It was David— he looked as though he was asleep.

I then took out my 35mm camera and took several photos of him. The guard extended his hand to me, helping me back upstairs. He looked at me and offered a warm smile. "I couldn't believe it either, not until I looked him in the face; that's when I knew it was David." We hugged each other and cried. We both agreed that David Ruffin would be greatly missed. Not just by people from Detroit, but by the whole world. David Ruffin was one of the baddiest Temptations that ever lived.

I had to pull myself together quickly and get ready for the big celebration. At 2:00 PM, I opened my doors to all my old friends who had traveled from Detroit for the party. Matthew Sr. was always the first one there and the last to leave; he loved my parties. We had a good time, and the boys were happy. My friends gave them words of encouragement, and I gave them plenty of love. As the evening wound down, I walked Matthew and his wife to their Aero Van. He leaned over and whispered in my ear, "I have lung cancer." I nearly fell out right there.

Suddenly, a day that had gone so well would end with tragic news like this. I was devastated.

My legs buckled under me. Looking up into his eyes, they were glossy from tears that hadn't fallen yet. I could see fear, an emotion I had never seen in him before. I was speechless and numb. He whispered, "The doctor told me this week. I have to undergo radiation and chemotherapy for six weeks, every day." I was unable to speak; I couldn't even process his words properly. I saw his lips move but couldn't retain what he was saying.

I turned to his wife, Alma, and she confirmed it with a nod. I put my arms around him and hugged him tight. I whispered in his ear, "You don't have to go through this alone. I'll be here for you." He smiled weakly and dropped his head. Matthew was a strong, independent man who didn't want any sympathy, and I didn't show him any. Instead, I showed him love. I showed him strength.

When the kids came home for the holiday and before the year ended, 1992 would prove to be the year that would separate the men from the women. It would be the most challenging year of my life. All of my sons were away at college, involved in their own lives. In the little spare time that I had, I was changing my bedroom furniture around. I thought this would maybe help relieve the nightmares of the abuse I was still suffering from.

Sometimes, they seem to be getting worse. I'd wake up crying in my sleep. They were becoming more and more common with time. I tried not to think of the time when I was raped by Donald Malone. I knew that he was still alive, but where? I asked those who remembered him and were still around if they heard anything from him. The answer all these years has always been no.

But I could tell he was still out there. I could still smell him and feel their touch. I thought many days about hiring someone to find him and do the same things to him that he'd done to me as a child. But on the flip side, I didn't want to get anyone, including myself, in trouble. So I'd say to myself, "Keep praying—'Vengeance is mine,' said the Lord. "Although Welton, his partner in this crime, was dead to me, it still wasn't enough. I'd lived with this all my life. I was tired of being afraid to go to sleep at night for fear that I would have a nightmare about that man who tormented me or nightmares about being beaten, raped, and sodomized. The pain and violent fights from the emotional abuse kept me up at night. I played some music to soothe my aching soul. I went to my Detroit old school library and played The Holidays' 1966 Double Jam.

"I'll Love You Forever." I continued to move things around my bedroom when I found Bird's telephone number. In the midst of things, I sprawled across the bed and gave her a call. We talked for an hour or so. Before we hung up the phone, she asked me if I had ever heard from Bobby, and I told her no and asked why she asked. Bird said that Bob tried to have sex with her when she was babysitting for me. She was just fourteen when it first started. She said that Bob exposed himself to her many times and that he put his hands on her and molested her on numerous occasions. I listened to her and felt bad for what happened. "Why didn't you tell me?" I asked her. Her reply was that she didn't want to cause any confusion; she thought it was her fault. I knew that she wasn't lying. "He's a pedophile," I said. She agreed, and then she described his penis to me in the same way I didn't care to remember—as being very, very small in size, like a cashew peanut, and uncircumcised.

Well, I know that 'God doesn't like ugly, and he doesn't care too much about pretty.' The truth to this story is that Bobby never made it to Soul Train; he wasn't even in the running. Don Cornelius never knocked at his door or acknowledged him in any way. All the people he mistreated when he thought he was going up, I know he saw coming down. I ran into my niece Cathy at the Piquette Market on Russell Street, and she told the same story as Bird. The last time I heard anything about Bobby, he was said to be preaching out the back of Cleaners on Linwood Avenue, with a roach clip hanging from his side pant pocket. The donations were so small that he could collect them in one hand.

March 1992.

It rained most of the summer of 1992—the kind of misty, warm rain that would make a person feel sad and blue. I really had to fight hard not to let the unpredictable weather get me down. I thank God that my home was bright in color; it really made the difference.

I missed my sons, and I worried about them to no end. My constant prayer was for God to cover them in His precious blood and to let no weapon formed against them prosper. "These are Your children," I prayed. "You are their Father; keep them safe, Lord." As independent as I was, I had to lean on God for a great many things that I couldn't control in my life. I had to rely on God Almighty for His guidance, protection, and strength. All of my sons lived more than an hour's ride away from me. I could no longer hear their laughter in the house; I couldn't see their faces, only in my mind. I walked the floors nightly, unable to sleep, rest, or eat. Praying and crying for their safety, thanking God for all that He's done and for all that He's going to do. I walked the halls and looked into their empty bedrooms. I touched their pillows where their heads used to lay; sometimes, I'd snuggle up in their beds. To get my mind off things and to help him out, I spent a lot of time with Matthew Sr., watching TV, barbecuing, playing cards, and attending doctor appointments. Sometimes I watched him work crossword puzzles, or I just checked in.

Kyham and I drove to Detroit at least four days a week.

Sometimes I'd bring fresh fruit, Ensure, ice cream, sherbets, corned beef sandwiches, baked fish—whatever came to mind. He told me to stop spending my money; all he wanted was my company. I could tell the treatments were taking a toll on him, and he knew it too. He was sad and blue most days. He told me that he had a lot of regrets, and the biggest one was when he signed the divorce papers my mother had issued through the court. In secrecy, he said, "I always loved your mother. I should have refused to sign the divorce papers; that would have forced her to stay married to me." Alma would call me, and I would have to go down to Detroit, sometimes twice a day, to try to make him eat something or to encourage him to fight to live. Some days, he'd close his lips really tight and turn his head like a child. After a while, he quit eating altogether. He said he didn't have an appetite. So, I called one of my friends and asked him to sell me a dime bag. He said that he would give me some to help with his appetite.

Matthew rolled it up like a champ, and soon he was eating again. "I learned how to roll cigarettes so well," he said, "because when I served in the United States Navy in 1944, I was shipped to Okinawa and didn't have cigarettes." I was determined to do whatever I could to help prolong his life.

August 1992

When I woke up this morning, I was feeling a little bit tired and unhappy. I drove Kyham to McDonald's for breakfast and then over to New Haven High. She had two years left before completion. Her goal was to be a veterinarian, and I wanted to make sure she had every opportunity to do just that.

At 11:07 p.m., my phone rang. Through the receiver, I heard the panicked voice of my son's friend, his words punctuated by screams. "The police—they're beating your sons! They're in handcuffs, and the officers… they've beaten them up." Oh God, I almost died right there. The commotion in the background was a cacophony of chaos. "Where are they?" I screamed, my hands fumbling for my keys and my feet slipping into my shoes in haste. "I don't know," he said, his voice breaking. "The police took them somewhere." Oh God, please don't let them kill my sons. I dialed Geri as fast as my trembling fingers allowed. "The police have them," I said, trying to keep my voice steady. "Call the state police, the Washtenaw police. Let them know we're aware. Tell them their mother is on her way. Keep them on the line until we get there." We ran out of the house. William drove; I couldn't have managed it. In the blink of an eye, all of my children were gone. God, please, I prayed, keep my children safe from any harm. Upon reaching Ypsilanti, Michigan, I rushed to Shawn's dorm room. The security police informed me of an icebreaker party that had escalated into a confrontation with the police. "Where are they?" I said, Please," my voice raw. "I need to find my sons." The hill behind the dorm was swarming with activity, the rain still pouring, and the side streets teeming with students. I called the police department, desperation clawing at my throat. "Terrance and Shawn," they said, "have been taken to the emergency room." Andre was nowhere to be found. I cried out, "Help me, Lord, please help me." I followed someone to the emergency room, and they ushered me back. Lord God, in heaven, I almost collapsed. My sons were alive; Terrance's head was split open from being beaten with a metal flashlight; Shawn's eyes had been gouged so bad I couldn't see the pupil; and Andre was being treated for a dislocated shoulder. I thanked God they were alive, but my sons had been handcuffed and beaten by the Washtenaw Police Department. Shawn, who was searching for his friend, discovered that the police had handcuffed him and were beating him. When Shawn asked why they were beating his friend, they cuffed him, threw him down the hill, and beat him. Terrance saw what happened to Shawn, and he went to help him, and they cuffed him and hit him in the head with the metal flashlight. Andre went to help his brothers, and they jumped him, cuffed him behind, and kept jerking in arms until they did bodily harm, dislocating his shoulder. All of my sons had been choked, called niggers, and beaten by the officers who swore to protect and serve. I was outraged, and after their release from the emergency room, I took my son home.

After ensuring the boys were settled, I took pictures—evidence of the night's harrowing events. Before retiring to bed, I kneeled, my knees pressing into the cold floor, and prayed earnestly to God.

"Please," I whispered, help me." The following morning, I called Channel 2 News, determined to shed light on the injustice. "I want the world to see what the police did to my sons," I declared. They responded with urgency, arriving immediately to interview my children. Then, I sought legal counsel, engaging the same lawyer that Dot had retained when she faced her own tribulations. We met for a consultation; I handed over a retainer fee of five thousand dollars and initiated a lawsuit against the police responsible for my kids' suffering. After the story aired on the news, "On the evening of Monday, October 5, 1992, I found myself kneeling at the foot of my bed, ascending like incense. Emotionally drained, I could barely stand, my hands grasping the walls for support. I wandered into the kitchen, seeking solace in a cup of hot lemonade. My mind was a fog; I was in a deep funk clouded by sleeplessness.

William, ever my rock, stayed by my side, his concern a silent shadow. He prepared dinner, but my appetite had fled. Retreating to my bedroom, I sank into the big chair, the weight of the world anchoring me. The 11:00 news flickered on, and with it came a blow I thought would collapse me. Eddie Kendrick, aged 52, had passed away. Lung cancer had claimed him in Birmingham, Alabama, at Baptist Medical Center Princeton. I sat motionless, numbness enveloping me. "My God, my God," I cried out, seeking divine intervention. The death of David had been a harbinger; I had sensed Eddie would follow. Acceptance eluded me. He had departed just 16 months after his dear friend. Detroit mourned; Eddie was one of our own. The radio stations—92.3, 107.5, and the venerable

WJLB—paid homage with tributes. Memories of Eddie cascaded through my mind—a poignant montage. I recalled the injustice at David's funeral, where Detroit's Finest had arrested Eddie over child support dues. In that moment, I felt they could have waited—they should have waited—until the final farewell was said.

On November 5, 1992, as I sat at Matthew's dining room table, the news profiled two white police officers. They were detained for questioning the beating death of a Detroit man, a motorist caught in the wrong place at the wrong time. During a routine traffic stop, the officers demanded he open his hand. Malice Green, the man in question, refused. And for that, they beat him— mercilessly, fatally. The officers, sworn to serve and protect, wielded their metal flashlights, nightsticks, and the butts of their guns with a brutality that belied their oath. Seven Detroit police officers were there—five stood by, passive spectators to the savage beating, while one joined in the frenzy. "12 to 14 blows to the head," the reports said. I scoffed bitterly. "Yeah, and I can sprout wings and fly." I recognized the west side area 23rd where this tragedy unfolded. The two ex-stress police officers had taken the life of a 35-year-old family man, a man with everything to live for. Compelled by a force I couldn't resist, I got into my car and drove to the scene of the crime on West Warren Avenue, nestled between two of the city's renowned barbecue joints— 'Green's' and 'Vickey's Bar-B-Que and Shrimp.' The sight that greeted me churned my stomach. I glanced over to the very spot where he had breathed his last. In disbelief, I watched city officials from the crime scene unit attempt to wash away the indelible marks of the night's events. They moved quickly, hosing down the bloody massacre without hesitation. The small pile of snow was stained with Malice Green's blood, his brain matter, and fragments of his face and head. The streets were alive with crowds of neighborhood residents; their presence was a testament to a community on edge, ready to rise against the darkness that had befallen the city. Yet, amidst the brewing storm, the officials worked swiftly and transparently, their actions a balm that kept the city's pulse steady. The tension was palpable; if justice was not served for the two officers— referred to derogatorily by some as 'Crackers'—the city was poised on the cusp of chaos. The Detroiters were resolute; this would not be another Rodney King. They would not stand idly by, allowing such transgressions to occur without consequence.

News cameras from every station flooded the streets, capturing the silent murmurs of a city in quiet turmoil. I found solace in prayer, seeking peace for the city and justice for Malice Green and his family. The two officers, who had sworn to protect and serve, were charged in the beating death—a fact too grim to warrant the mention of their names. As the reality of what had happened to my children replayed in my mind, I pondered over my home in November. Despite my love for it, it felt too small and constricting. What if my children needed a sanctuary to return to? The question haunted me. Driven by this need, I sought the help of a real estate agent. She was diligent, promising a house that would be a true home—a place with six bedrooms and ample space, soon to hit the market.

"Take a look," she urged. The appointment was set, and I drove to the address provided. The sight that greeted me was breathtaking—a grand structure with a welcoming front porch and a back deck, boasting two entrances. Stepping inside, I was overwhelmed. The beauty was undeniable, but the price was beyond my reach. Who would grant me a mortgage for such a voluminous, majestic property? The land stretched out, acres of serene beauty adjoining the well- manicured estate.

A long driveway led to the carport, a walkout from the family room. The kitchen, with its step- down nook, was bathed in beige—the ceramic floors flowing seamlessly throughout the house. Coco brown carpet embraced the tri-level farmhouse, a warm contrast to the cool tiles. A huge wood-burning stove stood proudly against the brick walls of the spacious step-down family room. All the original windows, doors, and fixtures were intact, a testament to the home's enduring charm. An old skeleton key, lodged in a keyhole, caught my eye—a relic of simpler times. The master bedroom was as vast as the entire house I currently reside in. This house sprawled over 2,500 square feet and was nestled within 11 acres of land, with an additional 39 acres available for purchase.

An English walnut tree graced the winding bend near the front driveway, standing sentinel over the property. The house itself, encased in black cement brick, was 87 years old. Yet, everything within had been remodeled, marrying history with modernity. Farm animals dotted the landscape: four horses, two mules, eight cows, and one bull—all to be sold separately. The asking price was

$169,000. As the real estate agent spoke, I nodded along, but internally, I had resigned myself to the belief that no one would grant me a mortgage for this house. "I can't afford this," I told myself, even as I fell irrevocably in love with the property. "I want to buy it for the kids," I thought, envisioning their return home. "Let's go back to my office," the agent suggested, "and you can make an offer to the seller." Shelly drafted the papers, and I signed the purchase agreement, handing over a $1,500 good faith deposit. I offered $141,000. From that moment on, I never glanced at another house—my heart was steadfastly set on this one. I would drive past the farmhouse often, each time sending up prayers, asking God to pave a way for me to acquire this house for my children. My prayers evolved into claims; I could see my children there, their laughter filling the rooms. One day, as I drove by, I noticed all the cars in the driveway departing simultaneously. I waited, then pulled into the now-vacant drive. Stepping out, I laid my hands on the house and claimed it in his mighty name," praying fervently, claiming it in Jesus' holy name, believing with all my heart that it would be ours. The boys returned home for the Thanksgiving holiday, but the air was heavy with an unspoken sorrow. It was our first Thanksgiving without the family, leaving a void that no festivity could fill. We gathered for a muted prayer and a dinner that remained largely untouched. I retreated to my solitude while the boys sought the company of friends in the village. I was a shell of myself, mentally and physically drained, with the weight of worry causing my clothes to hang loose.

I visited Matthew, hoping to coax him into eating. Alma told me my presence was his greatest comfort. Yet he was a shadow, his frame skeletal, and his spirit dimmed. We spoke of fishing; his voice was a faint echo of better days. His resignation was palpable, though he tried to mask it. My attempts to feed him were futile; I stayed by his side all day, offering the solace of my company. As night fell, I embraced him, promising to return the next day. On December 7, 1992, at 1:12 a.m., my phone shattered the silence. My heart leapt—it was Alma's voice that met my ear, her soft sobs conveying the news that Matthew Sr. had passed away quietly in his sleep.

In an instant, I was on my feet, and I hastened to the house. I entered his bedroom, and there he lay, still and serene, as if in slumber. I draped myself across his still-warm body, letting my tears flow freely. I remained there, keeping a silent vigil, until they came to take him away. A hollow emptiness echoed within me; I had lost not just a friend or a father figure, but a true human being. Matthew Sr. had his faults, but I believed he had tried to make amends with me.

The funeral was held at Thompson's on Dexter Avenue.

Brook Benton's song "Thank You, Pretty Baby," from 1959, is a personal favorite of mine and his.

Chapter 28

"Victory: God, I Give You the Glory"

On March 8, 1993, as if by divine intervention, I received a call: the house was mine. The closing was set for the following week. Upon discovering my race, the seller hesitated, his prejudices nearly derailing the sale. But in the end, he had no choice. I requested separate closings; I could not bear to sit across from a man so rooted in bigotry. As I brought the $14,000 to the closing, I reflected on my journey. From homelessness to owning three houses, I was a living testament to God's miracles—a thought that warmed me from within. I was so proud of myself, coming from nothing, that I couldn't stand it. Moreover, I was thankful to God for all He had done for me.

As difficult as my life had been, He never left me, and He always made a way. Then, on April 21, 1993, on Mrs. Brazil's birthday, she extended an invitation to me to attend a church revival— a sanctuary for the soul. They pitched a tent right there on the playground of an old school. She mentioned she had a surprise for me. Despite my reluctance, I knew I couldn't decline, especially that night.

The wrongs of my life assailed me, but in my desperation, I called upon the Lord for help. With a heavy heart, I got dressed. We gathered at her home and drove to the revival together, a convoy of hope amidst the shadows of grief. The congregation tried to lift my spirits, but the weight of my heart was too heavy. I collapsed at the altar; my tears were endless. Emory, Evelyn, and Marlene, ever the pillars, lifted me up and guided me back to my seat. They knew the weight I carried. To my amazement, I looked up to see Ozel draped in a white minister's garment, carrying a Bible. Ozel was a ordain Minister. Ozel's sermon resonated through the hallowed halls, a message of trust and faith in the Lord. "Ask God for what you want in your life and claim it," he proclaimed. But I, drained of all strength, could only whisper His name in a silent plea for solace. I was unraveling; my soul lay bare before God, pleading for forgiveness and understanding.

The Williams Brothers' hymn, "I've Learned to Lean," seemed a serenade to my plight, breaking me down further. Yet, as my life's trials flashed before me, I felt a shift—a lifting of the burdens that had long oppressed my heart. I threw my hands in the air and cried a river. Leaving the church, I felt a purity of spirit I had never known—a renewal from a lifetime of suffering. God's presence was undeniable; His existence was a beacon of hope. Outside, I looked up to the heavens, drawing in a deep, life-affirming breath. Upon my return, I saw the answer to my prayers. God had indeed brought all of my children safely home to me. "Ask, and you shall receive." Praise God!

To date, my children have gone on to complete high school, and they all have college degrees. I am in my fourth year of college, and I made the dean's list. And for all of you who said I wouldn't make it with my children—guess what? I did.

THE END

By The Grace Of God... Ending
By The time this book went to publication Everyone was Dead.

1. Emory Related to Drugs Evelyn Related to Drugs
2. Marlene Alcohol Cancer and her three children. She had two Daughter's Murdered.
3. Frank and Pickles Drug Overdose
4. Bird L. Drug Related Gramps- Murdered
5. Robert Kill by a Pit Bull Dog Bite Ted Aids- Drug Related
6. Elaine Murdered Drug Related Spunky
7. Corinthia
8. Dickey Bird Drug Related Michael Related to Car Accident Ike Martin Seizures
9. Diane Alcohol Related
10. Pee Wee Drug Related Diabetes Eric Alcohol Related
11. Lynn Kidney Drug Related Eldoris Alcohol Related Willie
12. Roger Drug Related
13. Pearlie Mae Alcohol Related Shirley Pringle Drug Related
14. Sam Drug Related
15. Winston Cancer Drug Related
16. Laura Cancer
17. Mrs. Wynn
18. Nanny Drug Related
19. The Whole entire immediate Brazil Family Everyone but Evan.
20. Virley Coulter and his brother Mother and Elder Travis Lettie
21. Scott Ma Dear Big Dot
22. Big Mama Yogi Cheryl Kimbery
23. Tee- Tee- Robbed and Murdered
24. Judy LaRue Heart attack on bench
25. Cousin Bird Alcohol Related
26. Ronnie Harris Drug Related
27. Junnie Drug Related
28. Harold Alcohol Related
29. Fred Hampton 21-Black Panther Party Assassinated

To You All I Dedicate This bad 1967- Jam by The Artistics "I'm Gonna Miss You."

Donald Malone Is Doing Time in A Federal Prison His Earliest Release Date is 2068. He Will Die In Prison. He Didn't Pay For What He Did To Me Or Did He?

God Has A Way To Even The Score.

To the degenerates who raped me, know this: Inside all my strength is still a little girl, that loves baby dolls. You didn't steal that part of my childhood from me. I was living on Prayers stored up for me by my mama.

Teddy, He Died a long agonizing miserable Death. God is Good. He Will always have my; sisters' blood on both of his hands.

The man's name is Norman P. The only reason I mentioned his pathetic name in my book is because I want everyone to know who he is and what he did to me.

He was mad because he couldn't break my spirit, grit, tenacity or determination.

And most of all because I wouldn't give myself to him willingly. He could see all of my good solid qualities; And himself lacking. He had been Debased since before his childhood.

I guess God chose the latter, because he is still alive. He is 92 years old. What he does not know is that I went back and stood on the side of his house three time to kill him.

Thank God he was not home.

The Man Smashed Up All Of My Records and destroyed my Suitcase Record Player. To Date I have replaced all my music. Yes, He Is Still Alive, and I know where he lives. "That man did things to me that only God knows about, but I lived to survive it." "Vengeance is mine saith the Lord."